Resistance and Persuasion

RESISTANCE AND PERSUASION

Edited by

Eric S. Knowles
University of Arkansas

Jay A. Linn
Widener University

LAWRENCE ERLBAUM ASSOCIATES, PUBLISHERS
2004   Mahwah, New Jersey   London

Senior Editor:	Debra Riegert
Cover Design:	Kathryn Houghtaling Lacey
Textbook Production Manager:	Paul Smolenski
Full-Service and Composition:	Westchester Book Services
Text and Cover Printer:	Sheridan Books, Inc.

Cover image is a 30" × 40" oil on canvas, entitled "Resistance," painted by Eric S. Knowles, 2003.

This book was typeset in 10/12 pt. Times, Italic, Bold and Bold Italic.
The heads are typeset in Americana, Americana Italic, Americana Bold, and Americana Bold Italic.

Lawrence Erlbaum Associates, Inc., Publishers
10 Industrial Avenue
Mahwah, New Jersey 07430
www.erlbaum.com

Library of Congress Cataloging-in-Publication Data

Resistance and persuasion / edited by Eric S. Knowles and Jay A. Linn.
    p. cm.
    Includes bibliographical references and index.
    ISBN 0-8058-4486-4 (casebound : alk. paper) — ISBN 0-8058-4487-2 (pbk. : alk. paper)
    1. Persuasion (Psychology)—Social aspects. 2. Opposition, Theory of. I. Knowles, Eric S., 1941– II. Linn, Jay A.

HM1196.R47 2004
303.3'42—dc22
    2003060740

Contents

Foreword

Do we need to convince you that persuasion is an important topic for the social sciences? Probably not. You know that humans are social beings. Our communication, psychology, social organization, political structures, market choices—in short, everything we do—is interpersonally coordinated. Persuasion is one of the important tools to achieve these alliances.

What about resistance? Do we need to convince you that resistance is the most important element in the persuasion process? Well, we believe it is. Resistance is an initial condition for persuasion. Without resistance, persuasion, like preaching to the choir, is unnecessary babble. It is the resistance that requires persuasion.

It is our view that resistance is the key element in persuasion. But it also is a neglected element. Most of the research from communication, marketing, social psychology, and political psychology has considered persuasion a way to increase the power of the message. Resistance reduction is a different side to the persuasion equation, one that has been relatively unexplored so far. We hope that this volume will focus attention on this other half—the neglected half—of the persuasion process.

CONCEPTION

We remember the moment this book was conceived. It was the first day of February, 2001, in San Antonio, Texas. The meeting of the Society for Personality and Social Psychology was just about to begin, and Eric heard Bob Wicklund and Jack Brehm talk about dissonance theory at the first attitudes preconference. Brehm had originated the idea of "reactance" 35 years before, and Wicklund had published an early book on this topic. Over the next two days, Eric talked to each of them about accomplishing persuasion by reducing resistance and asked them if they would (a) come to Fayetteville, Arkansas, to talk about this issue, and (b) contribute to a book that presents the ideas discussed. Both men were excited and full of ideas, and both said yes. Armed with these two lead authors, we set about writing a conference prospectus, inviting speakers, arranging funding, and eventually finding a publisher for a book that would explore influence mechanisms that work by removing resistance. Eventually, Bob Wicklund was unable to participate in this project, though he has much to say. Eric remembers fondly the spring weekend in 1991 that he spent at Bob's house in Bielefeld, Germany, discussing nearly everything worth discussing.

We held our conference on resistance and persuasion in Fayetteville on April 12–13, 2002. Twenty-four of the 31 chapter authors were in attendance, presented papers, and participated in lively discussions about the general topic and the specific chapters. This participation in the conference and in the discussions was very useful as authors turned their papers into chapters. We asked authors to attend to the general issues, such as the definitions of resistance, and to the issues raised in other chapters. We also exerted strong editorial control to ensure that these requests were followed. The result is a book that is much more coherent and integrated than most edited volumes.

ORGANIZATION OF THE BOOK

You will find four sections in this book. The first section, "Introduction," contains the introductory chapter (Chapter 1), which describes "The Importance of Resistance to Persuasion." It also describes the other chapters in the book in great detail. This introduction is followed by two multichapter sections. The second section presents five chapters that discuss "The Nature of Resistance in Persuasion" and focus on the definition and operation of resistance as an attitude (Chapter 2, Chapter 4), as an affective feeling (Chapter 3), and as an individual difference (Chapter 5, Chapter 6). The third section presents eight chapters that discuss various "Strategies for Overcoming Resistance." The first chapter in this section (Chapter 7) introduces a distinction between Alpha strategies and Omega strategies for persuasion. Alpha strategies attempt to overwhelm resistance by building up the desirable reasons that promote attitude change and compliance. Omega strategies, on the other hand, attempt to remove or deal with the resistance to persuasion or change. Omega strategies promote attitude change and compliance by reducing a person's reluctance. The seven other chapters in this section discuss other avenues for dealing with a person's resistance: Pushing a decision into the future (Chapter 8), using narratives to sidestep resistance (Chapter 9), forewarning a person of a persuasive attempt (Chapter 10), emphasizing positive thoughts about the message (Chapter 11), affirming the self (Chapter 12), training people to identify illegitimate messages (Chapter 13), and using resistance against itself, as studied in consumer psychology (Chapter 14). A final section in the book contains one chapter (Chapter 15) that puts the previous chapters into an integrated perspective and leads readers away from these chapters toward future, unstudied issues in resistance and persuasion.

TARGET AUDIENCE

This book is aimed broadly at those social sciences that study persuasion, including communication, marketing, political science, social psychology, journalism, advertising, and consumer psychology, and also at those arts and sciences that use persuasion. The target readers are professionals, professors, graduate learners of persuasion, and persuasion practitioners who are interested in the theoretical underpinnings of their practice. We see this as a must-have book in the professional library of these target readers. We have also designed it to be used in graduate courses and advanced undergraduate courses on social influence and persuasion. The integration, organization, and flow of the chapters are especially suited to a course format.

It is our hope that readers will be excited and invigorated by the ideas presented here, that researchers will be filled with new hypotheses and research questions, that practitioners will appreciate the value of addressing resistance as a persuasion tool, and that textbook writers will have more than enough material to create a new chapter or expanded section on resistance and persuasion.

ACKNOWLEDGMENTS

Many people contributed to this volume. First, we are indebted to the 31 authors who put considerable effort into the writing and revisions of their chapters. Second, we are extraordinarily grateful for the production and marketing programs at Lawrence Erlbaum Associates and Westchester Book Services that made these pages and put them in your hands. Third, we are grateful to our funding sources for the conference, the National Science Foundation and the Marie Wilson Howells Fund, who encouraged this project from the first moment they heard about it. Fourth, we need to thank the Omega Lab, our research group at the University of Arkansas, who sustained us through this book and who, for four days, were chauffeur, host, companion, gofer, and fan for the authors who attended the conference. Fifth, we appreciate the public relations and press that were provided so ably by Allison Hogge and our Omega Lab publicist, Elizabeth Hartman. Finally, specific individuals who need to be thanked for various tasks and encouragements are Steve Breckler, Dave Schroeder, Joel Freund, Angelo Welihindha, Christine Rufener, Heather Renfroe,

Renee Boeck, Amira Al-Jiboori, Karissa McKinley, Karen Naufel, Mary Lou Wommack, Cheryl Gober, Elizabeth Knowles, Debra Riegert, Susan Barker, and Karyn Slutsky.

—Eric S. Knowles, Fayetteville, Arkansas
—Jay A. Linn, Chester, Pennsylvania

Resistance and Persuasion

Introduction

1

The Importance of Resistance to Persuasion

Eric S. Knowles
University of Arkansas

Jay A. Linn
Widener University

This book explores persuasion by considering its antithesis: resistance. Resistance hounds persuasion the way friction frustrates motion. To accomplish the latter, you have to expect and, preferably, manage the former. It makes sense that those who desire to understand persuasion should also seek to understand the nature and operation of resistance to persuasion.

As the next 14 chapters show, the focus on resistance does more than supplement the study of persuasion. It opens new windows to the processes involved in persuasion and unlocks a storehouse of new influence strategies. The following chapters show how resistance can be reduced, and therefore persuasion achieved, by training people to be appropriately resistant, by postponing consequences to the future, by focusing resistance on realistic concerns, by forewarning that a message will be coming, by simply acknowledging resistance, by raising self-esteem and a sense of efficacy, and by consuming resistance. New insights, new influence strategies, and new facets of persuasion emerge from a focus on resistance.

DEFINITIONS OF RESISTANCE

Psychological resistance is a broad term, with a long and varied history, that refers to a variety of specific events. The term has been used to refer to the noncompliance with a directive (Newman, 2002), a desire to counteract someone else's attempt to limit one's choices (Brehm, 1966), unwillingness to achieve insight about the real nature of one's thoughts or feelings (Messer, 2002), avoidance of unpleasant or dangerous feelings (Perls, Hefferline, & Goodman, 1951), or the feeling of ambivalence about change (Arkowitz, 2002).

Perhaps it is fair to say that resistance is a concept with a clear nucleus and fuzzy edges. As editors, we asked authors to be attentive to the issue of definition, to articulate the definitions and definitional issues raised by their topic and approach. This first chapter will start the defining process generally and then proceed to discussing the varieties and dimensions of psychological resistance.

Webster's New World College Dictionary includes these four definitions of resistance: (a) "The act of resisting, opposing, withstanding, etc.," (b) "Power or capacity to resist," (c) "Opposition of some force . . . to another or others," and (d) "A force that retards, hinders, or opposes motion. . . ." The first of these four definitions references resistance as a behavioral outcome, the act of withstanding influence. The other three reference more motivational aspects of resistance, as a power or oppositional force.

Clear Core

Resistance to persuasion is familiar to anyone who has offered advice or counseling, delivered a sales pitch, or tried to enlist others in a plan of action. Resistance can be seen in a smirk, that stare of inattention, the sentence that begins, "Well, perhaps, but . . ." The clear core of the definition of resistance is that it is a reaction against change. It becomes evident in the presence of some pressure for change. McGuire (1964) set the stage for discussions of resistance to persuasion. He was interested primarily in increasing people's ability to resist unwanted influence, a concern shared by Sagarin and Cialdini (this volume). McGuire defined resistance to persuasion as the ability to withstand a persuasive attack. McGuire treated resistance as a variable potential (rather than kinetic) response, ready to spring forward when needed. It could be built up through inoculation or bolstering, perhaps diminished in other ways, but it was a property of the person, the potential to resist persuasion. McGuire's inoculation strategies increased resistance in two ways, first, by increasing motivation to resist, and second, by arming the person with the weapons needed to accomplish the resistance. The Sagarin and Cialdini (this volume) chapter details the importance of both of these features of resistance. Interestingly, we will see from the Sagarin and Cialdini chapter that the story does not end there. Training people to resist persuasion has other consequences that McGuire (1964) didn't anticipate. Sagarin and Cialdini's research shows that training people to resist illegitimate sources has the attendant effect of allowing them to be more easily persuaded by legitimate sources. Focusing resistance and providing success experiences at resisting illegitimate sources frees the trained participant to be more receptive to other, perhaps more appropriate and useful persuasion.

Outcome Versus Motive

Resistance has acquired a dual definition in psychology. On the one hand, it defines an outcome: the outcome of not being moved by pressures to change. On the other hand, it identifies a motivational state: the motivation to oppose and counter pressures to change.

In part, the distinction is driven by methodology, whether the research has access to the experience or just to the result. Several chapters in this volume employ meta-analyses, where various studies of attitude change are characterized and compared (Quinn & Wood, this volume; Johnson, Smith-McLallen, Killeya, & Levin, this volume). This methodology has to rely solely on the outcome of persuasion, whether and how much the persuasive attempt was effective. The reliance on the behavioral outcome raises an interesting definitional issue. In some cases a persuasive message, even a very strong one, has no effect on the recipient. A strong change attempt leaves the recipient unchanged. In other cases a persuasive message may produce a boomerang effect. The recipient changes in a direction *opposite* to the one advocated in the message. Are these two the same? Are they both resistance? Johnson et al. (this volume) tussle with this problem and decide to investigate boomerang effects separately from the absence of change.

Defining resistance as a motivational desire raises other issues. Motivations to oppose may not result in behavioral resistance. As Wegener, Petty, Smoak, and Fabrigar (this volume) and Tormala and Petty (this volume) discuss, resistance may not alter the outcome, but it may affect other reactions to the influence attempt.

To some extent the outcome and motivational definitions are theoretically linked. A motivation to oppose would promote the outcome of not changing. However, the two definitions are also not completely overlapping.

Resistance as Attitude

One model of attitude structure distinguishes three components: affective, cognitive, and behavioral. This tripartite model applies to resistance as well. "I don't like it!", "I don't believe it!", and "I won't do it!" are the affective, cognitive, and behavioral components of resistance, respectively. Some authors focus more on one component, some authors on another. Studies of the failure to comply with a request (e.g., Quinn & Wood, this volume; Johnson et al., this volume) reference resistance through the behavioral component. Studies of counterarguing to a persuasive message or evaluating outcomes in the future (e.g., Haugtvedt, Shakarchi, Samuelson, & Liu, this volume; Sherman, Crawford, &

McConnell, this volume; Wegener et. al, this volume) reference resistance primarily through the cognitive component. Studies of changes in preferences for alternatives or action (e.g., Knowles & Linn, this volume; Jacks & O'Brien, this volume) seem to place more emphasis on the affective components of resistance.

Source of Resistance

Although resistance is a response to pressures for change, the source of resistance is sometimes attributed more to the person, and sometimes it is attributed more to the situation. Many of the chapters in this volume identify or posit stable individual differences in resistance, and in doing so, presume that resistance to be largely a quality of the person (cf., Briñol, Rucker, Tormala, & Petty, this volume; Shakarchi & Haugtvedt, this volume), or the person's attitude (Wegener et al., this volume). As a stable quality of the person, resistance lies in wait, a potential response always ready to be enacted if needed.

Brehm's (1966; Brehm & Brehm, 1981) wonderful concept of "reactance" emphasizes a different source for resistance, an external source. Reactance, as used by Brehm (1966), is caused by external threats to one's freedom of choice. When a person senses that someone else is limiting his or her freedom to choose or act, an uncomfortable state of reactance results, creating motivation to reassert that freedom. This externally provoked contrariness initiates oppositional feelings and behaviors; the reactant person likes the forbidden fruit even more, and finds ways to enact the banned behavior. Two sets of factors determine the amount of reactance (Brehm, 1966; Brehm & Brehm, 1981). One set concerns the freedoms that are threatened. The more numerous and important the freedoms, the greater the reactance to losing them. A second set of factors concerns the nature of the threat. Arbitrary, blatant, direct, and demanding requests will create more reactance than legitimate, subtle, indirect, and delicate requests. Without the threat, there would be no resistant reaction, so reactance is, as the name implies, reactant, and thus stands in contrast to the forms of resistance that are more intrinsic, permanent parts of the person or attitude. The chapter by Fuegen and Brehm (this volume) illustrates new information about the reactant process. It apparently is more fragile than first thought—weak threats seem not to raise this reaction, and very strong threats apparently overcome it.

FOUR FACES OF RESISTANCE:
REACTANCE, DISTRUST, SCRUTINY,
AND INERTIA

As we think about the nature of resistance, we identify four different but probably related faces. We think of these not as different kinds of resistance, but as different perceptual stances toward it, much the same way an object viewed from four directions may present varied retinal projections but still be seen as the same entity.

Reactance

One face of resistance is the reactance described by Brehm (1966). This face of resistance recognizes the influence attempt as an integral element of resistance. Reactance is initiated only when the influence is directly perceived and when it threatens a person's choice alternatives. This view of resistance also emphasizes the affective ("I don't like it!") and motivational ("I won't do it!") sides of resistance.

Distrust

Another face of resistance spotlights the target of change, and it reveals a general distrust of proposals. People become guarded and wary when faced with a proposal, offer, or message to change. They wonder what the motive behind the proposal might be, what the true facts are. This face of resistance underlies both affective ("I don't like it!") and cognitive ("I don't believe it!") reactions to influence. We chose to describe this face as "distrust" rather than "paranoia" because some degree of this wariness seems legitimate. The persuader's goals may be divergent from the target's goals and may, in fact, be exploitive.

Scrutiny

A third face of resistance is a general scrutiny that influence, offers, or requests create. When people become aware that they are the target of an influence attempt, a natural reaction is to attend more carefully and thoughtfully to every aspect of the situation (Langer, 1989; Petty & Cacioppo, 1986). This is a form of resistance that puts emphasis on the proposal itself. The careful scrutiny of the proposal means that each point is examined more carefully and questioned more thoroughly. The strengths of an argument are appreciated and accepted, and to that extent the proposal is believed. But, the weaknesses of an argument are exposed, evaluated, and countered, and to that extent, the proposal is rejected. Several chapters in this volume emphasize this scrutiny face of resistance and illustrate the many ways that this primarily cognitive element ("I don't believe it!") works. Wegener et al.'s chapter on multiple routes to resistance to persuasion discusses the many, often subtle ways this form of resistance works. The scrutiny face is also discussed in the chapter by Johnson et al. (this volume) on the power of positive thinking and in the chapter by Haugtvedt et al. (this volume), which explores resistance in consumer psychology.

Inertia

A fourth face of resistance might be called inertia. This is a face that is not reactant to the proposer or the proposal, and it doesn't necessarily lead to greater scrutiny, distrust, or reactance. Inertia is a quality that focuses more on staying put than on resisting change. It is one face of the great equilibrium motive

(Heider, 1946) that attempts to keep the attitude system in balance. To the extent that a request, an offer, or a persuasive message asks for change in affect, behavior, or belief, the inertia of personality and attitude frustrates that change. However, this form of resistance has more in common with the drag of an anchor than with the antagonism of the provoked.

CONCLUSION

Resistance is the tug-of-war partner with persuasion. Just as it takes two opposing teams for a tug-of-war competition, resistance and persuasion are opposing yet integral parts of a persuasive interaction. However, treatments of persuasion in psychology, communication, rhetoric, political science, and marketing most often overlook, or at least underplay, the role of resistance in the process. Typically, when resistance is discussed, McGuire's (1964) research on instilling greater resistance through inoculation and bolstering is treated in a separate and isolated section. This segregation fails to appreciate the full implications of McGuire's contribution and the crucial role that resistance plays in all persuasion. McGuire (1964) identified the interplay between persuasive challenges and resistance to influence as a dynamic process, McGuire's system identified motivation and argument as the elements involved in change. If the person had few counterarguments and little motivation, then he or she was easily persuaded; but if motivation were increased and counterarguments made available, then influence could be resisted. This is a view that is echoed in the Knowles and Linn (this volume) chapter that explores the implications of this approach–avoidance model of persuasion. The key element is that complex situations like persuasive messages, offers, or commands set up conflicting motives. The ambivalence of the situation (Arkowitz, 2002) is one of its hallmarks. And, like any nonlinear system, the interplay of these opposing forces can yield interesting, unexpected, and sometimes paradoxical consequences.

A LOOK AHEAD

This book seeks to do two things. First, it strives to establish resistance as a legitimate, informative, and coequal member, along with the influence attempt, of the persuasive duo. The chapters as a set define, dissect, understand, and explain the roles of resistance in persuasion. As many of the chapters show, the processes of resistance are not simply the inverse of persuasion. Resistance has its own dynamic, often quite complex, often quite malleable. Second, this book demonstrates the benefits of adding resistance to the persuasive equation. As you will see in the chapters, there are many new revelations about persuasion made available by a focus on resistance. The chapters demonstrate a number of new ways that influence might be promoted or inhibited by focusing on resistance rather than on the persuasive message. We will see that simply acknowledging resistance goes part way to reducing it (Knowles & Linn, this volume; Wegener et al., this volume), that raising reactance to a message makes a strong message more persuasive (Haugtvedt et al., this volume), that training people to identify illegitimate sources of information makes them more persuaded by legitimate sources (Sagarin & Cialdini, this volume), that putting arguments into a narrative rather than a message increases their influence (Dal Cin, Zanna, & Fong, this volume), and that affirming the target seems to reduce resistance to persuasion in general (Jacks & O'Brien, this volume). These resistance-based influence approaches, other insights about resistance, and other strategies to create or combat change await you in the chapters ahead.

REFERENCES

Arkowitz, H. (2002). Toward an integrative perspective on resistance to change. *Journal of Clinical Psychology, 58,* 219–227.

Brehm, J. W. (1966). *A theory of psychological reactance.* New York: Academic Press.

Brehm, S. S., & Brehm, J. W. (1981). *Psychological reactance: A theory of freedom and control.* New York: Academic Press.

Heider, F. (1946). Attitudes and cognitive organization. *Journal of Psychology, 21,* 107–112.

Langer, E. J. (1989). *Mindfulness.* Reading, MA: Addison-Wesley.

McGuire, W. J. (1964). Inducing resistance to persuasion: Some contemporary approaches. In L. Berkowitz (Ed.), *Advances in experimental social psychology* (Vol. 1, pp. 191–229). New York: Academic Press.

Messer, S. B. (2002). A psychodynamic perspective on resistance in psychotherapy: Viva la resistance. *Journal of Clinical Psychology, 58,* 157–163.

Newman, C. A. (2002). A cognitive perspective on resistance in psychotherapy. *Journal of Clinical Psychology, 58,* 165–174.

Perls, F., Hefferline, R., & Goodman, P. (1951). *Gestalt therapy: Excitement and growth in the human personality.* New York: Julian.

Petty, R. E., & Cacioppo, J. T. (1986). *Communication and persuasion: Central and peripheral routes to attitude change.* New York: Springer-Verlag.

Webster's new world college dictionary (4th ed.). (1999). New York: Wiley.

Nature of Resistance
in Persuasion

2

Multiple Routes to Resisting Attitude Change

Duane T. Wegener
Purdue University

Richard E. Petty
The Ohio State University

Natalie D. Smoak
Purdue University

Leandre R. Fabrigar
Queen's University

As many of the chapters in this volume illustrate, attempts at persuasion might often benefit from techniques aimed at addressing the "resistance" forces working against acceptance of a persuasive appeal. For example, young smokers often resist messages aimed at getting them to stop smoking, preferring to believe that the highly publicized health risks are exaggerated or do not apply to them (e.g., Milam, Sussman, Ritt-Olson, & Clyde, 2000; see also Coleman, Stevenson, & Wilson, 2000). If one were able to convince young smokers that the risks do apply to them or that the risks are greater than they currently believe, this would certainly increase the effectiveness of an appeal that rests on these reasons not to smoke. "Addressing resistance" can also be substantially less direct. For example, Linn and Knowles (2002) increased the effectiveness of a persuasive appeal by simply acknowledging that the message recipient would probably want to disagree with the message (see also Knowles & Linn, this volume). Somewhat paradoxically, allowing people the "freedom to resist" appears to undermine the motivation to do so, consistent with what might be expected from reactance theory (Brehm, 1966).

In many situations, however, one of the primary goals of the communication is to create an attitude that *does* resist future attempts at change. For example, one of the most important challenges in the health domain is how to effect lasting changes in health-relevant behaviors (i.e., to create positive attitudes toward health-enhancing behaviors and negative attitudes toward risky behaviors that persist over time, in part by resisting attempts at further change; Petty & Cacioppo, 1996). As many parents can attest, they would want very much for their children to form lasting negative attitudes toward such behaviors as smoking and taking drugs and/or lasting positive attitudes toward such behaviors as regular exercise and eating a nutritious diet. Development of such attitudes would be one primary determinant of the behaviors that would keep those children healthy over the course of a lifetime (e.g., Albarracín, Johnson, Fishbein, & Muellerleile, 2001; Kraus, 1995; Sheeran & Taylor, 1999).

In fact, much of the classic work in attitude change has dealt with the possible ways to induce, rather than reduce, the resistance property of attitudes. For example, McGuire and Papageorgis (1961; see also McGuire, 1964; Papageorgis & McGuire, 1961) noted that some of our most cherished ideals (e.g., freedom of speech) and fundamental beliefs (e.g., the value of brushing one's teeth) were highly susceptible to change and thus needed to be made more resistant. In a pioneering program of research, McGuire examined the effects of providing either supportive or weak attacking information on future resistance to change. In this research, presentation of attacking information that could be refuted (either within the message or by message recipients themselves) enhanced resistance to attacks on frequent tooth brushing. The basic idea behind this research was that "cultural truisms" such as brushing one's teeth after every meal were generally endorsed but rarely attacked and therefore rarely defended. Attacks on the endorsed belief were thought to motivate counterarguing of the attack and generation of a rationale that would support the belief. Providing support directly was found to be less successful in producing later resistance. Interestingly, weak attacks along with refutations were often approximately equal in effect, regardless of whether the attacks and refutations directly addressed the arguments to be used in later attacks or not (McGuire, 1964; McGuire & Papageorgis, 1961; Papageorgis & McGuire, 1961; see also Szybillo & Heslin, 1973) although some studies have found significant advantages for refutations that match the content of later attacking messages (e.g., Tannenbaum, 1967). The applied significance of inoculation theory is clear, and inoculation treatments have also been shown to effectively increase resistance to development of risky health behaviors such as smoking (e.g., Pfau, Van Bockern, & Kang, 1992).

Like the research by McGuire and colleagues, much work in attitudes has regarded "resistance" as strongly tied to counterarguing of attacking messages. For example, work on forewarning of persuasive intent has focused on mechanisms such as anticipatory counterarguing as important in producing resistance to the upcoming message (e.g., Petty & Cacioppo, 1977; Quinn & Wood, this volume). Yet, there might be a variety of reasons for attacking messages to be ineffective. For example, messages might also be ineffective because recipients of the message engage in attitude bolstering (i.e., selective generation or recall of information supportive of their attitudes; Lewan & Stotland, 1961; Lydon, Zanna, & Ross, 1988; Briñol et al., this volume) or because they derogate the source of the message (e.g., Tannenbaum, Macauley, & Norris, 1966; Zuwerink

& Devine, 1996). In this chapter, we begin by discussing some different ways to think about what "resistance" is and from whence it comes. Within that context, we describe a variety of mechanisms that can result in resistance to change, paying special attention to the amount of information processing involved in those mechanisms. In so doing, we also present ongoing research that illustrates both thoughtful and nonthoughtful processes by which resistance can occur. The amount of thought that goes into opposing a message should be particularly important, in part because attitude change outcomes that involve high levels of information scrutiny generally have stronger and more enduring consequences than outcomes that involve lower levels of information scrutiny (Petty, Haugtvedt, & Smith, 1995). Learning about the processes that lead to resistance also puts one in a much stronger position to intervene and change a resistance outcome, because a process-level understanding of the phenomenon would often provide predictions about when the processes occur and what types of circumstances could limit or change the operation of those processes.

THE ATTITUDE STRENGTH BACKDROP

Over the past 10 to 15 years, there has been a great deal of interest in the overall "strength" of attitudes, with strength defined in terms of the forces the attitude can withstand and create. That is, Krosnick and Petty (1995) defined strength in terms of the persistence of the attitude over time (withstanding the force of time), the resistance of the attitude to attack (withstanding the force of opposing persuasive appeals), and the ability of the attitude to guide related thoughts and behavior (creating a force that guides cognition and action; see also Eagly & Chaiken, 1993, 1998; Petty & Wegener, 1998).

Many properties of attitudes have been identified as increasing attitude strength. For example, attitudes are more likely to guide behavior when they are accessible (i.e., when they come to mind quickly upon encountering the attitude object, see Fazio, 1995) and when they are based on high levels of attitude-relevant knowledge (e.g., Davidson, Yantis, Norwood, & Montano, 1985) or on beliefs that are consistent with the overall evaluation (Norman, 1975; see Petty & Krosnick, 1995, for reviews of many strength-related properties of attitudes).

Our own research on attitude strength has focused on the elaboration (thoughtful processing) of attitude-relevant information. Attitudes based on high, rather than low, levels of elaboration have been found to persist longer over time, to resist the opposing persuasive messages better, and to predict more accurately future behavior (see Petty, Haugtvedt, & Smith, 1995, for a review). For example, Petty, Haugtvedt, Heesacker, and Cacioppo (1995; discussed by Petty, Haugtvedt, & Smith, 1995) manipulated the personal relevance of a strong (compelling) persuasive message that was also attributed to three expert sources. Attitudes following the message were equally extreme for people who encountered the message under conditions of high and low personal relevance. However, these two groups were differentially affected by a second message on the same topic that argued weakly for the opposite view from that of the first message. The people for whom the topic was low in relevance (and who, presumably, arrived at their initial attitudes because of peripheral cues such as the expert sources in the first communication; Petty, Cacioppo, & Goldman, 1981) changed their attitudes more following the (second) weak opposing message than did people for whom the topic was high in relevance (whose attitudes were presumably based on careful processing of the strong message arguments). Similar effects have been observed when levels of elaboration have been indexed via relevant individual differences (Haugtvedt & Petty, 1992) such as "need for cognition" (NC; Cacioppo & Petty, 1982b).[1] According to the Elaboration Likelihood Model (ELM; Petty & Cacioppo, 1986a), this is because attitudes based on high levels of elaboration should have strongly interconnected cognitive and affective structures, structures that are not only internally relatively complex, but are also more likely to be linked to related attitudes and information (Petty, Haugtvedt, & Smith, 1995; see also Eagly & Chaiken, 1998). Such strong, interconnected structures should provide informational resources useful in defending the attitude from attack and should also create stronger motives to resist future changes in the attitude (e.g., because the interconnected structure could provide a larger number of elements supporting a general cognitive consistency, the undermining of which would be aversive, e.g., Abelson, Aronson, McGuire, Newcomb, Rosenberg, & Tannenbaum, 1968).

A critic might interpret these elaboration-resistance studies as showing simply that people high in elaboration (based on individual differences or manipulations of processing motivation) take on attitudes that are consistent with the arguments that are available in the entire setting (i.e., strong arguments on one side, and weak on the other), whereas people low in elaboration take on attitudes more consistent with the available cues (e.g., an expert source on each side of the issue). However, similar resistance effects of elaboration have also been found when the attacking message contains arguments as strong as those in the initial message. For example, Haugtvedt and Wegener (1994) used opposing messages pretested as equally strong and presented them to research participants in either a pro/con or con/pro order. For example, in one study, participants either received a message in favor of building new nuclear power plants followed by a message opposed to such plants or received the same messages in the reverse order. Therefore, the same messages sometimes served as the initial message and sometimes as the attacking message (thereby totally equating the strength of initial and attacking messages). Similar to the previous ELM research, participants either thought that nuclear power plants were being considered for construction in their own and neighboring states (high personal relevance) or in distant states (low personal relevance). Consistent with higher levels of resistance being associated with attitudes based on high levels of elaboration, Haugtvedt and Wegener (1994) found primacy effects (greater influence of first than second messages) when personal relevance was high, but found recency effects (less influence of first than of second messages) when personal relevance was low. In addition, when elaboration was high rather than low, attitudes were more highly correlated with thoughts listed by participants as having come to mind while reading the messages, and a larger number of direct counterarguments were generated and listed as coming to mind in response to the second (attacking) message.

High levels of elaboration of an initial attitude have also been shown to decrease later persuasion (i.e., to increase resistance) in face-to-face communication. For example, Shestowsky, Wegener, and Fabrigar (1998) provided people high and low in need for cognition (NC; Cacioppo & Petty, 1982b) with diverging information about a civil court case before the people were split into pairs with each pair including one person high in NC and the other low, to discuss the case and arrive at a consensus in their dyad. Shestowsky et al. expected that high-NC people would form opinions of the case that were based on higher levels of elaboration than for their low-NC counterparts. The diverging information about the case meant that the high- and low-NC people began their dyadic discussion disagreeing about the appropriate verdict in the case. Consistent with high levels of elaboration leading to greater resistance to change (as well as other related strength properties), the pre-discussion views of people high in NC better predicted the dyadic decisions.[2] Also, Johnston, Fabrigar, Wegener, and Rosen (2002) found that the level of elaboration (manipulated to be high or low using a combination of high personal relevance with low distraction or low personal relevance with high distraction) can influence the strength of majority versus minority influence effects in group discussions. Majority and minority opinions were created by distributing the same diverging descriptions of a civil case used by Shestowsky et al. (1998). As in much majority/minority research, in the Johnston et al. study, majority views best predicted group decisions. However, this majority influence pattern was enhanced if the majority also elaborated the initial information more than the minority. In contrast, if the minority elaborated more than the majority, it decreased the majority advantage in group decisions.

ALTERNATIVE WAYS TO DEFINE RESISTANCE

Perhaps the most typical approach to resistance, and the approach that has been illustrated in each of the preceding lines of research, has been to treat resistance as a property or quality of the attitude itself. As noted earlier, for example, the objective of McGuire's (1964) research was to increase the resistance to change of each "cultural truism." This was accomplished by enhancing both ability and motivation to counterargue the attacking message. In fact, this active counterarguing is also often implied by the term "resistance" (see Quinn & Wood, this volume). Treating resistance as due to the process of counterarguing might follow from the conception of resistance as a property of the attitude in that increases in elaboration (thinking) about the attitude object (which creates resistant attitudes) should activate related knowledge that can be used to counterargue later opposing messages. Just as highly elaborated attitudes are more likely to guide behaviors, attitudes based on extensive thought should also guide related information processing. This could often include interpreting information in opposing messages as failing to compel the person away from his or her existing opinions (see later discussion of use of attitudes in later information processing). Also, an attitude linked to many related attitudes and other knowledge structures might make people more motivated to maintain that attitude in face of attack.

In many circumstances, however, it might be useful to think about resistance somewhat more broadly (see also Petty, Tormala, & Rucker, in press). That is, in addition to resistance as a *property* (quality) of an attitude and as the active *process* of counterarguing, one might consider resistance as a *motive* or as a persuasion *outcome*. Consideration of resistance as an outcome of persuasive attempts would prompt a treatment of resistance that is more parallel to contemporary treatments of persuasion. As noted by Petty, Tormala, and Rucker (in press), resistance can be the result of many different processes.[3] Most important for the current discussion, we would emphasize that some of the processes that lead to resistance outcomes (i.e., relative lack of change) are more thoughtful than others. Just as it has been important to dissociate outcome from process in work on persuasion (see Petty & Wegener, 1999), it should be equally important to dissociate the resistance outcome from the responsible processes.

Resistance as an Outcome

In traditional studies of resistance to persuasion, the level of resistance for a particular attitude is indexed by the relative lack of change in the face of a persuasive appeal that attacks the person's initial attitude. For example, when comparing attitudes based on high versus low levels of elaboration, resistance of those attitudes to change has been indexed by the relative amount of change (with attitudes based on high levels of elaboration generally changing less than attitudes based on low levels of elaboration, e.g., Petty, Haugtvedt, et al., 1995). In many of these studies, there has been some movement toward the attacking message, but lack of full acceptance of the opposing view suggests that there have been at least some forces at work that resist change. Therefore, most resulting attitudes (which fall between the initial attitude and the position advocated by the attacking message) are the result of some persuasion—movement toward the message—and some resistance—lack of movement toward the message.[4] If resistance and persuasion can be thought of as part and parcel of the same outcome (i.e., if the same change in attitudes can be thought of in terms of amount of persuasion and in terms of amount of resistance), this would suggest that one should ask conceptual questions that are parallel for persuasion and resistance. Yet, because studies of resistance have tended to focus on resistance as a property of the attitude (or as the result of a specific process such as counterarguing), researchers have not generally asked questions about resistance that parallel the questions asked about persuasion.

As is well-documented in the attitudes domain, one persuasion outcome can occur for many different reasons. For example, imagine that one is studying reactions to an advertisement for a certain type of exercise equipment. Also, imagine that the ad results in more favorable attitudes toward the equipment when the ad is encountered in the middle of a funny situation comedy than when the ad is encountered within a more neutral, but equally popular, nature show. One might understand this outcome as increased persuasion occurring when message recipients are in a positive mood (e.g., Petty, Fabrigar, & Wegener, 2003). Yet, in contemporary persuasion research, such a conclusion would barely be a beginning. A natural question stemming from current dual-process (Chaiken & Trope, 1999) or multiprocess (Petty & Cacioppo, 1986a; Petty & Wegener, 1999) theories would be, "Which processes and factors led to the research outcome?" That is, happy mood could lead to positive attitudes because message recipients were not thinking much (because they were distracted or uninterested) and positive mood served as a peripheral cue (Petty & Cacioppo, 1986b) or heuristic (Cacioppo & Petty, 1982a; Chaiken, 1987; Schwarz & Clore, 1983). However, the same outcome (greater persuasion in a positive mood) could also come about: (a) if message recipients are thinking a lot, but positive mood biased the interpretation of ambiguous information about the product (e.g., Petty, Schumann, Richman, & Strathman, 1993) or served as a strong merit of the product (i.e., if the product was viewed more favorably because use of the product simply makes one feel good, see Petty, Cacioppo, & Kasmer, 1988); (b) if positive mood decreased processing of the message and the message contained rather weak arguments supporting purchase of the product (Schwarz, Bless, & Bohner, 1991); (c) if positive mood increased processing of the message and the message contained strong arguments supporting purchase of the product (Wegener, Petty, & Smith, 1995); or (d) if message recipients realize that positive mood can sometimes lead to negative biases (e.g., Dermer et al., 1979; Wegener, Petty, & Klein, 1994) and they attempt to correct (compensate) for this presumed bias (DeSteno, Petty, Wegener, & Rucker, 2000; Wegener & Petty, 1997).

According to the ELM, each of these processes would be most likely under a specific set of conditions. That is, the "cue effects" of mood would be most likely when motivation or ability to process is low. The "biased processing" and "argument" effects are most likely when motivation and ability are high (depending on the ambiguity of the object-relevant information, cf., Chaiken & Maheswaran, 1994, and the ease of processing the mood as an argument; see Wegener & Petty, 2001). The "amount of processing" effects are most likely when background levels of elaboration are not constrained to be high or low. Finally, according to the Flexible Correction Model, the correction effects are most likely when the issue of potential bias is salient to the message recipient (depending on factors such as the amount of previous experience with the perceived bias and relevant correction), and people are motivated and able to correct for the perceived bias (Wegener & Petty, 1997; Wegener, Dunn, & Tokusato, 2001; see Wegener & Petty, 2001, for a discussion of the multiple processes by which mood can influence post-message attitudes and judgments).

It is important to understand which process(es) led to a particular outcome, in part, because the process of change will help determine how long that change lasts, whether the change translates into changes in behavior, and whether the new attitude guides future information processing and judgment (e.g., Petty, Haugtvedt, & Smith, 1995). If the process was more elaborative (i.e., if the effect was due to biased processing, use of mood as an argument when processing is high, increases in thought about strong arguments, or effortful corrections for perceived negative biases), then the resulting attitude would be hypothesized to last longer and to guide future behavior, information processing, and judgment to a greater extent than if the process leading to the same judgment was less thoughtful. Of course, when elaboration is high, the resulting attitude is also hypothesized to resist future attempts at change better—resistance as a property (quality) of the attitude.

Knowing which process(es) leads to a persuasion outcome also equips one to predict which types of factors might influence when the outcome occurs, and how one might change or overcome that result. For example, if one finds that persuasion is the result of effortful processing, this implies that overcoming that persuasion would often be better accomplished through introducing substantive information that counters the implications of the message arguments rather than introducing a credible or attractive source that advocates an alternative position. However, if the persuasion result is coming about under conditions of relatively little thought, the introduction of new arguments might be less successful than the introduction of salient sources or other cues.

Parallel Treatment of Resistance

But what if message recipients successfully ward off any impact of the exercise ad? One could easily treat this resistance outcome in a manner that directly parallels the processes considered as responsible for the persuasion outcome. For example, what if one were to find relative lack of change by message recipients who received the exercise ad in a positive (comedy) program? These message recipients might have failed to change because they were unmotivated or unable to process the message and used some negative aspect of the source as a rejection cue (e.g., self-interest of the source making him or her appear untrustworthy). Alternatively, recipients might have engaged in more thoughtful (and biased) processing of the ad that led to counterarguing it and maintaining the original attitude. Lack of change could also spring from relatively high levels of processing of arguments that are relatively weak, or low levels of processing of arguments that are relatively strong. Finally, lack of change could result from corrections for perceived positive biases.[5]

Therefore, viewing resistance as an outcome can lead one to think about resistance questions in much the same way one thinks about persuasion questions. If most persuasion outcomes actually represent some level of persuasion (change toward the message) and some level of resistance (lack of change toward the message), then many of the process questions should be conceptually similar. Though generally discussed using "persuasion" terminology, reactions to most messages could be thought of as involving some resistance. After all, in a world with absolutely no resistance, people would completely accept the advocacy of all messages they receive. Of course, this does not happen, and likely for many different reasons. The task, then, for investigations of resistance is similar to the task in studies of persuasion—to discover the reasons why lack of change (or presence of change) occurred.

Effortful Versus Noneffortful Resistance

In some initial data, Haugtvedt and Wegener (2002) accumulated evidence of both effortful and noneffortful resistance to persuasive appeals. Part of this study was patterned after the Petty, Haugtvedt, et al. (1995) and Haugtvedt and Petty (1992) research mentioned earlier. That is, equal pre-attack attitudes were created for people at high and low levels of processing of an initial message. In the current case, amount of processing was influenced by a manipulation of personal relevance (Petty & Cacioppo, 1990), and the initial communication contained both strong arguments in support of the advocacy (establishment of a comprehensive exam graduation requirement) and a credible source (a Princeton Professor of Education). When research participants received an attacking message similar to the attacking messages used by Petty, Haugtvedt, et al. (1995) and Haugtvedt and Petty (1992)—weak arguments with credible sources—the results looked much like those previously obtained. That is, attitudes initially based on high levels of information processing were less likely to change in response to the opposing message. This pattern replicated the previous "active resistance" results in which "strong attitudes" led to counterarguing of attacking messages (e.g., Haugtvedt & Petty, 1992; Haugtvedt & Wegener, 1994). However, when the weak attacking message was presented by a noncredible source (i.e., a janitor from Michigan State University), both people for whom the topic was relevant and those for whom the topic was irrelevant changed relatively little in response to the attacking message (see Fig 2.1). This suggests that both change and lack of change in response to the attacking message were based in relatively peripheral processes for people who received the messages in conditions of low personal relevance. This also suggests that lack of change in the face of attack can be relatively thoughtful or nonthoughtful.

Such claims treat resistance outcomes as the result of process rather than as a property of the attitude per se. In certain respects, the idea that resistance can be relatively nonthoughtful or thoughtful might appear similar to the notion that

Credible Attack Source

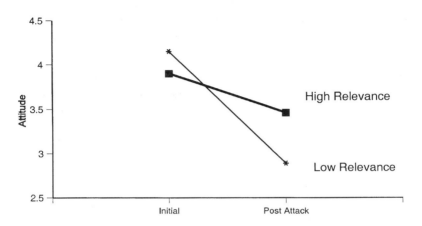

High Relevance

Low Relevance

Noncredible Attack Source

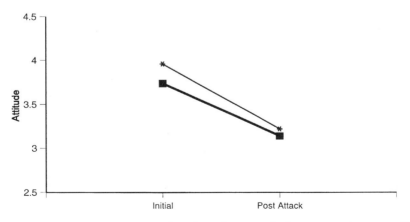

FIG. 2.1.   Resistance as a function of personal relevance and source of the attacking message (from Haugtvedt & Wegener, 2002).

"defense motivation" can be served by both "heuristic" and "systematic" processing (e.g., Giner-Sorolla & Chaiken, 1997). Consistent with our emphasis on multiple processes by which such outcomes can occur, however, we believe that one must also be careful not to make one particular motivation isomorphic with the outcome. Just as one can obtain an outcome because of different processes, the same outcome (or even the same process) could be the result of different motives.

Consider a researcher that attributes resistance outcomes to "defense motivation." The outcome (i.e., lack of change) or the process (e.g., source derogation or counterarguing) could come about because of a motive to "defend" the attitude, but it could also come about for other reasons. The presence or absence of such "defensiveness" might or might not covary with the outcome. For example, when one looks at the Petty, Haugtvedt, et al. (1995) data, one might assume that people with attitudes based on high levels of elaboration experience greater "defense motivation" when they encounter the attacking message, and that this is why they change less than people with attitudes based on low levels of elaboration. However, this assumption would not necessarily hold up well when considering the Haugtvedt and Wegener (2002) data described earlier. In that study, both defense "motivated" and "unmotivated" individuals (i.e., people with attitudes based on high and low levels of elaboration) change equally little when the attacking message is presented by a noncredible source. Therefore, if defense motivation is associated with elaboration, the Haugtvedt and Wegener (2002) data show resistance with little defense motivation. Alternatively, if one were to assume that elaboration is not associated with defense motivation, then the Petty, Haugtvedt, et al. (1995) data (and the credible source conditions of the Haugtvedt and Wegener [2002] study) show differences in amount of resistance without differences in defense motivation.

Equally important, one could imagine a variety of settings in which message recipients would want very much to keep their existing attitude, not because they are motivated to defend the attitude per se, but because they are highly motivated to hold correct or accurate attitudes (see Petty & Cacioppo, 1986b). Even if one were perfectly happy to adopt another position if it is correct, the current attitude might be kept precisely because the current attitude is believed to be correct (Petty, Priester, & Wegener, 1994; Petty & Wegener, 1999; see Petty, Tormala, & Rucker, in press, for a discussion of the various sources of a "resistance motive," including accuracy).

THOUGHTFUL AND NONTHOUGHTFUL USE OF ATTITUDES IN RESISTANCE

Even without considering "defense" or "resistance" motives, one could find similar resistance outcomes for more "cognitive" reasons. For example, attitude-relevant knowledge might predispose certain interpretations of information (Evans & Petty, 1998). That is, information that is at all ambiguous might be understood by using knowledge that inherently supports one's current attitude. In fact, rather than attributing biased processing of information to attitude-related knowledge per se, one might also think about various situations and ways in which people might use the evaluative implications of their attitudes in assessing new information. Consistent with the thrust of the rest of this chapter, use of one's current attitude could be relatively thoughtful or nonthoughtful.

Use of an attitude would be directly relevant to issues of resistance in that use of an attitude as a cue would generally be as a "rejection" cue (i.e., it would be unusual to receive a message that advocates exactly the attitudinal position one already espouses). Fabrigar, Petty, Wegener, Priester, & Brooksbank (2002) examined the thoughtful and nonthoughtful impact of existing attitudes on reactions to generally counter-attitudinal messages. At the beginning of the study, attitudes were measured regarding the building of additional nuclear power plants. Whereas most initial attitudes were somewhat favorable toward such plants, all research participants received a message that argued against nuclear power. Some participants encountered the written messages with little distraction and assumed that the proposed nuclear plants would be built in geographically close locations (high elaboration conditions), whereas other participants believed that plants were being proposed for distant locations and encountered the written messages while concurrently completing an auditory distraction task (low elaboration conditions).

A manipulation of argument quality showed that the elaboration manipulation was successful. That is, the quality of arguments (strong, mixed, or weak) influenced both post-message attitudes and thoughts to a greater extent when personal relevance was high and distraction was low than when personal relevance was low and distraction was high. Consistent with the message being counterattitudinal for most people, significantly more counterarguments (thoughts in opposition to the message) were generated in conditions of high rather than low elaboration. Also, the number of counterarguments was better predicted by premessage attitudes when elaboration was high rather than low.

The top panel of Fig. 2.2 presents the pre-message attitudes, post-message attitudes, and overall favorability of listed thoughts ([proarguments–counterarguments]/total topic-related thoughts) for people in the low-elaboration condition. These paths represent the impact of pre-message attitudes and thoughts controlling for the impact of argument quality. Pre-message attitudes significantly predicted both post-message attitude and thoughts, and thoughts predicted post-message attitudes. Because of the large sample size in the study, the significance of each path is not surprising. After all, the notion of an elaboration continuum in the ELM suggests that both "central" and "peripheral" processes will have at least some impact on attitudes everywhere on the continuum except the theoretical endpoints of the continuum (see Petty & Wegener, 1999). Consistent with the logic of the ELM, however, impact of "central merits" of the attitude object should increase with higher levels of processing, but impact of "peripheral cues" should decrease as processing increases.

Comparing the top and bottom panels of Fig. 2.2, one sees that direct impact of pre-message attitudes on post-message attitudes decreases as one goes from

Low Elaboration

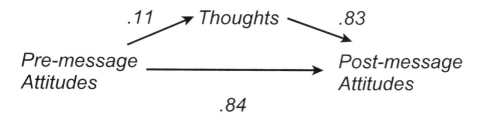

High Elaboration

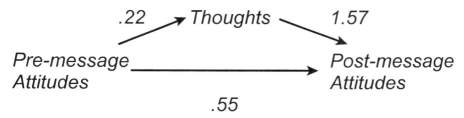

FIG. 2.2. Influence of pre-message attitudes on thoughts and post-message attitudes as a function of amount of elaboration (from Fabrigar, Petty, et al., 2002). Note: All presented regression coefficients are significant at $p < .01$.

the low-elaboration conditions to the high-elaboration conditions. Also, the impact of listed thoughts on post-message attitudes is greater in high- than in low-elaboration settings (see also Chaiken, 1980; Petty & Cacioppo, 1979). Just as importantly, the impact of pre-message attitudes on listed thoughts is greater in high- than in low-elaboration conditions. Therefore, the Fabrigar, Petty, et al. (2002) data suggest both thoughtful and nonthoughtful use of attitudes in information processing. When motivation and/or ability are lacking, attitudes can be used rather directly to reject (or, for some people, accept) the message advocacy. In such settings, the pre-message attitudes are not providing a strong guide for active resistance processes, such as counterarguing. When motivation and ability are higher, however, pre-message attitudes guide information processing, resulting in more negative cognitive responses to the message when pre-message attitudes are more negative toward the advocacy. Both thoughtful and nonthoughtful uses of attitudes increase the similarity between pre-message and

post-message attitudes. But, of course, the more thoughtful route to this resistance to change would be predicted to last longer and produce a stronger guide
to future thought and action. Therefore, the impact of prior attitudes provides
yet another example of a setting in which it is useful to go beyond a persuasion
(or resistance) outcome to learn about the process(es) responsible for the effect.

Consistent with prior treatments of resistance as a property of the attitude, it
could well be that "strong" attitudes create each of the current effects to a greater
extent than "weak" attitudes. A finding of attitude strength effects alone,
therefore, would not necessarily distinguish between thoughtful and nonthoughtful resistance processes. Incorporating the methodological tool of manipulating
argument quality would be perhaps the most valuable addition to many studies
of resistance (or, similarly, the manipulation of salient peripheral cues, such as
source credibility, e.g., Haugtvedt and Wegener, 2002).

ACCEPTANCE AND RESISTANCE PROCESSES

Our discussion thus far has illustrated thoughtful and nonthoughtful processes
in resistance outcomes. Thinking of resistance as the outcome of relative lack
of change, rather than as one particular process (i.e., counterarguing) or motive
(i.e., defense motivation), opens up the topic of resistance to many of the same
process questions common in the attitudes and persuasion literature more generally. That is, in many persuasion settings, there are likely to be potentially
thoughtful mechanisms of resistance (e.g., counterarguing weak arguments) as
well as nonthoughtful mechanisms of resistance (e.g., rejecting on the basis of
negative cues). But just as persuasion through thoughtful mechanisms lasts
longer and influences later thoughts and behavior to a greater extent than persuasion through nonthoughtful mechanisms (Petty, Haugtvedt, & Smith, 1995),
the same should be true of resistance through thoughtful versus nonthoughtful
means. In addition, knowing how and why someone resists change would presumably put one in a better position to create an effective persuasive appeal.
That is, similar to the focus of many chapters in this book, we would assert that
understanding resistance can set the stage for more effective attempts at persuasion. However, understanding the processes that underlie resistance also allows one to address a more traditional and equally important goal. That is,
understanding resistance can also lead to creation of more resistant attitudes in
areas that communicators find of crucial importance (e.g., health, education,
religion, etc.).

Although we have focused on the production of resistance, whereas the majority of chapters in this volume focus on reducing resistance, there is perhaps
at least one additional point of similarity between our approach and that of the
other chapters. In a variety of these chapters, resistance is treated as a somewhat
separate force or entity from persuasion or acceptance (e.g., see Fuegen &

Brehm, this volume; Jacks & O'Brien, this volume; Knowles & Linn, this volume). Similarly, in our approach, one might specify relatively thoughtful versus nonthoughtful *resistance* processes and relatively thoughtful versus nonthoughtful *acceptance* processes. These are often conceptually parallel. For example, as we noted earlier, counterarguing would often be a relatively effortful resistance mechanism. But, of course, one can also generate supportive cognitive responses in the process of effortfully scrutinizing information. And this "proarguing" would increase acceptance rather than resistance. In terms of relatively nonthoughtful resistance versus acceptance processes, one might compare source derogation (cf., Festinger & Maccoby, 1964) with source acceptance via heuristics such as "experts can be trusted" (Chaiken, 1987). As demonstrated by Fabrigar, Petty, et al. (2002; see earlier description), message recipients can use their own preexisting attitudes as either relatively simple rejection cues or more thoughtfully, as the attitudes and associated knowledge form the context in which message arguments are interpreted, scrutinized, and often rejected. Of course, in those circumstances where people receive messages that agree with their existing opinions, these attitudes could be used in thoughtful or nonthoughtful ways to accept the advocacy.

When one considers separable resistance and acceptance mechanisms, the process–outcome relation also might become a bit more complicated. For example, differences in persuasion outcome could be because of differences in resistance processes, acceptance processes, or both. For example, although the number of favorable cognitive responses might often be highly (negatively) correlated with the number of unfavorable cognitive responses, one could imagine certain outcomes being attributed primarily to the favorable or to the unfavorable thoughts.

In this context, it is also important to note that a variety of individual and situational factors could increase each of these types of mechanisms. For example, counterarguing can be increased by encountering weak rather than strong arguments (Petty & Cacioppo, 1979) or by receiving a message that disagrees more extremely with one's preexisting views (Brock, 1967). Interestingly, receiving a message from an expert source can either decrease the generation of counterarguments (Cook, 1969; if the person is open to persuasion, Hass, 1981) or increase the generation of counterarguments (if the person is already committed to his or her attitude position, see Hass, 1981). Consistent with our earlier discussion of motives, one should also note that each of the resistance processes could be enhanced by a variety of motives. For example, when a message consists of relatively weak arguments, counterarguing can be increased by increasing the motive to seek correct (accurate) attitudes in addition to increasing motives to defend the attitude. Similarly, resistance and persuasion outcomes could be influenced by a variety of other motives such as managing impressions (Chaiken, Liberman, & Eagly, 1989; Leippe & Elkin, 1987), preserving the fairness of decisions or procedures (Fleming, Wegener, & Petty, 1999), or defending disadvantaged groups (Petty, Fleming, & White, 1999). As with any other type of possible distinction in social psychology, the ultimate utility of

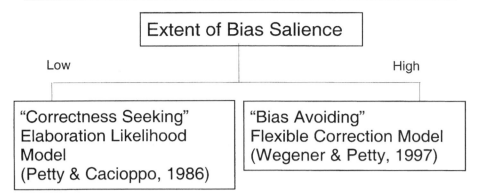

FIG. 2.3. Salience of bias as a moderator of "correctness seeking" (ELM) versus "bias avoiding" (FCM) processes.

making the distinction (in this case, between resistance versus acceptance processes or among different possible motives) is in the ability to predict and obtain differences in judgment outcomes or consequences of those judgments.

RESISTANCE AND CORRECTION

To this point, we have focused on persuasion processes (e.g., use of peripheral cues, scrutiny of central merits, counterarguing) that often occur when people are simply seeking "correct" attitudes. This "seeking," described in such theories as the ELM (Petty & Cacioppo, 1986b) and Heuristic-Systematic Model (HSM; Chaiken, Liberman, & Eagly, 1989), might be thought of as similar to the "promotion" orientation described by Higgins and colleagues (see Higgins, 1999) in that people are attempting to "approach" correct attitudes (see the left side of Fig. 2.3; Wegener & Petty, 2001). In seeking correct attitudes, however, people often end up using (or being affected by) factors of which they are unaware. For example, people might often fail to realize that their attitudes have been affected by the mood they experience when they encounter a persuasive appeal (Petty, Fabrigar, & Wegener, 2003; Wegener & Petty, 1996). In some circumstances, however, people might realize that there is something inappropriate or illegitimate about their reactions to social stimuli. For example, attention might be drawn to a cause of current mood (e.g., Schwarz & Clore, 1983), and people might believe that positive moods can make perceptions of social stimuli unduly positive (e.g., Petty & Wegener, 1993). If social perceivers come to realize the impact of "biasing" factors, they might focus more on "avoiding" these factors, rather than purely "seeking" information about the attitude object (see the right side of Fig. 2.3). In such cases, the processes described by models of bias correction might dominate or be added to the processes described by traditional persuasion theories.

Our own work on bias correction has been guided by the Flexible Correction Model (FCM; Wegener & Petty, 1997). Within this view, attempts at avoiding bias are guided by peoples' naive theories of bias. That is, people's perceptions of the bias at work should often guide their attempts at removing or avoiding that bias. So, if a person believes that positive moods make perceptions unduly positive, then realizing that one is in a positive mood could actually make one's judgments less positive (e.g., DeSteno et al., 2000). If, however, a person believes that the same positive mood makes judgments unduly negative, as they sometimes do (e.g., Dermer, Cohen, Jacobsen, & Anderson, 1979), then realizing that one is in a positive mood could make the person's judgments even more positive. It is important to note that these perceptions of bias need not be accurate assessments of the bias actually at work (e.g., Petty & Wegener, 1993; Wegener & Petty, 1995; Wilson & Brekke, 1994). Therefore, attempts at avoiding bias can sometimes decrease the ultimate bias in judgments, but they could also create or increase biases (depending on the accuracy of perceivers' theories of bias).

Recent attitudes research has illustrated the ability of bias correction to remove and to create biases. For example, Petty, Wegener, and White (1998) exposed message recipients to a counter-attitudinal message presented by either a likeable or dislikeable source. Consistent with past research (Chaiken, 1980; Petty, Cacioppo, & Schumann, 1983), source likeability (being irrelevant to the substantive merits of the position advocated) influenced attitudes only when motivation and ability to process were relatively low. Source effects were markedly different, however, when message recipients were asked not to let "non-message" factors (such as reactions to the source) influence their perceptions of the message advocacy. When alerted to possible bias, the source effects observed in low-elaboration conditions were eliminated. However, when alerted to the same possible bias, participants in high-elaboration conditions (who did not show any source bias when not alerted to potential bias) reported more favorable attitudes when the source was dislikeable rather than likeable. That is, corrections for a nonexistent bias actually created the opposing bias! The same source characteristic that produced relatively nonthoughtful resistance when thought was at low levels produced the highest levels of persuasion when thought was high and message recipients were concerned about possible bias.

These results illustrate a number of characteristics of theory-based corrections. As noted earlier, theories of bias need not be accurate to be used (or misused). In many circumstances, the perceived bias is used even when the perception of bias is far from accurate. Part of the problem for social perceivers is that they do not have a control group for social perceptions. For example, slightly negative views of a message advocacy might be appropriate given the person's assessment of the (counterattitudinal) information in the message. However, the same perception might be negatively biased by a dislikeable source, positively biased by a likeable source, or negatively biased by previous attitudes. It many settings, it is likely very difficult for social perceivers to tell when perceptions are biased and when they are not (cf., Nisbett & Wilson, 1977).

These results also show that "seeking" of correct attitudes can lead to different outcomes than attempts to "avoid bias." As previously studied by ELM and HSM researchers, people can sometimes seek correct attitudes in thoughtful ways, but at other times in nonthoughtful ways. When this seeking is thoughtful, effects of peripheral cues are less likely. Yet, efforts to avoid potential bias (it might often be the case that use of peripheral cues is seen as "undue" influence) can actually create the opposing bias in judgment. In some settings, "seeking correctness" and "avoiding bias" can result in similar outcomes (e.g., compare the Petty et al., 1998, low-thought conditions with correction instructions and the high-thought conditions without correction instructions). However, high levels of "seeking correctness" do not necessarily include explicit consideration of potential biases. If they did, then corrections following high-thought consideration of a persuasive message would be likely to be smaller or nonexistent in comparison with corrections following low levels of thought about the persuasive appeal.

Regarding the current emphasis on consequences of processes responsible for resistance effects, it is important to note that corrections could differ in the extent of elaboration that goes into that correction. In some cases, corrections could be guided by naive theories with little or no reconsideration of judgment-relevant information. At other times, however, theories of bias might be used to help the person interpret and (re)consider the implications of relevant information. Similar to the expectations for ELM-based persuasion processes, corrections based on higher levels of information processing are expected to result in stronger perceptions of the judgment target (i.e., perceptions that last longer over time, that better resist information aimed at changing that view, and that more strongly guide future information processing and behavior; see Wegener & Petty, 1997).

Some existing persuasion effects could be thought of as instances of bias correction. For example, Sagarin, Cialdini, Rice, and Serna (2002; Sagarin & Cialdini, this volume) taught social perceivers to identify "illegitimate" sources and to reject their messages. In addition, they found that perceivers were likely to do this primarily when they believed that they were susceptible to the "undue" positive influences of these sources. That is, similar to the processes outlined in the FCM (Wegener & Petty, 1997; Wegener et al., 2001), message recipients are most likely to avoid unwanted positive influences of illegitimate sources when they are motivated and able to identify and correct for those perceived biases. One might account for such effects using other explanatory mechanisms (see Sagarin et al., 2002), but the explicit alerting of message recipients to unwanted influences would seem likely to activate "bias avoiding" processes. Therefore, corrections for perceived positive biases, (e.g., in illegitimate positive sources) could increase resistance, whereas corrections for negative biases (e.g., a dislikeable source) could decrease resistance (e.g., Petty et al., 1998).

One might also think about studies of the sleeper effect (when messages are discounted upon presentation, but are later found to influence attitudes in a message-consistent direction; e.g., Gruder, Cook, Hennigan, Flay, Alessis, & Halamaj, 1978; Pratkanis, Greenwald, Leippe, & Baumgardner, 1988) as involving corrections for bias. That is, in many sleeper studies, the initial discounting of the message could be thought of as a correction for the perceived message-consistent effects of the message (see Priester, Wegener, Petty, & Fabrigar, 1999). For example, it might be likely that messages seen as having little influence (e.g., because they consist of weak arguments) would receive little discounting and therefore show little, if any, "sleeper effect" (cf., conditions for the sleeper effect laid out by Gruder et al., 1978). As noted by Priester et al., (1999), the relative persistence of effects of the message and the relative lack of persistence of effects of the discounting cue suggest that the sleeper effect requires relatively extensive processing of the initial message (see also Petty & Cacioppo, 1986a) with relatively low levels of effort given to the correction (discounting). In other words, the resistance instilled by the discounting cue is relatively short lived, in part, because the effort that went into that discounting (correction) was considerably less than that given to the processing of the message content. However, if one were to increase the processing that goes into the resistance-producing correction per se, then the resistance should persist to a greater extent. Of course, this persistence of resistance would decrease sleeper effects (see Priester et al., 1999).

SO, MESSAGE RECIPIENTS DID NOT CHANGE

From this ELM/FCM theoretical orientation, what would be the natural questions to ask after obtaining a "resistance" outcome? Put another way, what research questions might follow discovery of a technique that increases (or decreases) resistance? For example, after finding that attitudes change less if they have been previously attacked by a weak "inoculation" (McGuire, 1964), one might ask a number of relevant questions. One could ask "ELM" questions. Was the increased resistance effortful (e.g., because of counterarguing weak arguments or biased processing of ambiguous information) or noneffortful (e.g., because of focusing on rejection cues)? Did the resistance-producing intervention affect the amount of processing of the later attacking message? Was the resistance a product of message recipients using their existing attitudes to guide information processing and/or judgment, or were other factors responsible? Depending on whether the resistance was effortful, noneffortful, or the result of differences in amount of processing, various factors other than existing attitudes could be responsible for observed differences in post-attack attitudes.

Alternatively, one could ask "FCM" questions. For example, a resistance outcome could occur because the message recipient engaged in correction for some "undue" positive influence (e.g., an illegitimate source posing as an expert). Related questions would include whether the communication setting or message includes factors that make awareness of bias likely (e.g., a salient bias, personal or situational reminders of potential bias, accessible theories of bias).

The Importance of Studying Process

For both theory development and for applications, one might reasonably ask about the importance of identifying the specific processes that bring about the resistance outcome. For both the ELM and FCM, a large part of the utility of identifying processes would lie in the different consequences that are hypothesized to follow from the thoughtful versus nonthoughtful mechanisms. Attitudes based on higher levels of elaboration have been found to persist longer over time (e.g., Haugtvedt & Petty, 1992; Petty, Haugtvedt, et al., 1995, described in Petty, Haugtvedt, & Smith, 1995), to guide related judgments and behavior more strongly (e.g., Cacioppo et al., 1986; Petty et al., 1983), and to resist future attempts at change better (e.g., Petty, Haugtvedt, et al., 1995; Haugtvedt & Petty, 1992) than attitudes based on lower levels of elaboration. Furthermore, these effects are hypothesized to occur regardless of whether the thoughtful processes consist of seeking a reasonable attitude or of avoiding potential bias (see Wegener & Petty, 1997; Wegener et al., 2001). Therefore, in addition to dissociating outcome from process (i.e., acknowledging that the same persuasion or resistance outcome can occur for different reasons), the ELM and FCM emphasize the different consequences of holding attitudes that result from effortful versus noneffortful processing.

As noted earlier, the discovery of different processes can also put one in a much stronger position to predict when the outcome will or will not occur, and to produce conditions under which the outcome would change. For example, if a resistance outcome can be attributed to corrections for a salient positive "bias" (e.g., an attractive or seemingly expert source, cf., Sagarin et al., 2002), then factors that reduce the salience of bias should influence the outcome. Alternatively, if the setting is one in which the issue of bias is chronically salient (e.g., because people are told by the law or common culture to avoid bias, as in areas of discrimination in job hiring, or because the person has a great deal of practice dealing with a particular bias, Wegener & Petty, 1997), one might imagine explicitly alerting message recipients to possible opposing (negative) biases that would offset the resistance-producing corrections.

Emphases on process and consequences can be applied to both techniques that increase and those that decrease resistance. For example, one could ask whether acknowledgment of resistance (as done by Linn & Knowles, 2002) decreases resistance through relatively thoughtful means (e.g., by getting people to think about the strong reasons that might lead a person to maintain his or her opinion despite clear knowledge that the audience for the message will be negatively disposed toward the message) or through relatively nonthoughtful means (e.g., simply finding the source more likeable when message recipients' opinions are acknowledged). Of course, consistent with our ELM/FCM approach, acknowledgment of diverging opinions might sometimes reduce resistance through thoughtful means and, at other times, through nonthoughtful means. Importantly, however, distinguishing when the effects are thoughtful and when they are not would afford one much greater leverage in predicting when the effects of "undermining resistance" are likely to hold up over time and when they are not.

AUTHOR NOTE

Preparation of this chapter was supported by grants BCS 9520854 and BCS 0094510 from the National Science Foundation and by a grant to Leandre R. Fabrigar from the Social Sciences and Humanities Research Council of Canada.

NOTES

1. Previous research had shown that people high in NC tend to process attitude-relevant information more thoroughly than people low in NC when the situation does not constrain processing to be high or low (e.g., Cacioppo, Petty, & Morris, 1983).

2. More recently, Fabrigar, Carter, Wegener, and Shestowsky (2002) have found that this tendency for the views of high-NC people to drive group decisions is actually stronger in four person groups than in dyads. This result is consistent with the idea that larger groups provide greater opportunity for social loafing (Latané, Williams, & Harkins, 1979) by low-NC people who would prefer to engage less in the cognitively demanding task of group discussion (cf., Petty, Cacioppo, & Kasmer, 1985, as described by Cacioppo, Petty, Kao, & Rodriguez, 1986). The relative lack of strength of attitudes for people low in NC might also decrease motivation to share and/or defend the opinion when larger numbers of others are apparently willing to do so.

3. Also, the motive to maintain one's current attitude (i.e., the motive to resist) can have many different sources.

4. Of course, messages can sometimes result in movement away from the message, referred to as "boomerang" (e.g., Abelson & Miller, 1967).

5. Though beyond the scope of the current chapter, our analysis of resistance outcomes would also suggest that one might usefully study thoughtful versus nonthoughtful processes that result in boomerang. For example, some relatively simple processes such as source derogation might bring about boomerang when a source insults a message recipient (e.g., Abelson & Miller, 1967), but boomerang could also occur because of thorough counterarguing of a weak attempt to persuade (e.g., Petty, Haugtvedt, et al., 1995, described in Petty, Haugtvedt, & Smith, 1995). Boomerang could also result from "over-corrections" for perceived positive influences. Of course, consistent with the discussions to follow, the same variable (e.g., an insult, Abelson & Miller, 1967) could lead to relatively thoughtful boomerang in some settings and relatively thoughtless boomerang in others.

REFERENCES

Abelson, R. P., Aronson, E., McGuire, W. J., Newcomb, T. M., Rosenberg, M. J., & Tannenbaum, P. (1968). *Theories of cognitive consistency: A sourcebook*. Chicago: Rand McNally.

Abelson, R. P., & Miller, J. C. (1967). Negative persuasion via personal insult. *Journal of Experimental Social Psychology, 3*, 321–333.

Albarracín, D., Johnson, B. T., Fishbein, M., & Muellerleile, P. A. (2001). Theories of reasoned action and planned behavior as models of condom use: A meta-analysis. *Psychological Bulletin, 127*, 142–161.

Brehm, J. W. (1966). *A theory of psychological reactance.* New York: Academic Press.

Brock, T. C. (1967). Communication discrepancy and intent to persuade as determinants of counterargument production. *Journal of Experimental Social Psychology, 3,* 269–309.

Cacioppo, J. T., & Petty, R. E. (1982a). A biosocial model of attitude change. In J. T. Cacioppo & R. E. Petty (eds.), *Perspectives in cardiovascular psychophysiology* (pp. 151–188). New York: Guilford press.

Cacioppo, J. T., & Petty, R. E. (1982b). The need for cognition. *Journal of Personality and Social Psychology, 42,* 116–131.

Cacioppo, J. T., Petty, R. E., Kao, C. F., & Rodriquez, R. (1986). Central and peripheral routes to persuasion: An individual difference perspective. *Journal of Personality and Social Psychology, 51,* 1032–1043.

Cacioppo, J. T., Petty, R. E., & Morris, K. J. (1983). Effects of need for cognition on message evaluation, recall, and persuasion. *Journal of Personality and Social Psychology, 45,* 805–818.

Chaiken, S. (1980). Heuristic versus systematic information processing in the use of source versus message cues in persuasion. *Journal of Personality and Social Psychology, 39,* 752–766.

Chaiken, S. (1987). The heuristic model of persuasion. In M. P. Zanna, J. M. Olson, & C. P. Herman (Eds.), *Social influence: The Ontario Symposium* (Vol. 5, pp. 3–39). Hillsdale, NJ: Erlbaum.

Chaiken, S., Liberman, A., & Eagly, A. H. (1989). Heuristic and systematic information processing within and beyond the persuasion context. In J. S. Uleman & J. A. Bargh (Eds.), *Unintended thought* (pp. 212–252). New York: Guilford Press.

Chaiken, S., & Maheswaran, D. (1994). Heuristic processing can bias systematic processing: Effects of source credibility, argument ambiguity, and task importance on attitude judgment. *Journal of Personality and Social Psychology, 66,* 460–473.

Chaiken, S., & Trope, Y. (Eds.) (1999). *Dual-process theories in social psychology.* New York: Guilford Press.

Coleman, T., Stevenson, K., & Wilson, A. (2000). Using content analysis of video-recorded consultations to identify smokers' "readiness" and "resistance" towards stopping smoking. *Patient Education & Counseling, 41,* 305–311.

Cook, T. D. (1969). Competence, counterarguing, and attitude change. *Journal of Personality, 37,* 342–358.

Davidson, A. R., Yantis, S., Norwood, M., & Montano, D. E. (1985). Amount of information about the attitude object and attitude-behavior consistency. *Journal of Personality and Social Psychology, 49,* 1184–1198.

Dermer, M., Cohen, S., Jacobsen, E., & Anderson, E. A., (1979). Evaluative judgments of aspects of life as a function of vicarious exposure to emotional extremes. *Journal of Personality and Social Psychology, 37,* 247–260.

DeSteno, D., Petty, R. E., Wegener, D. T., & Rucker, D. D. (2000). Beyond valence in the perception of likelihood: The role of emotion specificity. *Journal of Personality and Social Psychology, 78,* 397–416.

Eagly, A. H., & Chaiken, S. (1993). *The psychology of attitudes.* Fort Worth, TX: Harcourt, Brace, Jovanovich.

Eagly, A. H., & Chaiken, S. (1998). Attitude structure and function. In D. Gilbert, S. Fiske, & G. Lindzey (Eds.), *The handbook of social psychology* (4th ed. pp. 269–322) New York: McGraw-Hill.

Evans, L., & Petty, R. E. (1998, May). *The effect of expectations on knowledge use.* Paper presented at the annual meeting of the Midwestern Psychological Association, Chicago.

Fabrigar, L. R., Carter, A. M., Wegener, D. T., & Shestowsky, D. (2002). Raw data. Queen's University, Kingston, Ontario.

Fabrigar, L. R., Petty, R. E., Wegener, D. T., Priester, J. & Brooksbank, L. (2002). Raw data. Queen's University, Kingston, Ontario.

Fazio, R. H. (1995). Attitudes as object-evaluation associations: Determinants, consequences, and correlates of attitude accessibility. In R. E. Petty & J. A. Krosnick (Eds.), *Attitude strength: Antecedents and consequences* (pp. 247–282). Mahwah, NJ: Erlbaum.

Festinger, L., & Maccoby, N. (1964). On resistance to persuasive communications. *Journal of Abnormal and Social Psychology, 68,* 359–366.

Fleming, M., Wegener, D. T., & Petty, R. E. (1999). Procedural and legal motivations to correct for perceived judicial biases. *Journal of Experimental Social Psychology, 35,* 186–203.

Giner-Sorolla, R., & Chaiken, S. (1997). Selective use of heuristic and systematic processing under defense motivation. *Personality and Social Psychology Bulletin, 23,* 84–97.

Gruder, C. L., Cook, T. D., Hennigan, K. M., Flay, B. R., Alessis, C., & Halamaj, J. (1978). Empirical tests of the absolute sleeper effect predicted from the discounting cue hypothesis. *Journal of Personality and Social Psychology, 36,* 1061–1074.

Hass, R. G. (1981). Effects of source characteristics on cognitive responses and persuasion. In R. E. Petty, T. M. Ostrom, & T. C. Brock (Eds.), *Cognitive responses in persuasion* (pp. 141–172). Hillsdale, NJ: Erlbaum.

Haugtvedt, C. P., & Petty, R. E. (1992). Personality and persuasion: Need for cognition moderates the persistence and resistance of attitude changes. *Journal of Personality and Social Psychology, 63,* 308–319.

Haugtvedt, C. P., & Wegener, D. T. (1994). Message order effects in persuasion: An attitude strength perspective. *Journal of Consumer Research, 21,* 205–218.

Haugtvedt, C. P., & Wegener, D. T. (2002). Raw data. Ohio State University, Columbus, OH.

Higgins, E. T. (1999). Promotion and prevention as a motivational duality: Implications for evaluative processes. In S. Chaiken & Y. Trope (Eds.), *Dual-process theories in social psychology* (pp. 503–525). New York: Guilford Press.

Johnston, L., Fabrigar, L. R., Wegener, D. T., & Rosen, N. (2002). Raw data. Queen's University, Kingston, Ontario.

Kraus, S. J. (1995). Attitudes and the prediction of behavior: A meta-analysis of the empirical literature. *Personality and Social Psychology Bulletin, 21,* 58–75.

Krosnick, J. A., & Petty, R. E. (1995). Attitude strength: An overview. In R. E. Petty & J. A. Krosnick (Eds.), *Attitude strength: Antecedents and consequences* (pp. 1–24). Mahwah, NJ: Erlbaum.

Latané, B., Williams, K. D., & Harkins, S. G. (1979). Many hands make light the work: The causes and consequences of social loafing. *Journal of Personality and Social Psychology, 37,* 822–832.

Leippe, M. R., & Elkin, R. A. (1987). When motives clash: Issue involvement and response involvement as determinants of persuasion. *Journal of Personality and Social Psychology, 52,* 269–278.

Lewan, P. C., & Stotland, E. (1961). The effects of prior information on susceptibility to an emotional appeal. *Journal of Abnormal and Social Psychology, 62,* 450–453.

Linn, J. A., & Knowles, E. S. (2002, May). *Acknowledging target resistance in persuasive messages.* Paper presented at the annual meeting of the Midwestern Psychological Association, Chicago, IL.

Lydon, J., Zanna, M. P., & Ross, M. (1988). Bolstering attitudes by autobiographical recall: Attitude persistence and selective memory. *Personality and Social Psychology Bulletin, 14,* 78–86.

McGuire, W. J. (1964). Inducing resistance to persuasion: Some contemporary approaches. In L. Berkowitz (Ed.), *Advances in experimental social psychology* (Vol. 1, pp. 191–229). New York: Academic Press.

McGuire, W. J., & Papageorgis, D. (1961). The relative efficacy of various types of prior belief-defense in producing immunity against persuasion. *Journal of Abnormal and Social Psychology, 62,* 327–337.

Milam, J. E., Sussman, S., Ritt-Olson, A. D., & Clyde, W. (2000). Perceived invulnerability and cigarette smoking among adolescents. *Addictive Behaviors, 25,* 71–80.

Nisbett, R. E., & Wilson, T. D. (1977). Telling more than we can know: Verbal reports on mental processes. *Psychological Review, 84,* 231–259.

Norman, R. (1975). Affective-cognitive consistency, attitudes, conformity, and behavior. *Journal of Personality and Social Psychology, 32,* 83–91.

Papageorgis, D., & McGuire, W. J. (1961). The generality of immunity to persuasion produced by pre-exposure to weakened counterarguments. *Journal of Abnormal and Social Psychology, 62,* 475–481.

Petty, R. E., & Cacioppo, J. T. (1977). Forewarning, cognitive responding, and resistance to persuasion. *Journal of Personality and Social Psychology, 35,* 645–655.

Petty, R. E., & Cacioppo, J. T. (1979). Issue-involvement can increase or decrease persuasion by enhancing message-relevant cognitive responses. *Journal of Personality and Social Psychology, 37,* 1915–1926.

Petty, R. E., & Cacioppo, J. T. (1986a). *Communication and persuasion: Central and peripheral routes to attitude change.* New York: Springer-Verlag.

Petty, R. E., & Cacioppo, J. T. (1986b). The Elaboration Likelihood Model of persuasion. In L. Berkowitz (Ed.), *Advances in experimental social psychology* (Vol. 19, pp. 123–205). New York: Academic Press.

Petty, R. E., & Cacioppo, J. T. (1990). Involvement and persuasion: Tradition versus integration. *Psychological Bulletin, 107,* 367–374.

Petty, R. E., & Cacioppo, J. T. (1996). Addressing disturbing and disturbed consumer behavior: Is it necessary to change the way we conduct behavioral science? *Journal of Marketing Research, 33,* 1–8.

Petty, R. E., Cacioppo, J. T., & Goldman, R. (1981). Personal involvement as a determinant of argument-based persuasion. *Journal of Personality and Social Psychology, 41,* 847–855.

Petty, R. E., Cacioppo, J. T., & Kasmer, J. A. (1985, May). *Effects of need for cognition on social loafing.* Paper presented at the annual meeting of the Midwestern Psychological Association, Chicago.

Petty, R. E., Cacioppo, J. T., & Kasmer, J. A. (1988). The role of affect in the Elaboration Likelihood Model of persuasion. In L. Donohew, H. E. Sypher, & E. T. Higgins (Eds.), *Communication, social cognition, and affect* (pp. 117–145). Hillsdale, NJ: Erlbaum.

Petty, R. E., Cacioppo, J. T., & Schumann, D. W. (1983). Central and peripheral routes to advertising effectiveness: The moderating role of involvement. *Journal of Consumer Research, 10,* 135–146.

Petty, R. E., Fabrigar, L. R., & Wegener, D. T. (2003). Emotional factors in attitudes and persuasion. In R. J. Davidson, K. Scherer, & H. H. Goldsmith (Eds.), *Handbook of affective sciences* (pp. 752–772). London: Oxford University Press.

Petty, R. E., Fleming, M. A., & White, P. H. (1999). Stigmatized sources and persuasion: Prejudice as a determinant of argument scrutiny. *Journal of Personality and Social Psychology, 76,* 19–34.

Petty, R. E., Haugtvedt, C. P., Heesacker, M., & Cacioppo, J. T. (1995). Message elaboration as a determinant of attitude strength: Persistence and resistance of persuasion. Unpublished manuscript, Ohio State University, Columbus, OH.

Petty, R. E., Haugtvedt, C. P., & Smith, S. M. (1995). Elaboration as a determinant of attitude strength. In R. E. Petty & J. A. Krosnick (Eds.), *Attitude strength: Antecedents and consequences* (pp. 93–130). Mahwah, NJ: Erlbaum.

Petty, R. E., & Krosnick, J. A. (Eds.) (1995). *Attitude strength: Antecedents and consequences.* Mahwah, NJ: Erlbaum.

Petty, R. E., Priester, J. R., & Wegener, D. T. (1994). Cognitive processes in attitude change. In R. S. Wyer & T. K. Srull (Eds.), *Handbook of social cognition* (2nd ed., Vol. 2, pp. 69–142). Hillsdale, NJ: Erlbaum.

Petty, R. E., Schumann, D. W., Richman, S. A., & Strathman, A. J. (1993). Positive mood and persuasion: Different roles for affect under high- and low-elaboration conditions. *Journal of Personality and Social Psychology, 64,* 5–20.

Petty, R. E., Tormala, Z. L., & Rucker, D. (in press). An attitude strength perspective on resistance to persuasion. In M. R. Banaji, J. T. Jost, & D. Prentice (Eds.), *The yin and yang of social cognition: Festschrift for William McGuire.* Washington, DC: American Psychological Association.

Petty, R. E., & Wegener, D. T. (1993). Flexible correction processes in social judgment: Correcting for context-induced contrast. *Journal of Experimental Social Psychology, 29,* 137–165.

Petty, R. E., & Wegener, D. T. (1998). Attitude change: Multiple roles for persuasion variables. In D. T. Gilbert, S. T. Fiske, & G. Lindzey (Eds.), *The handbook of social psychology* (4th ed., Vol. 1, pp. 323–390). New York: McGraw-Hill.

Petty, R. E., & Wegener, D. T. (1999). The Elaboration Likelihood Model: Current status and controversies. In S. Chaiken & Y. Trope (Eds.), *Dual-process theories in social psychology* (pp. 41–72). New York: Guilford Press.

Petty, R. E., Wegener, D. T., & White, P. (1998). Flexible correction processes in social judgment: Implications for persuasion. *Social Cognition, 16,* 93–113.

Pfau, M., Van Bockern, S., & Kang, J. G. (1992). Use of inoculation to promote resistance to smoking initiation among adolescents. *Communication Monographs, 59,* 213–230.

Pratkanis, A. R., Greenwald, A. G., Leippe, M. R., & Baumgardner, M. H. (1998). In search of reliable persuasion effects: III. The sleeper effect is dead. Long live the sleeper effect. *Journal of Personality and Social Psychology, 54,* 203–218.

Priester, J. R., Wegener, D. T., Petty, R. E., & Fabrigar, L. R. (1999). Examining the psychological processes underlying the sleeper effect: The Elaboration Likelihood Model explanation. *Media Psychology, 1,* 27–48.

Sagarin, B. J., Cialdini, R. B., Rice, W. E., & Serna, S. B. (2002). Dispelling the illusion of vulnerability: The motivations and mechanisms of resistance to persuasion. *Journal of Personality and Social Psychology, 83,* 526–541.

Schwarz, N., Bless, H., & Bohner, G. (1991). Mood and persuasion: Affective states influence the processing of persuasive communications. In M. P. Zanna (Ed.), *Advances in experimental social psychology* (Vol. 24, pp. 161–201). San Diego: Academic Press.

Schwarz, N., & Clore, G. L. (1983). Mood, misattribution, and judgments of well-being: Informative and directive functions of affective states. *Journal of Personality and Social Psychology, 45,* 513–523.

Sheeran, P., & Taylor, S. (1999). Predicting intentions to use condoms: A meta-analysis and comparison of the theories of reasoned action and planned behavior. *Journal of Applied Social Psychology, 29,* 1624–1675.

Shestowsky, D., Wegener, D. T., & Fabrigar, L. R. (1998). Need for cognition and interpersonal influence: Individual differences in impact on dyadic decisions. *Journal of Personality and Social Psychology, 74,* 1317–1328.

Szybillo, G. J., & Heslin, R. (1973). Resistance to persuasion: Inoculation theory in a marketing context. *Journal of Marketing Research, 10,* 396–403.

Tannenbaum, P. H. (1967). The congruity principle revisited: Studies in the reduction, induction, and generalization of persuasion. In L. Berkowitz (Ed.), *Advances in experimental social psychology* (Vol. 3, pp. 271–320). San Diego, CA: Academic Press.

Tannenbaum, P. H., Macauley, J. R., & Norris, E. L. (1966). Principle of congruity and reduction of persuasion. *Journal of Personality and Social Psychology, 3,* 233–238.

Wegener, D. T., Dunn, M., & Tokusato, D. (2001). The Flexible Correction Model: Phenomenology and the use of naive theories in avoiding or removing bias. In G. B. Moskowitz (Ed.), *Cognitive social psychology: The Princeton symposium on the legacy and future of social cognition* (pp. 277–290). Mahwah, NJ: Erlbaum.

Wegener, D. T., & Petty, R. E. (1995). Flexible correction processes in social judgment: The role of naive theories in corrections for perceived bias. *Journal of Personality and Social Psychology, 68,* 36–51.

Wegener, D. T., & Petty, R. E. (1996). Effects of mood on persuasion processes: Enhancing, reducing, and biasing scrutiny of attitude-relevant information. In L. L. Martin & A. Tesser (Eds.), *Striving and feeling: Interactions between goals and affect.* Mahwah, NJ: Erlbaum.

Wegener, D. T., & Petty, R. E. (1997). The Flexible Correction Model: The role of naive theories of bias in bias correction. In M. P. Zanna (Ed.), *Advances in experimental social psychology* (Vol. 29, pp. 141–208). Mahwah, NJ: Erlbaum.

Wegener, D. T., & Petty, R. E. (2001). Understanding effects of mood through the Elaboration Likelihood and Flexible Correction Models. In L. L. Martin & G. L. Clore (Eds.), *Theories of mood and cognition: A user's guidebook* (pp. 177–210). Mahwah, NJ: Erlbaum.

Wegener, D. T., Petty, R. E., & Klein, D. J. (1994). Effects of mood on high elaboration attitude change: The mediating role of likelihood judgments. *European Journal of Social Psychology, 24,* 25–43.

Wegener, D. T., Petty, R. E., & Smith, S. M. (1995). Positive mood can increase or decrease message scrutiny: The hedonic contingency view of mood and message processing. *Journal of Personality and Social Psychology, 69,* 5–15.

Wilson, T. D., & Brekke, N. (1994). Mental contamination and mental correction: Unwanted influences on judgments and evaluations. *Psychological Bulletin, 116,* 117–142.

Zuwerink, J. R., & Devine, P. G. (1996). Attitude importance and resistance to persuasion: It's not just the thought that counts. *Journal of Personality and Social Psychology, 70,* 931–944.

3

The Intensity of Affect and Resistance to Social Influence

Kathleen Fuegen
The Ohio State University

Jack W. Brehm
University of Kansas

Whether we contemplate the arguments that lead to divorce or those that involve international conflict, such as that between the Israelis and Palestinians or Pakistanis and Indians over Kashmir, we recognize that strong feelings are involved. Psychologists have assumed that such extraordinary conflicts require extraordinary methods to cause some reduction in the conflicting forces, and many attempts even with such methods have failed to be effective. While the research to be presented concerns feelings of somewhat lesser magnitude, we believe the results and the theory on which it is based point to a relatively simple method of ameliorating negative attitudes and reducing resistance to change.

Our approach to attitudes concerns the affective component and what controls its intensity. The prevailing view among psychologists studying attitudes is that an attitude is comprised of cognitions (facts, beliefs, and arguments), each of which can be weighted for its relevance to the attitude and for its importance to the individual holding the attitude. These cognitions give rise to one or more affects or feelings, and these affects have either a positive (approach) character, or a negative (avoidance or hostile) character. In other words, the motivational character of the affective states that derive from cognitions is either positive and aimed at promotion of the attitude object, or negative and avoidant or destructive of the attitude object. Hence, it is the affective component that is crucial in determining what kind of behavior occurs, if any, as a consequence of a person's holding the attitude.

An obvious implication of this conception of attitudes is that change in behavior can be accomplished by change in the cognitions that lead to the dominant affective responses. Indeed, this implication is what many social psychologists have long assumed to be the case—change the cognition and the attitude is magically changed. This is, of course, the model of attitude change referred to by Festinger (1964) when he commented on the apparent failure of attitude measures to predict behaviors (see also Ajzen & Fishbein, 1977; La-Piere, 1934; Wicker, 1969). While it is possible to cite several reasons why attitude measures failed to predict behavior (see Eagly & Chaiken, 1993), it has not become particularly clear why the cognitive elements of an attitude are insufficient in predicting behavior. There seems to be something wrong with this conception of attitudes.

What might be wrong with the tripartite model of attitudes? First, it is possible that cognition does not determine affect in a monotonic manner as is generally assumed, or that affect does not determine behavioral tendencies. Second, it may be that the main causal connection between cognition and affect runs in reverse, i.e., cognition results largely from affect, not vice versa (Murphy & Zajonc, 1993; Zajonc, 1980, 1984). For example, given an attitude object (e.g., air pollution), a negative affective state may occur immediately, which is then followed by the selection of supporting facts, beliefs, and arguments. In this chapter, we will argue that the cognitive component of an attitude is secondary to the affective component, and that research on attitude change may profit from a new approach. Instead of focusing on how to change a person's attitude with facts and arguments, it may be worthwhile to consider how we can alter his or her affective responses to an attitude object. Recent research on motivation and emotion illustrates the basis for our thinking and may be helpful in this regard.

THE INTENSITY OF MOTIVATION AND EMOTION

We know from earlier theorizing about motivation (e.g., Brehm & Self, 1989) and research by Wright and Biner and their associates (e.g., Biner & Hua, 1995; Wright, Contrada, & Patane, 1986; Wright, 1996) that the intensity of motivation is a cubic function of known difficulty of goal attainment. This relationship may be seen in Fig. 3.1.

The curve shows that when level of difficulty of goal attainment is unknown (far left of figure), motivational arousal is a direct function of the importance of the goal. For example, if an individual has the goal of repairing his or her car, then the motivation to achieve that goal will be at its maximum potential if there are no known impediments to the goal (i.e., if difficulty of repair is

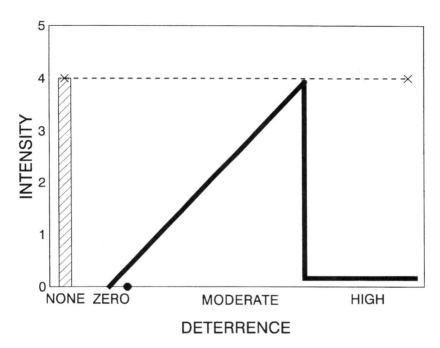

FIG. 3.1.   The intensity of motivation.

unknown). Following the curve to the right, if the individual learns that achieving the goal will be easy (e.g., repairs will be cheap and take less than 30
minutes), his or her motivational arousal will drop to a low level. This is because
little effort is necessary to achieve the goal. As difficulty of achieving the goal
increases, so does motivational arousal until it reaches an upper limit that is
determined by the importance of the goal (i.e., how much effort is the goal
worth?). If the individual decides that the goal of repairing the car is not worth
the effort required, or if he or she learns that the car is beyond repair, motivational arousal will decrease to a low level, presumably because the task will not
be carried out.

Recent work has shown that emotions function like motivational states, that
is, they urge one to do something (e.g., Frijda, 1986; Lazarus, 1991). Like any
motivational state, an emotion must overcome any factors that tend to block its
function. These factors may be called *deterrents*. A deterrent is simply any
reason for not feeling the way one does (Brehm, 1999). The stronger the deterrent, the more intense the emotion must be if it is to carry out its function. The
same curve that represents motivational arousal can be used to represent emo-

tional intensity by replacing motivational arousal with amount of emotion and replacing task difficulty with deterrents. When an event instigates an emotion such as anger, the intensity of that anger is modified by the presence or absence of deterrents. For example, if aggression against the instigator is easy, then the intensity of anger will tend to be low (little effort is required to carry out the function of the anger). As difficulty in aggressing increases, so does the intensity of anger. However, if there is no way to carry out the function of the anger (e.g., the instigator of the anger cannot be found), then the intensity will drop to a low level, presumably because nothing can be done. In other words, if we conceive of anger as a motivational state, then we can predict that its magnitude will be a nonmonotonic function of the difficulty of doing what it urges.

Experimental research has demonstrated that anger, sadness, and happiness may be modified in the same way as normal motivational states (e.g., Brehm, Brummett, & Harvey, 1999; Brummett, 1996; D'Anello, 1997; Silvia & Brehm, 2001). These studies all support the following theoretical contention (Brehm, 1999): When confronted with an instigation to a strong emotion, people who are also made aware of a deterrent to the function of that emotion report an intensity of feeling that is relatively low when a deterrent is low in magnitude, high when the deterrent is of greater magnitude, and low again when the deterrent is very high in magnitude. For example, in a study by D'Anello (1997), participants were induced to feel happy by receiving a free candy bar. They then played a lottery game where they lost the chance of winning a gift certificate worth $1, $2, $3, or $4 (deterrent manipulation). Participants in the control condition were exposed to the happiness induction but did not play the lottery. D'Anello found that happiness decreased from the control to the $1 condition (low deterrent), increased from the $1 to $2 condition (moderate deterrent), and then decreased from the $3 (moderate deterrent) to $4 (high deterrent) condition. The predicted cubic trend was reliable.

THE INTENSITY OF AFFECT

We believe it is but a short step to generalize from prior research on motivation and emotion to other intense, affective states. As an initial test of this generalization (Brehm & Miller, 2000), college students tasted chocolate truffles, a particularly delicious kind of candy, and at the same time, received news that tuition was to be raised either 2%, 8%, or 16% beginning the following semester. Figure 3.2 shows how positively participants reported feeling while tasting the chocolate. Compared to control participants who tasted the chocolate without hearing about a rise in tuition, those who heard of a 2% rise indicated relatively little liking for the chocolate; those who heard of an 8% rise liked the chocolate as much as control participants; and those who heard of a 16% rise indicated relatively little liking for the chocolate. Thus, some evidence exists that an affective state may vary in intensity as a function of deterrents to the affect.

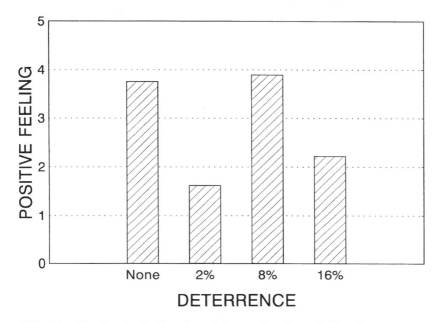

FIG. 3.2.   Positive feeling for chocolate as a function of tuition increases.

We endeavored to expand our inquiry of liking for chocolate to other attitudes with a strong affective component. In so doing, we hypothesized that the affective component of an attitude may be considered a motivational state. This seems reasonable insofar as affect urges us to approach or avoid (or, support or obstruct) an attitude object. If affect may be considered a motivational state, then affective intensity—or the strength of a feeling associated with an attitude— should be subject to the same laws as motivational intensity. Therefore, we predicted that affective intensity would be a joint function of both the potential strength of the feeling associated with the attitude object *and* reasons for not having that feeling (deterrents). Weak reasons (deterrents) will tend to reduce the intensity of the affective component. As the number or importance of reasons for not having the attitudinal feeling increases, so too will reported affective intensity up to a point where the reasons outweigh the affect associated with the attitude. Beyond that point, reported affect should decrease to a low level. Thus, to the extent that a person's attitude has a strong affective component, deterrents to the affect should influence the magnitude of the affective component in the same way as deterrents to emotions. As they increase in strength from zero, the affective component of the attitude should first be minimized, then grow to maximum strength, and then be overwhelmed.

We assume that deterrents to an affective state need not be related to the attitude issue. Deterrents are anything that inhibit or oppose the function of the affective state, including factors that threaten to draw attention away from it, such as

distracting stimuli, or factors that have the potential to create a completely different affective state, such as humor. Therefore, we predict that deterrents that are unrelated to the attitude issue, e.g., receiving an irrelevant gift certificate, can be
effective in reducing the strength of an affectively based attitude.

There are two conditions under which we may not observe the predicted
pattern. First, if the affective component of a person's attitude is not strong, or
if a person's attitude is primarily driven by cognitions about a given object, then
attitude change may be a linear monotonic—rather than non-monotonic—function of deterrents. In this case, greater change should occur with increasing
strength of influence attempts, particularly if these attempts emanate from a
credible source. Only when the affective component of an attitude is strong will
attitude change follow a pattern similar to what we have observed for emotions.
Second, it is conceivable that an attitude will be so strong that even the strongest
deterrent introduced will not be sufficient to reduce affective intensity to a low
level. Thus, affective intensity would continue to increase from a moderate to
a strong deterrent. Such a case is not inconsistent with our theory. All that is
needed to support the theory is for affective intensity to decrease in the presence
of a small deterrent and then increase as the magnitude of deterrence increases.
Theoretically, a sufficiently strong deterrent will cause a reduction in affective
intensity, though in practice, the strongest deterrent introduced may not be strong
enough to overwhelm the affect.

THE NATURE OF RESISTANCE

Resistance to persuasion, in keeping with the tripartite view of attitudes, can
originate in cognitive, affective, or behavioral factors, but we will confine ourselves to a brief consideration of those particularly relevant to our present focus
on affect. The fundamental affect of an attitude is normally associated with the
fundamental values represented by the person's position on the issue. Thus, a
major source of resistance to affective change concerns the extent to which such
change would require some change in, or reshuffling of, the relevant values.
Attitudes based on important values would normally be expected to be more
resistant to change than attitudes based on trivial values. Closely linked to that
resistance would be the importance of the freedom to hold a particular position
on an issue. Thus, any attempt to persuade a person to change her position on
an issue can run into resistance due to both the potential frustration of values
and the potential arousal of reactance. As will be seen in the following presentation of research, these two sources of resistance can be separated though they
will often work together. In either case, the present analysis concerning how
resistance can be reduced through the use of deterrents applies to affect due to
both frustration of values and reactance. In either case, the affect represents
aroused motivation, in the one case to satisfy important values, in the other, to
restore freedom. It is this state of affect or aroused motivation that causes resistance to influence.

The implication of affective intensity theory for resistance to persuasion is straightforward: Resistance is a function of the magnitude of deterrence. If we wish to reduce resistance to persuasion, all that is needed is a small deterrent to one's attitude. In the face of a small deterrent, little effort is required to achieve the goal of the attitude, and resistance will be minimized. Thus, a weak reason for not feeling as one does can be more effective in changing an attitude than a strong reason. Put another way, strong counterarguments are not necessary to reduce an individual's resistance to persuasion.

Study 1 was designed to test the predictions outlined above. Participants, college students, were presented with a provocative proposal: random drug testing for students. In addition, students were presented with no further comment on the issue, or they received either a weak, moderate, or strong endorsement of the proposal, and they were then asked to indicate their own position on the issue.

STUDY 1

Method

Introductory psychology students (34 females, 27 males) participated in exchange for course credit and within gender, participants were randomly assigned to one of four conditions. Participants were conducted through the experiment individually by a male experimenter. The participant first learned from an informed consent sheet that he or she would be asked to respond to a short questionnaire regarding a consumer item and a memorandum. After giving consent, the experimenter handed the participant an envelope containing a sheet of paper on which the statement of the issue, the endorsement (if any), and the dependent measure were included.

The sheet, entitled "Opinion Questionnaire," stated in the first paragraph that the university had again been cited as a "party place" rather than as one of the top academic institutions in the country. Members of the faculty and administration were considering ways to restore the good reputation of the university, and were interested in getting students' opinions regarding a particular proposal. Students were instructed not to put their names on the questionnaire.

In the next paragraph, entitled "Random Testing for Drugs," participants were told that each day when there were classes, a random sample of students would be required to report to the university health center for tests that would reveal the usage of illegal or harmful substances, including marijuana and alcohol. Students who showed any evidence at all of having used these substances would be required to participate in a rehabilitation program run by the local police department, and their parents would be notified.

The last item on the questionnaire was the dependent measure, a single attitude item asking, "To what extent do you support or oppose the above proposal?" Participants made their responses on an 11-point scale ranging from 5 (strongly support) through 0 (neither) to −5 (strongly oppose).

Between the proposal and the attitude measure, participants in the experimental conditions read a single sentence endorsement of the proposal. The endorsement was designed to provide weak, moderate, or strong support for the proposal. In other words, the weak endorsement was intended to act as a low deterrent to opposing the proposition, and at the other extreme, the strong endorsement was intended as a high deterrent to opposition.

Weak.   You probably will not like this proposition, but it may be necessary for the good of the university.

Moderate.   You probably will not like this proposition, but it could be very good for the university.

Strong.   You probably will not like this proposition, but it is absolutely necessary for the good of the university.

Participants in the control condition (no endorsement) simply read the proposal and gave their opinion.

After indicating their support or opposition to the proposal, participants placed the opinion questionnaire back inside the envelope and notified the experimenter. All participants were carefully debriefed before being excused. No consumer item was presented.

Results and Discussion

The mean responses to the attitude measure are presented in Fig. 3.3. Participants' opposition to random drug testing varied as a function of the strength of the endorsement for the proposal. As expected, opposition was high in the no deterrent condition, dropped in the weak endorsement condition, and then rose steadily in the moderate and strong endorsement conditions. The decrease in opposition from the control to the weak endorsement condition was marginally significant, ($t(57) = 1.85$, $p < .07$), while the increase in opposition from the weak to strong endorsement was significant ($t(57) = 2.62$, $p = .01$), as was the predicted quadratic function for all four conditions ($t(57) = 2.59$, $p = .01$). Theoretically, an even stronger endorsement in the high deterrence condition should result in a decrease in opposition to the proposal, but that effect was not obtained here.

While the mean pattern is consistent with the theory, it is of further interest to see the proportion of participants in each condition who originally opposed the proposition, and who did so after each of the endorsements. Omitting two participants who indicated no preference, the proportions of those opposed in the no, weak, moderate, and strong endorsement conditions were 79%, 50%, 64%, and 87%, respectively. Thus, participants' resistance to the proposal was at its lowest level when a weak endorsement was presented.

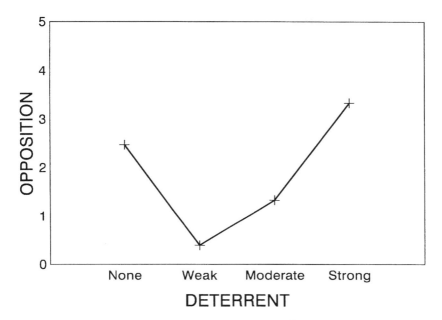

FIG. 3.3.   Opposition to random drug testing, Study 1.

Even though the results are in the anticipated pattern, there is the possibility that the effects are due not to deterrence, but rather to the instigation of reactance. Because the random drug testing might have been interpreted as a threat to an existent freedom, and the endorsements might have been interpreted as qualifiers of the threat, the pattern of effects might simply be due to differences in amount of reactance aroused. However, we do not believe reactance is a plausible explanation for these findings. If the differences between conditions are to be attributed to reactance, then these differences must indicate that freedom is almost completely restored in the Weak condition and not at all in the Strong condition. However, the content of the reasons for supporting the counter-attitudinal position does not differentially restore freedom. In fact, reactance should be worse in the Weak or Moderate condition than in the Strong condition, because only the Strong condition provides any justification for a threat to freedom.

This study provided a foundation from which to examine a variety of attitudes and deterrents. In our next study, we attempted to replicate these findings with a new proposal aimed at eliciting negative affect in participants and a new kind of deterrent. The new proposal concerned the implementation of exit exams for graduating students, and the deterrent was the gift certificate amount participants received after reading the proposal. We chose to use gift certificates as deterrents for several reasons. First, unlike the endorsements used in Study 1, the magnitude of gift certificates can be easily quantified. Second, gift certificates have been used successfully as deterrents in research on emotional intensity (Brummett, 1996; D'Anello, 1997; Silvia & Brehm, 2001). Third, unlike endorsements, gift certificates are irrelevant to the attitude issue. This is important because if the attitude issue and deterrent are not perceived as linked with one another, reactance may be less likely.

STUDY 2

Method

Eighty-two introductory psychology students (42 females, 40 males) participated in exchange for course credit. Nine participants were later excluded from analyses because of suspicion, misunderstanding the meaning of exit exams, or because they were leaving the university before the proposal would be implemented. The resulting sample was comprised of 39 females and 34 males.

Participants were conducted through the experiment individually by a male experimenter. After being escorted to a private room, the participant was handed a two-paragraph proposal written on university letterhead along with a large manilla envelope labeled "Questionnaire." The proposal was the same for all conditions, and the envelope contained the deterrent (if any). The experimenter asked the participant first to carefully read through the proposal, and then to open the envelope and complete the questionnaire. Participants placed the questionnaire back inside the envelope when finished and notified the experimenter. All were carefully debriefed before being excused.

The proposal began by stating that many faculty and administrators had become concerned that the university was losing its reputation as a high-quality educational institution. Accordingly, they proposed a plan in which all seniors would be required to take two exit exams before graduating: one comprehensive exam for the general school of study and one comprehensive exam for students' major field of study. Each exam would last approximately four hours, and students would be required to take their exams the week following spring break. A score of 90% on each exam would be required to pass, and students scoring below 90% would be required to retake the exam until they passed before being allowed to graduate.

The second paragraph explained that the psychology department was gathering student opinion on this matter, particularly the opinions of younger students who would be affected by exit exams. If the proposal was passed, exit exams would be implemented in one and a half years.

The dependent measures were in the envelope labeled "Questionnaire." The measures were the same as before, except that a second attitude measure was included. In addition to being asked the extent to which they supported or opposed the proposal, participants were also asked, "How do you feel about the above proposal?" Responses to both items were made on 11-point scales ranging from 5 (very positive feeling for the feeling item, strongly support for the support/oppose item) to 0 (neither) to -5 (very negative feeling for the feeling item, strongly oppose for the support/oppose item).

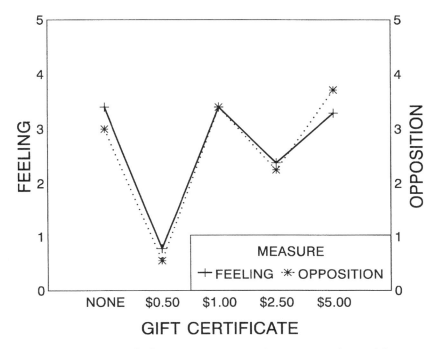

FIG. 3.4. Negative feeling/opposition to exit exams: Male participants, Study 2.

Participants in any of the four deterrent conditions found a gift certificate to the university food service affixed to the top of the dependent measures. Coupled with the gift certificate was an explanation stating that the gift certificates were left over from a research project with a local business, and that the experimenter was simply giving them away. Participants were told they could use the gift certificate in any way they chose. The four gift certificate amounts ($0.50, $1.00, $2.50, and $5.00) served as deterrents. Participants in the control condition received no gift certificate.

Results and Discussion

Figures 3.4 and 3.5 display male and female participants' mean feeling about and opposition to the proposal as a function of deterrent. As can be seen, males and females showed quite different patterns.

Among male participants, although negative feeling was not as strong as we had intended in the no deterrent condition ($M = -3.40$), the drop from the control condition to the weakest deterrent ($0.50) approached significance, $F(1, 29) = 3.83$, $p < .06$. Consistent with prediction, negativity toward exit exams increased in a marginally reliable way from the $0.50 condition to the

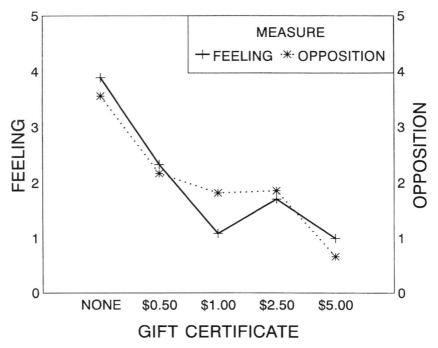

FIG. 3.5.   Negative feeling/opposition to exit exams: Female participants, Study 2.

$1.00 condition ($p < .06$). Negativity slightly decreased in the $2.50 condition and then slightly increased in the $5.00 condition, though neither change was significant. Largely because there was no significant decrease in negativity from the $1.00 condition, neither the quadratic nor cubic trend was significant, $ps > .22$. It is possible that $5.00 was not a sufficiently strong deterrent to overwhelm negative affect regarding exit exams. We believe that a stronger deterrent (e.g., $10) would have produced a reliable decrease in negativity from the $1.00 condition, but as the irrelevant deterrent increases in magnitude, it also tends to arouse suspicion about its purpose.

Figure 3.5 displays the mean values for female participants. Not surprisingly, the linear trend was significant, $F(1, 34) = 10.08$, $p < .01$. The decrease in negativity from the control to the $1.00 condition was significant ($p < .03$), and the decrease from the $2.50 to the $5.00 condition approached significance ($p < .09$). Unfortunately, among female participants there was no substantial increase in negativity from a small to a larger deterrent akin to the rise from $0.50 to $1.00 among male participants. Because distributions in some conditions were skewed, we also inspected medians. The medians for the control and each deterrent condition (-5, -4, -1, -3, 1) suggest that the $2.50 condition (median $= -3$) may have functioned as a moderate deterrent. Nevertheless, because of the large standard deviation in this condition, we are cautious in inferring its meaning to participants.

Study 2 replicated Study 1 (among male participants) and it extended research on affective intensity by using deterrents irrelevant to the attitude object. The results of this study show that any stimulus that has the potential to create an opposing affective state (e.g., positive rather than negative) may serve as a deterrent. In other words, the deterrent need not be related to the attitude object to alter an individual's affective state. To our surprise, gender differences emerged on this issue. This is despite the fact that we found no evidence of gender differences during pretesting. In fact, control condition means (see Figs. 3.4 and 3.5) indicate that female participants felt slightly more negatively than males toward exit exams (Ms -3.89 and -3.40, respectively, ns). In general, we would expect those with the strongest affect to provide the best support for the theory, but this is not what we found. We will return to the issue of participant gender differences in Study 3.

We suggested earlier that reactance would be less likely if participants perceived the attitude issue and the deterrent to be unconnected, though a skeptic may still argue that the increase in negativity toward exit exams in the $1.00 condition among males may reflect reactance rather than affective intensity. Such a person would again need to make an argument for why $0.50 would be sufficient to restore freedom but $1.00 would not be. Nevertheless, at this point we cannot rule out that some part of the negative responses in both Studies 1 and 2 may indeed be due to reactance. To examine further the relationship between reactance and affective intensity, we designed a new study in which we endeavored to deter support for a proposal designed to *help*, rather than hurt, students. This addresses reactance insofar as one should not feel threatened with the removal of a freedom one does not already have. Any increase in reported support for the proposal cannot be attributed to reactance but instead would support the theory of affective intensity.

In addition to creating a pro-attitudinal proposal, we made two additional changes to the next study. First, we used a new kind of deterrent: the proportion of others who were opposed to the proposal aimed to help students. Second, we examined the effect of issue involvement on support for the proposal. We did this by manipulating when the proposed change would take place: either in the following fall semester or in three years. We expected that affective intensity would be greater when the proposal would affect students directly (high involvement), and that in this condition we should find the strongest support for our theory.

STUDY 3

Method

To find issues about which students would have positive attitudes, twenty issues of potential interest to undergraduate students (e.g., abolishing attendance requirements in all classes, permitting the sale of alcohol at university sporting events) were presented to some introductory psychology students. After reading each issue, participants indicated their support or opposition on an 11-point scale ranging from +5 (strongly support) to −5 (strongly oppose). Four proposals that yielded the highest mean support ratings, greatest agreement among participants, and no gender differences were chosen for use in the main study. The issues were placing a freeze on tuition hikes ($M = 4.18$), lowering the cost of parking permits ($M = 3.53$), making it possible for students to have minors in all fields of study ($M = 3.47$), and extending hours at the university recreation center weight room ($M = 2.88$).

One hundred introductory psychology students (45 females, 55 males) participated in exchange for course credit. Within gender, participants were randomly assigned to one of eight conditions in blocks of eight.

Participants were conducted through the experiment individually by a female experimenter. At the start of the experiment, participants were escorted to a private room and told that the researchers were assessing student opinion on different issues concerning the university. Participants were given a sheet of paper listing the four issues selected from pretesting and were asked to place a check beside the issue that was "most important" to them. The experimenter noted the issue the participant checked and subsequently returned to the room with an envelope containing a questionnaire pertaining to that issue. Though the experimenter was clearly not blind to issue, she was blind to condition. She explained that the questionnaire was a survey of student opinion and that the participant should read through the questionnaire, indicate his or her response, and then place the questionnaire back inside the envelope. Each participant was carefully debriefed before being excused.

The "Opinion Questionnaire" was a single sheet of paper containing the proposal related to the issue participants marked as most important, the deterrent (if any), and the dependent measure. Participants read that an ad hoc committee of faculty and students was considering (the proposal), and the psychology department had been asked to gather student opinion. The proposals (in the high relevance condition) were as follows:

FREEZING TUITION HIKES: Effective the Fall semester of 2000, the University will not raise tuition for the next five years.

LOWERING PARKING PERMIT COSTS: Effective the Fall semester of 2000, the University will lower the cost of all parking permits by 30%.

MINORS IN ALL FIELDS OF STUDY: Effective the Fall semester of 2000, students will be able to get a minor in any field of study offered by the University.

EXTENDING WEIGHT ROOM HOURS: Effective the Fall semester of 2000, the Weight Room will be open to students from 6:00 A.M. to 10:00 P.M. every day.

In the low relevance condition, the proposals were identical, except that they were prefaced by the phrase "Effective academic year 2002–2003 . . ." (then three years away).

As in Study 1, participants indicated their support or opposition to the proposal on an 11-point scale ranging from +5 to −5 with endpoints labeled "Strongly support" and "Strongly oppose."

Between the proposal and the attitude measure, participants in the experimental conditions read a single sentence identifying a group in opposition to the proposal. The proportion of each group opposing the proposal was designed to serve as a weak, moderate, or strong deterrent to students' support for the proposal. For example, regarding the minors in all fields of study issue, a weak deterrent read, "A few members of the faculty are against this proposition, but most are neutral." The moderate deterrent read, "About half the faculty are against this proposition, and the rest are neutral." The strong deterrent read, "The vast majority of faculty are against this proposition, but a few are neutral." Participants in the control condition simply read the proposal and filled out the questionnaire.

Results and Discussion

Results are displayed separately for males and females in Figs. 3.6 and 3.7. Male participants were more strongly in favor of the proposal when the change would affect them personally (high relevance) than when it would most likely not (low relevance) (control condition Ms 4.71 and 3.43, respectively). Looking first at the high relevance condition, we see that support for the proposal was high in the no deterrent condition, dropped in the weak deterrent condition, rose in the moderate deterrent condition, and then dropped in the strong deterrent condition. The decrease in support from the control to the weak deterrent condition was significant, $F(1, 24) = 5.01$, $p < .04$, as was the increase in support from the weak to moderate deterrent condition, $F(1, 24) = 6.61$, $p < .02$. The predicted cubic trend was also significant, $F(1, 24) = 6.85$, $p < .02$. There were no significant effects in the low relevance condition. These results provide evidence that positive attitudinal affect can be deterred in a manner similar to negative affect, but only when the issue is highly involving to participants.

Consistent with findings from Study 2, female participants showed a different pattern from males. Rather than a cubic trend in the high relevance condition, female participants showed a linear trend, where support for the proposal de-

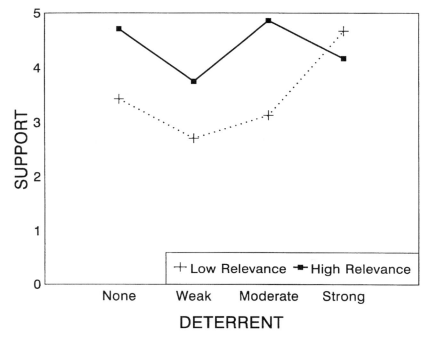

FIG. 3.6. Support for pro-attitudinal proposal: Male participants, Study 3.

creased with each successive deterrent, $F(1, 18) = 6.47$, $p < .03$. There were
no significant effects in the low relevance condition.

The reader may note from Fig. 3.7 that female participants' support for the
proposal did not differ appreciably depending on involvement. With the exception of the strong deterrent condition where support was weaker under high than
low relevance, female participants' support for the issue did not differ based on
whether they, personally, would be affected by the proposed changes. This
stands in contrast to male participants, whose support for the proposal was
greater (excepting the strong deterrent condition) when they personally would
be affected by the change. We have no ready explanation for these findings.
One may posit that female participants did not feel as strongly about the proposals as male participants, but the lack of significant gender differences in the
control condition and in pretesting data argue against this interpretation. It is
possible that female participants processed the proposal more cognitively than
males, forming an opinion based more on the proposal's likelihood of being
implemented than on their personal feelings about the proposal. Because we do
not know whether the gender difference is caused by the instigator of the affect
(i.e., something about the proposal), the nature of the deterrent, or by a combination of these, we cannot determine the meaning of the gender differences

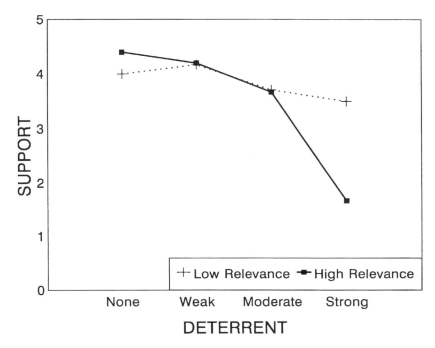

FIG. 3.7.   Support for pro-attitudinal proposal: Female participants, Study 3.

at this time. Further research in which instigator and deterrent are independently manipulated is needed.

STUDY 4

The final study examines the reactance issue along with the intensity of affect by measuring affective enjoyment of an item when a person has been exposed to an appeal designed to vary in emotional deterrent value. Put more simply, people who eat meat were shown more or less dramatic pictures of the slaughter of chickens and then asked how much they enjoyed eating meat.

When persuasive attempts involve obviously emotional material in order to make their case, there is the distinct possibility of two very different responses from the audience. If recipients see the persuasive attempts as threats to one or more of their freedoms, reactance can lead them to increase their opposition to the goal of the persuasion. If reactance were the only effect of the attempted persuasion, one would expect a monotonic increase in opposition to the persuasion, unless the persuasion was overwhelming, in which case there should be a strong decrease in opposition (see Fig. 3.8). However, given that affective states

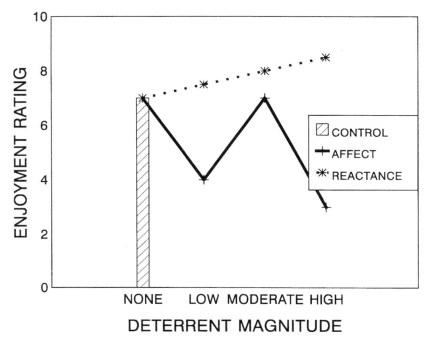

FIG. 3.8. Affective intensity vs. reactance.

may be involved in the issue on which persuasive attempts are made, the persuasive attempts may act as deterrents to one's feeling. In this latter case, a
weak reason for not feeling as one does should reduce the intensity of one's
feeling, while a moderately strong reason can raise one's intensity to its potential
level. On the other hand, a very strong reason could overwhelm one's affective
state and replace it with one that is altogether different (Figure 3.8). For example, if a person who liked coffee received information that new research had
shown that coffee would shorten one's life by either a month, a year, or 10
years, the person's positive affect for coffee could be reduced, pushed to its
maximum, or even eliminated, respectively. If only reactance were involved,
liking for coffee would be expected to increase with each increment in persuasive strength until the persuasion overwhelmed one's liking for coffee. In a
preliminary attempt to examine the possibilities of reactance versus deterrent
effects from persuasions, Elizabeth Price carried out the following project for
her senior honors thesis (Price, 2001). She is a vegetarian and particularly interested in the effect pictures of animal slaughter have on the attitude of meat
eaters.

Method

The research participants consisted of 40 volunteers, all meat eaters, from introductory psychology courses at the University of Kansas. The students received credit for their participation in the research. Participants within gender were randomly assigned to one of four conditions, making a total of 10 in each. Because females outnumbered males by three to one, we were unable to test for gender differences in this study.

Participants were individually taken into a private room and told they would receive a series of envelopes, each containing further instructions. Participants were asked to carry out each task and to notify the research assistant when they had finished. The first envelope contained a preliminary questionnaire designed to determine how frequently they ate meat and what kinds of meat they consumed (fish, poultry, pork, or beef). Participants were then given a second envelope containing another instruction sheet asking them to think of their favorite meat dish and to write a brief, descriptive paragraph summarizing why it appealed to them. They were told they would have up to 10 minutes to complete this task. Having completed the second set of instructions, participants were randomly assigned to one of four groups: no persuasion (control), weak, moderate, or strong persuasion.

Each participant assigned to one of the three persuasion groups received an envelope containing a photograph designed to be of low, moderate, or high persuasive strength. A simple label attached to the photograph described it as typical of those used to influence people not to eat meat, and that they should take a moment to look at it and then wait for the research assistant to return.

The photographs all depicted the same scene: a row of chickens recently killed in a slaughterhouse, with a man standing in the background holding a knife and wearing a bloodied apron. The image was chosen based on a series of prior ratings describing it as very graphic. By altering the brightness of the color, the picture was manipulated to the three levels. The weak persuasion photograph was printed almost in black and white, the moderate photograph in muted colors, and the strong photograph in bright colors.

After participants had two minutes to look at the photograph, they were given a fourth envelope containing an attitude questionnaire. Each question was accompanied by an 11-point response scale (0 = Not at all, 10 = Very Much or Extremely). The questionnaire was the same for all persuasion groups. The first three questions were designed to ascertain whether the photographs were perceived as having persuasive character: "To what extent did the picture present reasons for not eating meat?", "How dramatic did you find the picture?", "How persuasive was the content of the picture?" These were followed by items designed to measure the participants' attitudes toward eating different kinds of meat: "Please rate the attractiveness of the following meats: fish, poultry, chicken, beef, pork." The last question addressed a possible affective response of disgust: "How disgusted did the picture make you feel?"

TABLE 3.1
Checks on the Persuasiveness of the Pictures

Question	Intended picture strength			
	Weak	Moderate	Strong	N
How good the reason	3.7	3.4	5.1	10
How dramatic the picture[1]	4.3	2.9$_a$	6.2$_b$	10
How persuasive the picture[1]	3.4	2.6$_a$	5.5$_b$	10
Feeling of disgust	3.9	3.3	5.3	10

[1]$p_{quadratic} = .05$
Note. Within each measure, means with different subscripts differ at $p < .05$.

Those participants assigned to the control group received a questionnaire that omitted the questions pertaining to the picture. Following the procedure all participants were fully debriefed.

Results and Discussion

We were interested in the possibility that the more dramatic the picture that portrays animal slaughter, the more reactance will be aroused in viewers, producing a boomerang tendency in attitude change among meat eaters. Participants' mean responses to the four questions assessing the success of the manipulation showed little in the way of systematic responses, suggesting that the manipulations did not work well (Table 3.1). Analyses of participants' responses found only two reliable effects among the four questions for the three different pictures. As is apparent, while there is a tendency for the high persuasion picture to produce higher ratings, the effects are not as strong as one wants for evidence of a successful manipulation.

Despite the lack of consistent effects on participants' judgments of the pictures, there are clear differences in the pictures presented to them, and it would be of some interest if these pictures did not produce differences in their enjoyment of eating meat. We therefore proceeded to analyze the data just as if our manipulation checks had indicated success. Specifically, we looked at responses to two measures of enjoyment—enjoyableness of eating chicken and of eating beef, the two most popular kinds. Indeed, of the 40 participants, 14 chose chicken as their favorite meat while 22 chose beef, 3 chose fish, and 1 chose pork. There were no gender differences in meat preferences.

We anticipated that chicken lovers would respond more strongly to the propagandistic pictures than would those who loved beef, but responses of these two groups to the question about enjoyment of chicken did not differ, and their joint responses can be seen in Fig. 3.9. They show a boomerang effect to the moderately strong deterrent as would be expected from reactance theory. The mean enjoyment in response to the moderate picture was greater than enjoyment either with no picture or with the weak picture (*ps* < .05). However, in sharp reversal

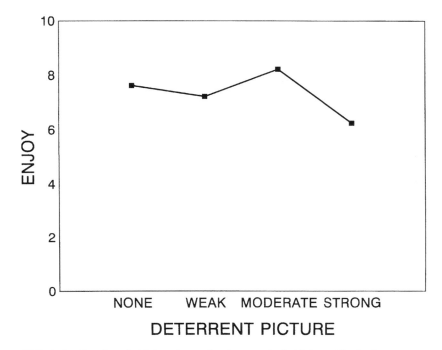

FIG. 3.9.   Beef and chicken lovers' enjoyment of chicken, Study 4.

of this reactance trend was reported enjoyment in response to the strong picture, which was lower than enjoyment in response to the moderate picture ($p < .01$). The quadratic trend, clearly visible from low to moderate to strong deterrent, was reliable at the 1% level, and the cubic trend was also reliable ($p = .05$). The cubic trend suggests that participants' responses were a joint function of reactance and intensity of affect processes.

   In contrast to this common response among chicken and beef eaters to the deterrent pictures, rated enjoyment of beef by chicken eaters showed no reliable effects or even trends, though enjoyment of beef by beef eaters revealed a strong cubic trend ($p < .02$), as seen in Fig. 3.10. While only the third leg of this cubic trend is by itself reliable ($p < .01$), the pattern is exactly what should be expected if the deterrent pictures are presented to people who have a strong affective response to the original stimulus, in this case, the beef. These data, based on cell Ns of 3 to 7, can hardly be called convincing, but they do suggest that propagandistic deterrents can have quite different effects, depending on how directly they attack a cherished value. Of course, we cannot be sure that these effects are not peculiar to differences between those who like chicken and those who like beef, or to pictures of hen slaughter as opposed to other kinds of animal slaughter that could have been presented. Nevertheless, the results certainly suggest that responses to this type of social influence attempt can be either positive

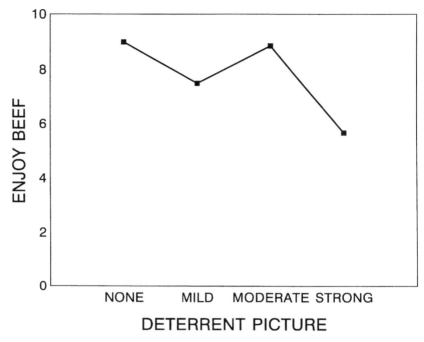

FIG. 3.10.   Beef lovers' enjoyment of beef, Study 4.

or negative depending on directness and strength of the influence attempt.

If one simply looks at the extent to which both chicken and beef lovers reported enjoying the meat they initially preferred more than the alternative (either beef or chicken), we find the following proportions: No Deterrent = 88%; Mild Deterrent = 44%; Moderate Deterrent = 78%; and Strong Deterrent = 25%. These data, again, reflect a cubic trend ($p < .05$). Participants' liking for their favorite meat tended to decrease in response to a mild deterrent, increase in response to a moderate deterrent, and decrease greatly to a strong deterrent.

Before moving on, we need to reconsider the manipulation checks, which suggested that the propagandistic pictures of chicken slaughter hardly differed from each other (see Table 3.1). In contrast, the effects of enjoyment of eating chicken or beef suggest that the pictures differed from each other in exactly the way intended, as attempted persuasions against eating chicken. This apparent puzzle is understandable and predictable from the theory about the intensity of emotion (Brehm, 1999). To the extent that measures of the success of manipulations are sensitive to affect, they will tend to show no differences when the affect elicited by the persuasive material is inconsistent with the affect created in dependent effects. The main dependent effects were those of enjoyment of eating chicken or beef, which were expected to be strong because these were participants' favorite meats. The affect that is appropriate to the propagandistic pictures is dislike or disgust, but this kind of affect is prevented from occurring by the dominant liking for meat. Similar effects have been reported (Brehm et al., 1999) for responses to gift certificates when the dominant affect is sadness: Positive affect regarding gift certificates occurred only when the gift certificate was large enough to do away with sadness. It is therefore perfectly plausible that the checks on the manipulations in the present research failed to show differences while the ratings of enjoyment of eating meat did.

GENERAL DISCUSSION

To summarize, these studies provide preliminary evidence that the intensity of affect associated with attitudes may function similarly to motivational and emotional intensity. Participants' attitude varied as a function of the attitude object and the strength of deterrents acting against the affective component of the attitude. In contrast to what traditional theories of attitude change would predict, attitudes did not linearly change as a function of the strength of the reasons for supporting or opposing a proposal. Rather, attitudes changed non-monotonically as a function of the forces acting against the affect. In Studies 1, 2, and 4, when the opposing force was weak (in the form of a weak endorsement, a small gift certificate, or a dulled photograph of graphic slaughter), opposition to a counter-attitudinal proposal decreased, relative to a control condition in which no deterrent was presented. In Study 3, *support* for a pro-attitudinal proposal similarly decreased in the presence of weak opposition. As mentioned earlier, we believe weak reasons for not feeling as one does reduce resistance to attitude change because they are perceived as presenting little challenge to the cherished attitude.

As reasons for not feeling the way one does increase in strength, so does resistance to attitude change. The intensity of one's affect is driven toward whatever maximum its instigation provides. Thus, a stronger endorsement, a more valuable gift certificate, and a more vivid photograph each increased affective intensity. Presumably, only when the strength of reasons for not having the attitudinal feeling outweighed the affect associated with the attitude did reported affect decrease to a low level.

Collectively, these studies also shed some light on how deterrents to an affective state cause reactance versus weakening or strengthening the intensity of one's affect. Though both processes are motivational in nature, they operate under different conditions. Results from Study 2 suggest that affective intensity varied as a function of the magnitude of deterrence, even when participants did not perceive the deterrent and issue as related. We have suggested that reactance is unlikely to occur when the deterrent is not perceived as connected with the issue. Offering further support that the results from the first two studies are not attributable to reactance, results from Study 3 showed that *support* for a pro-attitudinal proposal increased in the moderate deterrent condition (among males). Because one should not feel threatened with the removal of a freedom one does not already have, this increase cannot be attributed to reactance. Results from Study 4 suggest that reactance is more likely when a cherished value is directly threatened, i.e., when the deterrent is connected with the issue. We believe that the reason enjoyment of eating beef among beef lovers showed a cubic trend was because participants' freedom to eat beef was not directly threatened by pictures of chicken slaughter. By contrast, beef and chicken lovers' enjoyment of eating chicken revealed a trend more indicative of reactance: increased liking of chicken with increasingly vivid pictures of chicken slaughter, until the vividness of the slaughter overwhelmed liking. Together, these studies suggest that reactance is likely when a deterrent directly challenges a cherished value.

This research has important implications for the nature of persuasion. Persons wishing to persuade others have typically employed messages from credible sources replete with facts and strong arguments. The implication was that more information was better than less and that strong arguments were more effective than weak arguments (e.g., Eagly & Chaiken, 1993; Petty & Cacioppo, 1986). The research presented here may prompt a reinterpretation of this reasoning. Our theory makes the seemingly paradoxical prediction that fewer, weaker arguments will be more effective in reducing resistance to persuasion than many stronger arguments. It is argued that the most effective way to reduce an individual's affectively based resistance to persuasion is to provide a weak deterrent that does not directly threaten a cherished value. We do not believe that resistance to change is indicative of the strength of an attitude (see Wegner, Petty, Smoak, & Fabrigar, this volume). Even strongly held attitudes (evidenced by extreme negativity) may change significantly in the face of a weak endorsement of a counter-attitudinal proposal.

To conclude, extraordinary conflicts such as those between Israelis and Palestinians and Indians and Pakistanis may be ameliorated by less than extraordinary means. While we certainly recognize that these conflicts reflect deep historical and religious differences, we believe the principles we have outlined here regarding resistance to persuasion may be applied to a variety of situations in which negative attitudes are intense. If we wish to subdue conflict between nations, a small deterrent that does not directly threaten a cherished value may be effective in reducing the negative attitudes nations hold toward one another.

REFERENCES

Ajzen, I., & Fishbein, M. (1997). Attitude-behavior relations: A theoretical analysis and review of empirical research. *Psychological Bulletin, 84,* 888–918.

Biner, P. M., & Hua, D. M. (1995). Determinants of the magnitude of goal valence: The interactive effects of need, instrumentality, and the difficulty of goal attainment. *Basic and Applied Social Psychology, 16,* 53–74.

Brehm, J. W. (1999). The intensity of emotion. *Personality and Social Psychology Review, 3,* 2–22.

Brehm, J. W., Brummett, B. H., & Harvey, L. (1999). Paradoxical sadness. *Motivation and Emotion, 23,* 31–44.

Brehm, J. W., & Miller, K. (2000). *The effect of unpleasant news on the good taste of chocolate.* Unpublished manuscript, University of Kansas.

Brehm, J. W., & Self, E. (1989). The intensity of motivation. *Annual Review of Psychology, 40,* 109–131.

Brummett, B. H. (1996). *The intensity of anger.* Unpublished doctoral dissertation, University of Kansas.

D'Anello, S. C. (1997). *Paradoxical effects of losing money and experiencing a health threat on happiness intensity.* Unpublished doctoral dissertation, University of Kansas.

Eagly, A. H., & Chaiken, S. (1993). *The psychology of attitudes.* Fort Worth TX: Harcourt, Brace, Jovanovich.

Festinger, L. (1964). Behavioral support for opinion change. *Public Opinion Quarterly, 28,* 404–417.

Frijda, N. (1986). *The emotions.* Cambridge, England: Cambridge University Press.

LaPiere, R. T. (1934). Attitudes vs. actions. *Social Forces, 13,* 230–237.

Lazarus, R. (1991). *Emotion and adaptation.* New York: Oxford University Press.

Murphy, S. T., & Zajonc, K. B. (1993). Affect, cognition, and awareness: Affective priming with optimal and suboptimal stimulus exposures. *Journal of Personality and Social Psychology, 64,* 723–739.

Petty, R. E., & Cacioppo, J. T. (1986). The Elaboration Likelihood Model of persuasion. In L. Berkowitz (Ed.), *Advances in experimental social psychology* (Vol. 19, pp. 123–205). New York: Academic Press.

Price, E. (2001). *Graphic images as deterrents to the desire to eat meat.* Unpublished Honors Thesis, University of Kansas, Lawrence, KS.

Silvia, P. J., & Brehm, J. W. (2001). Exploring alternative deterrents to emotional intensity: Anticipated happiness, distraction, and sadness. *Cognition and Emotion, 15,* 575–592.

Wicker, A. W. (1969). Attitudes versus actions: The relationship of verbal and overt behavioral responses to attitude objects. *Journal of Social Issues, 25,* 41–78.

Wright, R. A. (1996). Brehm's model of motivation as a model of effort and cardiovascular response. In P. M. Gollwitzer, & J. A. Bargh (Eds.), *The psychology of action* (pp. 424–453). New York: Guilford.

Wright, R. A., Contrada, R. J., & Patane, M. J. (1986). Task difficulty, cardiovascular response, and the magnitude of goal valence. *Journal of Personality and Social Psychology, 52,* 837–843.

Zajonc, R. B. (1980). Feeling and thinking: Preferences need no inferences. *American Psychologist, 35,* 151–175.

Zajonc, R. B. (1984). On the primacy of affect. *American Psychologist, 39,* 117–124.

4

Resisting Persuasion and Attitude Certainty: A Meta-Cognitive Analysis

Zakary L. Tormala
Indiana University

Richard E. Petty
The Ohio State University

Imagine a typical political campaign battle in which two candidates are running against each other and hold opposing positions on most major issues. Now imagine that Eddie, an avid opponent of abortion rights, is exposed to a persuasive appeal from one of the candidates in which the candidate argues in favor of the woman's right to choose. Because this message is incongruent with Eddie's attitude, he generates counterarguments against it and thus resists attitude change. The present chapter asks whether when Eddie resists the advocacy, his initial attitude against abortion rights might still be impacted in other, subtle ways. Our specific interest is in the possibility that when Eddie resists persuasion, he might under specifiable conditions become more or less convinced of the validity of his own attitude. In other words, when people resist persuasive attacks, are there any implications for the certainty with which their original attitudes are held?

Over the years, attitude change researchers have been most concerned with making persuasion successful. Beginning with the seminal work on persuasion by Hovland, Janis, and Kelley (1953), considerable attention has been focused on developing models that predict the conditions under which persuasive communications will produce attitude change (see also Greenwald, 1968; McGuire, 1968; Petty, Ostrom, & Brock, 1981). The basic assumption underlying much of this work has been that if a persuasive message does not change the target attitude in terms of valence or extremity (i.e., the message has been resisted), it has simply failed. Even researchers interested in resistance to persuasion as a topic worthy of study in its own right (e.g., McGuire, 1964) appear to assume that once someone resists a persuasive message, the initial attitude has not been impacted.

In the present chapter, we argue against this view of resistance. We propose that when people resist persuasive attacks, their initial attitudes can change in terms of the certainty with which they are held. We argue that depending on the meta-cognitive inferences people form about their attitudes after a persuasive message is resisted, they can either gain or lose confidence in these attitudes.

WHAT IS RESISTANCE?

In the attitude change literature, many different meanings have been associated with the concept of resistance. Indeed, it can be viewed as an outcome, a process, a motivation, or a quality of attitudes or people (Petty, Tormala, & Rucker, in press). Perhaps the most common conceptualization of resistance has been as an *outcome*. In this sense, resistance refers to the absence of attitude change, or even attitude change away from the persuasive appeal (i.e., boomerang; see Johnson & Smith-McLallen, this volume).

As a *process*, resistance refers to the various mechanisms through which people prevent persuasive messages from changing their attitudes. Numerous mechanisms of resistance have been identified. For example, when exposed to a persuasive attack someone might generate counterarguments or negative thoughts (e.g., Brock, 1967; Killeya & Johnson, 1998; Petty, Ostrom, & Brock, 1981), bolster his or her initial attitude (e.g., Lewan & Stotland, 1961; Lydon, Zanna, & Ross, 1988), derogate the source of the message (e.g., Tannenbaum, Macauley, & Norris, 1966), or experience negative affect and attribute it to the message or source (e.g., Zuwerink & Devine, 1996). Recent research suggests that there may be individual differences in the mechanisms of resistance people use (Briñol, Rucker, Tormala, & Petty, this volume).

As a *motivation*, resistance refers to having a goal to resist attitude change or protect the existing attitude (see also Jacks & O'Brien, this volume; Knowles & Linn, this volume). Several specific motives have been identified as sources of resistance. For instance, reactance involves the motivation to maintain or restore freedom (Brehm, 1966). Consistency motives have also been implicated in this regard. According to cognitive dissonance (Festinger, 1957) and balance (Heider, 1958) theories, people are motivated to resist changing their attitudes when doing so will result in inconsistent cognitions. Resistance could also be guided by accuracy motives, which might lead a person to defend the current attitude if he or she is highly confident that it is correct (Petty & Wegener, 1999).

Finally, as a *quality*, resistance has been used to describe the types of people or attitudes that do not change. That is, certain types of people (e.g., those high in dogmatism or authoritarianism; Rokeach, 1960; Miller, 1965) are generally more difficult to persuade than others (for a more detailed discussion see Briñol et al., this volume). Similarly, certain types of attitudes—such as those that are high in certainty or accessibility—tend to be more resistant to persuasion than others (see Petty & Krosnick, 1995, for a review).

The focus of the present chapter is on the types of inferences people form about their own attitudes once the outcome of resistance has occurred. In addressing this question, though, our research touches upon resistance in all its forms. That is, we examine situations in which people are *motivated* to resist a personally relevant and counterattitudinal message. We then induce them to generate counterarguments against this message (*process*). Once people perceive that they have resisted persuasion (*outcome*), we explore the implications of this perception for the *quality* of their initial attitudes (i.e., how certain they are about the attitudes, how resistant the attitudes are to subsequent persuasion, and how well the attitudes predict behavioral intentions).

ATTITUDE CERTAINTY

Before turning to our studies, it is useful to discuss our primary dependent measure—attitude certainty. Attitude certainty refers to the sense of conviction with which one holds one's attitude, or one's subjective assessment of the validity of his or her attitude (Festinger, 1950, 1954; Gross, Holtz, & Miller, 1995). Research on attitude certainty has shown that it has numerous implications for other kinds of evaluative responding, including attitude-relevant behavior, an attitude's resistance to persuasion, and an attitude's temporal persistence. Fazio and Zanna (1978), for instance, examined the attitude–behavior relationship in a study addressing people's attitudes toward participating in psychology experiments. Participants were asked to report the number of psychology experiments in which they had previously participated, their attitudes toward psychology experiments, and the certainty with which they held these attitudes. At the end of the experimental session, the researchers allowed participants to volunteer for psychology experiments scheduled for later in the year. They found that the more certain participants were about their attitudes toward psychology experiments, the more these attitudes predicted volunteering for future participation. In other words, increased attitude certainty strengthened the relationship between attitudes and behavior.

Attitude certainty has also been shown to facilitate resistance to persuasion (e.g., Babad, Ariav, Rosen, & Salomon, 1987; Bassili, 1996; Krosnick & Abelson, 1992; Swann, Pelham, & Chidester, 1988; Wu & Shaffer, 1987). Bassili (1996), for instance, used a telephone survey to examine people's attitudes and attitude certainty with respect to three target issues. After respondents reported their attitudes toward each of these issues over the phone, they were challenged by a counterargument against the attitude they had expressed. Bassili found that high levels of attitude certainty enhanced resistance to persuasion on all three of the target issues as compared to lower levels of certainty—that is, the more certain people were, the less they changed in response to the argument against their attitude. In a separate study, Bassili (1996) also examined the temporal persistence of attitudes and found that the more certain respondents were about their attitudes, the more stable these attitudes were, or the less they changed, over a two-week period.

As this research suggests, attitude certainty is an important characteristic of people's attitudes that has very real consequences. Nevertheless, little prior research has explored the possible effects of resisting persuasion on attitude certainty. Although we know that certainty can enhance resistance, we know less of what the effect of resistance is on certainty. In other words, researchers have identified various other antecedents of attitude certainty (see Gross et al., 1995, for a review), but little is known about whether resisting a persuasive message can influence attitude certainty. In the following sections we outline our perspective. In brief, we believe that under some conditions resisting persuasion can lead to either an increase or a decrease in attitude certainty. Following our conceptual position, we describe some of the evidence we have obtained that is consistent with this view.

RESISTANCE AND INCREASES
IN ATTITUDE CERTAINTY

One intriguing possibility is that when people resist persuasion, the certainty with which they hold their initial attitudes can be augmented. We propose a meta-cognitive framework for this phenomenon, whereby when people resist persuasion they can perceive their own resistance and form corresponding inferences about their attitudes (e.g., feeling more certain that their initial attitude is correct). Following the logic of attribution theory, in the meta-cognition literature it is typically assumed that when people "observe" their thoughts or meta-cognitive experience, they only use this information to form a judgment if it is perceived to be diagnostic (see Strack & Föster, 1998, for a related discussion). When meta-cognitive information is deemed less diagnostic, reliance on it in forming a judgment is attenuated (e.g., Jacoby & Kelley, 1987; Schwarz, Bless, et al., 1991). In other words, just as salient situational explanations for someone else's behavior tend to dampen dispositional attributions about that person (see Gilbert, 1998, for a review), salient alternative explanations for one's own meta-cognitive experience can lead people to discount that experience or information.

We use the same attributional logic in an attempt to understand the role of meta-cognition in resistance to persuasion. We argue that increases in attitude certainty following resistance likely stem from a meta-cognitive attribution process, whereby people make inferences about their attitudes based on their perception of their own resistance. When people perceive that they have resisted persuasion, they might infer that their attitude is correct, and feel more certain about it. Indeed, if their attitude were incorrect, they should have changed it in the face of persuasion. Consistent with the attribution literature, however, we also postulate that people consider "situational" factors before reaching such conclusions about their attitudes. More specifically, resisting a persuasive attack viewed as cogent should confer more certainty about one's attitude than resisting an attack viewed as specious. A clearly weak attack is less challenging to one's attitude, and resistance to it might therefore be perceived as less diagnostic. That is, resisting a weak attack might indicate that one's attitude is correct, but it might also indicate that the message simply lacked the power to change even an erroneous attitude (thus leaving certainty unchanged). In short, when the weak nature of an attack provides a salient situational attribution for resistance, resistance becomes uninformative.

In sum, we propose that when people resist persuasion, they can detect their own resistance, form an inference that their attitude must be correct, and adjust for situational factors such as the perceived strength of the attack. Our framework suggests, then, that one situation in which resistance will increase attitude certainty is when the message recipient both believes the persuasive message has been resisted and views the resisted attack as reasonably strong. If one or both of these conditions are not met, attitude certainty is not expected to increase.

In a recent series of experiments we tested this possibility (Tormala & Petty, 2002). In each experiment we exposed undergraduates to a counter-attitudinal persuasive message promoting the implementation of senior comprehensive exams as a graduation requirement at their university (see Petty & Cacioppo, 1986). Participants were told that if they failed to pass these exams, they would not be allowed to graduate until they had successfully retaken them. All participants were told that we were conducting this research on behalf of their university to assess student reactions to the exam policy, and that in this capacity we would be asking them not only to report their opinions of comprehensive exams, but also to provide a list of the counterarguments they could raise against the proposal. Following these instructions, participants were presented with the persuasive message in favor of comprehensive exams, after which they listed their counterarguments, completed attitude measures, and indicated the extent to which they were certain about their attitudes.

Importantly, each experiment contained three basic message conditions: a perceived strong message condition, a perceived weak message condition, and a control condition. In the two persuasive message conditions, participants actually read the exact same message in favor of comprehensive exams. In both conditions, participants read more detailed versions of the following arguments (adapted from Petty & Cacioppo, 1986): Grades would improve if the exam policy were adopted, implementing the exams would allow the university to take part in a national trend, the average starting salary of graduates would increase, and implementing the exams would allow students to compare their

TABLE 4.1
Attitude, Attitude Certainty, and Attitude-Behavioral Intention Consistency

		Message condition	
Dependent Measure	Control	"Weak"	"Strong"
	Study 1		
Attitudes			
M	4.82_a	4.91_a	5.03_a
SD	1.52	1.80	1.91
Certainty			
M	5.10_a	4.33_a	6.16_b
SD	1.79	1.91	1.95
	Study 2		
Attitudes			
M	4.68_a	4.96_a	4.81_a
SD	1.96	1.73	1.86
Certainty			
M	4.83_a	4.78_a	5.39_b
SD	1.20	1.11	1.73
Attitude-Behavior			
r	$.68_a$	$.72_a$	$.89_b$

Note. Adapted from Tormala and Petty (2002). Means with the same subscript do not differ from each other (interpret within rows only).

scores with those of students at other universities. Although participants in both persuasive message conditions read the exact same arguments, their *perception* of these arguments was manipulated. In the "strong" message condition, participants were led to believe the proposal contained the strongest arguments the university could muster. In the "weak" message condition, participants were led to believe the proposal contained weak arguments, so that the researchers could collect students' reactions to all kinds of points that might be raised in support of the issue. Thus, participants in these conditions read the same message, but were induced to believe it was either strong or weak. In the control condition, participants were told about the possible exam policy, but then read an unrelated article and were not asked to think of counterarguments.

In the initial experiment using this paradigm, we examined the basic hypothesis that when people resist persuasion they become more certain, but only when the message they resist is believed to be strong. The data were highly consistent with this notion. First, as indicated in the top portion of Table 4.1, participants in both the perceived strong and perceived weak message conditions resisted persuasion. Resistance was indicated by the lack of significant difference between attitudes in either of these conditions and attitudes in the control condition, where a persuasive message was not even presented. There was, however, a significant effect of message condition on attitude certainty. As illustrated in

Table 4.1, certainty increased relative to the control when participants resisted a message they believed to be strong, but not when they resisted a message believed to be weak. This effect was particularly telling given that the "strong" and "weak" persuasive messages did not really differ in any substantive way, but only in whether they had been labeled as strong or weak.

In subsequent experiments we extended these findings. For example, using the same procedure as the first experiment, we conducted a study in which we also included a measure of behavioral intentions in order to determine if the certainty effects uncovered in our initial work had any implications for the attitude–behavior relationship. This experiment was essentially a replication of the first, but at the end of the session we asked participants how they intended to vote on the comprehensive exam issue if it were placed before undergraduates. To create a sensitive measure of voting intention, we asked participants to respond on a 9-point scale ranging from *definitely against* to *definitely in favor*. As indicated in the lower portion of Table 4.1, we replicated the attitude and attitude certainty effects from the first study, but also found that the findings had implications for the correlation between attitudes and voting intentions. Although the simple attitude–behavioral intention correlation was positive and significant in each condition, it was also moderated by message condition, such that it was significantly higher in the perceived strong message condition than in the other two conditions, which did not differ from each other. Importantly, then, we found that when people resist persuasion, their feelings of increased certainty can have ramifications for behavioral intentions. Such intentions are consequential in that they are highly predictive of actual behavior (Fishbein & Ajzen, 1975).

In a separate experiment, we also assessed the consequences of the certainty effect for resistance to subsequent persuasion. In this experiment, participants listed their counterarguments and reported their attitudes after a first message, which was identical to that used in the other studies. Then participants engaged in an unrelated filler task for approximately 15 minutes. Following the filler task, participants were exposed to a second persuasive message in the same direction as the first, but with new arguments. The amount of attitude change evinced in response to the second message served as a measure of resistance, such that less attitude change indicated greater resistance to the second message. The findings, illustrated in Fig. 4.1, matched our predictions based on the certainty effect. That is, participants were most resistant to the second attack after having resisted an initial attack believed to be strong. In fact, in this condition the difference between time 1 and time 2 attitudes was not significant. When participants resisted a message believed to be weak, however, attitude change from time 1 to time 2 was significant and equivalent to the amount of change in the control condition. Therefore, only when participants believed that they had resisted an initial strong message did they resist the second attack, even when that initial message was objectively no different from the one labeled as weak.

It is important to note that in each of these experiments we also examined the counterarguments participants generated against the comprehensive exam

72

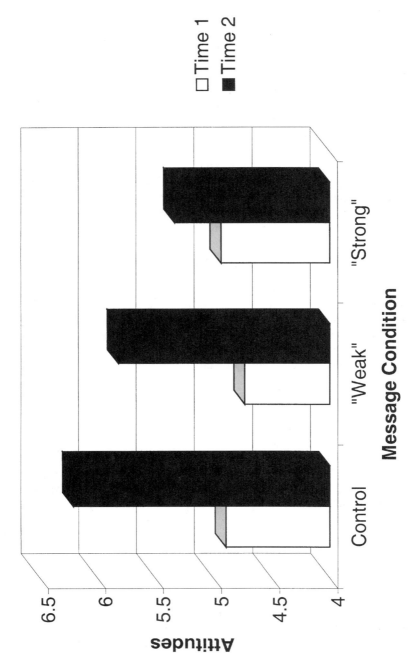

FIG. 4.1. Attitudes after first message (time 1) and after second message (time 2). (Adapted from Tormala & Petty, 2002).

proposal. Analysis revealed that there were no differences in any study in the number, quality, or focus of counterarguments generated. Thus, it appeared that participants were not resisting the message any differently when they thought it was strong versus weak, but they formed different inferences about their attitudes based on their *perception* that it was either strong or weak. In fact, in a separate experiment we found that participants did see the messages as differentially compelling depending on our perceived message strength manipulation, and they actually felt that their resistance had been more successful when the message was viewed as strong. What is more, these effects were moderated by people's perceptions of whether or not they had resisted persuasion. Only under conditions in which participants were led to believe they had resisted did certainty increase. When participants were led to believe they did not resist persuasion, certainty was unaffected. These findings are consistent with the notion that people must have the subjective perception that they have not changed their attitudes following a (strong) persuasive attack for certainty to be augmented.

RESISTANCE AND DECREASES IN ATTITUDE CERTAINTY

In other recent research (Tormala & Petty, 2003), we have explored the possibility that attitude certainty can also *decrease* when someone resists a persuasive attack. That is, under some conditions, meta-cognitive inferences might lead a person to conclude that his or her attitude is less correct, thus reducing confidence in it. We postulate more specifically that even when people objectively resist persuasion, they can become less certain about their initial attitudes if they believe they struggled to resist. For example, people can perceive that they have resisted a persuasive attack but also perceive that it was difficult to do so, or that the counterarguments they generated were specious. If people have the perception that a persuasive attack has only been resisted by the skin of their teeth, they might logically conclude that the initial attitude is less valid and thus become less certain about it. In essence, this perspective retains the attributional logic used to explain increases in attitude certainty but explores the impact of a new type of situational factor—the perceived efficacy of one's resistance. We suggest that in some situations people can perceive that they have resisted persuasion but also realize that they barely resisted and therefore lose confidence in their attitudes.

In an initial test of this possibility, we presented undergraduate participants with a counter-attitudinal persuasive appeal, again promoting the implementation of a new comprehensive examination requirement for graduation. After introducing participants to the issue, but before presenting them with the persuasive message, we asked them to report their attitudes and attitude certainty, based on what they knew right then. Participants were subsequently told that they would be allowed to read the proposal in favor of the comprehensive exam policy, and that we would be asking them to provide a list of the counterarguments they could raise against it. After reading the message, which contained the same arguments as in the experiments described earlier in the chapter, participants listed their counterarguments. Immediately following this procedure, participants were led to believe that the computer program they were using was designed to analyze their counterarguments as they were entered by comparing them to a larger pool of counterarguments generated by other participants earlier in the term. Participants were randomly assigned to receive bogus feedback, based on these ostensible comparisons, that their counterarguments were either strong or weak. Finally, participants completed time 2 measures of attitudes and attitude certainty.

Analysis of time 1 and time 2 attitudes indicated that there was no attitude change following exposure to the persuasive message. That is, participants resisted persuasion, as expected given that the message was counter-attitudinal and they were explicitly instructed to think of counterarguments. There was, however, a significant interaction on attitude certainty. As illustrated in Fig. 4.2, participants became significantly *less* certain of their attitudes after being led to believe they had generated specious counterarguments. When participants had been led to believe their counterarguments were strong, attitude certainty did not decrease, but rather was maintained at a relatively high level. Thus, the data from this experiment were consistent with the notion that under some conditions individuals can resist persuasion according to conventional standards (i.e., zero attitude change in response to a persuasive appeal), but lose confidence in their attitudes when they believe they did not do a good job resisting (i.e., their counterarguments were weak).

In this study we also examined the correspondence between participants' post-message attitudes and behavioral intentions. As a measure of behavioral intentions, we told participants that we would be attempting to solicit some volunteer assistance in making telephone calls to other undergraduates at the same university to inform them of the benefits of the comprehensive exam policy. Participants were asked to report how many phone calls they would be willing to make if we contacted them in the future, and responded on a 1–9 scale ranging from *0 calls* to *40 to 45 calls*. As expected, we found that attitudes were more highly correlated with behavioral intentions when participants were led to believe their counterarguments were strong, $r = .42$, $p < .05$, than when they were led to believe their counterarguments were weak, $r = .16$, $p = .42$. This finding suggests that the attenuation of certainty had real implications for other outcomes.

As in our earlier research (Tormala & Petty, 2002) there were no measurable differences in the counterarguments generated by participants across conditions. One intriguing question, however, is why did attitude certainty not increase when participants were led to believe they had generated compelling arguments against the persuasive attack? Two possible explanations for the lack of increase seem plausible. First, there was a potential ceiling effect in the strong counter-argument feedback condition. Pre-message certainty in that condition was ap-

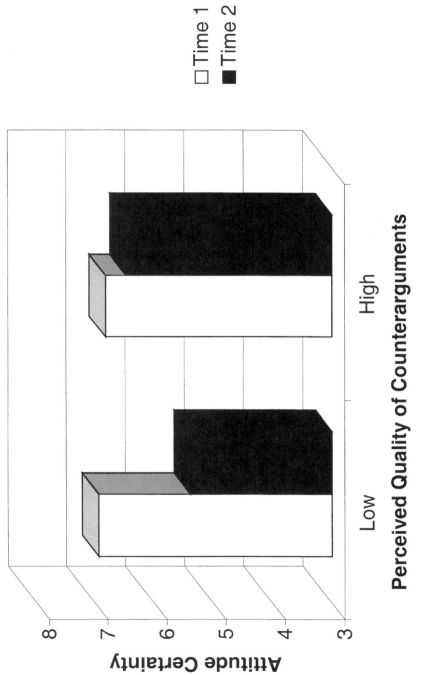

FIG. 4.2. Pre-message certainty (time 1) and post-message certainty (time 2) as a function of counterargument feedback.

proximately 7 on a 9-point scale. In other words, there was little room for substantial increase in certainty in that condition. Second, based on the Tormala and Petty (2002) findings, we would not necessarily expect attitude certainty to increase in that condition. A key finding in that research was that for people to become more certain about their attitudes after resisting persuasion, they must perceive that the persuasive attack they have resisted is a strong one. Perceived message strength was not manipulated in the present experiment. Moreover, the message that was used was moderate in strength, containing both strong and weak arguments. As a consequence, any spontaneous assessments of message strength were likely to produce ambiguous judgments. In short, perceptions of message strength may not have been high enough to elevate certainty in the strong counterargument condition.

Also provocative is the question of what happens when people truly *fail* to resist—for instance, when people attempt to counterargue a message but are ultimately persuaded by it. Recent research by Rucker and Petty (in press) provides one possible answer to this question. In a series of studies, Rucker and Petty found that when people attempt to resist a message that is extremely compelling, counterarguing can become quite difficult, thus opening the door for attitude change. Interestingly, Rucker and Petty found that when this occurs, people can become even more certain about their new attitudes than if they had not attempted to resist in the first place. That is, individuals who were persuaded when trying to resist were more confident in their new attitudes than were individuals who were changed to the same degree as a function of more objective thinking. From a meta-cognitive perspective, unsuccessfully attempting to resist an incoming attack appears to highlight the strength of the opposing attitudinal position, making people more certain that their new (changed) attitudes are correct and more likely that they will behave in accord with their attitudes in the future.

SUMMARY

As discussed earlier, we believe our findings follow from the meta-cognitive inferences people make about their own attitudes when they perceive that they have resisted persuasion. Following this logic, we suspect that when people resist persuasion with relative ease and "observe" this resistance, the default inference is probably that the initial attitude is correct, thus instilling confidence in that attitude. Importantly, though, this inference appears to be corrected to account for potential situational forces that may also have been at play. For example, people appear to take the perceived strength of the persuasive attack into consideration. When the attack is perceived to be strong, the inference that the attitude is correct is bolstered and people feel more certain about their attitude than they did before. When the attack is perceived to be weak, on the other hand, the inference that the attitude is correct is undermined because ambiguity remains as to whether a stronger attack would also have been resisted. Under these circumstances, attitude confidence does not increase.

People also appear to attend to perceptions of the strength of their own resistance. We found that people can become less certain of their attitudes when they believe the counterarguments they generated were not compelling. In other words, when people perceive that they have struggled to resist in some way, they can actually *lose* confidence in their initial attitude, even when by conventional standards they have resisted persuasion. We suspect that the subjective experience of difficulty resisting would produce similar effects.

Importantly, we have also shown that these effects on attitude certainty have implications for other forms of evaluative responding. In the first set of studies (Tormala & Petty, 2002) we found that by successfully resisting a message believed to be strong, people's attitudes can become more predictive of behavioral intentions and more resistant to later persuasion. When the resisted message was viewed as weak, resistance did not confer these same benefits. In the study examining reductions in attitude certainty (Tormala & Petty, 2003), we showed that this effect can be reversed. That is, when people resist persuasion but perceive that their resistance was not too compelling, they not only lose confidence in the attitude, but they also show a reduced willingness to rely on their attitudes when forming behavioral intentions. Therefore, even resisted attacks can have a hidden kind of success in terms of weakening the target attitude.

THE PRESENT FINDINGS IN CONTEXT

The current findings represent a potentially important contribution to the persuasion literature. Most traditional approaches to the study of persuasion have assumed that the story ends when persuasion is resisted—that is, the persuasive message has simply been unsuccessful. Thus, when resistance has occurred, inquiry has stopped. We question this assumption and suggest that in many cases inquiry might fruitfully *begin* when resistance has occurred. In other words, resistance itself appears to have many potentially important consequences. We have postulated and demonstrated that it can affect attitude certainty, attitude–behavior correspondence, and future resistance to persuasive attacks. We see these studies as having intriguing connections to other areas of persuasion research and social psychology more generally.

Inoculation Theory

The objective of the current chapter, like many other chapters in this volume, is to offer a fresh perspective on resistance to persuasion. Nevertheless, it is important to consider historical perspectives on resistance, and how our findings relate to other theoretical frameworks. In particular, our findings appear to have implications for McGuire's classic work on inoculation theory (McGuire, 1964).

In this work McGuire argued that people's beliefs can be inoculated against persuasive attacks through exposure to an initial attack that is easily resisted. In other words, inoculation theory suggested that when people resist an initial persuasive message, they sometimes become more resistant to future messages, presumably because they gain motivation and ability to build strong defenses. Although this enhanced resistance effect is similar on the surface to some of the findings discussed in the present chapter, the current conceptual framework is actually quite different from inoculation theory (see Petty et al., in press; Tormala & Petty, 2002, for more detailed discussion). Most importantly, our framework for future resistance to persuasion revolves around attitude certainty effects and the inferences people form about their attitudes after resisting an initial attack. By adopting this perspective, we are able to account not only for future resistance, but also for increased attitude–behavior consistency, and even cases in which the apparent strength of the attitude is reduced following initial resistance. In short, we simply note that our conceptualization of resistance differs from McGuire's innovative work on inoculation theory, and has potentially broader implications for people's future evaluative responding.

Minority Influence

Our findings might also have implications for the literature on minority influence and delayed attitude change (for a review, see Wood, Lundgren, et al., 1994). In some stimulating research in this domain, it has been found that persuasive attacks can sometimes fail to alter a target attitude in the immediate situation but still exert a delayed impact on that attitude. More specifically, researchers have found that people can resist persuasion from minority sources but evince delayed attitude change in the direction of the minority position as time passes, particularly if the minority message is strong and message recipients process it relatively extensively (e.g., Crano & Chen, 1998).

As described earlier, attitude certainty has a well-established association with attitude stability, or attitudinal persistence over time (e.g., Bassili, 1996). Given this association, and our finding that certainty can sometimes decrease after resistance has occurred, it seems reasonable to speculate that when people resist persuasive messages from minority sources, they might under some conditions become less certain about their attitudes than they initially were. Perhaps when people resist minority influence, they recognize that they did not resist by "legitimate" means—that is, they realize they resisted because of the minority status of the source even though the message itself was reasonably sound. As a result, they may have doubts about how easily they could have resisted had they actually attempted to counterargue the message. This, in turn, could create doubt about the validity of the initial attitude, thus destabilizing it or opening it up to change in the future. Considering the implications of the current framework for the minority influence literature may turn out to be a useful direction in future research.

The Self-Validation Hypothesis

The research described in this chapter may also have ties to other recent work in the area of meta-cognition. In work on the self-validation hypothesis, for instance, Petty, Briñol, and Tormala (2002) found that in addition to the two dimensions of thinking that have traditionally been examined in the persuasion literature—the amount and direction (valence) of issue-relevant thought—attitude change and resistance are also critically dependent on the confidence people have in their cognitive responses to persuasive messages. In some studies, Petty et al. (2002) assessed participants' cognitive responses to a persuasive message and then asked them to report their confidence in these cognitive responses. In other studies, the researchers experimentally induced participants to feel confidence or doubt in their thoughts about a persuasive message. This research revealed that participants' confidence in their thoughts moderated the impact of those thoughts on attitudes. When thoughts were primarily favorable, high confidence in thoughts increased persuasion relative to low confidence in thoughts. When thoughts were primarily unfavorable, however, the pattern was reversed, such that high thought confidence increased resistance relative to low thought confidence (see also Briñol & Petty, 2003; Tormala, Petty, & Briñol, 2002).

Although *thought* confidence was not directly assessed in the present research, the current findings might tie into the self-validation hypothesis. Indeed, one potential interpretation of the current research is that when people resist persuasion, this resistance has varying implications for attitude certainty depending on the confidence people have in their resistance thoughts, or counterarguments. When confidence in one's counterarguments is high (e.g., when an ostensibly strong attack has been resisted), attitude certainty increases (and attitudes may become even less favorable). When confidence in one's counterarguments is low (e.g., when the message or one's counterarguments are ostensibly specious), however, attitude certainty remains the same or even decreases. Consistent with this notion, we found in one experiment (Tormala & Petty, 2002, Experiment 2) that the attitude certainty effects are mediated by participants' perceptions of the effectiveness (or success) of their own resistance. Participants in that experiment reported that they had been more successful at counterarguing the message to the extent that the message was believed to be strong rather than weak, even though their counterarguments did not actually differ in any objective way.

Interestingly, the parallels between the present research and the self-validation research suggest an additional moderator of the present attitude certainty effects. In the work on the self-validation hypothesis, Petty and colleagues (2002) found that people attended to their meta-cognitive experience of thought confidence only when they were relatively high in the motivation to think (e.g., when message recipients were high in the need for cognition; Cacioppo & Petty, 1982). When the motivation to think was relatively low, confidence in thoughts did not appear to impact attitudes. Extending this finding to the present concerns, it is possible that the meta-cognitive perspective we have taken on resistance applies mainly to situations in which information processing activity is somewhat high. In each of the studies we have conducted thus far, it is reasonable to assume that elaboration likelihood was relatively high as participants were led to believe a personally relevant and counterattitudinal policy might be implemented at their own university. As explained by Wegener, Petty, Smoak, and Fabrigar (this volume), however, resistance can occur through a number of different mechanisms, many of which involve low effort thinking (e.g., relying on cues to reject the message). In accord with the self-validation findings (Petty et al., 2002), it is possible that when people resist persuasion with less elaborative information processing, attitude certainty is unaffected because under these conditions people are presumably paying less attention to their meta-cognitions. Furthermore, it is possible that had a less engaging topic been used, even an active method of resistance such as counterarguing would not have had the same implications (see Quinn & Wood, this volume, for additional discussion of the role of personal relevance in resistance to persuasion). In future research we will explore this issue systematically.

Implications for Self-Confidence

Finally, the argument has been made elsewhere that resistance has implications for the self-concept (e.g., Jacks & Devine, 2000; Jacks & O'Brien, this volume). Given this notion, and the present findings, we surmise that when people resist persuasion and become more (or less) certain about their attitudes, they might also become more (or less) confident about themselves, their general abilities and competencies, and so on. For example, when someone has the perception that he or she handily resisted a strong persuasive attack (particularly on an important topic), he or she might feel successful and generate positive attributions about the self, feeling prouder and more confident than ever. If, on the other hand, someone struggles to resist, he or she might interpret that struggle as a kind of failure and form negative attributions about the self, becoming less proud and less confident. Although this idea is speculative, the possibility suggests that resistance and the self-concept could be even more intertwined than researchers have previously realized.

CONCLUSION

Our perspective is that the studies described in this chapter open the door for new research examining the consequences of resistance to persuasion. Resistance often has been viewed as an outcome, indicating that a persuasive communication has failed to affect the target attitude. Although this is sensible, resistance also has many other dimensions, as the various chapters in the current volume attest. Indeed, the research described in this chapter suggests that in some cases at least, when a persuasive attack appears to have had no impact on the target attitude (i.e., the attack was resisted), it may actually have had a subtle yet important impact in terms of attitude certainty, attitude-relevant behavior, and the attitude's resistance to future change. In short, resistance can be viewed as a launching pad for further theoretical and empirical exploration.

REFERENCES

Babad, E. Y., Ariav, A., Rosen, I., & Salomon, G. (1987). Perseverance of bias as a function of debriefing conditions and subjects' confidence. *Social Behaviour, 2,* 185–193.
Bassili, J. N. (1996). Meta-judgmental versus operative indexes of psychological attributes: The case of measures of attitude strength. *Journal of Personality and Social Psychology, 71,* 637–653.
Brehm, J. W. (1966). *A theory of psychological reactance.* New York: Academic Press.
Briñol, P., & Petty, R. E. (2003). Overt head movements and persuasion: A self-validation analysis. *Journal of Personality and Social Psychology, 84,* 1123–1139.
Brock, T. C. (1967). Communication discrepancy and intent to persuade as determinants of counterargument production. *Journal of Experimental Social Psychology, 3,* 296–309.
Cacioppo, J. T., & Petty, R. E. (1982). The need for cognition. *Journal of Personality and Social Psychology, 42,* 116–131.
Crano, W. D., & Chen, X. (1998). The leniency contract and persistence of majority and minority influence. *Journal of Personality and Social Psychology, 74,* 1437–1450.
Fazio, R. H., & Zanna, M. P. (1978). Attitudinal qualities relating to the strength of the attitude-behavior relationship. *Journal of Experimental Social Psychology, 14,* 398–408.
Festinger, L. (1950). Informal social communication. *Psychological Review, 57,* 271–282.
Festinger, L. (1954). A theory of social comparison processes. *Human Relations, 7,* 117–140.
Festinger, L. (1957). *A theory of cognitive dissonance.* Evanston, IL: Row, Peterson.
Fishbein, M., & Ajzen, I. (1975). *Belief, attitude, intention, and behavior.* Reading, MA: Addison-Wesley.
Gilbert, D. T. (1998). Ordinary Personology. In D. Gilbert, S. Fiske, & G. Lindzey (Eds.), *Handbook of social psychology* (Vol. 2, pp. 89–150). Boston: McGraw-Hill.
Greenwald, A. G. (1968). Cognitive learning, cognitive response to persuasion, and attitude change. In A. G. Greenwald, T. C. Brock, & T. M. Ostrom (Eds.), *Psychological foundations of attitudes* (pp. 147–170). New York: Academic Press.
Gross, S., Holtz, R., & Miller, N. (1995). Attitude certainty. In R. E. Petty & J. A. Krosnick (Eds.), *Attitude strength: Antecedents and consequences* (pp. 215–245). Mahwah, NJ: Erlbaum.
Heider, F. (1958). *The psychology of interpersonal relations.* New York: Wiley.
Hovland, C. I., Janis, I. L., & Kelley, H. H. (1953). *Communication and persuasion: Psychological studies of opinion change.* New Haven, CT: Yale University Press.
Jacks, J. Z., & Devine, P. G. (2000). Attitude importance, forewarning of message content, and resistance to persuasion. *Basic and Applied Social Psychology, 22,* 19–29.
Jacoby, L. L., & Kelley, C. M. (1987). Unconscious influences of memory for a prior event. *Personality and Social Psychology Bulletin, 13,* 314–336.
Killeya, L. A., & Johnson, B. T. (1998). Experimental induction of biased systematic processing: The directed-thought technique. *Personality and Social Psychology Bulletin, 24,* 17–33.
Krosnick, J. A., & Abelson, R. P. (1992). The case for measuring attitude strength in surveys. In J. Tanur (Ed.), *Questions about questions* (pp. 177–203). New York: Russell Sage.
Lewan, P. C., & Scotland, E. (1961). The effects of prior information on susceptibility to an emotional appeal. *Journal of Abnormal and Social Psychology, 62,* 450–453.
Lydon, J., Zanna, M. P., & Ross, M. (1988). Bolstering attitudes by autobiographical recall: Attitude persistence and selective memory. *Personality and Social Psychology Bulletin, 14,* 78–86.

McGuire, W. J. (1964). Inducing resistance to persuasion: Some contemporary approaches. In L. Berkowitz (Ed.), *Advances in experimental social psychology* (Vol. 1, pp. 191–229). New York: Academic Press.

McGuire, W. J. (1968). Personality and attitude change: An information-processing theory. In A. G. Greenwald, T. C. Brock, & T. M. Ostrom (Eds.), *Psychological foundations of attitudes* (pp. 171–196). New York: Academic Press.

Miller, N. E. (1965). Involvement and dogmatism as inhibitors of attitude change. *Journal of Experimental Social Psychology, 1,* 121–132.

Petty, R. E., Briñol, P., & Tormala, Z. L. (2002). Thought confidence as a determinant of persuasion: The self-validation hypothesis. *Journal of Personality and Social Psychology, 82,* 722–741.

Petty, R. E., & Cacioppo, J. T. (1986). *Communication and persuasion: Central and peripheral routes to attitude change.* New York: Springer-Verlag.

Petty, R. E., & Krosnick, J. A. (Eds.). (1995). *Attitude strength: Antecedents and consequences.* Mahwah, NJ: Erlbaum.

Petty, R. E., Ostrom, T. M., & Brock, T. C. (Eds.) (1981): *Cognitive responses in persuasion.* Hillsdale, NJ: Erlbaum.

Petty, R. E., Tormala, Z., & Rucker, D. D. (in press). Resistance to persuasion: An attitude strength perspective. In J. T. Jost, M. R. Banaji, & D. Prentice (Eds.), *Perspectivism in social psychology: The yin and yang of scientific progress.* Washington, DC: American Psychological Association.

Petty, R. E., & Wegener, D. T. (1999). The Elaboration Likelihood Model: Current status and controversies. In S. Chaiken & Y. Trope (Eds.), *Dual-process theories in social psychology* (pp. 41–72). New York: Guilford.

Rokeach, M. (1960). *The open and closed mind.* New York: Basic Books.

Rucker, D. D., & Petty, R. E. (in press). When resistance is futile: Consequences of failed counterarguing for attitude certainty. *Journal of Personality and Social Psychology.*

Schwarz, N., Bless, H., Strack, F., Klumpp, G., Rittenauer-Schatka, H., & Simons, A. (1991). Ease of retrieval as information: Another look at the availability heuristic. *Journal of Personality and Social Psychology, 61,* 195–202.

Strack, F., & Förster, J. (1998). Self-reflection and recognition: The role of metacognitive knowledge in the attribution of recollective experience. *Personality and Social Psychology Review, 2,* 111–123.

Swann, W. B., Pelham, B. W., & Chidester, T. R. (1988). Change through paradox: Using self-verification to alter beliefs. *Journal of Personality and Social Psychology, 54,* 268–273.

Tannenbaum, P. H., Macauley, J. R., & Norris, E. L. (1966). Principle of congruity and reduction of persuasion. *Journal of Personality and Social Psychology, 3,* 233–238.

Tormala, Z. L., & Petty, R. E. (2002). What doesn't kill me makes me stronger: The effects of resisting persuasion on attitude certainty. *Journal of Personality and Social Psychology, 83,* 1298–1313.

Tormala, Z. L., & Petty, R. E. (2003). *Resisting persuasion by the skin of one's teeth: The hidden success of failed persuasive communications.* Unpublished manuscript. The Ohio State University.

Tormala, Z. L., Petty, R. E., & Briñol, P. (2002). Ease of retrieval effects in persuasion: A self-validation analysis. *Personality and Social Psychology Bulletin, 28,* 1700–1712.

Wood, W., Lundgren, S., Ouellette, J. A., Busceme, S., & Blackstone, T. (1994). Minority influence: A meta-analytic review of social influence processes. *Psychological Bulletin, 115,* 323–345.

Wu, C., & Shaffer, D. R. (1987). Susceptibility to persuasive appeals as a function of source credibility and prior experience with the attitude object. *Journal of Personality and Social Psychology, 52,* 677–688.

Zuwerink, J. R., & Devine, P. G. (1996). Attitude importance and resistance to persuasion: It's not just the thought that counts. *Journal of Personality and Social Psychology, 70,* 931–944.

5

Individual Differences in Resistance to Persuasion: The Role of Beliefs and Meta-Beliefs

Pablo Briñol
Universidad Autónoma de Madrid

Derek D. Rucker
The Ohio State University

Zakary L. Tormala
Indiana University

Richard E. Petty
The Ohio State University

Within the persuasion literature, the most common treatment of the term "resistance" involves the *outcome* of showing little or no change to a persuasive message, (e.g., McGuire, 1964). However, to understand resistance truly, one must recognize that the study of resistance is more than simply the outcome of a persuasive message. Petty, Tormala, and Rucker (in press; see also Tormala & Petty, this volume) noted recently that within the persuasion literature, resistance has also been examined as a psychological *process* (e.g., one can resist by counterarguing), a *motivation* (i.e., having the goal of not being persuaded), and a *quality* of an attitude or person (i.e., being resistant to persuasion).

Many of the chapters in the present volume discuss variables or situations that affect the outcome of resistance (e.g., Jacks & O'Brien, this volume; Tormala & Petty, this volume; Quinn & Wood, this volume), the process of resistance (e.g., Wegener, Petty, Smoak, & Fabrigar, this volume), or people's motivation to resist (e.g., Knowles & Linn, this volume). The present chapter differs in that our interest lies in identifying personality attributes or aspects of the individual related to resistance. We focus our discussion on individual differences in resistance expected to be constant across topics, sources, situations, and so on. Thus, we deal primarily with resistance as a quality of a person. In this chapter, we introduce a new meta-cognitive approach to understand individual differences in resistance.

That is, we examine individuals' meta-cognitions about their own resistance. We begin by providing a brief review of past work on individual differences in resistance, and we suggest that future research could benefit from adopting a meta-cognitive perspective. Finally, we present empirical evidence and apply the meta-cognitive framework to understand: how individuals' beliefs affect their actual resistance to persuasion (resistance as an outcome); the qualities an individual possesses (resistance as a quality); and the processes by which an individual chooses to resist (resistance as a process) when his or her goal is to resist (resistance as a motivation).

META-COGNITION

Meta-cognition refers to the study of thinking about thinking, or thoughts about thoughts. The topic of meta-cognition has received considerable theoretical and research attention, being considered one of the "top 100 topics" of psychological research (Nelson, 1992). According to Jost, Kruglanski, and Nelson (1998), social meta-cognition includes (a) beliefs about one's own mental states and processes as well as beliefs about those of other people, (b) momentary sensations as well as enduring naïve theories, and (c) descriptive beliefs about how the mind works and normative beliefs about how it ought to work.

It is necessary to distinguish between two qualitatively different aspects of meta-cognitive beliefs. First is the *nature of the belief itself*—What does a person believe about his or her thoughts and attitudes, or the type of person he or she is? For example, with respect to resistance, individuals might believe they are either difficult or easy to persuade. These beliefs need not be grounded in reality. For example, although there is ample evidence that explicit persuasive communications can change attitudes (e.g., Petty & Cacioppo, 1986) and that subliminal messages are ineffective (e.g., Vokey & Read, 1985), people still tend to believe that they can not resist the influence of subliminal information, whereas they think that they can control the influence of supraliminal persuasive communications. Consequently, people do not mind exposing themselves to strong persuasive arguments (that change their attitudes) but they prefer to avoid subliminal messages (that do not change their attitudes; see Wilson, Gilbert, & Wheatly, 1998). Similarly, individuals might believe that they are very resistant to persuasive attempts (or very easy to persuade), and these beliefs may be unrelated to the extent to which they actually resist different persuasive messages. A second aspect of a person's belief is a *value judgment of the belief.* Specifically, people may believe that it is either appropriate or inappropriate to possess the thoughts, attitudes, or the personality characteristics they believe that they have. We address both types of meta-cognition in this chapter.

Research on meta-cognition and resistance is in its infancy. As one example, in a recent series of studies, Petty, Briñol, and Tormala (2002) have shown that the confidence or doubt people have in the validity of their own thoughts can either increase or decrease resistance to persuasion depending on the nature of the thoughts elicited by the message (see also Briñol & Petty, 2003; Tormala, Petty, & Briñol, 2002). When people generate counterarguments against a persuasive message, for example, those counterarguments are more effective in instilling resistance when they are held with relatively high confidence. When people doubt the validity of their counterarguments, they are less effective in facilitating resistance. Conversely, when people generate mostly favorable thoughts to a message, increasing doubts in these favorable thoughts increases resistance. The literature on *attitude* confidence has also demonstrated that the overall confidence a person has in the validity or accuracy of his or her attitude has implications for resistance to persuasion. The more confident one is that his or her attitude is correct, the more motivated and willing one is to defend that attitude against persuasive attempts (see Gross, Holtz, & Miller, 1995; Petty & Wegener, 1999).

We propose that people's beliefs about their own personality might operate in a similar manner. That is, one's beliefs about one's personality dimensions might also be influenced by the perceived validity or appropriateness of those beliefs. For example, if an individual is aware of a belief she possesses regarding her personality but views this belief as inappropriate, she may attempt to correct for it, undermining or even reversing the impact of the personality characteristic. Furthermore, the perceived appropriateness of her belief may vary depending on contextual factors. As another example, an individual may believe that he is very resistant to persuasion in general and feel that being resistant is valid or appropriate. However, if the individual is on a jury panel he might consider this belief to be temporarily inappropriate and thus be motivated to control for its potential influence when forming a judgment.

The Flexible Correction Model (FCM; Petty & Wegener, 1993; Wegener & Petty, 1995, 1997) can be used to help us predict when people will correct for their default beliefs. The FCM asserts that correction will only occur when an individual both suspects the presence of some biasing agent and is motivated and able to exert the increased cognitive effort to compensate for it. Moreover, according to the FCM, attempts at avoiding or removing bias are guided by perceivers' naïve theories about the nature of the default belief or bias. To the extent that people become aware of a potential biasing factor and are motivated and able to correct for it, they consult their theory of the direction and magnitude of the bias and adjust their judgment accordingly (see also Wilson & Brekke, 1994). Interestingly, this can cause judgments to move in a direction opposite to people's presumed direction of bias (Wegener & Petty, 1997; 2001; Wegener et al., this volume). For example, if people think a positive mood has a favorable impact on their judgments, and they overestimate this bias, the corrected judgment can become less positive *or even negative* (e.g., Berkowitz et al., 2000; DeSteno, Petty, Wegener, & Rucker, 2000; Ottati & Isbell, 1996). In short, the default response may be for an individual to act in accordance with the belief he or she possesses unless the belief is salient and viewed as inappropriate.

In the present analysis, people who perceive themselves as resistant to per-suasion probably act resistant in many cases, showing little or no change in the face of persuasive messages. However, to the extent an individual believes it is inappropriate or invalid to possess the beliefs or characteristic he or she does (i.e., "I should not be 'resistant' in this situation"), the individual may attempt to correct for the trait. Thus, an individual who believes that he or she is resis-tant, but also that it is wrong to be resistant in a given situation, may act less resistant in that context. Importantly, however, this correction would require the motivation and ability to correct.

Although we are interested in people's beliefs about their own persuasibility because of the potential implications for resistance to persuasion, such beliefs may also play a central role in people's values and identities. For example, Schwartz's (1992) theory about universal human values is structured by two main motivational dimensions: The Self-Transcendence/Self-Enhancement di-mension and the Openness to Change/Conservation dimension. Importantly, the second dimension reflects a conflict between favoring change versus protection of stability. In consonance with the literature on personality (e.g., McCrae & Costa, 1997), this work implies that almost everyone may have beliefs about their own resistance to change and that such beliefs might be an integral part of the self-concept.

An interest in the study of what people believe about persuasion and the appro-priateness of such beliefs has recently motivated a considerable amount of work in applied fields, such as consumer behavior (e.g., Briñol, Petty, & Tormala, in press; Wright, 2002) and organizational behavior (e.g., Vonk, 1998). For instance, Fries-tad and Wright (1994) have argued that people's persuasion beliefs are an important determinant of how they deal with persuasion attempts. According to their view, people develop knowledge about persuasion and use this knowledge when interpreting and responding to ads or sales presentations, as well as when evaluating the effectiveness or appropriateness of such persuasion attempts. These lay beliefs about persuasion contain theories about the effects of different external or internal stimuli. People's beliefs about persuasion can influence the impres-sions of an influence agent (such as a salesperson), but only when the beliefs are made salient and people are able to think carefully about the information (Camp-bell & Kirmani, 2000). Despite this conceptual emphasis on people's beliefs about persuasion, very little is known about how these beliefs affect persuasion or resis-tance and the specific circumstances under which such influence might occur. For that reason, in the present chapter we will examine different beliefs about persua-sion and their consequences for resistance.

More specifically, in the present chapter we discuss individual differences in people's meta-beliefs about their own resistance and why acknowledging these individual differences can be advantageous in studying resistance. We present two lines of research. In the first set of studies, we examine individual differ-ences in whether people think they are generally resistant to persuasion or not, and the impact these meta-beliefs have on actual persuasion. Furthermore, in this line of research we also examine whether individuals ever attempt to correct for their beliefs. In the second line of research, we examine individual differences in people's beliefs about *how* they resist persuasion (beliefs about the processes of resistance they use) and the impact these beliefs have on actual resistance processes. However, before introducing our research on individual differences in meta-cognitive beliefs, we provide a brief overview of previous attempts to examine general individual differences in resistance.

INDIVIDUAL DIFFERENCES IN RESISTANCE: CLASSIC AND CONTEMPORARY RESEARCH

Classic Research

From prior literature, it is unclear whether a single general dimension of personality exists that makes some people more resistant to persuasion than others. However, research does suggest that there are clear individual differences in the degree to which people are persuaded by the same message. For example, McGuire found that across a wide array of topics, some individuals consistently changed a great deal, whereas others consistently changed only a small amount (McGuire, 1969).

Attempts to identify individual differences in persuasion originated in the early 1950s, when several scholars were focused on the study of different forms of cognitive rigidity—the stability of individuals' beliefs. One of the most ambitious attempts is represented by work on the "authoritarian personality" (Altemeyer, 1969). The authoritarian personality arose out of the idea that some people were predisposed to agree with statements related to the fascist ideology (Stagner, 1936). The initial measures of authoritarianism inspired similar measures, such as the Anti-Semitism Scale (Levinson & Sanford, 1944), the Ethnocentrism Scale (Adorno, Frenkel-Brunswik, Levinson, & Sanford, 1950), and the California F Scale (Adorno et al., 1950). As an alternative to the authoritarian personality, Rokeach (1954) developed the dogmatism scale, which was designed to measure individual differences in open versus closed belief systems.

There are some indications that authoritarianism measures, including dogmatism, can predict change in response to external pressures. For example, Crutchfield (1955) reported a correlation of .39 between authoritarianism and yielding to group pressure in a variation of the Asch (1956) conformity paradigm. Altemeyer (1981) also reported a correlation of .44 between authoritarianism and obedience in a replication of the Milgram (1974) obedience to authority paradigm. In both examples, individuals low in authoritarianism were more likely to resist group conformity and obedience pressures. These findings suggest that measures of authoritarianism can be partially useful in predicting susceptibility or resistance to social influence. Overall, however, reviewers of this work have argued that individual difference approaches to understanding cognitive rigidity have proven only marginally successful (Abelson, 1968; Wicklund & Brehm, 1976). Furthermore, these measures have rarely been applied to examine resistance to the more common verbal persuasive messages.

Contemporary Research

In recent times, researchers' interest in identifying general individual differences in resistance to persuasion has been rekindled. For example, Cialdini, Trost, and Newsom (1995) developed a measure of individuals' preference for consistency (the PFC Scale). This scale includes items such as "I typically prefer to do things the same way" and "I don't like to appear as if I am inconsistent." The scale has been found to be reliable in predicting individuals who would and would not be susceptible to cognitive consistency effects such as cognitive dissonance (Festinger, 1957) or the foot-in-the-door technique (Freedman & Fraser, 1966). However, the PFC is focused exclusively on situations where attitude change occurs as a result of cognitive inconsistency. The realm of attitude change involves numerous scenarios where persuasion is not based on consistency pressures (Petty & Cacioppo, 1981). For this reason, we consider work on consistency, as well as the original research on authoritarianism, to address the phenomena of individual differences in general resistance to persuasion.

Recently, several new scales have emerged to help plot individual differences in resistance. For example, Knowles and Linn (this volume) measure resistance by assessing three interrelated components: Reactance, Scrutiny, and Distrust. These measures assess the degree to which resistance takes the form of opposing influence, cautious thought, and skepticism, respectively. Although these scales appear promising, to date they have not been used to predict resistance to persuasive communications.

INDIVIDUAL DIFFERENCES
IN RESISTANCE:
A META-COGNITIVE APPROACH

Although past research has tried to identify stable individual differences related to resistance, researchers have for the most part failed to examine individual differences in people's beliefs about their own resistance to persuasion. One exception is recent research by Albarracín and Mitchell (2002). Albarracín and Mitchell proposed a measure of defensive confidence as a way to tap individual differences in resistance to persuasion. Defensive confidence refers to one's belief that one's own position can be defended and is assessed with items such as "I have many resources to defend my point of view when I feel my ideas are under attack," or "No matter what I read or hear, I am always capable of defending my feelings and opinions." According to Albarracín and Mitchell, the beliefs people have about their ability to defend their attitudes can moderate their approach to attitude-relevant information. Specifically, individuals who feel confident in their ability to defend their beliefs (i.e., high in defensive confidence) do not feel a need to ignore counter-attitudinal information. Individuals who do not feel confident about their abilities, however, prefer to avoid counter-attitudinal information.

This recent line of inquiry is suggestive in showing that the beliefs people have about their own abilities to defend their attitudes can influence information exposure. However, this research does not provide any information about how these specific beliefs influence information processing and yielding. We now turn to discuss how the more general beliefs people hold about their own resistance to persuasion can provide a direct predictor of attitude change. Specifically, we examine how individuals' meta-beliefs about their general susceptibility to persuasive attempts can affect their resistance to persuasive communications.

One way people's beliefs about their own resistance to persuasion might influence attitude change is by triggering relatively simple cognitive inferences. That is, people might sometimes rely on beliefs about themselves as relatively simple cues to behavior (or persuasion). In research on self-efficacy (e.g., Bandura, 1997), for instance, it has been shown that beliefs about self-efficacy can determine how information is processed, whether people engage in coping behaviors, how much effort will be expended in some task, and how long effort will be sustained in the face of obstacles and aversive experiences. For example, someone might say, "Since I can accomplish everything I want, I will be able to finish this tedious task." Similarly, people might rely on their beliefs about their own resistance and reason, "I am a person who is difficult to influence, so I am not going to change my opinion in response to this persuasive attempt." In the next section we describe several experiments conducted to test this notion.

Individual Differences in Perceived Persuasibility

In an initial test of the relationship between people's beliefs about their persuasibility and their actual persuasibility, we exposed college students to an editorial in favor of the idea of including more broccoli in their diet. Participants were asked to read the editorial and to write down all the thoughts that they had while reading the message. After completing the thought listing, participants reported their attitudes. Finally, all participants were asked to report their beliefs about how resistant they were in general on a series of scale items. Examples of such items included, "It could be said that I am an easy person to persuade," and "It is really hard to persuade me of something." As predicted, persuasion varied directly as a function of participants' beliefs regarding their own vulnerability to persuasion. That is, Experiment 1 showed that participants were less resistant to persuasion when they reported themselves as easily persuaded.

Interestingly, though, we also uncovered a boundary condition for this effect. Specifically, participants' beliefs only affected their responses to persuasion under relatively low-elaboration conditions. At the end of the experiment, participants were asked to report the extent to which the topic was personally relevant for them and the extent to which they had paid attention and thought carefully about the message. Participants' beliefs about persuasion and self-reported elaboration were treated as continuous factors in the regression analyses. As shown by a significant interaction between resistance beliefs and self-reported elaboration ($\beta = -.17$, $p = .05$), only those who were relatively low in elaboration (i.e., low personal relevance, low attention given) showed a direct impact of their beliefs regarding their own persuasibility. That is, low-elaboration participants showed significantly more attitude change when they thought they were low in resistance to persuasion ($M = 5.18$, $SD = 1.65$) than when they thought they were relatively high in resistance ($M = 6.33$, $SD = 2.22$), $t(46) = -2.03$, $p < .05$ (both variables split at the median). Participants who reported relatively higher levels of message elaboration did not change their attitudes as a direct result of their beliefs toward persuasion. In fact, high-elaboration participants tended to show more persuasion when they thought they were *high* in resistance to persuasion ($M = 7.88$, $SD = 2.23$) than when they thought they were relatively low ($M = 6.78$, $SD = 1.43$) in resistance, $t(37) = 1.69$, $p = .09$.

Taken together, these findings suggest that individuals' beliefs may have different effects on persuasion depending on the amount of elaboration. When elaboration is relatively low, participants use their beliefs about their own persuasibility as a cue, adjusting their attitudes in the direction of their beliefs. This pattern of results is consonant with previous research in persuasion (e.g., Albarracín & Wyer, 2000; Chaiken & Baldwin, 1981; see also Taylor, 1975; Wood, 1982). However, when elaboration is relatively high, participants showed no direct effect of their meta-beliefs. In fact, there was a tendency for a reverse effect, demonstrating more persuasion when people thought they were difficult to persuade. This pattern of results tentatively suggests that under high elaboration, participants might attempt to compensate or correct for the influence of their own self-views. If true, these findings would be consistent with prior research demonstrating that participants high in elaboration sometimes attempt to correct their judgments for biases to which they perceive they have succumbed, producing over-correction effects (e.g., DeSteno, Petty, Wegener, & Rucker, 2000; Wegener & Petty, 1995, 1997). This assumes, of course, that viewing oneself as very easy or difficult to persuade could be identified as inappropriate. In situations where this is not the case, correction is unlikely to occur.

In a second experiment, we developed a standardized instrument to measure people's beliefs about their own resistance to persuasion. First, we created a large pool of items designed to measure people's beliefs about their own susceptibility to persuasion. Based on initial analyses, we retained a set of items that composed the Resistance to Persuasion Scale (RPS). The RPS included the original items from Experiment 1 as well as other items, such as "I find my opinions to be changeable," "My opinions fluctuate a lot," and "It is hard for me to change my ideas" (reversed). High scores on the scale indicate less perceived resistance to persuasion. This scale was submitted to different samples of students at The Ohio State University and evinced excellent psychometric properties.

In our first formal test of the predictive power of the RPS, participants were asked to read the transcript of an editorial from a college radio station on the topic of a new state foster care program. The foster care program was described as a system designed to take care of children who came from broken homes, as well as children who were victims of parental abuse and neglect. All participants received a message in favor of the program. After reading the message, participants were asked to write down the thoughts they had while reading the message and to report their attitudes toward the proposal. Finally, participants completed the 18-item version of the Need for Cognition Scale (Cacioppo, Petty, & Kao, 1984) for the purpose of distinguishing between participants high and low in their motivation to elaborate the information. The need for cognition scale contains statements such as, "I prefer complex to simple problems," and "Thinking is not my idea of fun."

We predicted and found that individuals exhibited persuasion consistent with their own beliefs about their persuasibility when need for cognition was low, but people appeared to correct for their beliefs when need for cognition was high. That is, a significant interaction between resistance beliefs and need for cognition ($\beta = -40$, $p < .01$) revealed that participants low in need for cognition showed more persuasion with low ($M = 7.14$, $SD = 1.27$) rather than high ($M = 5.30$, $SD = 2.31$) scores on the RPS, $t(37) = -3.16$, $p < .01$. However, participants high in need for cognition tended to show more persuasion with high ($M = 6.93$, $SD = 1.60$) rather than low ($M = 6.28$, $SD = 1.43$) scores on the RPS, $t(37) = 1.26$, $p = .26$. These findings replicated our pilot study and provided initial support for the validity of the RPS. This experiment also provided further evidence regarding the multiple roles that persuasion beliefs can play in attitude change.

It is also worth noting that in both of the above experiments, we manipulated argument quality in the persuasive messages and it did not interact with participants' beliefs about their own general resistance. Also, across studies, the role that these beliefs played was unaffected by the topic of the message, the way in which elaboration was assessed, and the specific measure of resistance beliefs. However, in both experiments the key variable, beliefs about resistance to persuasion, was measured rather than manipulated. For this reason, we conducted a third experiment in which beliefs concerning resistance to persuasion were manipulated by providing participants with false feedback about their general resistance to persuasion. This experiment was designed to help establish the fact that one's beliefs about one's own persuasibility have a casual impact on persuasion.

Previous research suggests that individuals' beliefs about their attitudes can be manipulated and can ultimately affect resistance to persuasion. For example, Chaiken and Baldwin (1981) induced participants to believe they had strong beliefs in favor or against the environment by asking them to answer extreme statements in a bogus personality questionnaire. As expected, they found that participants used their manipulated beliefs to infer their attitudes. In more recent research, Albarracín and Wyer (2002) used false feedback to induce participants to believe they either supported or opposed the institution of comprehensive exams at their university. Albarracín and Wyer found that participants induced to believe that they supported the institution of comprehensive exams reported more favorable attitudes toward the policy than participants induced to believe that they opposed the policy.

In our third experiment, participants were seated in front of individual computers and informed that they were going to participate in two different research projects. They were told that the first portion of the study was designed to validate different psychological scales for future research interested in predicting people's personalities. Participants were then asked to fill out a questionnaire composed of 16 items, all of them endorsing extreme assertions of resistance to persuasion. These items were worded in an extreme way with the objective of biasing participants' responses in the opposite direction. For example, to induce participants to respond as being low in resistance to persuasion, they received items such as "I do not let anybody convince me of anything," "It is almost impossible for me to change my ideas," and "I have never changed the way I see something." On the other hand, participants in the high resistance to persuasion condition were asked to respond to items such as "I let anybody convince me of anything," "I find my opinions to be very changeable and malleable," and "My opinions always fluctuate a lot."

After completing the questions, participants were asked to wait for a few seconds while the computer processed their previous responses. During this period, participants completed the need for cognition scale. Following this, participants received false feedback on their personality. In the condition of low resistance to persuasion, participants were told they had characteristics such as flexibility, open-mindedness, ability to deal with change, and a willingness to consider others' opinions. In the high resistance to persuasion condition, participants were told they had characteristics such as being resistant to external influences, ability to defend their own points of view, holding consistent beliefs, and having a low vulnerability to outside influence. This false personality feedback has worked in the past to influence people's cognitive responses (see Petty & Brock, 1979).

As illustrated by Fig. 5.1, we found that the false feedback influenced peoples' beliefs and influenced their resistance to the persuasive information. Again, a significant interaction between resistance beliefs and elaboration emerged from the analysis ($\beta = -.24$, $p < .05$), such that participants low in need for cognition showed more attitude change when they were induced to believe that they were low in resistance to persuasion ($M = 5.62$, $SD = 1.77$) than when they thought that they were resistant to persuasion, ($M = 4.17$, $SD = 1.55$), $t(36) = -2.64$, $p < .05$. For participants high in need for cognition, however, attitude change tended to be greater when they were induced to believe that they were resistant to persuasion ($M = 6.54$, $SD = 2.09$) than when they were induced to believe

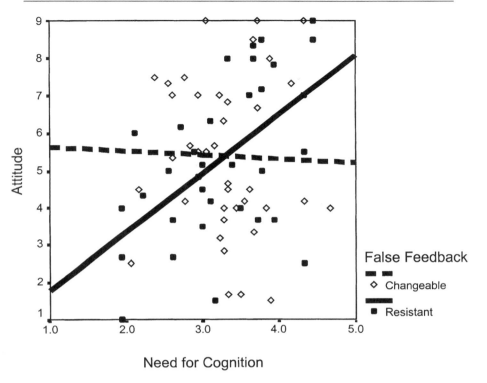

FIG. 5.1.   Attitude as a function of elaboration and beliefs about resistance to persuasion.

they were vulnerable to persuasion (M = 5.13, SD = 2.43), $t(35)$ = 1.89, p = .06. These results conceptually replicated our previous findings in which beliefs about resistance to persuasion were measured rather than manipulated.

In summary, our three experiments examining individuals' beliefs about their own resistance, whether measured or manipulated, all point to the same conclusion—people's beliefs about their own resistance impact actual resistance. Specifically, when elaboration is low, individuals who believe they are more resistant to persuasion show less attitude change than individuals who believe they are easily susceptible to persuasion. The fact that this occurs only under low-elaboration conditions suggests that, at least in the present experiments, these self-beliefs function as a cue for people to decide whether or not to adopt a message position. Just as people can rely on external cues when elaboration is low (e.g., source expertise or the mere number of arguments; see Petty & Cacioppo, 1986), they can also rely on more internal beliefs about themselves.

Potential Implications of Perceived Persuasibility

These initial findings open up many possibilities for further research and have implications for applied fields. For example, certain contexts in which individuals believe an attempt is being made to persuade them are likely to increase the accessibility of individuals' beliefs about their own resistance. Conventional wisdom suggests that more persuasion will be possible when people do not realize they are being exposed to a persuasive attempt. The present findings demonstrate that in certain scenarios (i.e., when elaboration is low and individuals believe they are resistant to persuasion) the conventional wisdom would be correct. A salient persuasive message would cause people to consult their persuasion beliefs, they would realize that they generally resist persuasion, and resistance would become more likely. However, our findings also suggest that if an individual believes that he or she is relatively easy to persuade, the activation of such beliefs might increase the impact of persuasive communications, at least under low-elaboration conditions.

In situations where people are more motivated to process, however, individuals may attempt to correct for their beliefs if they think that their natural tendencies are biasing. For example, judges or jury members are often assigned to the task of being as objective and fair as they possibly can. In this situation, individuals who recognize that they are typically resistant to persuasive attempts may become especially vigilant and try to keep an open mind when hearing testimony, statements, etc. These individuals may then become more accepting of arguments and information than usual, provided they have the motivation and ability to correct for their "resistance bias." The recognition and application of individuals' beliefs about persuasion is an interesting and exciting area for future research.

The present research also suggests that our perceptions of our own persuasibility are relatively malleable. It is possible to think that beliefs about persuasion might vary from one context to another, and thus one way to manipulate individuals' beliefs might consist of selecting precisely those contexts in which people believe they are more easily persuaded. Future research should explore these and other issues such as the antecedents of beliefs about persuasion and potential moderators of their effects. For example, in another line of research it has been found that normative beliefs that people hold about persuasion (i.e., beliefs that persuasion is good or bad) can interact with beliefs about persuasibility to predict attitude change (Briñol & Petty, 2002).

Other researchers have found that people's feelings or beliefs about themselves can increase or decrease vulnerability to persuasion, depending on situational factors. For example, Jacks and O'Brien (this volume) have found that feeling good about oneself (through self-affirmation) can, under specifiable conditions, decrease resistance. Moreover, Sagarin and colleagues (this volume) have found that increasing confidence in oneself by learning how to resist "invalid" persuasive attempts (e.g., from famous sources) can ironically make people more vulnerable to "legitimate" persuasive attempts (e.g., from expert sources). We would like to extend these arguments and posit that increasing confidence in oneself, through one mechanism or another, might increase or decrease resistance to persuasion depending on the type of beliefs the individual holds regarding his or her own persuasibility and the degree to which these beliefs are viewed as appropriate. Assuming the meta-beliefs are seen as appropriate, in a person who believes he or she is resistant to persuasion, increasing confidence should enhance resistance; for a person who believes he or she is easily persuaded, increasing confidence should reduce resistance. If a person views his or her default tendencies as inappropriate or biasing, however, and elaboration is relatively high, he or she may try to correct for these beliefs, and the pattern could be attenuated or even reversed.

In the remainder of this chapter, we explore the possibility that in addition to beliefs regarding the extent to which a person is resistant to persuasion, individuals' beliefs about *how* they resist can impact persuasion processes and outcomes. That is, we consider the possibility that the specific way in which people believe they resist persuasion might influence the way in which they actually respond to persuasive information under some conditions. We examine the association between people's perceptions of the effortful strategies they employ to resist persuasion, the actual strategies employed, and the consequences for attitude change.

INDIVIDUAL DIFFERENCES IN PERCEIVED RESISTANCE STRATEGIES

When a person wants to resist an advocacy, there are several processes a person can implement to defend his or her attitude against counter-attitudinal information. The individual might attempt to derogate or discredit the source of the information (e.g., Tannenbaum, Macauley, Norris, 1966; Zuwerink & Devine, 1996; see also Pratkanis, Greenwald, Leippe, & Baumgardner, 1988), or discount the message altogether (see Gruder, Cook, Hennigan, Flay, Alessis, & Halamaj, 1978). Resistance can also be achieved through selective attention to attitude-congruent information, or selective avoidance of attitude-incongruent information (Albarracín & Mitchell, 2002; Frey, 1986; Gilbert, 1993). Simply responding to a message with negative affect or irritation has also been found to enhance resistance (e.g., Cacioppo & Petty, 1979; Jacks & Devine, 2000; Zuwerink & Devine, 1996). As just discussed, individuals may also rely on their perceptions of their own persuasability to resist a message (i.e., "I am resistant to persuasion so I won't change my attitude."). These strategies, by nature, do not necessitate a great deal of thought to be implemented.

However, there are resistance strategies that do require considerable thought to execute. First, resistance might be accomplished by actively generating counterarguments or negative thoughts against the opposing viewpoint (e.g., Brock, 1967; Killeya & Johnson, 1998; Papageorgis, 1968; Petty & Cacioppo, 1977; see Petty, Ostrom, & Brock, 1981). For example, an individual in favor of capital punishment, when confronted with a message against capital punishment, may actively attempt to resist the message by finding fault in it. This individual actively searches for information about what is wrong with the opposing viewpoint.

A second effortful way to accomplish resistance is through attitude bolstering, or reinforcing one's own stance on an issue (Lewan & Stotland, 1961; Lydon, Zanna, & Ross, 1988). For example, an individual in favor of capital punishment might resist a message by actively thinking about everything that supports capital punishment. Rather than looking for fault in the opposing message (i.e., counterarguing), this individual seeks out merit in one's own viewpoint. For a similar distinction, see McGuire's discussion of supportive versus refutational resistance strategies (1964).

Although the multitude of resistance strategies is interesting and worthy of study, we first examined individual differences in attitude bolstering and counterarguing. These are both effortful resistance strategies likely to produce enduring resistance, but, as just surmised, they are fundamentally different approaches to resistance. We propose that one determinant of whether an individual will bolster or counterargue is the individual's own set of beliefs about how he or she resists persuasion. We now turn to discuss the construction of an individual difference scale to identify preferences for counterarguing versus attitude bolstering methods, and to discuss some consequences of these preferences.

Scale Construction

We began with a set of 25 items designed to measure preferences for resisting through bolstering versus counterarguing. Examples of items geared toward those who prefer to counterargue included, "When someone challenges my beliefs, I enjoy disputing what they have to say," and "I take pleasure in arguing with those who have opinions that differ from my own." Items geared toward those who prefer to bolster included, "When someone gives me a point of view that conflicts with my attitudes, I like to think about why my views are right for me," and "When someone has a different perspective on an issue, I like to make a mental list of the reasons in support of my perspective."

In our first study, 600 Ohio State University undergraduates completed the scale. We divided our sample into two groups of 300. The first group was used for the purpose of an exploratory factor analysis, and the second group was used for purposes of a confirmatory factor analysis. The exploratory factor analysis revealed clear support for two distinct factors that were only slightly positively correlated ($r = .20$). Based on parsimony and goodness of fit, 12 items were retained from the exploratory analysis for inclusion in the Bolster-Counterargue Scale (BCS). Six of the items were related to bolstering (factor one) and six were related to counterarguing (factor two). After developing the scale based on the exploratory analysis, a confirmatory analysis was carried out. The confirmatory analysis revealed that a two-factor solution with the same six items for the counterarguing and bolstering subscales fit the data well. The confirmatory analysis also found that the two factors showed a small positive correlation ($r = .18$).

The results of our first study suggest that the two-factor solution we obtained using the 12 items is reliable. The fact that the two factors are only slightly correlated suggests that preferences for bolstering and counterarguing are essentially orthogonal. Thus, an individual high in bolstering may be either high or low in counterarguing.

Scale Prediction

Having established that the BCS has good structural properties, we sought to examine its predictive utility. Past research has shown that when individuals are instructed to counterargue or bolster, attitude change is often attenuated (Killeya & Johnson, 1998; McGuire, 1964). Thus, we expected that individuals naturally inclined to bolster or counterargue would show less attitude change when confronted with a persuasive message. That is, higher scores on either of these dimensions should be associated with reduced attitude change. To examine the relationship between our scales and attitude change, an experiment was conducted.

In this experiment, all participants read an advertisement for "Brown's Department Store," reported their attitudes toward Brown's, and completed the BCS. Participants' scores on each subscale were calculated and then submitted to a regression to predict attitude change. As predicted, higher scores on the bolstering subscale were significantly associated with less attitude change ($\beta = -.27$, $p = .02$); similarly, higher scores on the counterarguing subscale were significantly associated with less attitude change ($\beta = -.25$, $p < .05$). There was no interaction between the bolstering and counterarguing subscales in predicting attitude change.

The results of this experiment provide initial evidence that individuals' perceptions of how they resist have implications for attitude change. The more individuals saw themselves as inclined to use a resistance method—whether bolstering or counterarguing—the less likely they were to succumb to a persuasive message. However, the experiment does little to distinguish between the bolstering and counterarguing subscales. Thus, based on this experiment, it is unclear whether our two scales predict the use of specific resistance strategies or simply a general preference for resistance. The fact that the correlation between the scales is low, however, supports the independence of the resistance strategies. Nevertheless, it would be useful to demonstrate that the subscales predict how people resist.

If the subscales predict how individuals resist persuasion, this should be apparent in the type of thoughts individuals generate when resisting a message.

Specifically, individuals high on the bolstering subscale should generate thoughts toward a message that represent arguments in favor of their position, as opposed to arguments against the opposing position. Likewise, individuals high on the counterarguing subscale should primarily generate thoughts that reflect arguments against the opposing position, rather than arguments in favor of their own position.

To test the influence of people's resistance preferences on actual thoughts, a second experiment was conducted. In this experiment, all participants were presented with a message advocating the adoption of senior comprehensive exams at their university. Participants were told that a policy of senior comprehensive exams would require them to pass an exam before they could graduate from their university, and that failing the exam would require the student to take additional classes (see Petty & Cacioppo, 1979). Thus, the topic was designed to be counter-attitudinal and create a situation in which participants were likely motivated to resist persuasion. After being informed about the exam policy, participants were given the arguments in favor of the exams, followed by the opportunity to list their thoughts about and attitudes toward the exam. Finally, all participants completed the BCS.

Replicating the findings of the first experiment, scores on both the bolstering subscale ($\beta = -.22$, $p = .06$) and counterarguing subscale ($\beta = -.25$, $p < .05$) were negatively correlated with attitude change. To examine participants' resistance methods, we coded thoughts as representing ideas bolstering their own position (e.g., "The current method of doing things already has the right balance of exams") or counterarguments against the message (e.g., "Implementing comprehensive exams will also cause a lot of unnecessary stress"). After coding the thoughts, we examined the predictive utility of our measures. The bolstering subscale was positively and significantly correlated with the number of bolstering thoughts: the higher an individual's preference for attitude bolstering, the more bolstering thoughts that were exhibited ($\beta = .30$, $p = .01$). The bolstering subscale was uncorrelated with the number of counterarguments generated ($\beta = -.02$, $p = .90$). Furthermore, the counterarguing subscale was positively correlated with the number of counterarguments generated: the higher an individual was in the preference to counterargue, the more counterarguments that were generated ($\beta = .22$, $p = .07$). However, the counterarguing subscale was uncorrelated with the number of bolstering thoughts generated ($\beta = .07$, $p = .55$). There was no interaction between the two scales in predicting thoughts. Thus, the results of the second experiment demonstrate that each subscale uniquely predicts the type of thoughts people generate when trying to resist a message.

In summary, the present research supports the idea that there are general differences in the extent to which people use different thoughtful resistance strategies, such as bolstering and counterarguing. The spontaneous generation of each type of cognitive response when trying to resist a message may vary from one individual to another, and the BCS may prove useful in assessing these individual differences. Furthermore, collapsing across the experiments, a simultaneous regression showed that both the counterarguing and bolstering scales uniquely predicted attitude change, even when controlling for the other. This suggests that each scale possesses unique predictability above the other.

These findings help us understand how peoples' beliefs about themselves can influence the method by which they resist persuasion, and they also raise new questions that should be addressed by further research. For example, it would be interesting to examine whether individuals who tend to bolster, versus counterargue, differ in their responses to specific influence strategies. On the one hand, bolstering may be more effective when individuals have little knowledge about an opposing viewpoint and thus are unable to counterargue. On the other hand, counterarguing may be more effective when individuals have knowledge about the opposing viewpoint and are able to dispute it, as the successful refutation of a message may add new counterarguments to individuals' counterpersuasion arsenal (for other implications of successful refutation, see Tormala & Petty, this volume). Also intriguing is the possibility that argument strength might have a differential impact on attitude change depending on someone's preferred resistance strategy. If a message is argued very cogently, for example, counterarguing may be quite difficult, so people who prefer bolstering over counterarguing may more effectively defend their attitudes in these contexts.

Future research may also examine whether there are situations in which people attempt to correct for the processing styles they perceive themselves to employ. In the present study, individuals were allowed to process the message in any manner they wished. However, if individuals were in a situation where objectivity was desired (such as the courtroom), and they saw their processing style as inappropriate, correction or overcorrection might occur as in the research using the RPS.

It would also be interesting to test whether these individual differences are operative across a variety of topics, or if individuals only use them when they are motivated to resist the message to some degree. For example, it is unclear at present how these scales would function in a situation where individuals actually wish to accept a message. If these scales only tap resistance strategies, they may not have much predictive power when a resistance motivation is absent. However, if these scales tap chronic dispositions, individuals may employ these strategies even when they wish to accept a message. This might lead individuals high on the counterarguing scale, for example, to be less likely to change their attitude even when attitude change is desired. This last point stresses the importance of considering resistance as a motivation in future research. Of course, before we conclude that the BCS assesses a chronic disposition, it would be important to assess its stability over time.

FUTURE DIRECTIONS:
MULTIPLE ROLES FOR VARIABLES

According to the ELM (Petty & Cacioppo, 1986), any *one* variable can have an impact on persuasion (or resistance) by serving in different roles in different situations. For example, past research has shown mood to play a variety of roles in persuasion (see Petty, DeSteno, & Rucker, 2001). When elaboration is low (e.g., low personal relevance), mood may serve as a simple cue. An individual may misattribute the mood to the message and subsequently show more persuasion when in a positive mood as compared to a neutral mood (Petty, Schumann, Richman, & Strathman, 1993). When elaboration is high (e.g., high personal relevance), mood can bias processing. For example, Petty et al. (1993) found that the thoughts of individuals in a happy mood were more positive than those of individuals processing the same message in a neutral mood. Finally, when elaboration is moderate, mood may determine the amount of processing. Wegener, Petty, and Smith (1995), for instance, found that happy individuals increased processing if they believed a message would maintain their happiness, but decreased processing if they believed a message would reduce their happiness (for a detailed description of these and other roles, see Petty, 1997; Petty & Wegener, 1998; Petty & Briñol, 2002).

In the present research, we found that individuals' beliefs about their own resistance affected attitude change by serving as simple cues (i.e., research on the RPS scale) or by influencing the type of processing (i.e., research on the BCS). However, beliefs about one's own persuasibility or how one processes information might take on different roles under varying degrees of elaboration. For example, consider beliefs about one's own persuasibility. If an individual perceives himself as difficult to persuade, elaboration is high, and his resistance is not seen as biasing, he may actually engage in more defensive processing of the message (e.g., more counterarguing, more bolstering) in an attempt to dismiss it. For example, if people are confronted with an attempt to change their core values about abortion, and elaboration is high, an individual may think, "I'm hard to persuade, and that's okay in this situation, so I'm going to counterargue this message!"

Likewise, individual differences on the BCS might play different roles as a function of elaboration. Our research on the BCS examined situations in which elaboration was relatively high, as everyone was instructed to process the message and had the resources to do so. When elaboration is moderate, however, these beliefs might determine the extent of message processing. Individuals who are high in counterarguing may process the message more, since processing the arguments would be necessary for counterargumentation to occur. Individuals who are high in bolstering, on the other hand, may be more likely to rehearse their preexisting attitude-relevant knowledge rather than process the message. Examining the multiple roles these beliefs can have is an intriguing and potentially important avenue for future research.

CONCLUSION

As early as the 1950s researchers attempted to understand individual differences in resistance to persuasion. Until recently, however, these measures have been relatively limited in scope. In the present chapter, we suggest a meta-cognitive approach to understanding people's general resistance tendencies. We presented some early evidence in this regard and focused on an examination of people's own beliefs about how resistant they are and the ways in which they resist persuasive attempts. Consistent with this meta-cognitive approach, we developed two new individual difference measures. The first measure, the Resistance to Persuasion Scale, assesses individual differences in people's perceptions of their own persuasibility. The second measure, the Bolster-Counterargue Scale, assesses individual differences in people's beliefs about what strategies they use to resist persuasion. The combination of both scales may provide a more complete instrument to assess general beliefs about persuasion.

The present research shows that beliefs about persuasion, measured by these scales and manipulated using false feedback, can play different roles in attitude change depending on the situation. When the elaboration likelihood is relatively low, individuals might use their beliefs about persuasibility as a cue to infer their response to persuasive messages. Under relatively high-elaboration conditions, beliefs about *how* a person resists persuasion can influence the actual thoughts a person has in response to a persuasive message, ultimately affecting attitude change. Finally, if elaboration is high and an individual's beliefs are seen as a source of bias, the individual might try to correct or adjust for the perceived bias.

In short, the current chapter argues for the utility of considering peoples' beliefs related to their own resistance and how they resist. The research presented has examined these perspectives in situations where an individual is likely to posses a motivation to resist. Continuing to examine resistance beliefs from these various angles will likely provide a more complete picture of the role such beliefs have in persuasion processes and outcomes.

REFERENCES

Abelson, R. P. (1968). Uncooperative personality variables. In R. P. Abelson, E. Aronson, W. J. McGuire, T. M. Newcomb, M. J. Rosenberg, & P. H. Tannenbaum (Eds.), *Theories of cognitive consistency: A source book* (pp. 648–651). Chicago: Rand McNally.

Adorno, R. W., Frenkel-Brunswik, E., Levinson, D. J., & Sanford, R. N. (1950). *The authoritarian personality*. New York: Harper.

Albarracín, D., & Mitchell, A. L. (2002). *Defensive confidence and approach to proattitudinal information: A study of individual differences*. Manuscript under review.

Albarracín, D., & Wyer, R. S. (2000). The congnitve impact of past behavior: Influences on beliefs, attitudes and future behavioral decisions. *Journal of Personality and Social Psychology, 79,* 5–22.

Altemeyer, B. (1981). *Right-wing authoritarianism*. Winnipeg, Canada: University of Manitoba Press.

Altemeyer, R. A. (1969). Balancing the F scale. *Proceedings of the annual convention of the American Psychological Association, 4,* 417–418.

Asch, S. E. (1956). Studies of independence and conformity: A minority of one against a unanimous majority. *Psychological Monographs, 70,* No. 9 (whole Number 416).

Bandura, A. (1997). *Self-efficacy: The exercise of control.* New York: W. H. Freeman & Co., Publishers.

Berkowitz, L., Jaffee, S., Jo, E., & Troccoli, B. (2000). Some conditions affecting overcorrection of the judgment-distorting influence of one's feelings. In J. P. Forgas (Ed.), *Feeling and thinking: The role of affect in social cognition.* Cambridge, England: Cambridge University Press.

Briñol, P., & Petty, R. E. (2002). *Persuasion knowledge: The role of normative beliefs.* Working Paper. Ohio State University, Columbus, OH.

Briñol, P., & Petty, R. E. (2003). Overt head movements and persuasion: A self-validation analysis. *Journal of Personality and Social Psychology, 84,* 1123–1139.

Briñol, P., Petty, R. E., & Tormala, Z. L. (in press). The self-validation of cognitive responses to advertisements. *Journal of Consumer Research.*

Brock, T. C. (1967). Communication discrepancy and intent to persuade as determinants of counterargument production. *Journal of Experimental Social Psychology, 3,* 296–309.

Cacioppo, J. T., & Petty, R. E. (1979). The effects of message repetition and position on cognitive responses, recall, and persuasion. *Journal of Personality and Social Psychology, 37,* 97–109.

Cacioppo, J. T., Petty, R. E., & Kao, C. F. (1984). The efficient assessment of "need for cognition." *Journal of Personality Assessment, 48,* 306–307.

Campbell, M. C., & Kirmani, A. (2000). Consumers' use of persuasion knowledge: The effects of accessibility and cognitive capacity on perceptions of an influence agent. *Journal of Consumer Research, 27,* 69–83.

Chaiken, S., & Baldwin, M. W. (1981). Affective-cognitive consistency and the effect of salient behavioral information on the self-perception of attitudes. *Journal of Personality and Social Psychology, 41,* 1–12.

Cialdini, R. B., Trost., M. R., & Newsom, J. T. (1995). Preference for consistency: The development of a valid measure and the discovery of surprising behavioral implications. *Journal of Personality and Social Psychology, 69,* 318–328.

Crutchfield, R. (1955). Conformity and character. *American Psychologist, 10,* 191–198.

DeSteno, D., Petty, R. E., Wegener, D. T., & Rucker, D. D. (2000). Beyond valence in the perception of likelihood: The role of emotion specificity. *Journal of Personality and Social Psychology, 78,* 397–416.

Festinger, L. (1957). *A theory of cognitive dissonance.* Evanston, IL: Row, Peterson.

Freedman, J. L., & Fraser, S. C. (1966). Compliance without pressure: The foot-in-the-door technique. *Journal of Personality and Social Psychology, 4,* 195–203.

Frey, D. (1986). Recent research on selective exposure to information. *Advances in Experimental Social Psychology, 19,* 41–80.

Friestad, M., & Wright, P. (1994). The persuasion knowledge model: How people cope with persuasion attempts. *Journal of Consumer Research, 21,* 1–31.

Gilbert, D. T. (1993). The assent of man: Mental representation and the control of belief. In D. M. Wegner & J. W. Pennebaker (Eds.), *Handbook of mental control* (pp. 57–87). Englewood Cliffs, NJ: Prentice Hall.

Gross, S., Holtz, R., & Miller, N. (1995). Attitude certainty. In R. E. Petty & J. A. Krosnick (Eds.), *Attitude strength: Antecedents and consequences* (pp. 215–245). Mahwah, NJ: Erlbaum.

Gruder, C. L., Cook, T. D., Hennigan, K. M., Flay, B. R., Alessis, C., & Halamaj, J. (1978). Empirical tests of the absolute sleeper effect predicted from the discounting cue hypothesis. *Journal of Personality and Social Psychology, 36,* 1061–1074.

Jacks, J. Z., & Devine, P. G. (2000). Attitude importance, forewarning of message content, and resistance to persuasion. *Basic and Applied Social Psychology, 22,* 19–29.

Jost, J. T., Kruglanski, A. W., & Nelson, T. O. (1998). Social metacognition: An expansionist review. *Personality and Social Psychology Review, 2,* 137–154.

Killeya, L. A., & Johnson, B. T. (1998). Experimental induction of biased systematic processing: The directed-thought technique. *Personality and Social Psychology Bulletin, 24,* 17–33.

Levinson, D. J., & Sanford, R. N. (1944). A scale for the measurement of anti-Semitism. *Journal of Psychology, 17,* 339–370.

Lewan, P. C., & Stotland, E. (1961). The effects of prior information on susceptibility to an emotional appeal. *Journal of Abnormal and Social Psychology, 62,* 450–453.

Lydon, J., Zanna, M. P., & Ross, M. (1988). Bolstering attitudes by autobiographical recall: Attitude persistence and selective memory. *Personality and Social Psychology Bulletin, 14,* 78–86.

McCrae, R. R., & Costa, P. T. (1997). Conceptions and correlates of openness to experience. In R. Hogan, J. Johnson, & S. Bringgs (Eds.), *Handbook of personality psychology* (pp. 825–847). San Diego, CA: Academic Press.

McGuire, W. J. (1964). Inducing resistance to persuasion: Some contemporary approaches. In L. Berkowitz (Ed.), *Advances in experimental social psychology* (Vol. 19, pp. 191–229). New York: Academic Press.

McGuire, W. J. (1969). The nature of attitudes and attitude change. In G. Lindzey & E. Aronson (Eds.), *Handbook of social psychology* (2nd ed., Vol. 3, pp. 136–314). Reading, MA: Addison-Wesley.

Milgram, S. (1974). *Obedience to authority.* New York: Harper & Row.

Nelson, T. O. (1992). *Metacognition: Core readings.* Boston: Allyn & Bacon.

Ottati, V. C., & Isbell, L. M. (1996). Effects of mood during exposure to target information on subsequently reported judgments: An on-line model of misattribution and correction. *Journal of Personality and Social Psychology, 71,* 39–53.

Papageorgis, D. (1968). Warning and persuasion. *Psychological Bulletin, 70,* 271–282.

Petty, R. E. (1997). The evolution of theory and research in social psychology: From single to multiple effect and process models. In C. McGarty & S. A. Haslam (Eds.), *The message of social psychology: Perspectives on mind in society* (pp. 268–290). Oxford; England: Blackwell Publishers, Ltd.

Petty, R. E., & Briñol, P. (2002). Attitude change: The Elaboration Likelihood Model. In G. Bartels & W. Nelissen (Eds.), *Marketing for sustainability: Towards transactional policy making* (pp. 176–190). Amsterdam: IOS Press.

Petty, R. E., Briñol, P., & Tormala, Z. L. (2002). Thought confidence as a determinant for persuasion: The self-validation hypothesis. *Journal of Personality and Social Psychology, 82,* 722–741.

Petty, R. E., & Brock, T. C. (1979). Effects of "Barnum" personality assessments on cognitive behavior. *Journal of Consulting and Clinical Psychology, 47,* 201–203.

Petty, R. E., & Cacioppo, J. T. (1977). Forewarning, cognitive responding, and resistance to persuasion. *Journal of Personality and Social Psychology, 35,* 645–655.

Petty, R. E., & Cacioppo, J. T. (1979). Effects of forewarning of persuasive intent and involvement on cognitive responses. *Personality and Social Psychology Bulletin, 5,* 173–176.

Petty, R. E., & Cacioppo, J. T. (1981). *Attitudes and persuasion: Classic and contemporary approaches.* Dubuque, IA: Wm. C. Brown.

Petty, R. E., & Cacioppo, J. T. (1986). *Communication and persuasion: Central and peripheral routes to attitude change.* New York: Springer-Verlag.

Petty, R. E., DeSteno, D., & Rucker, D. (2001). The role of affect in persuasion and attitude change. In J. Forgas (Ed.), *Handbook of affect and social cognition* (pp. 212–233). Mahwah, NJ: Erlbaum.

Petty, R. E., Ostrom, T. M., & Brock, T. C. (1981). *Cognitive responses in persuasion.* Hillsdale, NJ: Earlbaum.

Petty, R. E., Schumann, D. W., Richman, S. A., & Strathman, A. J. (1993). Positive mood and persuasion: Different roles for affect under high- and low-elaboration conditions. *Journal of Personality and Social Psychology, 64,* 5–20.

Petty, R. E., Tormala, Z., & Rucker, D. D. (in press). Resistance to persuasion: An attitude strength perspective. In J. T. Jost, M. R. Banaji, & D. Prentice (Eds.), *Perspectivism in social psychology: The yin and yang of scientific progress.* Washington, DC: American Psychological Association.

Petty, R. E., & Wegener, D. T., (1993). Flexible correction processes in social judgment: Correcting for context induced contrast. *Journal of Experimental Social Psychology, 29,* 137–165.

Petty, R. E., & Wegener, D. T. (1998). Attitude change: Multiple roles for persuasion variables. In D. Gilbert, S. Fiske, and G. Lindzey (Eds.), *The handbook of social psychology* (4th ed.). New York: McGraw-Hill.

Petty, R. E., & Wegener, D. T. (1999). The Elaboration Likelihood Model: Current status and controversies. In S. Chaiken & Y. Trope (Eds.), *Dual-process theories in social psychology* (pp. 41–72). New York: Guilford Press.

Pratkanis, A. R., Greenwald, A. G., Leippe, M. R., & Baumgardner, M. H. (1988). In search of reliable persuasion effects: III. The sleeper effect is dead. Long live the sleeper effect. *Journal of Personality and Social Psychology, 54,* 203–218.

Rokeach, M. (1954). The nature and meaning of dogmatism. *Psychological Review, 61,* 194–204.

Schwartz, S. H. (1992). Universals in the content and structure of values: Theoretical advances and empirical test in 20 countries. In M. P. Zanna (Ed.), *Advances in experimental social psychology,* Vol. 24 (pp. 1–65). San Diego, CA: Academic Press.

Stagner, R. (1936). Fascist attitudes: An exploratory study. *Journal of Social Psychology, 6,* 309–319.

Tannenbaum, P. H., Macauley, J. R., & Norris, E. L. (1966). Principle of congruity and reduction of persuasion. *Journal of Personality & Social Psychology, 3,* 233–238.

Taylor, S. E. (1975). On inferring one's attitude from one's behavior: Some delimiting condition. *Journal of Personality and Social Psychology, 31,* 126–131.

Tormala, Z. L., Petty, R. E., & Briñol, P. (2002). Ease of retrieval effects in persuasion: The roles of elaboration and thought-confidence. *Personality and Social Psychology Bulletin, 28,* 1700–1712.

Vokey, J. R., & Read, J. D. (1985). Subliminal messages: Between the devil and the media. *American Psychologist, 40,* 1231–1239.

Vonk, R. (1998). The slime effect: Suspicion and dislike of likable behavior toward superiors. *Journal of Personality and Social Psychology, 74,* 849–864.

Wegener, D. T., & Petty, R. E. (1995). Flexible correction processes in social judgment: The role of naïve theories in corrections for perceived bias. *Journal of Personality and Social Psychology, 68,* 36–51.

Wegener, D. T., & Petty, R. E. (1997). The Flexible Correction Model: The role of naïve theories of bias in bias correction. In M. P. Zanna (Ed.), *Advances in experimental social psychology* (Vol., 29, pp. 141–208). San Diego: Academic Press.

Wegener, D. T., & Petty, R. E. (2001). Understanding effects of mood through the Elaboration Likelihood and Flexible Correction Models. In L. L. Martin & G. L. Clore (Eds.), *Theories of mood and cognition: A user's guidebook* (pp. 177–210). Mahwah, NJ: Erlbaum.

Wegener, D. T., Petty, R. E., & Smith, S. M. (1995). Positive mood can increase or decrease message scrutiny: The hedonic contingency view of mood and message processing. *Journal of Personality and Social Psychology, 69,* 5–15.

Wicklund, R. A., & Brehm, J. W. (1976). *Perspectives on Cognitive Dissonance.* Hillsdale, NJ: Erlbaum.

Wilson, T. D., & Brekke, N. (1994). Mental contamination and mental correction: Unwanted influences on judgments and evaluations. *Psychological Review, 116,* 117–142.

Wilson, T. D., Gilbert, D. T., & Wheatley, T. P. (1998). Protecting our minds: The role of lay beliefs. In V. Y. Yzerbyt & G. Lories (Eds.), *Metacognition: Cognitive and social dimensions* (pp. 171–201). Thousand Oaks, CA: Sage Publications.

Wood, W. (1982). Retrieval of attitude-relevant information from memory: Effects on susceptibility to persuasion and on intrinsic motivation. *Journal of Personality and Social Psychology, 42,* 798–910.

Wright, P. (2002). Marketplace metacognition and social intelligence. *Journal of Consumer Research, 28,* 1–31.

Zuwerink, J. R., & Devine, P. G. (1996). Attitude importance and resistance to persuasion: It's not just the thought that counts. *Journal of Personality and Social Psychology, 70,* 931–944.

6

Differentiating Individual Differences in Resistance to Persuasion

Richard J. Shakarchi and
Curtis P. Haugtvedt
The Ohio State University

Attitude change and persuasion research has a rich history in the use of individual difference variables. The present volume by Knowles and Linn on the topic of resistance is no exception. Throughout this volume, authors have used individual variables in the service of better understanding the processes of interest. At first glance, some of the individual difference variables may look like they measure overlapping constructs. For example, consideration of future consequences (Strathman, Boninger, Gleicher, & Baker, 1994) may share similarities with need for cognition (Cacioppo, Petty, & Kao, 1984), in that both scales portend to measure tendencies toward deliberation and elaborative thought. Similarly, as noted by Haugtvedt, Shakarchi, Samuelson, and Liu (this volume), transportability (Dal Cin, Zanna, & Fong, 2002) may be closely related to self-referencing (Haugtvedt, 1994) because both scales try to capture the extent of personal involvement in a strategic communication. In addition, some of the scales noted in this volume are relatively new and/or currently under development.

TABLE 6.1
Scale Reliability Coefficients, Means, and Standard Deviations (SD)

Scale	Std. Alpha	Mean	SD
Need to Evaluate	.8157	51.81	9.05
Need for Cognition	.8748	60.48	11.21
Self-Referencing	.8481	30.34	5.59
Resistance to Persuasion	.8213	51.38	8.53
Consideration of Future Consequences	.8036	42.80	6.82
Bolster-Counterargue	.8268	42.64	7.45
Bolster	.8339	22.44	4.27
Counterargue	.8597	20.20	5.25
Transportability	.8499	60.51	12.46

METHOD

To explore the relationship of these various individual difference measures with one another, we recruited 376 undergraduates at The Ohio State University to complete the following scales for course extra credit: Need to Evaluate (Jarvis & Petty, 1996; 16 items); Need for Cognition—short version (Cacioppo et al., 1984; 18 items); Propensity to Self-Reference (Haugtvedt, 1994; 8 items); Resistance to Persuasion (Briñol, Rucker, Tormala, & Petty, this volume; 16 items); Consideration of Future Consequences (Strathman et al., 1994; 10 items); Bolster-Counterargue (Briñol et al., this volume; 12 items); and Transportability (Dal Cin, Zanna, & Fong, this volume; 18 items). All items were rated on a 5-point response scale, based on the scale anchors provided by the respective authors of each measure. See Appendix 1 for a complete listing of the items and respective scale anchors for these seven individual difference measures.

RESULTS

Internal Reliability

After appropriate reverse-scoring, a standardized Cronbach's alpha was calculated for each individual difference measure in order to assess the internal reliability of each measure. In the case of the Bolster-Counterargue Scale, alphas were calculated both for the entire measure and for each subscale. These alphas are reported in Table 6.1, along with respective means and standard deviations (SD). As expected, all of the measures displayed high inter-item correlations and standardized reliability coefficients greater than .80.

The analyses also indicated that the two subscales of Bolster-Counterargue are independently reliable, each with an alpha greater than .80. This suggests that although correlated significantly at $r = .227$ (see Table 6.2), the two subscales could function independently of one another. (That the subscales' alphas exceeded the alpha for the entire scale suggests that, perhaps, the two subscales *should* be treated as independent.)

Discriminant Validity

The relationship between measures (including their subscales) is presented in Table 6.2. Almost every measure was significantly correlated with every other measure; only three measures were not correlated ($r < .01$ in Table 6.2). The smallest significant correlation was .144, between Self-Referencing and the Counterargue subscale, and the largest correlation (excluding scales with their subscales) was .47, between Consideration of Future Consequences and Need for Cognition.

The evidence from these correlations indicated that these individual difference measures are not completely orthogonal and may overlap significantly in some areas. To investigate further the properties of these measures, the data were entered into an exploratory factor analysis. The goal of this analysis was to determine whether these measures and their subscales would emerge reliably, or whether the conceptual and statistical overlap noted previously would suggest conceptually distinct dimensions underlying several of these measures.

Factor analyses were conducted to extract 7- and 8-factor solutions. An 8-factor solution would be consistent with an approach that treated the Bolster and Counterargue subscales as distinct factors, whereas a 7-factor solution would collapse these into a single scale.

The quartimax-rotated 8-factor solution provided strong evidence for the independence of these scales and subscales from one another. Almost every item of each scale and subscale loaded orthogonally onto a unique factor that represented the item's respective individual difference measure, with no other meaningful pattern of loadings. In fact, the 8-factor solution demonstrated close fit, $RMSEA = 0.045$, $CI = (0.044, 0.047)$.

Beyond establishing the independence of the various individual difference measures included in the factor analysis, this seemed to provide evidence that the Bolster and Counterargue subscales are independent. Based on the presentation of the Bolster-Counterargue Scale by Briñol et al. (this volume), we expected that the Bolster and Counterargue subscales would load onto a single factor, representing a common underlying psychological construct. However, an 8-factor solution could create the appearance that these subscales were independent if the inter-item correlations were not very high. We sought to test the interdependence of the Bolster and Counterargue subscales through a 7-factor analysis, which would force the subscales to load together if they shared significant common variance.

In fact, the 7-factor solution supported the independence of these subscales: Consistent with the evidence of scale reliability and correlations the Bolster and Counterargue subscales of the Bolster-Counterargue Scale (Briñol et al., this volume) loaded orthogonally. Furthermore, the 7-factor solution provided weaker factor structure than the 8-factor solution for the remaining scale items,

TABLE 6.2

Correlations Among Individual Difference Measures and Subscales

	Need to Evaluate	Need for Cognition	Self-Referencing	Resistance to Persuasion	Consideration of Future Consequences	Bolster-Counterargue	Bolster	Counterargue	Transportability
Need to Evaluate	1.000	.353	.261	.425	.250	.430	.269	.395	.263
Need for Cognition	.353	1.000	.219	.081	.470	.305	.165	.301	.338
Self-Referencing	.261	.219	1.000	.153	.229	.315	.374	.144	.288
Resistance to Persuasion	.425	.081	.153	1.000	.285	.294	.263	.205	.070
Consideration of Future Consequences	.250	.470	.229	.285	1.000	.174	.251	.044	.196
Bolster-Counterargue	.430	.305	.315	.294	.174	1.000	.730	.831	.237
Bolster	.269	.165	.374	.263	.251	.730	1.000	.227	.223
Counterargue	.395	.301	.144	.205	.044	.831	.227	1.000	.155
Transportability	.263	.338	.288	.070	.196	.237	.223	.155	1.000

Note. All correlations above 0.1 are significant at $p < .01$. All correlations below 0.1 are not statistically significant.

suggesting that the 8-factor solution provided the best fit to the data, and that the Bolster and Counterargue subscales should be treated as independent scales.

CONCLUSION

Our conclusions regarding the various individual difference measures relevant to resistance are very positive. Each measure has high internal validity and seems to make theoretically independent contributions in measuring individual differences. Furthermore, we agree with Briñol et al. that the Bolster-Counterargue Scale seems to have two distinct subscales, and we suggest that, rather than conceptualizing the subscales as interdependent, they may be used independently of one another.

APPENDIX 1

Need to Evaluate (Jarvis & Petty, 1996)
(scale: *extremely uncharacteristic of you to extremely characteristic of you*)
1. I form opinions about everything.
2. I prefer to avoid taking extreme positions.
3. It is very important to me to hold strong opinions.
4. I want to know exactly what is good and bad about everything.
5. I often prefer to remain neutral about complex issues.
6. If something does not affect me, I do not usually determine if it is good or bad.
7. I enjoy strongly liking and disliking new things.
8. There are many things for which I do not have a preference.
9. It bothers me to remain neutral.
10. I like to have strong opinions even when I am not personally involved.
11. I have many more opinions than the average person.
12. I would rather have a strong opinion than no opinion at all.
13. I pay a lot of attention to whether things are good or bad.
14. I only form strong opinions when I have to.
15. I like to decide that new things are really good or really bad.
16. I am pretty much indifferent to many important issues.

Need for Cognition (Cacioppo, Petty, & Kao, 1984)
(scale: *extremely uncharacteristic of you to extremely characteristic of you*)
1. I prefer complex to simple problems.
2. I like to have the responsibility of handling a situation that requires a lot of thinking.
3. Thinking is not my idea of fun.
4. I would rather do something that requires little thought rather than something that is sure to challenge my thinking abilities.

5. I try to anticipate and avoid situations where there is a likely chance I will have to think in depth about something.
6. I find satisfaction in deliberating hard for long hours.
7. I only think as hard as I have to.
8. I prefer to think about small daily projects to long-term ones.
9. I like tasks that require little thought once I've learned them.
10. The idea of relying on thought to make my way to the top appeals to me.
11. I really enjoy a task that involves coming up with new solutions to problems.
12. Learning new ways to think doesn't excite me very much.
13. I prefer my life to be filled with puzzles that I must solve.
14. The notion of thinking abstractly is appealing to me.
15. I would prefer a task that is intellectual, difficult, and important to one that is somewhat important but does not require much thought.
16. I feel relief rather than satisfaction after completing a task that required a lot of mental effort.
17. It's enough for me that something gets the job done; I don't care how or why it works.
18. I usually end up deliberating about issues even when they do not affect me personally.

Propensity to Self-Reference (Haugtvedt, 1994)
(scale: *extremely uncharacteristic of you to extremely characteristic of you*)
1. I find that thinking back to my own experiences always helps me understand things better in new and unfamiliar situations.
2. I think it is easier to learn anything if only we can relate it to ourselves and our experiences.
3. When I read stories, I am often reminded of my own experiences in similar circumstances.
4. I often find myself using past experiences to help remember new information.
5. I think it is easier to evaluate anything if only we can relate it to ourselves and our experiences.
6. I always think about how things around me affect me.
7. In casual conversations, I find that I frequently think about my own experiences as other people describe theirs.
8. When explaining ideas or concepts to other people, I find that I always use my own experiences as examples.

Resistance to Persuasion Scale (Briñol, Rucker, Tormala, & Petty, this volume)
(scale: *extremely uncharacteristic of you to extremely characteristic of you*)
1. I am strongly committed to my own beliefs.
2. My own beliefs are very clear.

   3. It is hard for me to change my ideas.
   4. I usually do not change what I think after a discussion.
   5. I find my opinions to be changeable.
   6. After participating in an informal debate, I always have the feeling that I was right.
   7. It could be said that I am likely to shift my attitudes.
   8. I often vary or alter my views when I discover new information.
   9. After forming an impression of something, it's often hard for me to modify that impression.
  10. My ideas are very stable and remain the same over time.
  11. I have never changed the way I see most things.
  12. What I think is usually right
  13. My opinions fluctuate a lot.
  14. I often have doubts about the validity of my attitudes.
  15. If it is necessary I can easily alter my beliefs.
  16. I have often changed my opinions.

Consideration of Future Consequences (Strathman, Boninger, Gleicher, & Baker, 1994)

(scale: *extremely uncharacteristic of you to extremely characteristic of you*)

   1. I consider how things might be in the future, and try to influence those things with my day to day behavior
   2. Often I engage in a particular behavior in order to achieve outcomes that may not result for many years.
   3. I only act to satisfy immediate concerns, figuring the future will take care of itself.
   4. My behavior is only influenced by the immediate (i.e., a matter of days or weeks) outcomes of my actions.
   5. My convenience is a big factor in the decisions I make or the actions I take.
   6. I am willing to sacrifice my immediate happiness or well-being in order to achieve future outcomes.
   7. I think it is important to take warnings about negative outcomes seriously even if the negative outcome will not occur for many years.
   8. I think it is more important to perform a behavior with important distant consequences than a behavior with less-important immediate consequences.
   9. I generally ignore warnings about possible future problems because I think the problems will be resolved before they reach crisis level.
  10. I think that sacrificing now is usually unnecessary since future outcomes can be dealt with at a later time.
  11. I only act to satisfy immediate concerns, figuring that I will take care of future problems that may occur at a later date.
  12. Since my day to day work has specific outcomes, it is more important to me than behavior that has distant outcomes.

Bolster-Counterargue Scale (Briñol, Rucker, Tormala, & Petty, this volume)
(scale: *extremely unlike me to extremely like me*)
1. When someone challenges my beliefs, I remind myself why my beliefs are important to me.
2. When someone has a different perspective on an issue, I like to make a mental list of the reasons in support of my perspective.
3. When someone gives me a point of view that conflicts with my attitudes, I like to think about why my views are right for me.
4. When someone tries to change my attitude toward something, I try to think about things that support the attitude I already have.
5. When confronted with an opposing viewpoint, I think it's good to think about my values and beliefs.
6. When information contradicts my beliefs, I think of all the reasons in support of my beliefs.
7. When someone challenges my beliefs, I enjoy disputing what they have to say.
8. I take pleasure in arguing with those who have opinions that differ from my own.
9. When someone gives me a point of view that conflicts with my own, I like to actively counterargue their point of view.
10. When someone presents a view that differs from my own, I don't like to engage in a debate.
11. I don't like to challenge people with views that differ from my own.
12. When information challenges my beliefs, I don't like to actively counterargue it.

Transportability Scale (Dal Cin, Zanna, & Fong, this volume)
(scale: *strongly disagree to strongly agree*)
1. I can easily envision the events in the story.
2. I find I can easily lose myself in the story.
3. I find it difficult to tune out activity around me.
4. I can easily envision myself in the events described in a story.
5. I get mentally involved in the story.
6. I can easily put stories out of my mind after I've finished reading them.
7. I sometimes feel as if I am part of the story.
8. I am often impatient to find out how the story ends.
9. I find that I can easily take the perspective of the character(s) in the story.
10. I am often emotionally affected by what I've read.
11. I have vivid images of the characters.
12. I find myself thinking of other ways the story could have ended.
13. My mind often wanders.
14. I find myself feeling what the characters may feel.
15. I find that events in the story are relevant to my everyday life.

16. I often find that reading stories has an impact on the way I see things.
17. I easily identify with characters in the story.
18. I have vivid images of the events in the story.

REFERENCES

Cacioppo, J. T., Petty, R. E., & Kao, C. F. (1984). The efficient assessment of "need for cognition." *Journal of Personality Assessment, 48*(3), 306–307.

Dal Cin, S., Zanna, M. P., & Fong, G. T. (February, 2002). *Perciever-based and stimulus-based individual differences in transportation.* Symposium paper presented at the third annual meeting of the Society of Personality and Social Psychology, Savannah, GA.

Haugtvedt, C. P. (1994, February). *Individual differences in propensity to self-reference: Implications for attitude change processes.* Paper presented at the first Winter Meeting of the Society for Consumer Psychology, St. Petersburg, FL.

Jarvis, W. B. G., & Petty, R. E. (1996). The need to evaluate. *Journal of Personality and Social Psychology, 70*(1), 172–194.

Strathman, A., Boninger, D. S., Gleicher, F., & Baker, S. M. (1994). Constructing the future with present behavior: An individual difference approach. In Z. Zaleski (Ed.), *Psychology of future orientation.* Scientific Society of the Catholic University of Lublin, no. 32, (pp. 107–119).

Strategies for Overcoming Resistance

7

Approach–Avoidance Model of Persuasion: Alpha and Omega Strategies for Change

Eric S. Knowles
University of Arkansas

Jay A. Linn
Widener University

"The Lord God said, . . . 'of the tree of the knowledge of good and evil you shall not eat. For in the day that you eat of it you shall die.' "

(Genesis, 2:15)

"But the serpent said to the woman, 'You will not die.' "

(Genesis, 3:4)

Persuasion is among the oldest of human experiences. It is the lubricant of social organization, the medium of interpersonal coordination. Because of this, the study of persuasion is at the core of social psychology, communication, rhetoric, advertising, and public relations.

This chapter develops an approach–avoidance model of attitudes and judgments, and it explores its ramifications for change and persuasion strategies. The approach–avoidance model implies two different tactics for change. Alpha strategies, which are widely known and have been the focus of much past research, attempt to persuade by increasing the approach forces. An offer or a message can be made more attractive by adding incentives, creating more convincing reasons, finding more credible sources, and so on. Omega strategies, which are relatively understudied and a primary focus of this book, attempt to persuade by decreasing avoidance forces. Thus, Omega change strategies work by removing or disengaging someone's reluctance to change.

The book of Genesis reports the first persuasive messages used to change someone's behavior. The serpent said to Eve, "You will not die!" Notice that the serpent did not say, "Great things come from the knowledge of good and evil," or "Trust me, I'm an expert in the benefits of knowledge," or "Eat of the tree and you will get not only knowledge, but also beautiful clothes." No, the serpent said, "I know you're afraid of the possibility of death, and I want you to know that death will not happen." The serpent used an Omega change strategy to deal directly with Eve's resistance. The serpent's Omega strategy was successful and, according to Genesis, changed human experience profoundly.

APPROACH–AVOIDANCE MODEL

Kurt Lewin (1951) told a story of a child at a beach whose toy floated in the surf at the water's edge. The child ran toward the ocean to retrieve the toy. But as she got closer, the pounding of the surf and the splashing of the waves began to scare her. She stopped 10 steps from the toy and was immobilized there. If she went further back, up the beach, her desire for the toy would impel her forward. If she went closer, the danger of the surf would push her back. She was stuck between approach and avoidance.

This story of the child with the toy epitomizes the approach–avoidance conflict and illustrates its various facets: (1) The goals, such as retrieving the toy, are complex events, with multiple meanings. Retrieving the toy means not only recapturing one's possession, but also putting one's self at risk. Most situations, attitude objects, messages, and offers are complex events, engaging many meanings and motives. (2) The meanings vary in many ways—in valence of affect, in breadth of applicability, in depth of engagement. Nonetheless, motives generally can be separated into two classes (Lewin, 1947, 1958). Those that promote movement toward the goal can be thought of as approach motives. Those that inhibit movement toward the goal can be thought of as avoidance motives. (3) Approach and avoidance motives may be of very different quality and aim, as is the attractiveness of the toy and the aversiveness of the surf. These two sets of forces may attend to different aspects of the goal or the situation. (4) Goals are acted on in context, not in the abstract. The desire for the toy is not a detached wish; it is a desire for this toy in this context. It is a desire that can only be understood at this time, in this place, in this way, and with these conditions and constraints.

Dollard and Miller (1950; Miller, 1944, 1959) formalized Lewin's descriptions into a sort of psychological gravitational model (Knowles, 1989). They believed that when one was far away from a goal, the approach cues were more salient than the avoidance cues. But as one moved closer to the goal, the avoidance gradients arose more steeply than the approach gradients. Dollard and Miller's (1950) famous depiction of these qualities showed a crossover point; closer than this point, the avoidance gradient has greater force than the approach gradient. This crossover point is the equilibrium point that froze Lewin's child at the beach, making her unable to move forward for fear of the surf, but unable to move away because of wanting the toy.

The Dollard and Miller approach–avoidance conflict model describes a basic mixed motive situation that characterizes numerous social interactions. We see this model applied to spatial behavior (Knowles, 1980), to optimal distinctiveness (Brewer, 1991), to group behavior (Wheeler, 1966), and to self-regulation (Forster, Grant, Idson, & Higgins, 2001). In this chapter, we apply the approach–avoidance model to the process of attitude, attitude change, and persuasion (see also, Knowles, Butler, & Linn, 2001). The model we apply is this: (1) Goals, attitude objects, offers, and opinions are complex stimuli that engage multiple motives. (2) Some of these motives are approach motives, pushing opinions and behaviors toward the goal. Others of these motives are avoidance motives, pushing opinions and behaviors away from the goal. (3) When the approach forces are greater in total strength or salience than the avoidance forces, then there is movement toward the goal. But when the approach forces are less compelling than the avoidance forces, then there is no movement toward the goal and perhaps even movement in the opposite direction. (4) To persuade or foster movement toward a goal, a change agent may increase approach forces or decrease avoidance forces.

TWO STRATEGIES FOR CHANGE

The approach–avoidance model has a number of implications. One implication, the one we focus on here, is that there are two fundamentally different ways to create change, two different strategies for promoting movement toward some goal. Alpha strategies promote change by activating the approach forces, thereby increasing the motivation to move toward the goal. In contrast, Omega strategies promote change by minimizing the avoidance forces, thereby reducing the motivation to move away from the goal.

Alpha Strategies

The empirical study of influence has focused almost exclusively on the study of Alpha strategies. Most influence texts review the many ways to make goals more desirable. Table 7.1 lists a number of these general strategies. We will only briefly mention them here, including a few key referents. We refer readers desiring more thorough treatments and discussions to Cialdini (2001), O'Keefe (2002), Perloff (2003), Pratkanis and Aronson (2001), Wilson (2002), or any general-survey social psychology text.

TABLE 7.1
Alpha Persuasion Strategies

Make messages more persuasive	Create strong arguments that justify and compel action (Petty & Cacioppo, 1986).
Add incentives	Add extra inducements for compliance, including interpersonal ones such as being liked for your opinion or choice.
Increase source credibility	Make the source more expert or attractive to increase their persuasiveness.
Provide consensus information	Show that many, many people are doing it, thinking it, wanting it.
Emphasize scarcity	Tell the target that few exist for only a short time. Scarcity makes the opportunity more attractive.
Engage a norm of reciprocity	Small gratuitous favors obligate the recipient to reciprocate, but you control the avenue of reciprocation.
Emphasize consistency and commitment	Create small actions or reframe the target's prior actions to appear consistent with the requested behavior.

Make Messages More Persuasive

The classic, first-line strategy for persuasion is improved rhetoric. When people are willing and able to listen to a message, strong arguments are more persuasive than weak arguments (Langer, 1989; Petty & Cacioppo, 1986; Pollock, Smith, Knowles, & Bruce, 1998). Petty and Cacioppo (1986) have shown that messages are more persuasive when they give more cogent reasons for an action or belief, when they raise someone's interest in listening to the message, and when the are phrased in a way that allows easy understanding.

Research has identified additional characteristics that affect the persuasiveness of messages. The vividness of a message (Frey & Eagly, 1993), the appeal of the messages to fear and emotion (Block & Keller, 1997; Maddux & Rogers, 1983; Rogers, 1983), and the use of humor in the message (Duncan & Nelson, 1985; Smith, Haugtvedt, & Petty, 1994) have all been explored, showing some conditions when these variables increase persuasion yet other circumstances when they decrease persuasion. Arguments are more persuasive when generated by listeners themselves than when merely read or heard (Gregory, Cialdini, & Carpenter, 1982). And, of course, reasonable arguments heard repeatedly are more persuasive than arguments heard only once (Haugtvedt, Schumann, Schneier, & Warren, 1994; Schumann, Petty, & Clemons, 1990).

Add Incentives

Another common way to promote change is to sweeten the deal by lowering the cost or by adding other inducements. "Free gifts," bonuses for "acting now," and other versions of the "that's-not-all" technique are effective sales strategies. Burger (1986) showed that the deal needs only to appear sweeter, not to actually be sweeter. Thus, people were more likely to purchase a 75-cent cupcake with a free cookie than they were to purchase a cupcake and cookie combination for 75 cents! The incentives need not be only monetary or product related. Thus, a persuader may imply that friendship or respect will be an added bonus to the deal (Cialdini, 2001).

Increase Source Credibility

Generally, a message will be more persuasive when delivered by a more expert or trustworthy source (Hovland & Weiss, 1951). Other source character-istics that influence persuasion are similarity to the target (Byrne, 1971) and the attractiveness of the source (Chaiken, 1979; Shavitt, Swan, Lowery, & Wanke, 1994). Source credibility may be less influential when people have the desire or ability to scrutinize the message (Petty & Cacioppo, 1986).

Provide Consensus Information

Often people use other people's actions as referents for what is appropriate and desirable (Sherif & Sherif, 1956). Cialdini (2001) calls this the influence principle of "social proof." The perception that other people find an alternative attractive often increases a person's appreciation of that alternative. Fads and panics are extreme examples. Thus, one Alpha strategy is to let people know that an alternative is the most popular, or that others have also made this selec-tion. Of course, people have a competing desire to think of themselves as unique, so this strategy can backfire unless carefully and subtly applied (Snyder & Fro-mkin, 1980).

Emphasize Scarcity

Making a person think that there are only a few items left, or that time for a decision is limited, can sometimes be an effective Alpha strategy. Scarcity is the ignition for several processes (Cialdini, 2001; Pratkanis & Aronson, 2001). First, scarcity implies social consensus that the item is desirable, that it is scarce because other people want it. Second, scarcity implies competition, and obtain-ing a scarce good implies that one has won the competition. Third, scarcity, especially time scarcity, burdens the decision-making processes, generally pro-ducing more heuristic-based decision processes.

Engage a Norm of Reciprocity

The opportunity to pay off an interpersonal obligation or debt is another sort of incentive that may make an offer more attractive. This Alpha strategy involves doing a small favor for someone before making a request of that person. The small favor creates a relationship (Dolinski, Nawrat, & Rudak, 2001) and engages a norm of reciprocity, an obligation to return the favor (Gouldner, 1960). Regan (1971) found that offering a potential customer a soft drink doubled the sales of raffle tickets that were two-and-a-half times more expensive than the drink. This reciprocation effect occurred even when the salesperson was relatively unfriendly.

Cialdini, Vincent, Lewis, Catalan, Wheeler, and Darby (1975) proposed that the door-in-the-face influence technique worked because of reciprocal concessions. The influence agent makes a very large request that is declined by the person. Then the agent revises her offer down, putting reciprocation pressure on the target to revise his answer up. Any action that an influence agent makes to agree with or serve the customer may increase the customer's obligation to reciprocate (but see also O'Keefe, 1999). Offering a drink, opening a door, agreeing with one's selection, and giving a gift may all increase the pressure to reciprocate.

Emphasize Consistency and Commitment

Another incentive for complying is the opportunity to be consistent with ones' sense of self or with one's prior actions. Inconsistency appears to be a threat to self-esteem. Getting people to commit to an opinion or action is an effective way to increase compliance with a later request (Dillard, 1991; Festinger, 1957). The greater the similarity of content between the small request and the later request, the more persuasive is the foot-in-the-door effect (Freedman & Fraser, 1966). Commitment is a powerful glue, cementing the person to a course of action. Cialdini, Cacioppo, Bassett, and Miller (1978) showed that initial commitments to an ambiguous course of action (e.g. participating in an experiment) can low-ball people into actions that they would not accept if they had full information (e.g. the experiment starts at 7:00 A.M.).

Omega Strategies

As rich as the influence literature is with examples of Alpha strategies for change, it is spare in examples of Omega strategies. The main thrust of this chapter is to bring together and label the variety of influence strategies that operate by reducing resistance to change. Table 7.2 lists these strategies. Because this literature is more diffuse and less well known, we will discuss each of these strategies in greater detail than the Alpha strategies. You will see that we journey through a broad range of literature, including that by authors who have looked

TABLE 7.2
Omega Persuasion Strategies

Sidestep resistance	Redefine interaction as not involving influence, e.g., a consultancy, a conversation.
Address resistance directly	Address sources of reluctance by lowering costs, counterarguing concerns, or offering guarantees.
Address resistance indirectly	Build confidence, esteem, and self-efficacy to remove reluctance.
Distract resistance	Distract attention to interfere with counterarguing the message.
Disrupt resistance	Disrupt complacency to bring attention to the message.
Consume resistance	Provide prior opportunities to resist or be critical.
Use resistance to promote change	Frame message so that resistance to it promotes change, e.g., paradoxical prescriptions, reverse psychology.

at change strategies in clinical psychology, social psychology, communications, and marketing.

Sidestep Resistance

Most people sense that the most effective strategy to use on resistance is not to raise it in the first place. There are a variety of things one can do to sidestep resistance.

Redefine Relationship. Jolson (1997) instructed salespeople to avoid resistance by redefining the sales interaction as a long-term consultation. Thus, an insurance agent calls not to sell you insurance, but to help you assess the ways your assets might be at risk, to see how your need for protection might have changed over the past several years. Straight (1996) advised salespeople to redefine all sales pitches as a cooperative interaction, beginning by exploring the interests and needs of the buyer to see if a mutually acceptable basis for doing business can be established. Redefining the sales pitch as a cooperative interaction or as a consultation is a way of sidestepping the resistance that would be raised by a sales call. The "buyer beware" wariness does not translate into "consultee beware!" (Alessandra, 1993).

A "consultation" has many implications. First, it implies that both consultant and target are working cooperatively on the target's goals. By implication, the target is in charge and, therefore, has less need to be wary. Second, a consultancy defines the situation more as a communal relationship (Clark, Mills, & Corcoran, 1989; Mills & Clark, 1994), which focuses attention away from negotiating an equitable exchange to developing a common plan. Third, a consultancy implies a longer-term relationship with more opportunities for interaction than a sales call. A long-term relationship implies that there will be future opportunities to reciprocate or repair any inequities that may result from this interaction.

Depersonalize the Interaction.   Which raises more resistance: "People should contribute to this charity!" or "You should contribute to this charity!"? Strategies that take the recipient's self out of the interaction, but preserve the message, sidestep a source of resistance. They minimize the impact of the current request either by making the request seem smaller or by making it seem less important.

Watzlawick (1987) reported working with a patient who had severe writer's block. Running up against a final deadline to complete his doctoral dissertation, the patient was agitated, depressed, and blocked. Obviously the dissertation, the deadline, and his inaction activated a great deal of anxiety. Watzlawick reported getting the patient to engage in a series of playful and unusual homework assignments. Together, therapist and patient devised silly social gaffs that the patient could experience, such as ordering an egg roll from a Mexican restaurant and asking a library to sell him a book. Over the course of several weeks, Watzlawick engaged the patient's intellect and creativity in devising cute, harmless, and engaging social errors. Eventually, the patient called to cancel an appointment because he was too busy writing his dissertation. Watzlawick's analysis was that the patient's anxiety was so strong that it caused him to avoid and resist any direct discussion of the fear of failure behind his procrastination. Watzlawick found an engaging activity, ostensibly unrelated to the writer's block or impending deadline, that nonetheless dealt with the fear of failure. The devised faux pas demonstrated that (a) failure and success are under one's control, and (b) the embarrassment and social disapproval that results can be managed and even experienced through an analytic eye.

In a similar vein, Milton Erickson often devised stories, sort of therapeutic parables, for resistant patients (Erickson, Rossi, & Rossi, 1976; Rosen, 1991). The stories were apparently about external or inconsequential people and events (e.g., "I once knew someone who. . . ."), but the content and resolution of each story was carefully crafted to mirror the patient's plight and to identify a path out of the predicament. Because the story ostensibly was not about the patient, it did not engage the resistance that would be sparked by an explicit discussion and prescription for the patient's dilemma. Dal Cin, Zanna, and Fong (this volume) analyze the narrative as an Omega strategy and show how the compellingness of the narrative sidesteps people's resistance to the message (see also, Green & Brock, 2002; Strange, 2002).

Minimize the Request.   The foot-in-the-door technique (Freedman & Fraser, 1966) may sidestep resistance by employing small incremental changes rather than one large change. The foot-in-the-door technique begins with a small, initial request that raises relatively little resistance and then it moves to larger and larger requests. Although the effectiveness of the foot-in-the-door is usually attributed to increasing commitment and to a target's self-perception as a co-operator, both of which may result from accepting the early small requests, the incremental approach also sidesteps resistance by making each request smaller. To move from no request to a small request and from a small request to a large request may seem like a smaller total change than does moving from no request to a large request in one jump.

Breaking a large, unreasonable request down into smaller, more acceptable steps is one of the ways that Stanley Milgram (1965) used to create extraordinary compliance in his obedience studies. He asked people assigned to the role of "teacher" to deliver seemingly fatal shocks as punishment to a "learner" who repeatedly failed at a task. Rather than saying, "Give this guy 450 volts!", Milgram's experimenter said, "The learner made another error. He needs another shock, 15 volts stronger than the last one." The slippery slope of incremental increases makes it hard to resist giving just 15 volts more than the last time.

The even-a-penny-will-help social influence technique (Cialdini & Schroeder, 1976) provides a third example of minimizing a request. Solicitors went door-to-door in Phoenix and Tempe, Arizona, to collect money for the American Cancer Society. When solicitors asked, "Would you contribute? Even a penny will help!", they received donations from 50% of the households as opposed to 29% when they simply asked, "Would you contribute?" Importantly, the average donation was quite similar in both conditions. Thus, the phrase "Even a penny will help" served to reduce people's reluctance to donate without greatly changing how much they decided to donate. The mechanism appears to be that the "even a penny" addition made the request seem smaller and, thus, less necessary to resist (Brockner, Guzzi, Kane, Levine, & Shaplen, 1984; Reingen, 1978; Weyant & Smith, 1987).

Raise the Comparison. Another way to reduce resistance to a plan is to introduce a comparison that makes the original offer seem more attractive, e.g., "While you are considering this half-caret ring, I just want you to see this beautiful one-caret ring." The comparison becomes an "anchor" or reference point from which the original offer is judged. A high anchor reduces resistance to the price by changing the implicit comparison price from zero (not buying the product) to some higher value (the high anchor price).

The "door-in-the-face" influence technique may work this way. It involves making a large request that is almost certain to be rejected before making the request that one wants to be accepted. The target's refusal of the large request makes acceptance of the smaller request more likely (Cialdini et al., 1975). Cialdini et al. attribute the effectiveness of the door-in-the-face to the norm of reciprocity, but another mechanism of the door-in-the-face technique is to provide a very high reference anchor for the target request. A request for $1 may engender resistance because it is compared to the alternative of not giving at all. A request for $10 that has been refused may create less resistance because the request for $1 seems like a bargain in comparison to the $10.

Burger (1986) thought that invoking a high judgmental anchor might be one of the processes that explain why a price reduction is effective. Telling a customer that an item used to be $1 but is now only 75 cents makes it more attractive than simply telling a customer that the item sells for 75 cents. The function of the high anchor is to reduce resistance to the price by changing the implicit comparison price from zero (not buying the product) to some higher value (the original price). The shopper returns loaded down with purchases from a store-wide 50%-off sale and says, "Look at all the money I saved!"

Thomas Mussweiler's (2000, 2002) research suggests that a variety of high numerical anchors might make a request seem more reasonable, even when the anchors are unrelated to the request, e.g., "There are two hundred uses for this eight-dollar item!" and "Eighty thousand customers have purchased this thirty-dollar service."

Pushing the Choice Into the Future.   The more distant a choice is, the more it is determined by hope and aspiration and the less by fear and inconvenience. Thus, offers are more likely to be accepted if they require future action than if they require immediate action, e.g., "Buy now, pay later!", "Could I borrow your truck for the third Saturday of next month?", or "Let's start Weight Watchers, not now, but three months and four days from now." Sherman, Crawford, and McConnell (this volume) describe the many ways this technique works.

The basic phenomenon, that distant choices are more determined by approach forces and close choices are more determined by avoidance forces, follows from Dollard and Miller's (1950) notion that avoidance gradients fall more quickly than approach gradients as psychological or temporal distance from the goal increases. Imagining future behavior minimizes the niggling negative aspects of a choice and magnifies the broader purposes and values of the choice (Liberman & Trope, 1998; Sagristano, Trope, & Liberman, 2002). People predict the future optimistically. Thus, people will assume that they can more easily and effectively serve as committee chairman next year than next week. People who are asked if they will vote in a future election report a very high intention to vote, much higher than the actual turnout. However, the act of making a prediction can be "self-anchoring." Greenwald, Carnot, Beach, and Young (1987) have shown that people who are called and asked if they will vote in the next election (several days away) do report a very high intention to vote, and because of this prediction actually do vote more than people who were not asked to predict.

Address Resistance Directly

Resistance that is raised by a request, an offer, or a message can be addressed directly. To do this, identify the source of resistance and remedy it.

Guarantees.   One Omega strategy that addresses resistance directly is the guarantee. A money-back guarantee doesn't make the refrigerator any larger, colder, more efficient, or stylish. What a guarantee does is address and remove some of the customer's fears involved with buying a product. What if it doesn't work? What if it doesn't fit? What if it looks terrible?

Sam Walton, founder of Wal-Mart, had his stores institute a no-questions-asked, money-back guarantee. Just return the item and you will get a refund. Walton guessed that the increased sales prompted by the return policy would greatly outweigh the added expense of returns and refunds. The customer, looking at some product, asks "Is this the kind I need?", "Will it fit?", "Does it match?", and puts the item in the shopping cart knowing that the item can always be returned. Walton (1992) said, "The two most important words I ever wrote were on that first Wal-Mart sign: 'Satisfaction Guaranteed.' They're still up there, and they have made all the difference" (pp. 316–317). This Omega strategy is one of the things that has made Wal-Mart the largest retail corporation in the world.

Guarantees help reduce any reluctance. If one's partner is worried about feeling trapped at a party, one could say, "Anytime you want to go, just wave at me, and we'll leave immediately."

Counterarguing Resistance. Persuasion research has examined addressing resistance directly in its study of the persuasiveness of one-sided versus two-sided communications (Hovland, Lumsdaine, & Sheffield, 1949; Insko, 1962; Lumsdaine & Janis, 1953). Most of these studies have used political issues, such as abortion or gun control, and messages that attempt to sway opinion rather than instigate behavior. A one-sided message advocates one alternative, giving reasons for believing it. A two-sided message advocates this same alternative and gives the same reasons, but it also refutes the opposing side. As such, the two-sided message includes an Omega element, identifying arguments opposed to the side advocated and directly countering these claims.

Two-sided messages seem to be generally more effective than one-sided messages in situations where listeners would be resistant enough to the message to think of the counterarguments themselves. For instance, higher-educated listeners and listeners who were initially opposed to the direction advocated in the message respond better to two-sided messages (Hovland et al., 1949; Faison, 1961). Two-sided messages are not always effective, however. Sometimes they lead to less change in the advocated direction, but these situations seem to be ones in which the refutations introduce resistance that was not initially there.

Address Resistance Indirectly

Resistance may be dealt with more indirectly by taking away the need for resistance. Several chapters in this book present excellent examples of this Omega strategy.

Raise Self-Esteem. Jacks and O'Brien (this volume) report that self-affirmation reduces people's resistance to persuasion. That is, people who have been praised, reminded of crowning accomplishments, or allowed to succeed at a task are more likely to agree with, that is, less likely to resist, an unrelated persuasive message. The Jacks and O'Brien study suggests that activities that build up people's sense of efficacy, self-esteem, or confidence have the added effect of making people less wary. This makes psychological sense. If a person feels efficacious and accomplished, these feelings imply that the person can overcome any difficulty. These indirect strategies reduce resistance by reducing the need to be resistant.

Focusing Resistance. Sagarin and Cialdini (this volume) report that training people to be critical of advertisements and to identify credible and noncredible sources for messages has two effects. First, training sometimes made people more resistant to illegitimate advertisements, especially if their susceptibility to influence had been demonstrated clearly. Second, the training made people less resistant to legitimate and appropriate sources. People who have been trained to be critical of advertisements end up being more persuaded by legitimate ads than do people who have not been trained. It is as if a general wariness that untrained participants applied to all advertisements was lifted from the legitimate ads after training. People who are provided with a sense of power, efficacy, control, and competence seem to have less need to be wary. They are more confident that they can handle or repair any breach.

Pratkanis (2000) suggests another strategy that indirectly disables resistance. He reminds us that influence is an interaction between two people who cast each other into specific roles (see also, Dolinski et al., 2001). Assuming the role of "teacher" implicitly demands that the other person take the role of "learner"; the role of "expert" implies that the other person take the role of "novice." Pratkanis observes that an influencer can disable a target's resistance by casting the resister in the role of "expert." Thus, the car salesman can say to the resistant customer, "Well, you drive for a living, so you know what an advantage it is that this car has the best breaking of any vehicle in its class!" Ascribing the "expert" role to the customer places the customer in a double-bind. To keep his status as an expert, the customer has to agree with the salesperson. Presumably, recasting the customer in a traditionally persuasive role (e.g., "Well, you're a teacher, you can explain better than I can why this is the best alternative") disables the customer's resistance and/or the customer's willingness to employ whatever resistance he might have.

Distract Resistance

Counterarguing of messages can be reduced by distractions (Haaland & Venkatesan, 1968; Petty & Brock, 1981). Festinger and Maccoby (1964) first demonstrated that a counter-attitudinal message can be more effective if presented with a distraction. Festinger and Maccoby's persuasive message argued against the Greek system on campus, and the recipients of this message were college fraternity members. When the recipients heard the message and viewed the speaker, they were less persuaded than when they heard the message but viewed a cartoon. Festinger and Maccoby speculated that the cartoon distracted the recipients from counterarguing the message, but Festinger and Maccoby had no direct measure of this process.

Petty, Wells, and Brock (1976) reasoned that distraction would interfere with any thoughts that the recipients had about a message. If the thoughts were predominantly counterarguments, then distraction would interrupt this resistance and make the message more effective than the same message without distraction. If the thoughts were primarily positive, then distraction would interfere with these supportive elaborations, making the message less effective than the same message without distraction. Petty et al. (1976) had participants monitor intermittent, distracting lights while listening to a message about university tuition. Petty et al. demonstrated that distraction reduced thinking about the message, making a poor message more effective and a good message less effective than with no distraction.

Petty and Cacioppo's (1986) Elaboration Likelihood Model of attitude change accounts for these findings very well. Participants who are able to process a message can attend to and think about the message. For these undistracted people, who use "central route" processing, the quality of the message has a major influence on their subsequent attitude about the issue. Participants who are unable to process a message because they are distracted or made busy by a second task are less influenced by the quality of the message and rely more on superficial, "peripheral" aspects of the message or situation to form an attitude. Distraction, in short, moves people from central route to peripheral route processing.

These considerations assume that distraction is sufficient to interfere with thinking about the message, but weak enough not to obscure the message. Distraction can boomerang, of course, and lead to no persuasion. If a distraction is too intense, then (a) it becomes the focus of attention, and (b) the message fails to even register.

Disrupt Resistance

Our consideration of distraction and disruption has been informed by Milton H. Erickson's conversational approach to hypnosis (Erickson, Rossi, & Rossi, 1976). Erickson realized that people who showed up in his office to be hypnotized were nonetheless resistant to the idea. They were caught in an approach–avoidance conflict. Consciously, they desired hypnosis enough to show up at the office, but unconsciously, they were still wary enough to resist a direct induction. Erickson developed a number of ways to counteract and deactivate the resistance so that the desire to be hypnotized could be met.

One class of hypnotic induction techniques employed "confusion" as the deactivating mechanism (Erickson, 1964; Gilligan, 1987). Confusion techniques started with a reasonable, unconfusing story that unfolded according to an expected script. When the patient was at ease with the story and where it was going, Erickson would insert an unexpected and confusing element and follow it immediately with a direct request to go into trance. Erickson believed that the confusion did two things. First, the confusing statements drew critical attention, as the patient tried to figure out what Erickson meant, leaving little attention left over to resist the induction. Second, the confusing statements created an uncomfortable uncertainty about what was happening, an uncertainty that the patient could alleviate by following the hypnotic suggestion.

Gilligan (1987) tells a story about a patient who came from a long distance to be hypnotized by the famous therapist, Erickson. Upon entering Erickson's office, the patient extended his hand in greeting. Erickson took the hand, shook it the normal three times, then shook it another five times, more slowly. Then, still holding on to the patient's hand, he raised his hand up to the level of their heads and said, "You are here to be hypnotized. You may go into a trance now." Erickson reported that the patient immediately went into a trance and the session began.

In another example (Rosen, 1991, pp. 79–80), a prominent physician, a particularly resistant patient, a came to Erickson for hypnotic treatment. The physician began by insisting that Erickson hypnotize him, a challenge that was a harbinger of failure. Erickson tried several commonplace techniques and, as expected, they all failed. Then Erickson went to his housekeeper, a young woman named Ilse, who was a frequent and easy hypnotic subject. He put Ilse into a somnabulistic trance, brought her into the room with the physician, raised Ilse's hand over her head, and left it in that position. Then Erickson said, "Ilse, go over there next to the man. I want you to stand like that until you put him into a trance. I'll come back in fifteen minutes" (Rosen, 1991, p. 79). Rosen reports that when Erickson returned, the physician was also in a deep trance. Rosen's explanation was that the physician was intent on resisting every active hypnotic induction, but he became confused by and unable to resist Ilse who was completely inactive. A second element in this induction was that the physician had focused his resistance on Erickson and was not able to shift easily to resist another agent.

Erickson's consideration of conversational hypnotism can be very informative for social influence (Sherman, 1988). It focuses on the words, meanings of words, and phrasing within the message. Erickson's hypnotic techniques have been applied to sales situations in a very thorough and detailed book by Moine and Lloyd (1990) entitled *Unlimited Selling Power: How to Master Hypnotic Selling Skills*. The book similarly focuses on the microprocesses of persuasion.

Erickson's confusion techniques are different from the distractions used in the typical attitude change experiment, and they seem to invoke different processes. Whereas external distractions, such as flashing lights, overwhelm thoughts about the message, the disruptions that Erickson used to create confusion (a) are part of the message, (b) create confusion about the meaning of the message, and (c) promote a reframing of the meaning of the message.

Santos, Leve, and Pratkanis (1994) demonstrated a confusion technique applied to panhandling. Panhandling student experimenters who asked for "some change" received a donation 44% of the time. Being specific and asking for "a quarter" raised this rate to 64%. Being confusing—asking for "37 cents"— produced the highest rate of compliance, at 75%. The "37 cent" request was a central part of the message, invoked confusion about the reason for the specificity, and resulted in people thinking that the requester had a specific purpose in mind.

This process of a disruption promoting a reframing of the meaning of a situation is the process of change described in Action Identification Theory (Vallacher & Wegner, 1985, 1987; Nowak & Vallacher, 1998). Vallacher and Wegner (1985) described an "Action Identification" as a label applied to an action sequence. The label invokes a schema and a script for action. Golf may be skill mastery for one person, but exercise for another. Once an identification snaps in, it assimilates facts and interpretations to it. Thus, it is very hard to change an action identification.

Vallacher and Wegner noted that to replace one action identification with another, one has to first disrupt the active identification. When an action identification is disrupted, when it doesn't work for the present situation, the person moves to a lower level, more detailed, and with more particular identification of action. Thus, when "driving the golf ball" produces a pronounced slice, the golfer moves attention to lower-level action identifications, to "setting the overlapping grip," "assuming the correct stance," "keeping the head down," and so on. Once lower-level action identifications regain control over the action sequence, then identification can move back to a higher level, but it may be a different higher level, a new conceptualization, a reframing.

Vallacher and Wegner conducted a number of studies to show this process of disrupting an action identification, moving the attention to lower-level identifications, then providing a reframing of the lower-level actions. In one study, students were instructed to eat Cheetos with their hands or with a pair of chopsticks (Vallacher & Wegner, 1985). In another study, students had to drink coffee out of a normal cup or a custom mug made unwieldy by a pound of shot in its base. Students drank this coffee while listening to a persuasive message that reported that coffee drinkers are the kind of people who seek stimulation or who avoid stimulation. The disruption of the normal activity made participants more susceptible to a persuasive message about the activity. The unwieldy mug made the message more persuasive, whereas a normal cup did not.

Davis and Knowles (1999) applied the disruption techniques of Erickson (1964) and Vallacher and Wegner (1985) to a sales situation, using a procedure they called the disrupt-then-reframe technique. In this technique, a reasonable and understandable offer is disrupted in a minor way by using an odd phrase or a slight speech dysfluency that is followed immediately by a persuasive message. They found that the message was more persuasive following the speech disruption than without the speech disruption.

Davis and Knowles had experimenters go door-to-door selling note cards for a local charity. In the normal sales condition, the experimenters ended their pitch by saying, "We're selling this pack of eight note cards for three dollars. They are a bargain. Would you buy some?" They sold cards to about 35% of the households. In the disrupt-then-reframe condition, experimenters said, "We're selling this pack of eight note cards for three hundred pennies. They are

TABLE 7.3
Three Studies of the Disrupt-then-Reframe Technique

Condition	Study 1	Study 2	Study 3
DTR (disrupt-then-reframe)	65%	70%	65%
"They're three hundred pennies. They're a bargain."			
Price only	35%	25%	30%
"They're three dollars"			
Reframe only	35%	30%	—
"Three dollars. They're a bargain."			
Disrupt only	—	35%	—
"They're 300 pennies."			
Reframe-then-disrupt	—	—	25%
"They're a bargain at three hundred pennies."			

a bargain. Would you buy some?" Sales nearly doubled, to 65% of the households. Davis and Knowles replicated this study with several comparison groups. Table 7.3 shows the various studies, comparison groups, and percentage sales. The disruption by itself and the reframe by itself failed to increase sales. The increased sales occurred only when the disruption was followed by the reframe. Particularly telling were low sales in the condition where the reframe occurred before the disruption. Saying that the cards "were a bargain at three hundred pennies" produced 25% sales, whereas saying that the cards "at three hundred pennies were a bargain" produced 65% sales.

The effect is not due to a frame of reference mechanism, comparing 300 to 3, or pennies to dollars. We have replicated this basic pattern selling "halfcakes" instead of "cupcakes" with the reframe, "They are delicious," and collecting charitable donations by requesting "money some" rather than "some money" when the reframe is "It could save a life." The effect is also not due to the experimenters' appearing more deserving or likeable because of the disruption, as in a "pratfall effect" (Aronson, Willerman, & Floyd, 1966). Videotapes of experimenters showed that the disruption had no significant effect on any judgment about or evaluation of the experimenter.

Our current work tries to tease apart the process at work to make these disruptions such powerful catapults for the reframing message. Erickson (1964) believed that his confusion techniques operated by interfering specifically with resistance. Erickson's explanation is reminiscent of Gilbert's (1991) two-stage model of judgment.

Gilbert (1991) described what he calls a "Spinozan" two-stage process of understanding a situation or communication. The first stage, which is comprehension of the situation, is only affirmative. It requires acceptance of the premise. To constitute and code a situation or experience, one first has to comprehend it uncritically, at face value, as if it were true. So, even an absurd statement like "My dog is a Buddhist" cannot be understood except as a truth. Once the manifest meaning of the utterance or situation has been comprehended, the experience becomes available for evaluation and consideration in a second evaluation stage. Stage two is where the experience is evaluated for internal and external coherence, compared to other facts and knowledge. The evaluative stage is where augmenting and discounting occur in attributions, where counterarguing is initiated. Grice (1975) made a similar point about language comprehension involving an appreciation of the literal meaning of an utterance, followed by an evaluation of the implication of the utterance. Grice argued that because it is impossible for a dog to be a Buddhist in the literal sense, we would search the statement more deeply for some metaphorical or ironic meaning.

In Gilbert's (1991) Spinozan theory, the two stages also differ in how easily they occur. The comprehension stage occurs automatically as an inherent part of meaning acquisition. It can't be avoided. The evaluation stage is under more cognitive and motivational control, and it requires more mental effort to accomplish. Because of this effort differential, a cognitive load, a distraction, or a lack of volition will interfere with the second stage, but not the first. A disruption of the second stage would leave intact the uncritical acceptance of the situation or utterance from the first stage. Thus, Gilbert's (1991) theory implies that a message disruption that occupies attention and interferes with evaluation would promote an uncritical acceptance of the message.

One of our recent studies began to assess this process (Linn & Knowles, 2002a). We showed people a very short, 30-second, home-made commercial for Tom's of Maine toothpaste. We chose Tom's toothpaste because it was commercially available but not widely known among our participants. (We appreciate the support and assistance that Tom's of Maine gave us in this project). Half the people saw an advertisement that ended with a statement that Tom's toothpaste was as effective as other toothpastes in fighting cavities. The other half heard the same thing about Tom's "mouthpaste." We selected "mouthpaste" as a disruptive, novel, and unexpected statement. Our purpose was to see whether the disruptive statement would create a general arousal or attentiveness to the message, or if it would take attention away from the message. Participants were asked to watch the commercial, but also to watch for a flash of yellow light. They were told to press a key as soon as they detected a flash. For half the participants the flash occurred early in the commercial; for the other half it occurred near the end of the commercial, immediately after the word "mouthpaste" or "toothpaste." Participants took longer to push the button after the disruptive word (1059 msec) than after the normal word (896 msec). It seems that a small disruption draws some attention away from the message. Our current research continues to investigate the role that Gilbert's (1991) Spinozan process plays in producing these subtle disruption effects.

Consume Resistance

Some part of resistance is a motivational process. It energizes responses. Resistance may express itself in action ("I won't do it!"), in affect ("I don't like it!"), and in cognition ("I don't believe it!"). But the character of resistance is that it applies energy against movement.

Muraven and Baumeister (2000; Baumeister, Muraven, & Tice, 2000) proposed that self-regulation is a limited ego resource that can become depleted with use. It seems to us that resistance to change is another form of self-regulation that is governed by this theory. Muraven and Baumeister (2000) outlined four assumptions of the ego-depletion model: (a) self-regulation is a limited resource, not infinite (Baumeister, Bratslavsky, Muraven, & Tice, 1998), (b) exercising self-control consumes this limited resource (Muraven, Tice, & Baumeister, 1998), (c) self-regulatory energy can be replenished, but at a slower rate than it is consumed, and (d) repeated exercise of self-control increases the capacity of the resource pool, just as exercise of a muscle strengthens the muscle (Muraven & Baumeiseter, 2000).

Muraven and Baumeister's ego-depletion theory of self-control, if it applies to resistance, implies that people should be less able to resist second requests than first requests (Dillard, 1991). Another way of saying this is that a request should be more effective later in a sequence than earlier in a sequence.

Political Advertisement Study.   To evaluate this process, we conducted a study of reactions to political advertisements (Knowles, Brennan, & Linn, 2002). We asked friends and family from around the country to videotape evening television shows the week before the November 2000 general elections in the United States. From these videotapes we identified a number of 30- to 45-second political ads that showed state or local candidates. We eliminated attack ads and used only ads that described the candidate and where he or she stood on issues. We showed the ads to some students and chose nine focal ads that were fairly noncontroversial, that were easily criticized or counterargued, and that were not strongly identified with a political party.

Undergraduate research participants viewed seven ads. They were asked to watch each ad and to tell their reaction to the advertisement (1 = terrible to 9 = wonderful) and to the candidate (1 = extremely unfavorable to 9 = extremely favorable). We thought that this rating task would introduce a critical evaluative stance toward each advertisement.

One of the seven advertisements was selected for more extensive evaluation, including completion of a Bivariate Evaluation and Ambivalence Measure (BEAMs; Cacioppo, Gardner, & Bernston, 1997) of feelings about the candidate. The BEAMs involved ratings (0 = Not at all to 4 = Extremely) on 16 adjectives, eight positive (e.g., "favorable," "pleasant," "comfortable") and eight negative (e.g., "negative," "bad," "opposing"). Although Cacioppo et al. (1997) suggest using the positive and negative adjectives as separate scales, we found them to be substantially correlated, $r = -.51$, and so combined them into a single scale by reverse scoring the negative adjectives.

Participants saw these ads under four conditions. One-fourth of the participants saw the focal ad first in the sequence. In this "First Ad" condition, participant's resistance should be strong and undiminished, and thus ready to apply wholeheartedly to the advertisements. Strong resistance here means that participants should have a relatively low evaluation of the first ad.

Other participants saw the focal ad last in the sequence of seven ads. In this "Last Ad" condition, participants had critically evaluated six other ads before seeing the focal ad. If their resistance had been depleted by this task, these participants should be less critical of the last ad.

Two other conditions followed the same pattern as the "Last Ad" condition, except that before the last ad, participants viewed a 12-minute travelogue about Fiji. This travelogue described a vacation to Fiji and showed many things to do. In the "Last Ad Accepting" condition, we asked participants to view the videotape and record what they liked about the vacation and which activities they found fun. In the "Last Ad Critical" condition, we asked participants to view the travelogue critically, listing when the narrator was deceptive and how the vacation as shown could go wrong. Whereas we expected the Last Ad condition to have a positive evaluation of the political advertisement because the six prior ads had consumed resistance, we expected the Last Ad Accepting condition to free participants from their critical stance and thereby allow the resistance to rebuild. The Last Ad Critical condition, which continued to use up a person's resistance, would not see this rebuilding. This thinking led to the expectation that evaluation of the political candidates should be relatively positive in the Last Ad and Last Ad Critical conditions, and relatively negative in the First Ad and Last Ad Accepting conditions. Eighty-seven people saw one of these four conditions. In addition, each participant saw one of three different ads as the focal ad for their more extensive judgments. The three ads, although liked differently, showed the same effects of conditions and therefore aren't discussed further.

The first analysis of the BEAMs evaluation showed disappointing results. The First Ad ($M = 11.67$) and Last Ad ($M = 9.01$) had very similar and not significantly different evaluations. However, when we took into account the participant's general level of skepticism about political advertisements, a different picture emerged. Participants had indicated their agreement with two statements: "I am skeptical of what a political advertisements says" and "Political advertisements can't be trusted." People who agreed with both statements were classified as high on skepticism ($n = 47$) and the remainder were classified as low on skepticism ($n = 40$).

When the level of skepticism was included in the analysis, the patterns showed an interesting interaction of condition with skepticism, $F(3, 62) = 3.20$, $p = .029$. As shown in Table 7.4, the participants low in skepticism showed the predicted pattern of results. These people, who told us they had relatively little resistance to political ads, were able to be critical of the first ad, leading to a moderate evaluation of the candidate ($M = 9.23$), but were not able to sustain this level of resistance through the series of seven ads, coming to like the same ad when it appeared in the last position ($M = 15.98$). However, giving them a rest period of 12 minutes where they looked at a travelogue uncritically allowed them to again become critical ($M = 3.06$). In contrast, when they were asked to continue being critical, by disparaging the travelogue, these low-skepticism participants were more positive about the final political ad ($M =$

TABLE 7.4
Effects of Repeated Exposure to Political Ads on BEAMs Evaluation of
Candidate

Condition	Low-skepticism participants	High-skepticism participants	All participants
First ad	9.23	14.00	11.61
Last ad	15.98	2.17	9.07
Last after acceptance	3.06	2.43	2.74
Last after criticism	12.25	5.22	8.74

12.25). These results are entirely consistent with the pattern expected from the idea that resistance is a quickly consumable but slowly replenishable resource.

The highly skeptical participants showed a very different pattern. Their most accepting evaluation was for the ad that came first ($M = 14.00$). Ads that came later, after these skeptical participants had evaluated six advertisements, were invariably given very low evaluations. The repeated experience of criticizing ads seemed only to warm participants up to their resistance. A lag of 12 minutes was not enough to dissipate it. These skeptical people seemed to have a much deeper resource of resistance to apply to these ads and to the travelogue film. Our tasks did not deplete it, as they did for less skeptical participants.

Invoking resistance in the hopes of consuming it may work for people who have little resistance or little practice at using their resistance. Offering the same opportunity to skeptical people, however, may prime the pump of a deep reservoir of resistance.

Use Resistance to Promote Change

Often, resistance is obstinate but not very discerning. When resistance is a prepotent and undiscriminating response, it can be used against itself. The vernacular calls this "reverse psychology," telling people not to do what you really want them to do.

Reverse Psychology. Paul Nail (2002; Nail, MacDonald, & Levy, 2000) gave this strategy the complex name "strategic self anti-conformity." This deceptive form of influence occurs when one says publicly the opposite of what one privately wants. The purpose of this deception is to get another person who is acting in a contrary way to do what one secretly wants.

A branch of psychotherapy called Strategic Therapy emphasizes these sorts of paradoxical interventions (Haley, 1973). Milton Erickson (Erickson, Rossi, & Rossi, 1967; Rosen, 1991; Zeig, 1982) discussed a number of resistance-based change techniques.

Erickson (Erickson & Rossi, 1975; Rosen, 1991) recounted his first well-remembered intentional use of reverse psychology from his early boyhood. He saw his father trying to lead a calf into the barn on their farm. The calf balked at the door, planted her feet, and refused to enter. Erickson laughed at the sight, which produced a challenge from his father for him to do better. Erickson accepted the challenge, went over to calf, grabbed her tail, and pulled as hard as he could away from the barn. The calf resisted and pulled Erickson through the barn door.

Reverse psychology is a dangerous strategy to adopt willy-nilly because you are pulling in the wrong direction, advocating against one's private interests. Targets of the influence attempt or onlookers could take one's actions at face value and act in accordance with your stated wishes, thereby thwarting your private desires. Reverse psychology, to be effective, requires that the persuader has (a) almost certain knowledge that the recipient will, in fact, resist any statement and (b) no compunction about lying or misrepresenting his or her private interests.

Paradoxical Interventions. Fortunately, there are a number of more straightforward, less deceptive ways to use resistance to promote change (Ghadban, 1995). The basic strategy is for the persuader (rather than the recipient) to specify a target for resistance. By specifying a useful target, or at least a benign target for the recipient's resistance, the persuader can constrain, control, and even use the resistance to promote change.

Rosen (1991) described one case where a 280-pound woman came to Erickson to lose weight. She described a list of previous attempts to reduce her weight in which she had struggled to reach a weight goal, only to relax upon reaching the goal and to relapse, gaining beyond her starting weight. Erickson asked her to commit to an unusual therapeutic course and to follow through with it no matter how bizarre it sounded. The patient agreed. Erickson's prescription was for the woman to gain weight until she tipped the scale at 300 pounds. The woman protested but complied. She and Erickson planned meals and snacks and watched her gain weight. She protested and complained but she continued until one day the scale in Erickson's office registered over 300 pounds. At that point, Erickson allowed her to relax her effort and relapse in the opposite direction, which she did, and well below her original weight. Apocryphal perhaps, but this story illustrates how resistance might be redirected. Erickson saw that in this person's conflict over weight, will power won the battle, but resistance won the war. He suspected that this dynamic was more powerful than the direction of the change, so he created a new and paradoxical goal that could be won in the short term by will power but lost in the long term by the more powerful resistance.

Watzlawick, Weakland, and Fisch (1988) made a distinction between first-order and second-order change. First-order change works within the parameters of an established system. Established systems are calibrated for equilibrium. Thus, when you are cold, put on a sweater. When you are lonely, seek friends. First-order changes work fine until they don't. When they no longer work, they become conundrums where the attempted solution becomes the problem, as in the case of the 280-pound woman who visited Erickson. The first-order change of dieting to lose weight did not work for her.

Watzlawick et al. say that cases where the intended solution has itself become a problem most likely require a second-order change, where the system is changed or replaced. Second-order influence often sounds paradoxical or bizarre at first hearing because its focus is on the nonworking solution, not on the original problem. Thus, the insomniac is advised to try to stay awake, the dieter is advised to stop trying to lose weight, and the anxious patient is advised to set aside an hour to concentrate on being anxious.

Paradoxical suggestions work when they provide a focus for a person's resistance. You may be able to think of other ways to provide a focus for a person's resistance. For instance, if you ask students to read an article for next week's class, you are implicitly structuring the acceptance (read the article) and the resistance (do not read the article) for them. But, if you ask students to read an article slowly and carefully, you have restructured the acceptance slightly (read the article slowly and carefully), but more importantly have restructured the resistance (read the article quickly). Students who are contrary or reactant to influence can now express these motivations in a more benign way, due to how the request is structured.

The structuring of resistance is subtle and important. If a real estate salesperson says to a couple, "This house may be more than you can afford," the potential buyers can only resist this statement by looking carefully at their finances, which will probably find some support for the agent's statement. But, if the real estate salesperson says, "This house may be more than you want," the buyers can resist immediately and strongly by looking at their desires. As any real estate agent knows, there may be many houses that are more than a client thinks she can afford, but there are few that are more than a client wants. The Omega strategy here is to recognize where the resistance lies, then to structure the request so that the resistance promotes, or at least is benign to, the change.

Acknowledging Resistance.   One of the ways to turn resistance against itself is to acknowledge it. Usually persuaders are reluctant to mention resistance, mistakenly believing that to identify it and label it is to give it power and credence. The approach–avoidance conflict theory of persuasion proposes that a persuasive message raises both an accepting consideration of the message and a counteractive resistance to that message. Although the message is overt, the resistance is to some extent covert, automatic, and hidden. However, if resistance is present, it is already powerful. Acknowledging the resistance, labeling it, and making its role overt may have the paradoxical effect of defusing its power and rendering that resistance less influential. We have conducted two studies to investigate whether acknowledging the resistance in a message would make the message more persuasive (Linn & Knowles, 2002b).

In the first study, we devised four short persuasive messages, simple assertions attributed to a source, such as "A professor of medicine said recently,

'Within 50 years, the average life expectancy will pass 100 years,' " followed by a measurement of how much participants agreed with the proposition. We had 234 undergraduates read these statements. Half the people read the statement as above, the other half read the same statement preceded by an acknowledgment of resistance, e.g., "You're not going to believe this, but . . ." The four statements advocated a long life expectancy, lunar effects on lunacy, psychokinesis, and higher tuition producing better education. As Table 7.5 shows, all four versions that acknowledged resistance had higher acceptance scores than the versions that did not. However, only the statement concerning tuition reached statistical significance by itself. Upon reflection, this pattern of results made sense: If the effect of acknowledgment was to reduce resistance, there had to be some degree of resistance there to begin with. Students, at least those in our lab, cared strongly only about the tuition they paid for their education. The other topics were unimportant to them.

We conducted a second study in an attempt to (a) replicate the acknowledgment effect for the tuition question, and (b) extend it to another issue about which our student participants cared deeply—the inadequacy of campus parking. We had 369 students read the two statements, one with the acknowledgment, the other without, and register their opinions about the issues. In both cases, the students in the control condition had a very negative opinion about the issue. The means for the parking question (3.34 on a 9-point scale) and for the tuition question (2.46 on a 9-point scale) indicated a great deal of resistance to these propositions. In both cases, including a simple acknowledgment of this resistance raised the attitude rating by at least half a point.

This acknowledgment-induced change in these opinions is interesting in several regards. First, these findings demonstrate attitude change without persuasion (Mark P. Zanna, personal communication, February 1, 2002). There was no persuasive attack or counterargument directed at the resistance. It was merely acknowledged. Second, the findings imply that mentioning resistance in a message does not empower it, but rather seems to diffuse it. We didn't convince anyone that they should pay more for their education, but including the acknowledgment did remove some of the resistance to this notion.

Choices. If a person is going to be resistant to a suggestion, one effective strategy may be to offer that person a choice between alternatives. If there is only one alternative, then acceptance and resistance are focused on that alternative, creating the approach–avoidance conflict. However, offering a person a choice between alternatives allows that person to separate the acceptance and the resistance and to apply them to different alternatives. The motivation to resist is satisfied in the rejected alternative at the same time that the approach motivation is satisfied in the accepted alternative. Thus, for children who are resistant to bedtime, the sensitive parent asks, "Do you want to brush your teeth first or do you want to put on your pajamas first?"

Erickson and Rossi (1975) described this general strategy as the alternative-choice double-bind. The child sees a choice and feels the efficacy of making a

TABLE 7.5

Paradoxical Acknowledgment

Statement	Control	(without brackets)	Paradox	(with brackets)	Sig of diff
Study 1	Mean	SD	Mean	SD	
Dr. Stubblefield, a university physicist, says, "Most people [don't think so, but they] have the ability to move objects through mental effort."	2.46	1.96	2.85	2.22	$t(232) = 1.41$ $p = .16$
The psychiatric nurse at Charter Vista Hospital says, "[It's really weird and sounds bizarre, but] when it is a full moon our psychiatric patients get crazier than at other times."	4.29	2.65	4.45	2.33	$t(232) = 0.48$ $p = .63$
A professor of medicine said recently, "[You're not going to believe this, but] within 50 years, the average life expectancy will pass 100 years."	5.31	2.37	5.60	2.39	$t(232) = .93$ $p = .35$
A Dean of Students at the university says, "[I know you will not want to agree with this, but] if students paid a little more tuition, they would get a much better education."	2.13	1.66	3.31	2.17	$t(232) = 4.57$ $p < .01$
Study 2					
A Dean of Students at the university says, "[I know you will not want to agree with this, but] if students paid a little more tuition, they would get a much better education.' "	2.46	1.61	3.31	2.10	$t(367) = 4.34$ $p < .01$
Dr. Stubblefield, a facilities planner for the university, says, "[I know you will not want to agree with this, but] parking at the University of Arkansas is easier and cheaper than at most universities."	3.34	1.60	3.84	1.93	$t(360) = 2.67$ $p < .01$

Note. Means = rating of agreement (1 = not at all ... 9 = very much) choice and gaining its rewards, but it is a double-bind in the sense that both alternatives bind the chooser to the same outcome, in this case going to bed. When a jeweler asks a patron whether she prefers sapphires or rubies, or a car salesman asks a customer if he is considering a red car or a silver car, choosing either alternative moves the shopper closer to a sale.

Cialdini (2001), Dillard (1991), and others have looked at choice as creating a commitment to an alternative. Commitment to the chosen alternative is part of the process. However, the alternative-choice double-bind also works by providing a separate target for the person's resistance. The customer's motivation to resist the car salesman or the child's motivation to resist bedtime is refocused on the rejected alternative. Resisting by rejecting one alternative provides a satisfaction, a sense of efficacy, a sense of being critical and discerning.

A number of Alpha strategies have this secondary characteristic of taking a person's resistance and refocusing it in a more benign way. For instance, the door-in-the-face technique includes an element of providing a focus for resistance. The large request is offered in the hopes that it will be rejected and thereby serve as a release for the target's resistance to influence.

Erickson and Rossi (1975) made a useful observation about double-binds and, more generally, about using resistance against itself. They reported Erickson as saying, "It took me a long time to realize that when the double bind was used for personal advantage it led to bad results. When the double bind was employed for the other person's benefit, however, there could be lasting benefit" (p. 144). Erickson and Rossi presumed that the effectiveness of these paradoxical techniques rests on a presumption of promotive collaboration, where the agent and the target are both working for mutual self-interest. When the encounter becomes implicitly defined as a win–lose or antagonistic situation, the target's resistance is uncontrollable and attempts to manipulate it are ineffective or counterproductive.

CONCLUSION

The simplest of models can have rich lessons. In this chapter we have explored the approach–avoidance conflict model of attitudes for implications about attitude change and persuasion. The first implication is that offers, messages, advertisements, commands, requests, or other opportunities for compliance, persuasion, or attitude change are psychologically complex events, engaging multiple and usually conflicting motives. A request affords both opportunities and dangers (Higgins, 1999, 2001; Forster, Grant, Idson, & Higgins, 2001). The recipient of the request is motivated to approach the opportunities, but to avoid the hazards.

A second implication of the approach–avoidance conflict model is that the resulting behavior depends on which motivational direction is strongest. If the desire to approach the opportunities is stronger than the desire to avoid the hazards, then the behavior will be selected, persuasion or attitude change will occur. But the selection will be conflicted, the behavior will be adopted with some trepidation, because the avoidance forces are still present. If the avoidance forces outweigh the approach forces, then the behavior will be refused, but with some regret because approach forces are still present.

A third implication of the approach–avoidance conflict model is that there are two different ways to promote change. One way is to increase the approach motivation. We call these the Alpha strategies because they are usually the first type considered. Certainly they are the type that the persuasion field has studied the most. The second way to promote change is to decrease the avoidance motivation. We call these the Omega strategies because their focus is on reducing resistance. Omega was selected both because it is the symbol for resistance and because it implies that these strategies are more subtle, among the last considered.

The Alpha strategies for persuasion are well known and form the mainstay of most discussions of persuasion (Cialdini, 2001; Perloff, 2002). The Alpha strategies involve making the offer more attractive through reasoning, more credible sources, or added incentives. The added incentives can be direct, as in the case of bonuses or price reductions, but they can also be indirect, as in the case of implying scarcity, emphasizing prior commitment, or invoking reciprocal obligations.

This chapter has concentrated on the Omega strategies for persuasion and change. We introduced the term *Omega strategies* to describe persuasion strategies that work primarily by addressing a person's resistance. We found a number of Omega strategies in a variety of places that have not previously been recognized, organized, or compared. Some of the Omega strategies were quite direct, such as counterarguing the reasons to resist or providing guarantees against undesirable outcomes. Others were indirect, such as bolstering a person's self-esteem, or disrupting resistance. Others were counterintuitive, such as acknowledging resistance. This chapter has identified seven types of Omega strategies.

Type 1 Omega strategies are sidestepping strategies that work by avoiding or minimizing resistance. There is a variety of strategies of this kind, including redefining the relationship or interaction away from a persuasion interaction to something more benign or collaborative, depersonalizing the interaction so that consequences of compliance would seem to be lessened, minimizing the request so that there is apparently less to react against, raising the comparison so that an offer is compared to something more onerous or costly, and, finally, pushing the choice into the future where higher-level advantages and opportunities become more salient and the lower-level hassles and inconveniences recede in importance. We suspect that we have not exhausted all the ways that resistance may be minimized. Other versions of the sidestepping strategies remain to be discovered and described.

Type 2 Omega strategies address resistance directly. These are the strategies that attempt to identify the nature of the resistance and then intervene to change that resistance. We described two such strategies. The first is counterarguing the resistance, that is, using a message that provides reasons for not being resistant. The second version is the guarantee, where the sources of resistance are eliminated by contract.

Type 3 Omega strategies address resistance indirectly, by taking away the need to be resistant. We found two clear examples, both represented by chapters in this book. One strategy was to raise self-esteem through self-affirmation (Jacks & O'Brien, this volume). The other was to provide training in appropriate resistance to illegitimate persuasion (Sagarin & Cialdini, this volume). Both strategies appear to reduce general wariness, especially to reasonable and appropriate persuasive messages.

Type 4 Omega strategies distract the recipient while they are receiving a message. This technique has been much studied in social psychology because of its theoretical implications (Petty & Cacioppo, 1986). Distractions are disturbances that interfere with thinking about a message, but are not so strong that they interfere with encoding the message. As Petty et al. (1976) noted, distraction interferes with all thinking, and so makes a message more persuasive if that message produces negative and resistant thoughts; but it also can make a message less persuasive if that message engenders positive and supportive thoughts.

Type 5 Omega strategies involve small disruptions in the message, disruptions that bring attention back to the message. These seem to work in different ways than distraction. We suspect they work by disrupting a script-based, mindless processing of the message, and orienting attention again to the message.

Type 6 Omega strategies attempt to consume resistance, that is, to reduce resistance by using it up. Repeated requests, messages, or activities that call upon one's ego resources can deplete those resources (Baumeister et al., 1998; Muraven & Baumeister, 2000). Our research found this to be the case for people who were not habitually skeptical, but we also found that skeptical people seemed to have more of a resource that was harder to use up.

Type 7 Omega strategies are the paradoxical strategies that seem to turn resistance against itself. We discussed reverse psychology, paradoxical interventions, acknowledging resistance, and providing choices as examples of this Omega strategy. What binds these disparate examples together is that they each accept a person's resistance and attempt to redirect it, rather than to minimize, counter, or interfere with it.

We suspect that this discussion of Omega strategies has expanded the kit of persuasion tools for most readers. These seven Omega strategies expand our understanding of persuasion by focusing on the resistance side of the persuasion equation. These are strategies that work, not by increasing the motivation, reason, or incentives to engage in a behavior, but by decreasing the motivation, reasons, or incentives not to engage in that behavior. We hope that this chapter will introduce this perspective to the persuasion literature and to you as a researcher, practitioner, and consumer of persuasion. Is the task complete? Certainly not! In this chapter, we introduced this perspective, initiating the search for and definition of Omega strategies for persuasion. The journey begins, not ends with this chapter. We fully expect that researchers will find an eighth or ninth strategy, will separate strategies we have combined, or will combine strategies that we have separated.

The serpent said to Eve, "You will not die!", choosing an Omega strategy to persuade her rather than an Alpha strategy. The distinction between Alpha and Omega strategies raises many important questions. For instance, when would an Alpha strategy be more productive and when would an Omega strategy be more compelling? Also, would the two strategies complement each other, leading to a more powerful persuasion attempt, or would they interfere with each other, making the combination less effective than either alone? There are many interesting and unanswered questions about the choice between Alpha and Omega strategies to persuasion. We have tried in this chapter to define the Omega approach to persuasion and to open the door to questions such as these. We hope that you find the Omega approach a useful addition to the persuasion literature, one that adds insight to the persuasion process, one that provides a clearer rationale for a new class of persuasion techniques, and one that opens the door to new issues for research.

AUTHOR NOTE

Preparation of this chapter and much of the research reported was supported by a National Science Foundation Grant, BCS-0091867, to the first author. The authors, not the National Science Foundation, are responsible for the opinions and conclusions reported here.

REFERENCES

Alessandra, A. J. (1993). *Collaborative selling: How to gain the competitive advantage in sales.* New York: Wiley.

Aronson, E., Willerman, B., & Floyd, J. (1966). The effect of a pratfall on increasing interpersonal attractiveness. *Psychonomic Science, 4,* 227–228.

Baumeister, R. F., Bratslavsky, E., Muraven, M., & Tice, D. M. (1998). Ego depletion: Is the active self a limited resource? *Journal of Personality and Social Psychology, 74,* 1252–1265.

Baumeister, R. F., Muraven, M., & Tice, D. M. (2000). Ego depletion: A resource model of volition, self-regulation, and controlled processing. *Social Cognition, 18,* 130–150.

Block, L. G., & Keller, P. A. (1997). Effects of self-efficacy and vividness on the persuasiveness of health communication. *Journal of Consumer Psychology, 6,* 31–54.

Brewer, M. B., (1991). The social self: On being the same and different at the same time. *Personality and Social Psychology Bulletin, 17,* 475–482.

Brockner, J., Guzzi, B., Kane, J., Levine, E., & Shaplen, K. (1984). Organizational fundraising: Further evidence on the effect of legitimizing small donations. *Journal of Consumer Research, 11,* 611–614.

Burger, J. M. (1986). Increasing compliance by improving the deal: The that's-not-all technique. *Journal of Personality and Social Psychology, 51,* 277–283.

Byrne, D. (1971). *The attraction paradigm.* New York: Academic Press.

Cacioppo, J. T., Gardner, W. L., & Bernston, G. G. (1997). Beyond bipolar conceptualizations and measures: The case of attitudes and evaluative space. *Personality and Social Psychology Review, 1,* 3–25.

Chaiken, S. (1979). Communicator physical attractiveness and persuasion. *Journal of Personality and Social Psychology, 37,* 1387–1397.

Cialdini, R. B. (2001). *Influence: Science and practice* (4th ed.). Boston: Allyn and Bacon.

Cialdini, R. B., Cacioppo, J. T., Bassett, R., & Miller, J. A. (1978). Low-ball procedure for produing compliance: Commitment then cost. *Journal of Personality and Social Psychology, 36,* 463–476.

Cialdini, R. B., & Schroeder, D. (1976). Increasing compliance by legitimizing paltry contributions: When even a penny helps. *Journal of Personality and Social Psychology, 34,* 599–604.

Cialdini, R. B., Vincent, J. E., Lewis, S. K., Catalan, J., Wheeler, D., & Darby, B. L. (1975). Reciprocal concessions procedure for inducing compliance: The door-in-the-face technique. *Journal of Personality and Social Psychology, 31,* 206–215.

Clark, M. S., Mills, J., & Corcoran, D. M. (1989). Keeping track of needs and inputs of friends and strangers. *Personality and Social Psychology Bulletin, 15,* 533–542.

Davis, B. P., & Knowles, E. S. (1999). A disrupt-then-reframe technique of social influence. *Journal of Personality and Social Psychology, 76,* 192–199.

Dillard, J. P. (1991). The current status of research on sequential-request compliance techniques. *Personality and Social Psychology Bulletin, 17,* 283–288.

Dolinski, D., Nawrat, M., & Rudak, I. (2001). Dialogue involvement as a social influence technique. *Personality and Social Psychology Bulletin, 27,* 1395–1406.

Dollard, J., & Miller, N. E. (1950). *Personality and psychotherapy.* New York: McGraw-Hill.

Duncan, C. P., & Nelson, J. E. (1985). Effects of humor in a radio advertising experiment. *Journal of Advertising, 14,* 33–40.

Erickson, M. H. (1964). The confusion technique in hypnosis. *American Journal of Clinical Hypnosis, 6,* 183–207.

Erickson, M. H., & Rossi, E. L. (1975). Varieties of double bind. *American Journal of Clinical Hypnosis, 17,* 143–157.

Erickson, M. H., Rossi, E. L., & Rossi, S. (1976). *Hypnotic realities: The induction of clinical hypnosis and forms of indirect suggestion.* New York: Irvington.

Faison, E. W. J. (1961). Effectiveness of one-sided and two-sided mass communications in advertising. *Public Opinion Quarterly, 25,* 468–469.

Festinger, L. (1957). *A theory of cognitive dissonance.* Evanston, IL: Row, Peterson.

Festinger, L., & Maccoby, N. (1964). On resistance to persuasive communications. *Journal of Abnormal and Social Psychology, 68,* 359–366.

Forster, J., Grant, H., Idson, L. C., & Higgins, E. T. (2001) Success/failure feedback, expectancies, and approach/avoidance motivation: How regulatory focus moderates classic relations. *Journal of Experimental Social Psychology, 37,* 253–260.

Freedman, J. L., & Fraser, S. C. (1966). Compliance without pressure: The foot-in-the-door technique. *Journal of Personality and Social Psychology, 4,* 195–202.

Frey, K. P., & Eagly, A. H. (1993). Vividness can undermine the persuasiveness of messages. *Journal of Personality and Social Psychology, 65,* 32–44.

Ghadban, H. (1995). Paradoxical intentions. In M. Ballou (Ed.), *Psychological interventions: A guide to strategies* (pp. 1–19). Westport, CT: Preager.

Gilbert, D. T. (1991). How mental systems believe. *American Psychologist, 46,* 107–119.

Gilligan, S. G. (1987). *Therapeutic trances: The cooperation principle in Ericksonian hypnotherapy.* New York: Brunner/Mazel.

Gouldner, A. W. (1960). The norm of reciprocity: A preliminary statement. *American Sociological Review, 25,* 161–178.

Green, M. C., & Brock, T. C. (2002). In the mind's eye: Transportation-imagery model of narrative persuasion. In M. C. Green, J. J. Strange, & T. C. Brock (Eds.), *Narrative impact: Social and cognitive foundations* (pp. 315–341). Mahwah, NJ: Erlbaum.

Greenwald, A. G., Carnot, C. G., Beach, R., & Young, B. (1987). Increasing voting behavior by asking people if they expect to vote. *Journal of Applied Psychology, 72,* 315–318.

Gregory, W. L., Cialdini, R. B., & Carpenter, K. M. (1982). Self-relevant scenarios as mediators of likelihood estimates and compliance: Does imagining make it so? *Journal of Personality and Social Psychology, 43,* 89–99.

Grice, H. P. (1975). Logic and conversation. In P. Cole & J. L. Morgan (Eds.), *Syntax and semantics: Vol. 3. Speech acts* (pp. 41–58). New York: Seminar Press.

Haaland, G., & Venkatesan, M. (1968). Resistance of persuasive communications: An examination of the distraction hypotheses. *Journal of Personality and Social Psychology, 9,* 167–170.

Haley, J. (1973). *Uncommon therapy: The psychiatric techniques of Milton H. Erickson, M.D.* New York: Norton.

Haugtvedt, C. P., Schumann, D. W., Schneier, W. L., & Warren, W. L. (1994). Advertising repetition and variation strategies: Implications for understanding attitude strength. *Journal of Consumer Research, 21,* 176–189.

Higgins, E. T. (1999). Promotion and prevention as a motivational duality: Implications for evaluative processes. In S. Chaiken & Y. Trope (Eds.), *Dual-process theories in social psychology* (pp. 503–525). New York: Guilford.

Higgins, E. T. (2001). Promotion and prevention experiences: Relating emotions to nonemotional motivational states. In J. P. Forgas (Ed.), *Handbook of affect and social cognition* (pp. 186–211). Mahwah, NJ: Erlbaum.

Hovland, C. I., Lumsdaine, A. A., & Sheffield, F. D. (1949). *Experiments in mass communication* (pp. 201–227). Princeton, NJ: Princeton University Press.

Hovland, C. I., & Weiss, W. (1951). The influence of source credibility on communication effectiveness. *Public Opinion Quarterly, 15,* 635–650.

Insko, C. A. (1962). One-sided versus two-sided communications and counter-communications. *Journal of Abnormal and Social Psychology, 65,* 203–206.

Jolson, M. A. (1997). Broadening the scope of relationship selling. *Journal of Personal Selling and Sales Management, 17,* 75–88.

Knowles, E. S. (1980). An affiliative conflict theory of personal and group spatial behavior. In P. B. Paulus (Ed.), *The psychology of group influence* (pp. 133–188). Hillsdale, NJ: Erlbaum.

Knowles, E. S. (1989). Spatial behavior of individuals and groups. In P. B. Paulus (Ed.), *The psychology of group influence* (2nd ed., pp. 53–86). Hillsdale, NJ: Erlbaum.

Knowles, E. S., Brennan, M., & Linn, J. A. (2002). *Consuming resistance to political ads.* Manuscript in preparation. University of Arkansas, Fayetteville, AR.

Knowles, E. S. Butler, S., & Linn, J. A. (2001). Increasing compliance by reducing resistance. In J. P. Forgas & K. D. Williams (Eds.), *Social influence: Direct and indirect processes* (pp. 41–60). Philadelphia: Psychology Press.

Langer, E. J. (1989). *Mindfulness.* Reading, MA: Addison-Wesley.

Lewin, K. (1947). Frontiers in group dynamics: Concept, method and reality in social science; Social equilibria and change. *Human Relations, 1,* 5–42.

Lewin, K. (1951). Frontiers in group dynamics. In D. Cartwright (Ed.), *Field theory in social science: Selected theoretical papers by Kurt Lewin* (pp. 188–237). New York: Harper.

Lewin, K. (1958). Group decision and social change. In G. E. Swanson, T. M. Newcomb, & E. L. Hartley (Eds.), *Readings in social psychology, rev. ed* (pp. 459–473). New York: Holt.

Liberman, N., & Trope, Y. (1998). The role of feasibility and desirability considerations in near and distant future decisions: A test of temporal construal theory. *Journal of Personality and Social Psychology, 75,* 5–18.

Linn, J. A., & Knowles, E. S. (2002a). *The effect of a small disruption on attention.* Unpublished manuscript, University of Arkansas.

Linn, J. A., & Knowles, E. S. (2002b, May). *Acknowledging target resistance in persuasive messages.* Paper presented at the Midwestern Psychological Association Convention, Chicago.

Lumsdaine, A. A., & Janis, I. L. (1953). Resistance to "counterpropaganda" produced by one-sided and two-sided "propaganda" presentations. *Public Opinion Quarterly, 17,* 311–318.

Maddux, J. E., & Rogers, R. W. (1983). Protection motivation and self-efficacy: A revised theory of fear appeals and attitude change. *Journal of Experimental Social Psychology, 19,* 469–479.

Milgram, S. (1965). Some conditions of obedience and disobedience to authority. *Human Relations, 18,* 57–76.

Miller, N. E. (1944). Experimental studies in conflict. In J. McV. Hunt (Ed.), *Personality and the behavior disorders* (Vol. 1). New York: Ronald.

Miller, N. E. (1959). Liberalization of basic S-R concepts: Extensions of conflict behavior, motivation, and social learning. In S. Koch (Ed.), *Psychology: A study of a science* (Vol. 2, pp. 196–292). New York: McGraw-Hill.

Mills, J., & Clark, M. S. (1994). Communal and exchange relationships: Controversies and research. In R. Erber & R. Gilmour (Eds.), *Theoretical frameworks for personal relationships* (pp. 29–42). Hillsdale, NJ: Erlbaum.

Moine, D. J., & Lloyd, K. L. (1990). *Unlimited selling power: How to master hypnotic selling skills*. New York: Prentice Hall.

Mussweiler, T. (2000). Overcoming the inevitable anchoring effect: Considering the opposite compensates for selective accessibility. *Personality and Social Psychology Bulletin, 26,* 1142–1150.

Mussweiler, T. (2002). The malleability of anchoring effects. *Experimental Psychology, 49,* 67–72.

Muraven, M. R., & Baumeister, R. F. (2000). Self-regulation and depletion of limited resources: Does self-control resemble a muscle? *Psychological Bulletin, 126,* 247–259.

Muraven, M., Tice, D. M., & Baumeister, R. F. (1998). Self-control as limited resource: Regulatory depletion patterns. *Journal of Personality and Social Psychology, 74,* 774–789.

Nail, P. R. (2002). *Proposal of a double diamond model of social response.* Unpublished manuscript. Southwestern Oklahoma State University.

Nail, P. R., MacDonald, G., & Levy, D. (2000). Proposal of a four-dimensional model of social response. *Psychological Bulletin, 126,* 454–470.

Nowak, A., & Vallacher, R. R. (1998). *Dynamical social psychology* (Ch. 7, Dynamics of social influence, pp. 217–249). New York: Guilford.

O'Keefe, D. J. (1999). Three reasons for doubting the adequacy of the reciprocal-concessions explanation of door-in-the-face effects. *Communication Studies, 50,* 211–220.

O'Keefe, D. J. (2002). *Persuasion: Theory and research.* Thousand Oaks, CA: Sage.

Perloff, R. M. (2003). *The dynamics of persuasion.* Mahwah, NJ: Erlbaum.

Petty, R. E., & Brock, T. C. (1981). Thought disruption and persuasion: Assessing the validity of attitude change experiments. In R. E. Petty, T. M. Ostrom, & T. C. Brock (Eds.), *Cognitive responses in persuasion* (pp. 55–79). Hillsdale, NJ: Erlbaum.

Petty, R. E., & Cacioppo, J. T. (1986). *Communication and persuasion: Central and peripheral routes to attitude change.* New York: Springer-Verlag.

Petty, R. E., Wells, G. L., & Brock, T. C. (1976). Distraction can enhance or reduce yielding to propaganda: Thought disruption versus effort justification. *Journal of Personality and Social Psychology, 34,* 874–884.

Pollock, C. L., Smith, S. D., Knowles, E. S., & Bruce, H. J. (1998). Mindfulness limits compliance with the That's-not-all technique. *Personality and Social Psychology Bulletin, 24,* 1153–1157.

Pratkanis, A. R. (2000). Altercasting as an influence tactic. In D. J. Terry & M. A. Hogg (Eds.), *Attitudes, behavior, and social context: The role of norms and group membership* (pp. 201–226). Mahwah, NJ: Erlbaum.

Pratkanis, A. R., & Aronson, E. (2001). *Age of propaganda: Everyday use and abuse of persuasion* (Rev. ed.). New York: W. H. Freeman & Co.

Regan, D. T. (1971). Effects of a favor and liking on compliance. *Journal of Experimental Social Psychology, 7,* 627–639.

Reingen, P. H. (1978). On inducing compliance with requests. *Journal of Consumer Research, 5,* 96–102.

Rogers, R. W. (1983). Cognitive and physiological processes in fear appeals and attitude change: A revised theory of protection motivation. In J. T. Cacioppo & R. E. Petty (Eds.), *Social psychophysiology: A sourcebook* (pp. 153–176). New York: Guilford.

Rosen, S. (1991). *My voice will go with you: The teaching tales of Milton H. Erickson, M.D.* New York: Norton.

Sagristano, M. D., Trope, Y., & Liberman, N. (2002). Time-dependent gambling: Odds now, money later. *Journal of Experimental Psychology: General, 131,* 364–376.

Santos, M. D., Leve, C., & Pratkanis, A. R. (1994). Hey buddy, can you spare seventeen cents? Mindful persuasion and the pique technique. *Journal of Applied Social Psychology, 24,* 755–764.

Schumann, D. W., Petty, R. E., & Clemons, D. S. (1990). Predicting the effectiveness of different strategies of advertising variation: A test of the repetition-variation hypothesis. *Journal of Consumer Research, 17,* 192–202.

Shavitt, S., Swan, S., Lowery, T. M., & Wanke, M. (1994). The interaction of endorser attractiveness and involvement in persuasion depends on the goal that guides message processing. *Journal of Consumer Psychology, 3,* 137–162.

Sherif, M., & Sherif, C. W. (1956). *An outline of social psychology.* New York: Harper & Brothers.

Sherman, S. (1988). Ericksonian psychotherapy and social psychology. In J. K. Zeig & S. R. Lankton (Eds.), *Developing Ericksonian psychotherapy* (pp. 59–90). New York: Brunner/Mazel.

Smith, S. M., Haugtvedt, C. P., & Petty, R. E. (1994). Attitudes and recycling: Does the measurement of affect enhance behavioral prediction? *Psychology and Marketing, 11,* 359–374.

Snyder, C. R., & Fromkin, H. (1980). *Uniqueness: The human pursuit of difference.* New York: Plenum.

Straight, D. K. (1996). How to benefit by straight shooter selling. *American Salesman, 41,* 10–15.

Strange, J. J. (2002). How fictional tales wag real-world beliefs: Models and mechanisms of narrative influence. In M. C. Green, J. J. Strange, & T. C. Brock (Eds.), *Narrative impact: Social and cognitive foundations* (pp. 263–286). Mahwah, NJ: Erlbaum.

Vallacher, R. R., & Wegner, D. M. (1985). *A theory of action identification.* Hillsdale, NJ: Earlbaum.

Vallacher, R. R., & Wegner, D. M. (1987). What do people think they're doing? Action identification and human behavior. *Psychological Review, 94,* 2–15.

Walton, S. (1992). *Sam Walton: Made in America.* New York: Bantam.

Watzlawick, P. (1987). If you desire to see, learn how to act. In J. Zeig (Ed.), *The Evolution of Psychotherapy* (pp. 91–100). New York: Brunner/Mazel.

Watzlawick, P., Weakland, J. H., & Fisch, R. (1988). *Change: Principles of problem formation and problem resolution.* New York: Norton.

Weyant, J. M., & Smith, S. L. (1987). Getting more by asking for less: The effects of request size on donation of charity. *Journal of Applied Social Psychology, 17,* 392–400.

Wheeler, L. (1966). Toward a theory of behavioral contagion. *Psychological Review, 73,* 179–192.

Wilson, S. R. (2002). *Seeking and resisting compliance: Why people say what they do when trying to influence others.* Thousand Oaks, CA: Sage

Zeig, J. K. (1982). *Ericksonian approaches to hypnosis and psychotherapy.* New York: Brunner/ Mazel.

8

Looking Ahead as a Technique to Reduce Resistance to Persuasive Attempts

Steven J. Sherman
Indiana University—Bloomington

Matthew T. Crawford
University of Bristol, England

Allen R. McConnell
Miami University, Oxford, Ohio

Social influence always involves resistance on the part of the target of influence. Regardless of the pressures toward acceptance of the influence, there is always a countervailing force in the form of resistance that reduces the likelihood of persuasion being effective. Successful influence, then, will be achieved only when the forces toward acceptance are greater than the forces stemming from resistance. As Knowles and Linn (this volume) so aptly point out, bringing about a situation where the forces toward acceptance are greater than the forces toward resistance can be achieved either by increasing the positive forces for persuasion or by decreasing the resistance that prevents persuasion.

Like other chapters in this book, we will focus on techniques to increase persuasion by decreasing resistance. A variety of techniques are discussed in this book that vary in their nature (e.g., cognitive versus affective) and in their subtlety (e.g., direct versus indirect). These techniques include interrupting resistance (Knowles & Linn, chapter 1 of this volume), using resistance paradoxically against itself (Knowles & Linn), persuasive message factors (Briñol, Rucker, Tormala, & Petty, this volume; Tormala & Petty, this volume; Wegener, Petty, Smoak, & Fabrigar, this volume), affect induction (Feugen & Brehm, this volume), forewarning (Quinn & Wood, this volume), self-affirmation (Jacks & O'Brien, this volume), positive thinking (Johnson, Smith-McLallen, Killeya, & Levin, this volume) and threats to self-image (Sagarin & Cialdini, this volume). We focus on a different technique—contemplation of the future as people make decisions in the present. We shall demonstrate that thinking about possibilities in the future can serve as a powerful force to overcome resistance to persuasion. The goal of this chapter is to demonstrate that future focus can be an effective technique for reducing resistance to persuasion, and to begin to uncover the affective, cognitive, and motivational reasons that underlie successful persuasion. Following a discussion of counterfactual generation, we shall consider prefactual thinking, especially anticipated regret, and its possible role in increasing and decreasing resistance to change. Then, we will broaden the focus to consider how techniques that involve thinking about the future can generally reduce resistance to social influence.

LAYING THE FOUNDATION: COUNTERFACTUAL THINKING

The initial ideas for this chapter have their roots in earlier work that we and others have done in the area of counterfactual thinking. Following the seminal paper by Kahneman and Miller (1986), which described the development of counterfactual comparison standards, there was a virtual explosion of research into when, why, and with what effects people generate alternatives to reality (see Roese & Olson, 1995). This research identified the antecedent conditions for counterfactual thinking, the mutations of reality that are most likely, the emotional consequences of counterfactual thinking, and the functions of counterfactual generations (Markman, Gavanski, Sherman, & McMullen, 1993, 1995; Roese, 1994).

While most of this work focused on counterfactuals for negative outcomes that had already occurred in the past ("What might have been, if only—"), some folks were beginning to investigate the interesting possibility that people might anticipate future regret by imagining their future actions, the possible negative outcomes of those actions, and counterfactual thoughts that would follow these future negative outcomes (Gleicher, Boninger, Strathman, Armor, Hetts, & Ahn, 1995; McConnell et al., 2000; Miller & Taylor, 1995). Engaging in prefactual thinking and anticipating future regret for various choices and outcomes would affect decision strategies because people would be motivated to reduce the likelihood and the amount of future regret.

Several studies seem to indicate that people indeed anticipate future regret under certain circumstances and that such prefactual thinking affects choices. For example, Boninger, Gleicher, and Strathman (1994) asked participants to think about either the consequences of using the insurance option in a game and finding out that it was unnecessary versus not using the insurance option in the game and finding that it *was* necessary. The specific prefactual that participants generated very much affected their insurance purchase decision in the direction that would reduce the regret elicited by that prefactual. Similar results were reported by Taylor (1989) and by Simonson (1992).

Regret theory (Bell, 1982; Loomes & Sugden, 1982) explicitly outlined the role of prefactual thinking in decision making. These theorists argued that anticipation of different amounts of regret for choices that might turn out badly is an important part of the choice process itself. In addition to assessing the absolute level of pleasure or pain associated with an outcome, people are also concerned with minimizing future regret for their choices. Recent studies have focused on this process of regret aversion. Zeelenberg, Beattie, Van der Pligt, and de Vries (1996) found that people prefer gambling choices where the outcomes of alternative gambles will never be learned. This avoids any possibility of future regret. Larrick and Boles (1995) and Ritov (1996) have also demonstrated that the anticipation of regret and the motivation to minimize future regret can explain choices when the future is uncertain (see also Bar-Hillel & Neter, 1996; Tykocinski & Pittman, 1998).

Based on this diverse research, it is clear that anticipated regret can very much affect the decisions that people make in the present. The principle that is operating is a relatively simple one: By anticipating future feelings, people can act in the present so as to minimize their future regret. We wondered whether this seemingly powerful tendency could possibly explain one of the most fascinating phenomena identified by social psychologists, the tendency to react against the suggestions and demands of others such that when others "push" one alternative, it can actually increase the likelihood of choosing other alternatives. This phenomenon, cognitive reactance, has been shown to be a strong and robust reaction to social influence pressure (Brehm, 1966).

ANTICIPATED REGRET AND COGNITIVE REACTANCE

Imagine a situation where an individual can choose between Alternative A and Alternative B. Someone tells this individual that she should really choose Alternative A. This has the paradoxical effect of increasing the likelihood (compared to the base-rate) that the individual will choose Alternative B. Brehm (1966) explained cognitive reactance in terms of a motivation to reinstate freedom of choice. Whenever one's freedom to do something is threatened or eliminated, one will act so as to reinstate that freedom. Telling people to choose Alternative A threatens their freedom to choose Alternative B, and the best way to reestablish this freedom is to actually choose Alternative B.

This reinstatement of freedom explanation has remained pretty much intact over the years as the explanation for cognitive reactance. In light of the recent work on anticipated regret, we wondered whether there might be a feasible alternative explanation. We proposed that reactance findings might be reconceptualized in terms of the anticipation of the amounts of future regret for compliance versus reactance. That is, the choice to go against the dictates of another may be due, in part, to the amount of future possible regret that is anticipated for negative consequences after choosing either the "forbidden" or the "promoted" alternative. In that individuals reliably go against the demands of the other, it seemed possible that they anticipate greater regret if negative outcomes follow compliance with the dictates of another than if the same negative outcomes follow defiance against the dictates. To minimize future regret, individuals will exhibit reactive behavior rather than compliance.

We examined our anticipated regret possibility as a way to understand why and the conditions under which people would show resistance to the dictates of another person. We were particularly interested in two issues. First, do people *spontaneously* anticipate regret when making decisions? In all the studies of anticipated regret cited above, either participants were directly instructed to anticipate future regret or conditions were established that made it very likely that people would focus on future outcomes and feelings. Second, by focusing specifically on interpersonal persuasion situations where people are "pushed" to make a particular choice, situations that typically arouse cognitive reactance, we could determine whether anticipated regret was a factor in reactant behaviors.

EMPIRICAL INVESTIGATIONS

As a first step, it was important to investigate perceptions of post-decision regret experienced by people who did or did not follow the dictates of another and experienced a negative outcome. To examine this, participants were asked to read scenarios that featured two individuals who were each debating between purchasing one of two stocks (Kahneman & Miller, 1986). Both protagonists received advice from one of three types of sources: a stranger, a friend, or a stockbroker. One of the individuals in the scenario (Mr. Paul) followed the advice, whereas the other (Mr. George) reacted against the advice. Both individuals learned that had they chosen the other stock, they would have been better off by $1200. If compliance followed by a negative outcome is seen as leading to more regret than reactance followed by the same negative outcome, we should find that the compliant actor (Mr. Paul) would have more regret attributed to him than would the reactive actor (Mr. George).

In addition, the different experimental conditions examined whether the source of the directive was important in affecting the amount of regret that one is seen as feeling for either complying with, or reacting against, another's edict. In the majority of the research on reactance involving social threats, the threatening agent is a stranger. We were interested in examining regret as a response to the directives of a high-expertise source (stockbroker), a well-liked source (friend), and a neutral target (a stranger). People should expect greater regret following an undesirable outcome if one complies with a stranger instead of complying with an expert or a liked other. That is, the salience of the "if only

TABLE 8.1
Amount of Regret Attributed to Compliant and Reactive Scenario Actors

| | Which actor feels more regret? | |
	Compliant	*Reactive*
Dichotomous judgment of regret		
Stockbroker	14%	86%
Friend	26%	74%
Stranger	42%	58%
Continuous ratings of regret		
Stockbroker	5.16	7.19
Friend	5.85	7.04
Stranger	6.04	6.65

I hadn't listened to that person . . ." counterfactual would be stronger for a stranger than for a target who is greater in expertise or likability, producing greater regret in the former case relative to the latter two cases. It is probably quite unusual for one to follow the stock advice of a complete stranger (compared to a friend or a stockbroker), and counterfactual thinking is more likely to follow from atypical events (Kahneman & Miller, 1986; Wells & Gavanski, 1989). Judgments of regret for protagonists who reacted against the other target should be greater for the high-expertise target (i.e., someone who should know what they are doing) than for the other two targets. That is, it is easier to kick oneself for not going along with the advice of an expert. Such an effect is in part due to the fact that going against the advice of an expert is a choice that increases the a priori probability of a negative outcome.

Contrary to our initial expectations that compliance leads to a greater attribution of regret than reactance (thus providing an alternative explanation for reactance effects), the actor who resisted the persuasive attempt (i.e., reactive behavior) was perceived as feeling more retrospective regret than the actor who complied. That is, it is *not* the case that observers feel that compliance will lead to greater potential regret than will reactance. These results suggest that reactance is not a strategy to minimize future regret in persuasion situations. As can be seen in Table 8.1, the predictions for target type were confirmed—greater regret for complying with a stranger than for complying with an expert or a friend, and greater regret for reacting against an expert than against a friend or a stranger. This pattern of results was replicated in a number of other scenario-style studies that varied in domain (e.g., gambles, lotteries), level of threat, and protagonist (e.g., third party versus self). Across these various studies, resistance to the persuasive message—in the form of reactive behavior—was perceived as resulting in greater retrospective regret than was compliant behavior (Crawford, Lewis, McConnell, & Sherman, 1998).

Although these findings may seem at odds with the fact that reactance is often observed in persuasion situations (Brehm & Sensenig, 1966; Heller, Pallak, & Picek, 1973; Snyder & Wicklund, 1976; Worchel & Brehm, 1971) and at odds with our prediction of reactance as a response to anticipated regret, they are not necessarily incompatible. To our knowledge, no research on reactance in choice situations has involved an examination of post-outcome perceptions of regret. In the scenario studies, we assessed participants' judgments about how people would feel *after* the negative outcomes were known. The reactance literature, as well as our account of reactance, involves the influences on people's behavioral choices *before* the outcomes are known. Earlier in the development of our reasoning, we argued that what would drive reactant behavior would be a predecision anticipation of regret. That is, in anticipation, future feelings of regret for negative outcomes after following someone else's directives would be perceived as greater than these feelings of regret for negative outcomes after reacting against them. This involves the anticipation of future regret rather than the perception of regret after the fact.

It may be that predictions of future regret do not match the post-outcome inferences made by observers in the scenario studies. Moreover, it may even be the case that predictions or postdictions of regret do not match actual regret that is experienced by compliant and reactant people. Indeed, there is research consistent with this possibility, including work by Gilbert, Pinel, Wilson, Blumberg, and Wheatley (1998) on errors in affective forecasting. In their work, they found that people misanticipate the extent to which they will feel negative emotions following events such as experiencing a romantic break-up, having a preferred gubernatorial candidate lose the election, or assessing blame when reading a vignette about a child's death. Thus, Gilbert et al. (1998) found that people's expectations about how they will feel if certain events occur may not correspond to how they actually feel after those events transpire. Gilovich and Medvec (1995) also reported that the things that people eventually regret most are not necessarily the things for which they anticipated the most regret.

These studies raise the intriguing possibility that people may misanticipate their future feelings, make decisions based on such (mis)anticipation, and then actually experience different (and perhaps worse) feelings than were anticipated. That is, a certain level of regret based on compliance or reactance may be anticipated prior to a decision, and this expectation may influence behavior, but the expectation of regret may not match what is actually experienced following an undesirable outcome.

If anticipation of future regret plays a role in whether one complies with the dictates of another person, we must consider not only the accuracy but also the spontaneity of the anticipation of regret. Researchers who investigate the effects of anticipated regret on decisions make the assumption, at least implicitly, that regret is anticipated spontaneously when one is faced with a decision. Anticipated regret can affect one's tendency to comply with or react against an influence attempt only if one spontaneously considers future regret when deciding what to do. It is possible that individuals make decisions based upon only what is salient *at the time* of the decision, and if the possibility of regret is not salient, then its anticipation may not enter into the decision-making process.

TABLE 8.2
Anticipated Regret and Choice Data

		Team pushed by other persons	
		Team X	Team Y
Anticipated Regret			
Team chosen	Team X	4.10	4.81
	Team Y	5.20	4.31
Choice (percentages):			
Anticipated regret condition:			
	Team X	73	26
	Team Y	27	74
No anticipated regret condition:			
	Team X	32	85
	Team Y	68	15

Note. From Crawford, McConnell, Lewis, and Sherman (2002)

To examine the issues of the spontaneity of anticipated regret and its role in compliance or reactance to persuasive attempts, we (Crawford, McConnell, Lewis, & Sherman, 2002) presented two equally attractive alternatives, i.e., football teams, on which to gamble. Participants were "pushed" to choose one team (e.g., Team X) by another student (actually a confederate) in the experiment. Participants were told, "You definitely have to pick Team X." Half of the participants (the anticipated regret condition) completed measures of anticipated regret that explicitly directed them to consider how much regret they would feel if they chose Team X and Team Y won, and how much regret would they feel if they chose Team Y and Team X won. From our previous scenario studies, we expected that participants in this experimental setting would anticipate greater regret for reactive, rather than for compliant, behavior. That is, when Team X is pushed, participants would anticipate greater regret for choosing, and losing, with Team Y (i.e., reactance) than they would if they chose Team X and lost (i.e., compliance). The results confirmed these predictions. As can be seen in the top portion of Table 8.2, in the anticipated regret condition, our participants anticipated greater regret for choosing the threatened alternative and losing than for choosing the promoted alternative and losing. That is, our participants expected to feel greater regret after a loss following defiance than after a loss following compliance.

To examine whether the anticipation of regret affected subsequent choices, participants were asked to select the team that they wanted to bet on to win. We expected that in the anticipated regret condition, following their consideration of future regret, participants would select the promoted alternative in an attempt to minimize their potential regret following a loss. If resistance to the persuasive attempt is seen as potentially more aversive than compliance (as the anticipated regret data indicated), then participants in the anticipated regret condition should minimize regret by complying with the push. As can be seen in the lower portion of Table 8.2, the choice data support this contention. That is, when participants were explicitly focused on the possibility of future regret, they were significantly more likely to comply with the persuasive attempt. In fact, over 73% of the participants in this condition complied with the influence attempt.

What of the participants who were not explicitly focused on the possibility of future regret? If regret is spontaneously anticipated, then those who were not directed to consider regret should show the same pattern of choice as the anticipated regret condition participants. This did not occur. When not focused on future regret, participants showed resistance to the persuasive attempt. That is, when one alternative was promoted, these participants were significantly more likely to show reactance, preferring to choose the threatened alternative. In fact, these participants reacted against the dictates of the other more than 76% of the time. Thus, participants who anticipated regret prior to making their choices showed a markedly different pattern of results (i.e., compliance) than did participants who were not asked about future regret (i.e., reactance).

Following selection of a team, all participants learned that their chosen team had lost. All participants then reported their current level of regret immediately after learning the outcome of the game. Across all of our participants, compliant behavior led to more regret after the fact than did reactance. Importantly, the interaction between choice and whether regret had been anticipated prior to making the choice was not significant. That is, greater regret was experienced following compliance than reactance regardless of whether or not participants were directed to think about the possibility of future regret. Although these results do not support our contention that reactance effects may be reinterpreted in terms of anticipated regret, it does appear that in response to an influence attempt, people do not spontaneously consider the possibility of future regret. However, if focused on that possibility, they (mis)anticipate the regret that they would feel in response to reactive behaviors, which leads them toward a behavior that results in greater actual regret after the fact. Thus, having people anticipate future regret is a way to increase compliance with a "push" and to overcome resistance to being influenced.

As we have seen, whenever one is trying to persuade another person to act, there is resistance (in the form of psychological reactance) that is aroused. It is necessary to overcome this resistance if the persuasive attempt is to be successful (Knowles & Linn, this volume). Simply asking people, prior to their behavioral choice, to anticipate the regret that they might feel in the future for complying with versus reacting against the persuasive attempt appears to be one way to overcome the resistance and increase compliance.

Are there other ways to overcome the resistance that occurs when the freedom to do something is perceived as having been threatened or eliminated? There is evidence that if the reactance aroused in a persuasive attempt situation can be overcome, not only does compliance increase, but also choice of a promoted course of action increases to a level greater than is observed in the absence of any threat to freedom. Imagine once again that you have the choice between Alternative A and Alternative B, and imagine again that an agent of influence tells you that you "really have to choose Alternative A." As we know, such a persuasive attempt has the effect of increasing the likelihood of your choosing Alternative B. Further imagine another condition where, prior to your choice, another person (actually a confederate of the experimenter) responds to this threat to freedom by saying "I haven't made up my mind. It's my choice, and I'll choose what I want." This reinstatement of personal freedom, a release from reactance, actually increases the percentage of participants who comply with the influencing agent's push for Alternative A even more than it does for a group that never had its freedom threatened (Worchel & Brehm, 1971). Thus, the arousal of reactance and the subsequent reduction of this resistance by the release from reactance is an effective way to increase compliance.

Indeed, such a reinstatement of perceived choice may be exactly why the "high choice" condition in cognitive dissonance experiments is so effective in leading to attitude change (Linder, Cooper, & Jones, 1967). At first, the participant's freedom to choose what to write or to say is threatened. However, by focusing on the seeming degree of personal freedom to write or say what one wishes, the threat is negated and a great deal of persuasion results.

These findings suggest that any direct attempt at persuasion involves two quite different and opposite effects—an arousal of resistance that decreases compliance and a positive persuasive impact that increases compliance. The former generally predominates when there are threats to perceived freedom; but if this resistance component can be negated, as through the induction of considerations of future regret (Crawford et al., 2002) or by the reinstatement of perceived choice (Worchel & Brehm, 1971), compliance can be dramatically increased.

PERSUASIVE ATTEMPTS ELICIT DUAL PROCESSES: REACTANCE AND COMPLIANCE

Although reactance has primarily been understood as a phenomenon where threat to choice induces a motivation to reinstate freedom (Wright & Brehm, 1982; cf., Heilman & Toffler, 1976), very little speculation about the underlying processes associated with reactance and responses to it have been articulated. We propose that influence situations involving reactance and compliance can be fruitfully understood by considering them in a dual-process framework (Chaiken & Trope, 1999). Specifically, we suggest that reactance against an influence attempt is a spontaneous, relatively automatic process. Threats to freedom, like other motivated responses, such as dissonance (Festinger, 1957), drive reduction (Hull, 1951), and goal-directed behavior (Kruglanski, 1996), often influence behavior without there being conscious mediation or awareness. On the other hand, we propose that the compliant behavior observed in our anticipated regret condition is a more controlled process. (However, other instances of compliant behavior, such as the click, whirr phenomenon discussed by Cialdini (1993), certainly involve automatic and nonconscious processes.)

As we have seen, people do not seem to anticipate regret spontaneously in advance of making decisions, and when they do, their behavior becomes compliant rather than reactive (Crawford et al., 2002). That is, we found that people do not appear to anticipate the regret they may feel in an influence situation unless explicitly directed to do so. Those who made their choice *immediately* after receiving the influence attempt revealed reactance by picking the football team *not* pushed by the other student. However, those participants who considered anticipated regret after the push complied with (rather than reacted against) the other student's edict. Thus, it appears that reactance was the spontaneous response to the influence attempt, but compliance was observed when decision makers were induced to consider additional information (in this case, future feelings of regret) before making their decision.

Although our findings suggest that reactance is spontaneous, one may wonder why reactance would be a relatively automatic process. We would argue that mainstream, Western culture values autonomy, self-determination, and independence (e.g., Bandura, 1997; Fiske, Kitayama, Markus, & Nisbett, 1998; Ryan & Deci, 2000; Triandis, 1995), and that the importance of these values is reinforced often and from a very early age. Thus, the need for autonomy becomes a chronic construct that automatically guides behavior (Higgins, King, & Mavin, 1982). Even though compliance may not be a spontaneous response in influence situations, it certainly may triumph in decision making once more controlled processes are invoked. For example, if people explicitly consider how much regret they might feel following an undesirable outcome if they follow or if they do not follow another's demands, their focus may shift from concerns about "me losing my freedom" to "me feeling bad for the actions *I choose* to take." Consciously choosing a course of action that rejects another's request is likely perceived as increasing the sense of volition, action (vs. inaction), and thus blameworthiness for one's bad decision, making the prospect of choosing an independent course of action that results in now-considered failure especially unattractive (Gilovich & Medvec, 1995; Kahneman & Miller, 1986; Markman et al., 1995). To the extent that decision makers focus on how their not going along with another's demand is *an action they are taking* that could result in undesirable consequences, they may find compliance more attractive. Again, this line of reasoning is consistent with our empirical findings (Crawford et al., 2002).

Even though this analysis suggests that compliance in reactance-evoking situations results from controlled rather than from automatic processes, we suspect that this might not always be the case. For instance, people who chronically anticipate the future and think about its consequences might spontaneously consider future feelings before making decisions. For instance, Gleicher et al. (1995) found that an individual difference, consideration for future consequences (CFC), reliably predicted those who engage in prefactual thinking when anticipating how current decisions will affect the future. Those greater in CFC, for example, were more likely to buy insurance to minimize potential future regret. We hypothesize that those greater in CFC may be more likely to anticipate regret spontaneously, similar to our anticipated regret condition participants, and thus be relatively more likely to comply with rather than react against another's demands even when not explicitly asked to consider anticipated regret. This possibility is still consistent with our dual-process assertion, but this process account predicts that compliance may be a relatively more automatic process for some people than it is for others.

It is interesting to consider this dual-process explanation for reactance-evoking situations because most contemporary models of attitudes and persuasion are dual process in nature as well (e.g., Chaiken, Liberman, & Eagly, 1989; Petty & Cacioppo, 1981; Petty & Wegener, 1998). For instance, targets of persuasion attempts emphasize controlled processes in attitude formation and persuasion (e.g., rely on argument quality) instead of automatic processes (e.g., use heuristic cues) when they have sufficient cognitive resources (Petty, Wells, & Brock, 1976), are greater in need for cognition (Cacioppo & Petty, 1982), and are in negative moods (Schwarz & Clore, 1996). Similarly, we might expect that people who have sufficient cognitive resources, are greater in need for cognition, and are in negative moods would be relatively less likely to show reactance and be more likely to think about the future, to misanticipate future regret for compliance versus reactance, and thus be more likely to comply in influence situations (yet, perhaps ultimately be less satisfied). Indeed, the case of negative mood may be especially relevant to the present analysis. Explicitly asking people to consider future negative consequences and anticipated regret may increase their negative mood, which may bring about more controlled processing, resulting in compliance. Thus, less reactance and more compliance may result because negative mood encourages the use of effortful, controlled processes (Schwarz & Clore, 1996), and because focusing on anticipated regret may emphasize concerns about how one's own volitional actions (i.e., going against another's request) may lead to a bad outcome rather than focusing on concerns about losing one's freedoms.

ANTICIPATED REGRET AS
A COMPLIANCE TECHNIQUE

The most important aspect of the findings of our research (Crawford et al., 2002) is that anticipated regret can be used as an effective technique in persuasion situations to help overcome resistance to the persuasive attempts of others and reduce reactance to those attempts. Some agents of influence are well aware of this technique. People selling life insurance typically ask potential customers to imagine the regret they would feel (interestingly, after they have died) if they were to die suddenly and their families were left without the financial capacity to ensure a good quality of life. The seller is in essence telling customers to imagine the large amount of regret they would feel from making a certain choice (forgoing insurance) and having the outcome turn out badly.

Persuasion always takes place in the face of some resistance. Whether one is a Freudian psychologist, an insurance salesperson, or a social psychologist trying to understand attitude change and influence, the presence of resistance to change is obvious. The trick is to overcome this resistance. Our findings indicate that one possibility is to use a focus on future regret as a way to overcome resistance to influence. By associating future regret with reactance, the forces of resistance are weakened, and compliance is more likely. This idea that anticipated regret could function as a technique to overcome resistance to being influenced was an appealing one. We then wondered whether other known effective techniques for inducing compliance and overcoming resistance might function through a similar process of anticipated regret. In addition, this consideration takes us beyond cognitive reactance and is applicable to other forms and bases of resistance as well.

Scarcity. When we are told that something is scarce, it is almost certain to create the thought of missing out on an opportunity. This focus on scarcity is clearly evident in the world of sales and marketing. There are statements of "last day of sale" and "only a limited supply." There is the ubiquitous clock on the Home Shopping Network, showing that one has only a very limited time to call in for the current offer.

Several lines of social psychological research have focused on the demonstration of scarcity as an effective compliance technique and on the processes by which this technique works. Cialdini (1993, 1994) outlined scarcity as one of his principles by which interpersonal influence is effective. He proposed that objects and opportunities appear more valuable when they are less available, even if those objects and opportunities have little intrinsic attraction for us. Cialdini offered two interpretations for the effects of scarcity on persuasibility. The first account involves the use of a simplifying principle or heuristic—"If it is scarce, it must be valuable." This interpretation of the effectiveness of scarcity involves an increase in the attractive forces that promote persuasion.

Cialdini (1993, 1994) offered a second interpretation of the power of scarcity that is much closer to our focus on anticipated regret. He suggested that as things become less and less available, we perceive a loss of freedom to have them. "If I don't comply and purchase it now, this object will be unavailable in the future, and I will very much regret not having it." To preserve our freedom (à la reactance theory), we must buy the item before it is too late. In other words, it may be an anticipation of future regret that explains why scarcity is an effective way to overcome resistance to being influenced. The knowledge of a product's scarcity may well elicit thoughts of anticipated regret if the item is not purchased right now. This interpretation is based on inducing future regret for resisting the persuasive attempt. Thus, in this case, scarcity works by weakening the forces of resistance through the anticipation of future regret for noncompliance (Knowles & Linn, this volume). Obviously, this has much in common with our analysis of anticipated regret as a technique for inducing compliance.

There has been some empirical work on the effects of scarcity. Ditto and Jemmott (1989) demonstrated a scarcity principle in evaluative judgments such that identically described medical conditions are evaluated as more detrimental when they involve rare conditions. Likewise, scarce positive health assets are rated as more beneficial than are more common assets. Although the findings of Ditto and Jemmott (1989) indicate strong effects of scarcity, they are not in the realm of interpersonal persuasion, and thus extrapolation to compliance settings must be done with caution.

Brannon and Brock (2001a) examined the effects of scarcity in the realm of the effectiveness of persuasive messages. They found that responses to persuasive messages led to more extreme attitudes (both positive and negative) when the message was about a seemingly rare attribute that the participant supposedly possessed rather than a more common attribute. Interestingly, Brannon and Brock (2001a) offered an explanation that is opposite to the simplifying heuristic explanation offered by Cialdini (1993, 1994). They proposed that thoughtful, elaborative processes are used for information about scarce attributes. These thoughtful, systematic processes might well be evoked by the anticipation of regret for missing out on a scarce item. Thus, the forces that weaken resistance to influence also lead to greater systematic processing. This proposal implies that if the basic evaluative information in a persuasive message about a product or act is strong, compliance would be greater if the product were scarce, due to the systematic processing of the information. However, if the evaluative information is weak or negative, scarcity would lead to less compliance. In fact, exactly such effects of scarcity in a compliance setting have been recently reported by Brannon and Brock (2001b). Thus, scarcity can overcome resistance to compliance when the reasons for compliance are compelling. This finding that compliance is more likely when effortful processing is induced and persuasive arguments are strong is consistent with our dual-process explanation of influence situations.

Fear Appeals. For many years, both social and health psychologists have tried to draw firm conclusions about the effects of the fear level of an appeal on the degree of persuasibility or compliance (Leventhal, 1970; Rogers, 1983). Fear is a future-oriented emotion. Thus, to the extent that fear is an effective way to induce social influence and to overcome resistance to persuasion, it is because of its ability to focus recipients of communications on negative future consequences. By associating negative affect with resistance to persuasion, fear appeals can weaken this resistance. Thus, fear appeals may share certain processes with the already discussed techniques of anticipated regret and scarcity.

Early research indicated that moderate levels of fear appeals were most effective (Leventhal, Watts, & Pagano, 1967; Rogers, 1983). Low levels of fear did not portray negative enough future scenarios to motivate participants to comply. High levels of fear may have frightened participants too much and increased resistance and defensive avoidance. A recent meta-analysis showed that strong fear appeals produce high levels of susceptibility to persuasion (Witte & Allen, 2000). In addition, strong fear appeals also motivate adaptive danger control actions, such as message acceptance, and maladaptive fear control actions, such as defensive avoidance or reactance. Thus, strong fear appeals combined with high-efficacy messages produce the greatest influence, whereas strong fear appeals combined with low-efficacy messages produce the greatest levels of defensive avoidance (Witte & Allen, 2000). This is reminiscent of the effects of scarcity, where high scarcity plus strong messages are the most effective, whereas high scarcity plus weak messages are the least effective. Perhaps strong fear appeals also work by inducing systematic and elaborative processing, which again is consistent with our dual-process explanation of influence situations.

Consideration of the effects of fear appeals demonstrates clearly the push–pull nature of compliance and persuasion that we noted previously in our discussion of the effects of release from reactance and of the dual-process nature of persuasion attempts—both a tendency to go along with the influence induction and a tendency to resist it. With fear arousal as a compliance technique, there are two different kinds of resistance that must be overcome—the inherent resistance to any persuasion attempt plus the defensive resistance caused by the arousal of fear. When the outcomes are too horrible to imagine, participants may resist careful consideration of the entire message.

In relating fear appeals to the anticipated regret technique, one might propose that there is a certain aspect of anticipated regret to fear appeals (i.e., "If you continue to smoke, all these horrible things will happen to you, and you will regret it"). On the other hand, it seems clear that fear appeals focus a person far more on the future outcome itself rather than on the future regret that might follow that future outcome. Thus, it occurs to us that we may be dealing with effects that are far more general than the use of anticipated regret as a compliance technique in situations that elicit cognitive reactance. We shall now propose that many kinds of considerations of the future, in addition to regret, scarcity, and fear, may be effective in inducing compliance. We shall discuss several of these more general techniques.

THINKING ABOUT THE FUTURE AS A GENERAL COMPLIANCE TECHNIQUE

Predicting the Future

As we have seen, directly asking someone to do something, or telling them what to do, is generally ineffective in gaining compliance. This ineffectiveness is in large part due to the resistance aroused by trying to force one's will on someone. Sherman (1980) identified a simple yet effective strategy for avoiding this resistance. Instead of directly asking people to do something, one simply asks them to predict what they *would* do *if* someone were to ask them to do it. Sherman (1980) found that compared to a control group that was simply asked to execute the behavior, participants who were asked to predict what they would do were terribly wrong in their predictions—and they were consistently wrong in the direction of overpredicting socially desirable behaviors. For example, when people were directly asked to devote an afternoon's time to help a charity some time during the current semester, only 2% complied with the request. However, when asked to predict what they would do if someone asked them to devote an afternoon to help a charity, 40% predicted that they would agree to help. Of course, most of these people were wrong in their prediction, given that only 2% who were directly asked agreed with the request. More importantly, this error of prediction was self-erasing. That is, when participants who had made predictions were actually called (under different circumstances) a couple of weeks later and were asked to devote an afternoon to help a charity, 38% complied (mainly those who had predicted that they would help if asked). Thus, the compliance rate was increased by 36% by simply asking participants to predict their own future behavior before presenting them with the full-blown request. This result has been replicated for a number of different behaviors. Compliance rates have been increased for agreement with requests to sing the Star-Spangled Banner (Sherman, 1980), for voting in elections (Greenwald, Carnot, Beach, & Young, 1987), for recycling (Sprott, Spangenberg, & Perkins, 1999), and for eating healthful food (Sprott, Fisher, & Spangenberg, 2001).

Why do predictions of future behavior increase compliance rates? The key to increasing compliance rates by predicting the future is that the prediction of a behavior arouses less resistance than actually committing to the behavior. It is simply far easier for one to predict that one will do something than to agree to do it. Agreeing to an action in the "hypothetical future" is benign and one need not resist any direct persuasive attempt. Thus, the technique of increasing compliance through future prediction works by diminishing the negative aspects associated with compliance. In this way, resistance is weakened.

Importantly, once the (mis)prediction is made, the likelihood of subsequently agreeing to the full-blown request is greatly increased. This technique of reducing resistance by first asking for a benign request has some similarities with the foot-in-the-door technique (Cann, Sherman, & Elkes, 1975; Freedman & Fraser, 1966). With that technique, some minor request is asked for (and almost always agreed to) prior to asking the target request, which is a more time-consuming request. The agreement to the initial small request increases (compared to a control group) compliance to the larger request quite significantly. The difference between the prediction technique and the foot-in-the-door technique is that the former involves prediction and compliance requests for exactly the same behavior. The foot-in-the-door technique involves requests for two different behaviors in the two phases. In addition, the prediction technique asks participants to anticipate the future and to think about what they might do at a later time. Thus, this technique has much in common with the anticipated regret, the scarcity, and the fear techniques that have already been discussed. All of these involve an anticipation of a future event in order to increase compliance with a request.

Several process explanations have been offered to explain the self-erasing error of prediction effect. Commitment and consistency (Cialdini, Reno, & Kallgren, 1990), norm salience (Sherman, 1980), and impression management (Tedeschi, Schlenker, & Bonoma, 1971) have all been offered as explanations. More recently, Spangenberg, Sprott, Obermiller, and Greenwald (2002) have proposed a dissonance reduction interpretation. They suggest that the self-prediction makes salient the discrepancy between one's principles and one's past behaviors that were in violation of these principles. This dissonance is subsequently reduced by compliance with the actual later request.

Regardless of the correct explanation for the effectiveness of the prediction technique for overcoming resistance and increasing compliance, the important point for now is that this is another example of how anticipation of the future can increase the likelihood that a person will comply with a request or be otherwise influenced to do something by weakening the resistance to social influence. The idea that thinking across time might be used as a general technique to overcome resistance to persuasion is also consistent with the known effects of imagining and explaining hypothetical future events.

Imagining and Explaining Hypothetical Future Events

Similar to the effects of predicting the future on subsequent judgments and behavior, simply imagining or explaining the future can increase one's subjective likelihood that an event will occur. Thus, Carroll (1978) asked participants to imagine one or the other outcome of the 1976 presidential election (prior to its occurrence). Those who imagined a victory by Carter judged that outcome as more likely, and those who imagined a Ford victory judged that Ford was more likely to win. Similarly, asking participants to imagine and explain a hypothetical victory by one or the other team in an upcoming football game very much influenced their judgments of who would win the game, with the team imagined as winning being seen as more likely to actually win (Sherman, Zehner, Johnson, & Hirt, 1983).

Imagining and explaining a hypothetical future event can affect not only one's judgments of the probability of future events, but also one's actual future behavior as well. Sherman, Skov, Hervitz, and Stock (1981) had participants imagine and explain their own hypothetical future success or failure at an upcoming anagram task. Those who explained success performed significantly better than did a control group that explained nothing. Interestingly, a group that explained failure and then stated explicit expectations also outperformed the control group—perhaps due to resistance to and reactance against the possibility of failure.

Most important for our current concerns, simply imagining engaging in a future behavior has the effect of increasing compliance rates with a later request regarding that behavior. Gregory, Cialdini, and Carpenter (1982) asked participants to imagine themselves subscribing to a cable television service and enjoying the benefits of the service. These participants were significantly more likely later to agree to sign up for a cable service than were people who simply received information about the service but did not imagine using it.

Through what process does explaining and imagining a hypothetical future event have its effects? Koehler (1991) proposed that explaining and imagining a specific outcome or event leads the person to establish what is described as a focal hypothesis. Once a focal hypothesis is established, the person adopts a "conditional reference frame" under which the hypothesis is assumed to be true. By evaluating the hypothesis in a biased way (Klayman & Ha, 1987) and by not adjusting properly from an assumed truth (Gilbert, Krull, & Malone, 1990), the person ends up believing in the focal hypothesis and behaving in ways (including compliance) consistent with the truth value of the focal hypothesis. The biasing effects of testing a hypothesis include differential prominence of aspects of the event, one-sided interpretation of evidence, and an incomplete search for information. Consistent with the "conditional reference frame" interpretation, Anderson (1982; Anderson & Sechler, 1986) reported that asking participants to consider the alternative possibilities eliminates the effects of imagination or explanation. Considering alternatives prevents the adoption of a focal hypothesis, along with its subsequent biasing effects on judgment and behavior. In addition, imagining a future compliant act may reduce the negative thoughts and feelings associated with the act. In this way, resistance to an influence attempt in the future is weakened, and compliance increases.

With regard to the effects of predicting future behavior, we have seen that the mere act of asking someone if he or she (hypothetically) would agree to a request in the future if asked to do something increases compliance rates to a subsequent request. We now suggest that directly asking someone to commit to do something in the future as opposed to right now can also substantially increase compliance rates. Such an effect would strongly indicate that thinking about oneself and one's surrounding circumstances in the future is not the same as thinking about oneself right now. More specifically, such an effect would suggest that less resistance to influence is elicited when a request is made for some time in the future. Just as in the effects of misprediction of the future, where it seems easier to say "yes" to something that is not real than to something that has immediate and more than hypothetical consequences, it may be easier to say "yes" to something that is not imminent. As we shall see, one reason why this effect occurs is that people misconstrue the future in terms of how difficult it might be to carry out a request. That is, it seems easier to do something when that something is not near at hand than it does when the time to do it is right now. Several lines of research and theorizing are relevant.

The Planning Fallacy

Buehler, Griffin, and Ross (1994) investigated people's predictions of the time that it would take to complete various tasks. It comes as no surprise to any one of us who has ever committed to write a chapter (including the present one) that people greatly underestimate their completion times. Buehler et al. (1994) demonstrated that this effect occurs because people tend to focus on future plan-based scenarios rather than on relevant past experiences. In fact, instructions to connect relevant past experiences with their predictions eliminated the overly optimistic predictions about how long tasks would take. Thus, without specific instructions to focus on the past, the act of predicting the time or ease of completion for a task evokes a future orientation about how a task may be done rather than a past orientation where valuable information from similar past procrastination experiences might be gained. In addition, motivations in the form of rewards for getting things done early in the future only exacerbate the planning fallacy—that is, the time predicted to complete a task is reduced more by motivation than are actual completion times (Buehler, Griffin, & MacDonald, 1997).

Importantly, from our point of view, these overly optimistic completion estimates about the time it will take and the ease of doing things greatly increase the likelihood that we will agree to requests of all types—provided that these requests do not require immediate action. A similar effect of temporal perspective on judgments has been investigated by Gilovich, Kerr, and Medvec (1993). They measured the degree of confidence that people have in their prospects for future success. They found that confidence decreases dramatically as the "moment of truth" approaches. For example, students think that they will do much better on midterm exams when asked on the first day of class than when asked on the day of the exam. Gilovich et al. (1993) interpret this effect as due to the fact that people tend to feel more accountable for their assessments as the time to perform approaches, and thus they focus more and more on possible causes of failure. In addition, when a task is to be done far in the future, one might well make unrealistic and overly optimistic assessments of future preparatory effects. Things seem easier in the future because there is so much time available to prepare and to get things accomplished.

Although neither Buehler et al. (1994) nor Gilovich et al. (1993) investigated the implications of their findings for the degree to which people will be influenceable or compliant, we feel that there is a clear connection. To the extent that people perceive that future tasks will be done more quickly and easily than is actually the case (Buehler et al., 1994), and to the extent that they feel confident that they can complete a task successfully (Gilovich et al., 1993), they ought to be more likely to be persuaded to do something if it is not required until a future date than if it is a request for compliance at the present time. Both perceptions of ease of completion and confidence in the success of completion should help overcome resistance to persuasive attempts, and these perceptions are likely for requests about the future.

The findings of Gilovich et al. (1993) have an additional implication for compliance requests that are for some time in the future. They suggest that confidence in successful completion increases monotonically as time before the "due date" increases. This finding implies that compliance rates will generally increase as the amount of time until the requested behavior is due increases. We shall now turn to a point of view that addresses this very issue.

Temporal Construal

Liberman and Trope (1998) have considered how people think about the future as a function of how far in the distance that future extends. According to their temporal construal theory, distant future situations are construed at a higher level than are near future situations. That is, people focus on the general, abstract, and central features of events that are in the far future, but on specific, concrete, and low-level features for events in the near future. For example, consider whether you might agree to a request to take part in a symposium sometime in the future. According to Liberman and Trope (1998), if the symposium is one year from now, you are likely to focus on abstract aspects of the symposium, such as its interest value and what you might learn. On the other hand, if the symposium is two weeks from now, you will be more likely to focus on specific and concrete aspects such as the ease of getting to the symposium site or the cost of travel.

In support of temporal construal theory, Liberman and Trope (1998) have shown that the value of an event is more positive in the distant future than the near future when the value associated with the high-level construal (i.e., the abstract features) is more positive than the value associated with the low-level construal (i.e., the specific features); and the value of an event is less positive in the distant future than in the near future when the value associated with the high-level construal of an event is less than the value associated with the low-level construal. These findings were replicated and extended in a series of experiments by Trope and Liberman (2000). They found that feasibility (a low-level feature) carries more weight for judgments of an event in the near future, whereas desirability (a high-level feature) carries more weight for events in the distant future. More specifically, participants are more likely to choose a difficult but interesting course assignment when the temporal distance is long, but they are more likely to choose an easy but uninteresting assignment when the temporal distance is short.

The implications of temporal construal theory are extremely interesting. The theory suggests, for example, that moral principles are more likely to guide decisions for the distant future than for the immediate future, whereas difficulty, cost, and situational pressures are more likely to be important for decisions about the near future. What is the relevance of temporal construal theory for our current interest in the role of thinking about the future on rates of compliance? For one thing, Liberman and Trope (1998) suggested that time constraints are a low-level of construal of an activity. Thus, people give little weight to time constraints in planning for the distant future, and they are thus more likely to plan to do and agree to do more things for the distant future, even incompatible activities. This suggests that it will be easier to secure greater compliance for requests about the distant future, in line with the ideas of Buehler et al. (1994) and Gilovich et al. (1993). In addition, because there is less resistance to compliance for the distant future than for the near future, one might propose that in order to increase compliance rates, strategies that aim at resistance reduction would be more effective for near-time decisions than for distant decisions, whereas strategies that increase the attraction forces that promote persuasion would be more effective for distant decisions than for near decisions. This would be compatible with the view of distant decisions as focusing on promotion considerations and near decisions focusing on prevention decisions (Higgins, 1998).

Although such a difference in promotion versus prevention focus is feasible, things may not be so simple. Both low-level (near future) and abstract (distant future) considerations can involve both promotion and prevention aspects. For example, low-level considerations of the reasonable cost of a trip can be framed as a way to promote savings or to prevent costly expenses. It might make more sense to consider that both low-level, concrete and high-level, abstract considerations of compliance can involve forces that promote persuasion as well as forces that weaken resistance. What is important is that both kinds of attempts to increase persuasion (promoting persuasion and weakening resistance) in the near future will be most effective if they involve concrete features, whereas both kinds of attempts to increase persuasion in the distant future will be most effective if they involve abstract features. Thus, temporal construal theory suggests that the framing of the compliance request will very much affect the rates of compliance differentially for the near and the distant future. For requests in the distant future, one should focus on promoting the positive, abstract features of the object of the request, such as its desirability, or on weakening resistance based on high-level features, such as moral considerations. However, to secure compliance for requests in the near future, one should focus on the positive, low-level, concrete features, such as ease and feasibility, or on weakening resistance based on low-level features, such as high cost.

CONCLUSION:
TAKING STOCK OF RESISTANCE

We began this chapter by noting that compliant behavior becomes more likely either when the attractiveness of persuasion is enhanced or when the resistance to persuasion is diminished. In particular, we emphasized that focusing people on the future can greatly erode resistance to influencing agents' demands in the present. Whereas many in the persuasion literature have emphasized making persuasive appeals more attractive (e.g., Briñol, Rucker, Tormala, & Petty, this volume; Cialdini, 1993, 1994; Tormala & Petty, this volume; Wegener, Petty,

Smoak, & Fabrigar, this volume), our approach has been to consider the other half of the persuasion equation: reducing resistance (Fuegen & Brehm, this volume; Knowles & Linn, chapter 1, this volume; Quinn & Wood, this volume; Jacks & O'Brien, this volume). It seems appropriate at this point to take some stock in what our findings and theorizing say about resistance and its importance.

In general, we view resistance as a response by an individual that attempts to eliminate or reduce the impact of another's influence attempt. Resistance is often based on motivational factors (Jacks & O'Brien, this volume), although cognitive, information-processing factors may be involved as well. Moreover, although resistance may involve conscious and controlled decisions and behaviors, we have focused more on resistance as a spontaneous response to social influence situations. Whether it is because people instinctively wish to maintain perceptions of choice and control (e.g., Brehm, 1966; Worchel & Brehm, 1971), because they do not automatically consider future regret (Crawford et al., 2002), or because they are driven by situational heuristics such as scarcity (e.g., Cialdini, 1993, 1994), it seems that thinking less is often linked to resisting more. Indeed, our proposed dual-process account of reactance and compliance is based on this reasoning. There are, undoubtedly, many ways to shift people away from this more spontaneous response, and we have argued that getting them to think more about the future is especially beneficial in reducing resistance. In particular, predicting the future, imagining and explaining hypothetical future events, avoiding the consideration of an ominous future too painful to consider, capitalizing on the planning fallacy, and considering the abstract, long-term positives of the situation focus people away from the immediate unattractiveness of compliance to a new decision set where compliance seems more reasonable, less costly, and easy to accept. What is true but not apparent to decision makers focused on the future is that there are many pitfalls on the road to these futures that may have been crafted by the influencing agent, which, if known to the decision maker, would make compliance far less attractive. However, like a good magician or politician, an influencing agent who focuses people away from "the action" makes acceptance more compelling and resistance less imperative.

We began this chapter by focusing on cognitive reactance as one important manifestation of resistance. We saw how the anticipation of future regret can diminish the tendency toward reactance. As we considered other compliance techniques, such as scarcity and fear appeals, and as we considered the effects on compliance of focusing on future behavior and events, it became clear that the reduction of resistance by considering the future was more general than the overcoming of cognitive reactance.

There are many different causes or bases of resistance to social influence: resistance based on restriction of freedom or threatened loss of control; resistance based on the regret anticipated for compliance followed by a bad outcome; resistance based on defensive avoidance; resistance based on aversion to change, such as the status quo bias; resistance based on a perceived potential loss of power or status as an outcome of becoming the target of a successful influence attempt. All these bases and manifestations of resistance that can be elicited by a persuasion attempt can be weakened to increase persuasion. We believe that an increase in future as opposed to present focus can weaken all these various forms of resistance, thus increasing compliance.

As this chapter has indicated, time and its consideration is a critically important aspect of many diverse social psychological phenomena. Where one is psychologically on the rubber band of time very much affects decision making, construal of events, confidence, emotions, and biases in memory and judgment (Johnson & Sherman, 1990). Now we see the possibility that, in addition, thinking across time has importance for overcoming resistance to social influence. Those who are savvy to these effects will find that subtle suggestions to reflect on the future or to think more deeply about down-the-road consequences will influence choices in the present. And to those readers who still remain unconvinced, we suggest that you consider how much regret you might feel if you later conclude that we were right all along.

AUTHOR NOTE

Preparation of this chapter was supported by Research Scientist Award K05 DA00492 from the National Institute on Drug Abuse to the first author and grant MH60645 from the National Institute of Mental Health to the third author.

REFERENCES

Anderson, C. A. (1982). Inoculation and counter-explanation: Debiasing techniques in the perseverance of social theories. *Social Cognition, 1,* 126–139.

Anderson, C. A., & Sechler, E. S. (1986). Effects of explanation and counterexplanation on the development and use of social theories. *Journal of Personality and Social Psychology, 50,* 24–34.

Bandura, A. (1997). *Self-efficacy: The exercise of control.* New York: W. H. Freeman & Co., Publishers.

Bar-Hillel, M., & Neter, E. (1996). Why are people reluctant to exchange lottery tickets? *Journal of Personality and Social Psychology, 27,* 2001–2014.

Bell, D. E. (1982). Regret in decision making under uncertainty. *Operations Research, 30,* 961–981.

Boninger, D. S., Gleicher, F., & Strathman, A. (1994). Counterfactual thinking: From what might have been to what may be. *Journal of Personality and Social Psychology, 67,* 297–307.

Brannon, L. A., & Brock, T. C. (2001a). Scarcity claims elicit extreme responding to persuasive messages: Role of cognitive elaboration. *Personality and Social Psychology Bulletin, 27,* 365–375.

Brannon, L. A., & Brock, T. C. (2001b). Limiting time for responding enhances behavior corresponding to the merits of compliance appeals: Refutations of heuristic-cue theory in service and consumer settings. *Journal of Consumer Psychology, 10,* 135–146.

Brehm, J. W. (1996). *A theory of psychological reactance.* New York: Academic Press.

Brehm, J. W., & Sensenig, J. (1966). Social influence as a function of attempted and implied usurpation of choice. *Journal of Personality and Social Psychology, 4,* 703–707.

Buehler, R., Griffin, D., & MacDonald, H. (1997). The role of motivated reasoning in optimistic time predictions. *Personality and Social Psychology Bulletin, 23,* 238–247.

Buehler, R., Griffin, D., & Ross, M. (1994). Exploring the "planning fallacy": Why people under-estimate their task completion times. *Journal of Personality and Social Psychology, 67,* 366–381.

Cacioppo, J. T., & Petty, R. E. (1982). The need for cognition. *Journal of Personality and Social Psychology, 42,* 116–131.

Cann, A., Sherman, S. J., & Elkes, R. (1975). Effects of initial request size and timing of a second request on compliance: The foot in the door and the door in the face. *Journal of Personality and Social Psychology, 32,* 774–782.

Carroll, J. S. (1978). The effect of imagining an event on expectations for the event: An interpretation in terms of the availability heuristic. *Journal of Experimental Social Psychology, 14,* 88–96.

Chaiken, S., Liberman, A., & Eagly, A. H. (1989). Heuristic and systematic information processing within and beyond the persuasion context. In J. S. Uleman & J. A. Bargh (Eds.), *Unintended thought* (pp. 212–252). New York: Guilford.

Chaiken, S., & Trope, Y. (1999). *Dual-process theories in social psychology.* New York: Guilford.

Cialdini, R. B. (1993). *Influence: Science and practice* (3rd ed.). New York: HarperCollins.

Cialdini, R. B. (1994). Interpersonal influence. In S. Shavitt & T. C. Brock (Eds.), *Persuasion: Psychological insights and perspectives* (pp. 195–217). Needham Heights, MA: Allyn & Bacon.

Cialdini, R. B., Reno, R. R., & Kallgren, C. A. (1990). A focused theory of normative conduct: Recycling the concept of norms to reduce littering in public places. *Journal of Personality and Social Psychology, 58,* 1015–1026.

Crawford, M. T., Lewis, A. C., McConnell, A. R., & Sherman, S. J. (1998). Anticipated regret, choice, and retrospective counterfactual regret. Paper presented at the eighth biennial meeting of the Social Psychologists of Indiana, South Bend, Indiana.

Crawford, M. T., McConnell, A. R., Lewis, A. C., & Sherman, S. J. (2002). Reactance, compliance, and anticipated regret. *Journal of Experimental Social Psychology, 38,* 56–63.

Ditto, P. H., & Jemmott, J. B., III (1989). From rarity to evaluative extremity: Effects of prevalence information on evaluations of positive and negative characteristics. *Journal of Personality and Social Psychology, 57,* 16–26.

Festinger, L. (1957). *A theory of cognitive dissonance.* Evanston, IL: Row, Peterson.

Fiske, A. P., Kitayama, S., Markus, H. R., & Nisbett, R. E. (1998). The cultural matrix of social psychology. In D. T. Gilbert, S. T., Fiske, & G. Lindzey (Eds.), *The handbook of social psychology* (4th ed., Vol. 2, pp. 915–981). New York: McGraw-Hill.

Freedman, J. L., & Fraser, L. C. (1966). Compliance without pressure: The foot-in-the-door technique. *Journal of Personality and Social Psychology, 4,* 195–202.

Gilbert, D. T., Krull, D. S., & Malone, P. S. (1990). Unbelieving the unbelievable: Some problems in the rejection of false information. *Journal of Personality and Social Psychology, 59,* 601–613.

Gilbert, D. T., Pinel, E. C., Wilson, T. D., Blumberg, S. J., & Wheatley, T. P. (1998). Immune neglect: A source of durability bias in affective forecasting. *Journal of Personality and Social Psychology, 75,* 617–638.

Gilovich, T., Kerr, M., & Medvec V. H. (1993). Effect of temporal perspective on subjective confidence. *Journal of Personality and Social Psychology, 64,* 552–580.

Gilovich, T., & Medvec, V. H. (1995). The experience of regret: What, when and why. *Psychological Review, 102,* 379–395.

Gleicher, F., Boninger, D. S., Strathman, A., Armor, D., Hetts, J., & Ahn, M. (1995). With an eye toward the future: The impact of counterfactual thinking on affect, attitudes, and behavior. In N. J. Roese & J. M. Olson (Eds.), *What might have been: The social psychology of counterfactual thinking* (pp. 283–304). Mahwah, NJ: Erlbaum.

Greenwald, A. G., Carnot, C., Beach, R., & Young, B. (1987). Increasing voting behavior by asking people if they expect to vote. *Journal of Applied Psychology, 72,* 315–318.

Gregory, W. L., Cialdini, R. B., & Carpenter, K. M. (1982). Self-relevant scenarios as mediators of likelihood estimates and compliance: Does imagining make it so? *Journal of Personality and Social Psychology, 43,* 89–99.

Heilman, M. E., & Toffler, B. L. (1976). Reacting to reactance: An interpersonal interpretation of the need for freedom. *Journal of Experimental Social Psychology, 12,* 519–529.

Heller, J. F., Pallak, M. S., & Picek, J. M. (1973). The interactive effects of intent and threat on boomerang attitude change. *Journal of Personality and Social Psychology, 26,* 273–279.

Higgins, E. T. (1998). Promotion and prevention: Regulatory focus as a motivational principle. *Advances in Experimental Social Psychology, 30,* 1–46.

Higgins, E. T., King, G. A., & Mavin, G. H. (1982). Individual construct accessibility and subjective impressions and recall. *Journal of Personality and Social Psychology, 43,* 35–47.

Hull, C. L. (1951). *Essentials of behavior.* New Haven, CT: Yale University Press.

Johnson, M. K., & Sherman, S. J. (1990). Constructing and reconstructing the past and the future in the present. In E. T. Higgins & R. M. Sorrentino (Eds.), *Handbook of motivation and cognition: Foundations of social behavior* (Vol. 2, pp. 482–526). New York: Guilford.

Kahneman, D., & Miller, D. T. (1986). Norm theory: Comparing reality to its alternatives. *Psychological Review, 93,* 136–153.

Klayman, J., & Ha, Y. W. (1987). Confirmation, disconfirmation, and information in hypothesis testing. *Psychological Review, 94,* 211–228.

Koehler, D. J. (1991). Explanation, imagination, and confidence in judgment. *Psychological Bulletin, 110,* 499–519.

Kruglanski, A. W. (1996). Motivated social cognition: Principles of the interface. In E. T. Higgins & A. W. Kruglanski (Eds.), *Social psychology: Handbook of basic principles* (pp. 493–520). New York: Guilford.

Larrick, R. P., & Boles, T. L. (1995). Avoiding regret in decisions with feedback: A negotiation example. *Organizational Behavior and Human Decision Processes, 63,* 87–97.

Leventhal, H. (1970). Findings and theory in the study of fear communications. In L. Berkowitz (Ed.), *Advances in experimental social psychology* (Vol. 5, pp. 119–186). New York: Academic Press.

Leventhal, H., Watts, J. C., & Pagano, F. (1967). Effects of fear and instructions on how to cope with danger. *Journal of Personality and Social Psychology, 6,* 313–321.

Liberman, N., & Trope, Y. (1998). The role of feasibility and desirability considerations in near and distant future decisions: A test of temporal construal theory. *Journal of Personality and Social Psychology, 75,* 5–18.

Linder, D. E., Cooper, J., & Jones, E. E. (1967). Decision freedom as a determinant of the role of incentive magnitude in attitude change. *Journal of Personality and Social Psychology, 6,* 245–254.

Loomes, G., & Sugden, R. (1982). Regret theory: An alternative theory of rational choice under uncertainty. *The Economic Journal, 92,* 805–824.

Markman, K. D., Gavanski, I., Sherman, S. J., & McMullen, M. N. (1993). The mental simulation of better and worse possible worlds. *Journal of Experimental Social Psychology, 29,* 87–109.

Markman, K. D., Gavanski, I., Sherman, S. J., & McMullen, M. N. (1995). The impact of perceived control on the imagination of better and worse possible worlds. *Personality and Social Psychology Bulletin, 21,* 588–595.

McConnell, A. R., Niedermeier, K. E., Leibold, J. M., El-Alayi, A. G., Chin, P. P., & Kuiper, N. M. (2000). "What if I find it cheaper someplace else?": Role of prefactual thinking and anticipated regret in consumer behavior. *Psychology and Marketing, 17,* 281–298.

Miller, D. T., & Taylor, B. R. (1995). Counterfactual thought, regret, and superstition: How to avoid kicking yourself. In N. J. Roese & J. M. Olson (Eds.), *What might have been: The social psychology of counterfactual thinking* (pp. 305–331). Mahwah, NJ: Erlbaum.

Petty, R. E., & Cacioppo, J. T. (1981). *Attitudes and persuasion: Classic and contemporary approaches.* New York: Springer-Verlag.

Petty, R. E., & Wegener, D. T. (1998). Attitude change: Multiple roles for persuasion variables. In D. T. Gilbert, S. T. Fiske, & G. Lindzey (Eds.), *The handbook of social psychology* (4th, ed., Vol. 1, pp. 323–390). New York: McGraw-Hill.

Petty, R. E., Wells, G. L., & Brock, T. C. (1976). Distraction can enhance or reduce yielding to propaganda: Thought disruption versus effort justification. *Journal of Personality and Social Psychology, 34,* 874–884.

Ritov, I. (1996). Probability of regret: Anticipation of uncertainty resolution in choice. *Organizational Behavior and Human Decision Processes, 66,* 228–236.

Roese, N. J. (1994). The functional basis of counterfactual thinking. *Journal of Personality and Social Psychology, 66,* 805–818.

Roese, N. J., & Olson, J. M. (1995). *What might have been: The social psychology of counterfactual thinking.* Hillsdale, NJ: Erlbaum.

Rogers, R. (1983). Cognitive and physiological processes in fear appeals and attitude change: A revised theory of protection motivation. In J. T. Cacioppo & R. E. Petty (Eds.), *Social psychophysiology: A sourcebook* (pp. 153–176). New York: Guilford.

Ryan, R. M., & Deci, E. L. (2000). Self-determination theory and the facilitation of intrinsic motivation, social development, and well-being. *American Psychologist, 55,* 68–78.

Schwarz, N., & Clore, G. L. (1996). Feelings and phenomenal experiences. In E. T. Higgins & A. W. Kruglanski (Eds.), *Social psychology: Handbook of basic principles* (pp. 433–465). New York: Guilford.

Sherman, S. J. (1980). On the self-erasing nature of errors of prediction. *Journal of Personality and Social Psychology, 39,* 211–221.

Sherman, S. J., Skov, R. B., Hervitz, E. F., & Stock, C. B. (1981). The effects of explaining hypothetical future events: From possibility to probability to actuality and beyond. *Journal of Experimental Social Psychology, 17,* 142–158.

Sherman, S. J., Zehner, K. S., Johnson, J., & Hirt, E. R. (1983). Social explanation: The role of timing, set and recall on subjective likelihood estimates. *Journal of Personality and Social Psychology, 44,* 1127–1143.

Simonson, I. (1992). The influence of anticipating regret and responsibility on purchase decisions. *Journal of Consumer Research, 19,* 105–118.

Snyder, M. L., & Wicklund, R. A. (1976). Prior exercise of freedom and reactance. *Journal of Experimental Social Psychology, 12,* 120–130.

Spangenberg, E. R., Sprott, D. E., Obermiller, C., & Greenwald, A. G. (2002). *Self-prophecy as dissonance reduction.* Unpublished manuscript. Washington State University.

Sprott, D. E., Fisher, R., & Spangenberg, E. R. (2001). Using the self-prophecy effect to promote socially desirable consumption: The role of normative beliefs. Unpublished manuscript. Washington State University.

Sprott, D. E., Spangenberg, E. R., & Perkins, A. W. (1999). Two more self-prophecy experiments. In L. Scott & E. Arnould (Eds.), *Advances in consumer research* (Vol. 25, pp. 621–626). Provo, UT: Association for Consumer Research.

Taylor, B. (1989). *Mental stimulation and the anticipation of regret.* Unpublished master's thesis. Princeton University, Princeton, NJ.

Tedeschi, J. T., Schlenker, B. R., & Bonoma, T. V. (1971). Cognitive dissonance: Private ratiocination or public spectacle? *American Psychologist, 26,* 685–695.

Triandis, H. C. (1995). The self and social behavior in differing cultural contexts. In N. R. Goldberger & J. B. Verloff (Eds.), *The culture and psychology reader.* New York: New York University Press.

Trope, Y., & Liberman, N. (2000). Temporal construal and time-dependent changes in preference. *Journal of Personality and Social Psychology, 79,* 876–889.

Tversky, A., & Kahneman, D. (1974). Availability: A heuristic for judging frequency and probability. *Cognitive Psychology, 5,* 207–232.

Tykocinski, O. E., & Pittman, T. S. (1998). The consequences of doing nothing: Inaction inertia as avoidance of anticipated counterfactual regret. *Journal of Personality and Social Psychology, 75,* 607–616.

Wells, G. L., & Gavanski, I. (1989). Mental simulation of causality. *Journal of Personality and Social Psychology, 56,* 161–169.

Witte, K., & Allen, M. (2000). A meta-analysis of fear appeals: Implications for effective public health campaigns. *Health Education and Behavior, 27,* 591–615.

Worchel, S., & Brehm, J. W. (1971). Direct and implied social restoration of freedom. *Journal of Personality and Social Psychology, 18,* 294–304.

Wright, R. A., & Brehm, S. S. (1982). Reactance as impression management: A critical review. *Journal of Personality and Social Psychology, 42,* 608–618.

Zeelenberg, M., Beattie, J., Van der Pligt, J., & de Vries, N. (1996). Consequence of risk aversion: Effects of expected feedback on risky decision making. *Organizational Behavior and Human Decision Processes, 65,* 148–158.

9

Narrative Persuasion and Overcoming Resistance

Sonya Dal Cin, Mark P. Zanna, and
Geoffrey T. Fong
University of Waterloo

Narratives are ubiquitous. Consider the vast numbers of people who are consuming stories at any given time. Casual observation of rush-hour passengers on the subway in Toronto (and we imagine those in Chicago, New York, and Paris) reveals a large number of commuters reading newspapers, magazines, and novels. At the same time, commuters driving the city's major highways are listening to the radio—hearing stories about what is happening in the world. Children in day care and at school spend part of the day reading (or being read) stories, selected as age-appropriate and noncontroversial in their content, lest impressionable youth be led astray. Meanwhile, adults at home avidly tune in to soap operas. After school and after work, millions of people around the world switch on the television, expecting to be entertained by dramas, comedies, and "reality" television.

This proliferation of stories is hardly surprising if one considers that stories have been with us throughout our history. Cave paintings at Lascaux (c. 17000–15000 B.C.E.) that predate the development of literacy tell stories of hunts and animals. About 330 B.C.E. Aristotle discussed the power of Greek tragedy in his *Poetics* (trans. 1996). Centuries later, Jesus used parables to teach morality and religion. The written versions of these oral narratives are reproduced in various versions of the Bible—the best-selling book of all time (Internet Public Library,

2002). During the Renaissance, Shakespeare wrote dramatic comedies, tragedies, and histories that still draw theater crowds to this day.

Given the popularity and diversity of narrative, it seems naïve to imagine that narrative does not serve some sort of positive function. If we didn't enjoy narratives, if they didn't have some benefit for us, would we be inclined to watch as much television as we do? Would Hollywood films generate profits in the millions of dollars? It seems unlikely. Scholars in a variety of disciplines have investigated the nature of narrative and our relationship with it. A wide body of research indicates that narratives have an influence on their readers. (In using the terms *reading, watching,* and *listening* we intend for the reader to understand that the processes apply regardless of the media in which the narrative is presented and consumed.) Narratives touch our emotions (e.g., Oatley & Gholamain, 1997), impact what we believe (Green & Brock, 2000), teach us new behaviors (see Slater, 2002, for a review), and shape our cultural identity (Jacobs, 2002). Indeed, there is little doubt in the minds of many that narratives can be persuasive. On one hand, parents read their children Aesop's fables or Brothers Grimm fairy tales, hoping to instill morals and ethics; on the other hand, they petition school boards to ban books they feel are a bad influence.

For years, communication initiatives known as education entertainment—the systematic use of stories (on television, radio, or other media) to promote specific behaviors—have been in place around the world (Slater, 2002). Even the U.S. government is in on the action—the Office of National Drug Control Policy (ONDCP) has identified the entertainment industry as a key player in disseminating anti-drug messages by incorporating these themes into storylines (ONDCP, 2000). Indeed, the ONDCP has negotiated with networks to allow inclusion of anti-drug storylines on popular series in lieu of providing discounted advertising slots (Forbes, 2000). Although outcome–evaluation of education entertainment has its limitations (Slater, 2002), research in social psychology has begun to demonstrate persuasion empirically through narrative (e.g., Strange & Leung, 1999; Green & Brock, 2000). The psychological mechanisms of narrative persuasion are not yet well understood, but theorists from a variety of disciplines are working toward this goal (see Green, Strange, & Brock, 2002, for a review).

If narratives can be persuasive, then we might begin to consider the situations in which narrative persuasion may prove particularly useful. The goal of the current chapter is to consider the possible role of narratives in overcoming resistance—people's motivated effort to defend an attitude against change. Specifically, how might the use of narrative persuasion strategies work better than the use of traditional advocacy messages? Is narrative more effective than the most state-of-the-art rhetoric? Indeed, similar to our own thinking, Slater (2002) has suggested that "Use of narratives, in fact, may be one of the only strategies available for influencing the beliefs of those who are predisposed to disagree with the position espoused in the persuasive message" (p. 175). We would extend this argument and suggest that narratives can be a useful strategy in challenging strong attitudes, that is, attitudes that people hold quite fiercely and confidently, and that are most resistant to change (Petty & Krosnick, 1995). We believe that narrative messages have an impact on weak attitudes, but by definition, weak attitudes are not particularly difficult to change using rhetorical persuasion strategies. It is strong attitudes—those that truly elicit resistance—that demand more effective persuasive tools. Our discussion of narrative persuasion is therefore concerned with overcoming resistance when attitudes are strong. It is our belief, for the reasons we outline below, that narratives will prove to be especially effective in the battle to change strong attitudes.

THE WHYS AND HOWS OF NARRATIVE PERSUASION

Why might narrative persuasion strategies be especially suited to overcoming resistance? We believe that there are two general means by which narratives might overcome resistance, each of which reflects a variety of specific processes. First, narratives may overcome resistance by reducing the amount and effectiveness of counterarguing or logical consideration of the message. Second, narratives may overcome resistance by increasing identification with characters in the story.

Narratives should reduce counterarguing in a number of ways. First, narratives may overcome *biased processing* (Petty & Cacioppo, 1986) in response to counter-attitudinal messages. When presented with a communication advocating a position with which we do not agree, there is a tendency to ignore the message, counterargue the information, or belittle the source. Petty and Cacioppo report that resistance to persuasion tends to increase when there is forewarning of either the message content or of persuasive intent (see also Quinn & Wood, this volume). In rhetorical communications, such as public service announcements and political speeches, we tend to be aware of either the communicator's intent to persuade us, the counter-attitudinal quality of the message, or both. With regard to the perception of persuasive intent, we argue that in general, narratives might be more effective than rhetoric because the former are not seen as persuasive attempts. We don't go to a movie or pick up a novel expecting to be influenced on a particular issue; rather, we expect to be entertained.

Also, the structure of narratives may impede forewarning of a counter-attitudinal message. A story often unfolds with some degree of suspense—it is not always clear what situation might next befall a protagonist or how that protagonist will react to it. "Predictable" is commonly used as a criticism in popular film reviews. Studies have shown that individuals avoid attending to information that is incongruent with their existing attitudes (e.g., Sweeney & Gruber, 1984). Narratives may be less vulnerable to this selective exposure because specific messages might not be apparent until it is too late. Although an antiabortionist might avoid a film about Roe v. Wade, this same person might willingly go to a film that is not about the abortion issue per se, but unbeknownst to the viewer, contains a subplot with a pro-choice message. Thus, narratives may be inherently suited to the presentation of messages seeking to change strong attitudes because they "get under the radar" of our efforts to protect these attitudes.

The content of narrative arguments may also be more difficult to discount than that of rhetorical arguments. Narratives are often concerned with relating the life experiences of other people, be they real or fictional. As Slater (2002) suggested, it may be especially difficult to counterargue the lived experiences of another real or fictional person. Although one might be able to argue against hypothetical examples ("That would never happen"), it is much more difficult to argue against another's "real" experiences as conveyed in a narrative. It is true that the experiences of fictional characters are not real. However, experiences of fictional characters that are construed as being plausible may be equally difficult to refute. As Green and Brock (2002) have noted, plausibility seems to be the yardstick by which we measure truth—the implausible must be untrue, regardless of whether it is fact or fiction, whereas the plausible, if not true, at least *could* be.

Narrative also differs from rhetoric in the way that messages are communicated. Whereas the aim of advocacy is to present clear, logical, specific arguments, the aim of narrative is to tell a story. In a narrative, beliefs are often implied as opposed to stated explicitly. This may inhibit counterarguing because it leaves the reader with no specific arguments to refute.

Implied beliefs, however, are not the only means by which narrative may inhibit counterarguing. We agree with others (e.g., Green & Brock, 2000; Slater, 2002), that the cognitive and emotional demands of absorption into a narrative leave readers with little ability or motivation to generate counterarguments. Absorption into a narrative is believed to be a convergent process, where all mental faculties are engaged in the narrative experience (Green & Brock, 2000). We lose access to real-world facts and suspend disbelief. Such a constriction of cognitive capacity should make it exceedingly difficult to scrutinize messages in the narrative and to generate counterarguments. The ability to counterargue is impaired not only because we have a limited amount of cognitive attention to devote to the endeavor, but also because many of the arguments we would call to mind are inaccessible. Add to this a lack of motivation brought about by a desire to remain engaged with the narrative (which counterarguing would necessarily disrupt), and counterarguing a narrative message should become increasingly difficult as absorption increases.

If narrative messages are less threatening than comparable rhetoric, then we may have a very powerful persuasive tool at our disposal. One of us (Zanna, 1993) has argued that resistance should result when listeners are faced with arguments that support an attitudinal position that falls outside their latitude of acceptance. That is, people have some degree of "wiggle room"—a latitude of acceptance—around their attitudes (see Sherif & Hovland, 1961). The latitude of acceptance can vary in size, from very narrow (indicating a fairly rigid attitudinal position) to very wide (indicating a more flexible attitudinal position). On either side of the latitude of acceptance lie latitudes of rejection—attitudinal positions that are unacceptable or objectionable because they are considered too extreme. Consider the following example: People hold very different opinions on gay rights. On one end of the spectrum one finds those who feel that gay and lesbian relationships should not be recognized as legitimate, or indeed, should be outlawed. At the opposite end of the spectrum one finds those who feel that gay and lesbian relationships are as valid as heterosexual relationships, and that gays and lesbians should be legally able to marry. Between these two extreme attitudinal positions is a continuum of attitudes where the attitude of any given individual can fall, and each individual has a unique latitude of acceptance around this attitude. For example, John and Sally may both agree that gays and lesbians should be allowed spousal-type pension benefits, but John is willing to accept calling a same-sex union "marriage" whereas Sally is not. Including same-sex unions in the definition of marriage is an attitudinal position that falls outside Sally's latitude of acceptance.

Zanna (1993) has argued that to overcome this type of resistance, it is necessary to avoid closed-mindedness on the part of those we are trying to persuade. That is, one should ideally seek to present an argument that is fairly extreme without making listeners aware of its extremity. Using rhetorical means of persuasion, this may be accomplished by presenting a message that claims to support a generally acceptable position, but that actually supports a more extreme and possibly objectionable position—the so-called "Marc Anthony gambit": After the assassination of Caesar, Shakespeare's Marc Anthony, knowing his Roman audience loathed the dead emperor, began a speech with the words, "I come to bury Caesar, not to praise him." (*Julius Caesar,* III. ii. 75) He then proceeded to do exactly what he claimed he would not. By not raising the red flags of resistance in his fellow countrymen, Anthony managed to present counter-attitudinal arguments that may have otherwise earned him the same fate as Caesar. We believe that narratives might be ideally suited to this type of "under the radar" persuasive attempt. As we have already mentioned, the counter-attitudinal message in a narrative may unfold so slowly, be so unexpected, be so subtle, that the reader fails to realize that the message falls within his or her latitude of rejection. We argue that to the extent that a narrative challenges an existing attitude without throwing up the barriers of closed-mindedness, we should find attitude change in the direction of the persuasive attempt.

Thus, narratives may indeed be useful in overcoming resistance by reducing negative thoughts associated with the persuasive message. In addition, we argue that narratives may also function by increasing positive thoughts about a behavior or an attitude object. This would be especially true if a liked protagonist behaves in a particular way or endorses a particular attitude, creating a positive association with the action or the attitude. Identifying with a story character may result in persuasion in a number of ways.

We know from research on rhetorical persuasion that a liked source can be more persuasive under conditions in which it is more difficult to process arguments (Petty & Cacioppo, 1986). We have already suggested some reasons why narratives, by their very nature, may limit the desire and ability to scrutinize messages. In addition, many narratives are visual presentations (e.g., film and television) in which the speed of the message is controlled, and this has implications for persuasion. Chaiken and Eagly (1983) found that a likeable source was more persuasive when the speed of exposure to rhetorical messages was forced (i.e., when presented on audio or video tape) than when the participants were allowed to self-pace the speed of exposure (i.e., when the same message was presented in written form). Therefore, it seems highly plausible that liking for a protagonist might be an important mediator of persuasion in the narrative context, especially when exposure is not self-paced.

In contrast to our argument that films may be more persuasive than books, Green and Brock (2002) have hypothesized that books may be more persuasive than films. They argue that self-pacing results in greater involvement (transportation) in response to the story because it allows for greater development of powerful images and participatory responses from the reader. Transportation into the narrative in turn causes narrative persuasion. We feel that both of these hypotheses regarding the importance of self-pacing (and, by extension, the format in which the narrative is presented) are plausible, and plan to investigate further the role of pacing in narrative persuasion.

But liking may be only part of the equation. Liking requires only positive sentiment—we like our friends, we like certain actors, we like our family members. Identification, however, requires more than just liking. It requires *likeness* (perceived similarity) to a character, or some desire to be *like* the character (Oatley, 2002; Slater, 2002). We may like a particular character but feel that his or her attitudes or behavior are not relevant to our own lives. For example, we might read a story about an older woman who is rediscovering the dating scene after her husband leaves her for a younger woman. We may like this character, we may feel sympathy for her, and we may be convinced that philandering husbands are evil, yet it is possible that none of us will identify with her. Why? Perhaps she is too different from us, her life experiences too different from our own; none of us is an older woman, or none of us seeks to be in her position. Along with Oatley and Slater, we believe that identification may be a key component in narrative impact. We agree that identification may not only lead to empathy and cognitive rehearsal of the beliefs, but that it may also, as Slater suggests, directly impact *behavior* and behavioral intentions by changing self-efficacy beliefs and making specific attitudes more accessible.

Thus, the narrative context may be especially suited to overcoming resistance to persuasion. We believe the power of narrative lies in reducing the amount and effectiveness of counterarguing and through identification with narrative characters that leads to positive associations with specific beliefs and behaviors.

TRANSPORTATION INTO THE STORY: THE PROCESS OF NARRATIVE-BASED BELIEF CHANGE

In keeping with current research on narrative persuasion, we suggest that the impact of narrative messages on readers' attitudes is dependent on the extent to which a reader becomes involved with the narrative. Researchers have discussed this concept of absorption into a narrative (e.g., Gerrig, 1993; Green & Brock, 2000; Green, Strange, & Brock, 2002). Green and Brock (2000) termed this phenomenon *transportation*—"a convergent process, where all mental systems and capacities become focused on events in the narrative" (p. 701). Our thoughts are centered on the story, we respond emotionally to the characters and events, and we picture the events as they unfold. To measure transportation, Green and Brock developed a scale designed to capture what are believed to be the major dimensions of transportation (Gerrig, 1993): cognitive attention to the story (e.g., "I was mentally involved in the narrative while reading it"), emotional involvement (e.g., "The narrative affected me emotionally"), feelings of suspense (e.g., "I wanted to learn how the narrative ended"), a lack of awareness of the surroundings (e.g., "While I was reading the narrative, activity going on in the room around me was on my mind"; reverse scored item), and existence of mental imagery (e.g., "While reading the narrative I had a vivid image of Katie," p. 704).

Using this scale, Green and Brock (2000) conducted studies supporting their contention that narratives can be persuasive to the extent that they transport their readers. Readers were presented with one of several short stories and were then asked how transported they were by the narrative. For example, participants in several studies read a short story entitled "Murder at the Mall," excerpted and paraphrased from a nonfiction bestseller dealing with the physiology of dying (Nuland, 1994). The following is a portion of the story participants read:

> . . . little Christine began tugging at Joan's hand to attract her attention to the mechanical pony rides, begging to be taken over there. Leaving Katie with the others, Joan and her younger sister headed toward the rides. Just as they reached the pony, Joan heard a hubbub from somewhere behind her and then a child's shrill scream. She turned, dropped Christine's hand, and advanced a few feet toward the sound. People were scattering in all directions, trying to get away from a large, disheveled man who stood over a fallen little girl, his outstretched right arm pummeling furiously away at her. Even through the haze of her frozen incomprehension, Joan knew instantly that the child lying on her side at the crazed man's feet was Katie. At first, she saw only the arm, then realized all at once that in its hand was clutched a long bloody object. It was a hunting knife, about seven inches long. Using all his strength, up and down, up and down, in rapid pistonlike motions, the assailant was hacking away at Katie's face and neck.
> . . . Two men suddenly appeared from somewhere beyond the margins of the tableau and grabbed at the killer, shouting as they tried to wrestle him down. But

he could not be deterred—with psychotic determination, he kept stabbing at Katie. Even when one of the men began aiming powerful heavy-booted kicks at his face, he seemed not to notice, though his head was being knocked from side to side by the force of the blows. A policeman ran up and seized the knife wielding arm; only then did the three men manage to subdue the struggling maniac and pin him to the ground.

The story continues with a powerful account of Katie's final moments, and we learn that Katie's assailant was a psychiatric patient with a history of violence who was out on a day pass. After reading the story and completing the transportation scale, readers provided evaluations of the major characters in the story and reported the extent to which they agreed or disagreed with specific beliefs implied by the narrative. For example, readers were asked to evaluate whether Katie and her attacker were good or bad, or whether they agreed or disagreed with statements such as "Psychiatric patients who live in an institution should be allowed to go out in the community during the day." Finally, participants were asked to identify *false notes* in the stories (statements that were contradictory or did not make sense).

Green and Brock (2000, Experiment 2) found that more transported participants identified fewer *false notes* than did less transported participants. Thus, the more readers reported being transported by the narrative, the more they failed to see errors or faulty arguments in that narrative. This lends support to the idea that being transported involves a certain degree of suspension of disbelief or logical inattention.

Green and Brock (2000) also found that the more transported participants were, the more they tended to endorse beliefs implied by the narrative. For example, across a number of studies, participants who were more transported after reading "Murder at the Mall" were significantly more likely to agree that psychiatric patients should have their freedoms restricted than were participants who were less transported. In an ancillary study, Green and Brock (Experiment 1) showed that preexisting beliefs did not predict transportation. That is, it was not the case that those whose attitudes were consonant (or dissonant) with the beliefs implied in the story were more transported by the story. Taken together, these findings suggest that transportation can lead readers to adopt beliefs that are consistent with those communicated by the narrative, independent of their initial attitudes.

Green and Brock's (2000) findings are consistent with our argument that narratives are persuasive and that messages in the narrative may not be well scrutinized. Also, participants' beliefs about whether the narrative was factual or fictional had no impact on either transportation or persuasion—supporting the hypothesis that narratives may indeed be judged on their plausibility.

INDIVIDUAL DIFFERENCES
IN TRANSPORTABILITY

Our own research in transportation focuses on the role that individual differences may play in narrative persuasion. We began with a simple observation that some individuals seem to be readily and deeply transported by narratives, whereas others do not seem to experience the same level of transportation. We call this individual difference *transportability*. We feel that transportability serves as a moderator that is unique to narrative persuasion. That is, other things being equal, transportability should predict who is persuaded by narrative appeals, such that those high in transportability should be more persuaded by a narrative than those low in transportability. In contrast, transportability should not predict the extent to which one is persuaded by traditional rhetoric or advocacy messages.

To measure this construct, we created two versions of a Transportability Scale, one worded to assess transportability for reading materials and one worded to assess transportability for visual materials such as films. Working from the premise that transportability is a generalized tendency toward being transported, we designed the Transportability Scale as an adaptation and extension of Green and Brock's (2000) Transportation Scale. Whereas the Transportation Scale is designed to measure transportation at a specific time, in response to a specific narrative, the Transportability Scale asks participants to generalize across stories and contexts. The Transportability Scale applicable to printed material is reproduced in Table 9.1.

In a study assessing the validity of our transportability measure (Dal Cin, Zanna, & Fong, 2002), we administered the scale to a large group of introductory psychology students in an extra-credit assignment booklet. Standardized Cronbach's alpha for both versions ranged from .87 to .88. Ten-week test-retest reliabilities ranged from .62 to .64 (all $ps < .001$), indicating that the Transportability Scale is quite stable over time. We also found that the two versions (reading material and film) of the Transportability Scale were correlated, $r = .66$, $p < .001$, but this correlation was somewhat less than might be expected, given the similarity of the items. Indeed, inspection of the raw data showed that there are individuals who report being much more transportable in response to books than in response to films (and vice versa).

Several weeks after administration of the Transportability Scales, we brought some of the students in to the lab, presented them with narratives that varied in quality and format (written stories vs. video clips), and measured the extent to which they were transported and the extent to which they endorsed beliefs espoused in the stories. Our measure of transportation was a narrative-specific version of our Transportability Scale. That is, the items were the same as those in the Transportability Scale (Table 9.1), but the tense was changed to the present and specific story titles and characters' names were inserted where appropriate.

Table 9.1

Transportability Scale

When reading for pleasure:
1. I can easily envision the events in the story.
2. I find I can easily lose myself in the story.
3. I find it difficult to tune out activity around me. (Reversed)
4. I can easily envision myself in the events described in a story.
5. I get mentally involved in the story.
6. I can easily put stories out of my mind after I've finished reading them. (Reversed)
7. I sometimes feel as if I am part of the story.
8. I am often impatient to find out how the story ends.
9. I find that I can easily take the perspective of the character(s) in the story.
10. I am often emotionally affected by what I've read.
11. I have vivid images of the characters.
12. I find myself accepting events that I might have otherwise considered unrealistic.
13. I find myself thinking what the characters may be thinking.
14. I find myself thinking of other ways the story could have ended.
15. My mind often wanders. (Reversed)
16. I find myself feeling what the characters may feel.
17. I find that events in the story are relevant to my everyday life.
18. I often find that reading stories has an impact on the way I see things.
19. I easily identify with characters in the story.
20. I have vivid images of the events in the story.

The film version of the Transportability Scale contains the same items as above, with syntactical changes designed to reflect the change in media being considered. For example, the prompt is changed to "When watching movies/videos for pleasure," and the word "reading" is replaced with "watching."

Both versions are scored on a scale of 1 through 9 (Strongly Disagree–Strongly Agree). Items 3, 6, and 15 are reverse scored.

We used two short stories and two movie clips as stimuli. One of the short stories was "Murder at the Mall" and the other was another short story used by Green and Brock (2000) entitled "Two Were Left" (Cave, 1942), which describes a test of loyalty between an Inuit boy and his dog. Green and Brock reported that these two stories differ in the extent to which they transport readers, and we hoped to demonstrate that transportability predicts transportation at varying levels of text quality. We also wanted to broaden the research on transportation by including film-based narratives in our study. We selected two major motion pictures, *A Time to Kill* and *Norma Rae*. We then selected scenes from each film and had them professionally edited to produce a self-contained "mini-movie." For example, the film *Norma Rae* tells the story of a woman working in a textile mill in the American south and her struggle to unionize her workplace. Our edited version included scenes that conveyed the general plot of the story but eliminated subplots and noncentral details. In the dramatic final scene, Norma Rae's employers fire her for her union organizing activities. As she is escorted out, she stands on a table in the center of the mill and holds up a sign that reads "UNION," and in support, her coworkers shut down their machines. In our version of *A Time to Kill*, viewers see the story of an African-American

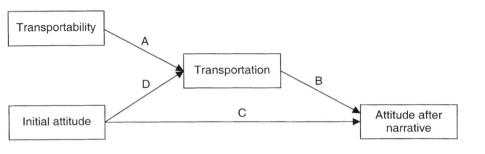

FIG. 9.1   Narrative-based belief change as a function of transportability, transportation, and attitude.

man on trial for killing the white men who assaulted his young daughter.

After participants were exposed to each narrative, we measured the extent to which they were transported by that narrative. We then asked them to agree or disagree with a variety of statements that reflected themes in the narrative. For example, after reading "Murder at the Mall" participants responded to statements like "Psychiatric patients who live in an institution should be allowed to go out in the community during the day" (reverse scored; Green & Brock, 2000, p. 705), and after watching *Norma Rae* participants responded to statements such as "Workers should fight for their rights, even if they lose their jobs over it."

As expected, we found mean differences in transportation across the four narratives ($F = 19.04$, $df = 3, 261$, $p < .001$). The most transporting narrative was our film clip from *A Time to Kill* ($M = 6.34$, $SD = 1.13$), followed by the short story "Murder at the Mall" ($M = 6.16$, $SD = 1.20$). The least transporting narratives were our film clip from *Norma Rae* ($M = 5.76$, $SD = 1.30$) and the short story "Two Were Left" ($M = 5.54$, $SD = 1.10$). This suggests that qualities of the stories themselves contributed to transportation, at least in part.

We also examined the relation between transportability, transportation, and beliefs. A typical result is illustrated in Fig. 9.1. We found that the Transportability Scale predicted the extent to which readers reported being transported by specific narratives. That is, participants who reported a greater tendency to become involved in narratives were more transported by the stories than were participants who reported a lesser tendency to become involved in narratives (Path A, Fig. 9.1). This relation between transportability and transportation was consistent across all four narratives ($Bs = .37$ to 48; $ps < .001$). The two versions of the Transportability Scale (written material vs. film) were equally predictive of transportation in response to narratives of different modalities. We plan to explore the specificity of transportability and its relation—or lack of relation—to transportation in future studies.

Consistent with Green and Brock's (2000) findings, transportation to particular stories in turn predicted the endorsement of beliefs advocated in the story (Path B, Fig. 9.1). For example, after reading "Murder at the Mall," in which a psychiatric patient kills a little girl, more transported readers tended to endorse statements calling for restrictions on the freedom of psychiatric patients. After watching the film clip from *Norma Rae,* which illustrates unfair working conditions and promotes workers' rights, more transported viewers tended to endorse pro-worker attitudes to a greater extent than did their less transported counterparts. Although participants' initial attitudes (measured weeks before, along with transportability) were correlated with their attitudes following the narrative (Path C, both $Bs = .47$; $ps < .001$), initial beliefs had no effect on transportation (Path D, $Bs = -.08$ to $.16$; $ps > .05$). Most importantly, the effect of transportation on subsequent attitudes remained significant even when accounting for preexisting attitudes (Path B, $Bs = .28$ to $.30$, $ps < .003$), indicating belief change. Occasionally, we found a zero-order correlation between transportability and specific beliefs following exposure to the narrative. However, in all cases, the relation between transportability and subsequent beliefs was entirely mediated by transportation.

In sum, we found support for the hypothesis that narrative persuasion, through transportation, is determined by features of both the reader and the narrative. We found that people vary in the extent to which they are transported by narratives, and that some narratives tend to transport readers more than others. We also found that the predisposition to be transported (transportability) reliably predicts the extent to which participants are transported by a particular story—the more transportable participants reported being more engrossed in the stories than the less transportable participants.

FUTURE DIRECTIONS

Although research has begun to shed light on the nature of narrative persuasion, we feel that there are a number of important questions that have yet to be addressed. Specifically, and in keeping with the theme of this volume, we believe that research into the use of narratives to overcome resistance is not only theoretically interesting, but also crucial in a media-saturated culture. Advertisers long ago realized that consumers have grown weary of commercials and blatant advertisements. (With the introduction of the remote control, it is a wonder that anyone sees commercials at all anymore). Possibly, as a consequence, advertisers decided that product placements—having a character in a film drink a certain beverage or drive a certain car—could lead to increased sales. There are also millions of dollars being spent to lobby Hollywood to include pro-social storylines in its television series (e.g., National Campaign to Prevent Teen Pregnancy, 2001). Yet we have little understanding of how, or indeed if, these strategies work.

We argue that the time has come to pit narrative against rhetoric, and to demonstrate that narrative can be effective and can "get under the radar" that detects persuasive attempts. We also suggest that future research identify how, when, and for whom narrative persuasion overcomes resistance. It is important that we determine whether narrative persuasion is indeed different from rhetorical persuasion—that each is characterized by different moderators and mediators. Some support for unique moderators currently exists; Green and Brock (2000) found that need for cognition, a well-established moderator of rhetorical persuasion (Petty & Cacioppo, 1986), does not moderate narrative persuasion. Similarly, we believe that our construct of transportability, which we have found moderates narrative belief change, will not moderate belief change in response to rhetorical persuasion attempts. Using transportability, we should be able to identify the people for whom narratives may be a particularly effective means of overcoming resistance. With regard to unique mediators, we feel that transportation should fail to serve as a mediator in rhetorical persuasion though it does mediate narrative persuasion. Furthermore, mediators of rhetorical persuasion (e.g., number of counterarguments generated in response to the message) should fail to mediate the effects of narrative persuasion. We look forward to empirical research exploring these hypotheses.

Beyond these theoretical questions, we see a vital need for social psychologists to begin applied research into the effects of narratives on attitudes and behavior. Narratives are being used to sell values and it is imperative that we evaluate the effectiveness of these attempts. Recent research on tobacco control has found that smoking is highly prevalent in feature films (e.g., Sargent, Tickle, Beach, Dalton, Ahrens, & Heatherton, 2001). In addition, there is research supporting the contention that positive depictions of tobacco use in film do indeed result in more favorable attitudes toward smoking and smokers (Dal Cin, Gibson, Zanna, & Fong, 2003; Gibson & Maurer, 2000; Pechmann & Shih, 1999). Happily, although popular narratives are persuasive on the "benefits" of smoking, Pechmann and Shih reported that including an antitobacco message before a film increases resistance to these pro-smoking images. This leaves us with some support for our belief that narrative persuasion functions, at least in part, by obscuring the persuasive intent of the communicator. Once alerted to the presence of pro-smoking images in the film, Pechmann and Shih's adolescent participants seemed much less willing to swallow the message. It seems clear that message placement in public narrative has the power to influence us.

This influence may occur in very subtle ways. We are currently examining whether narratives can change implicit attitudes. Implicit attitudes (Greenwald & Banaji, 1995) reflect the unconscious, automatic associations a person has toward attitude objects, such as members of visible minorities (e.g., Son Hing, Li, & Zanna, 2002). Oatley and his colleagues (Oatley, 2002; Oatley & Gholamain, 1997) have discussed the emotional impact of narratives on their readers, and the identification readers develop with characters. The strength of the affective component of an attitude is directly related to resistance; that is, the stronger the affective component of the attitude, the more resistant the attitude is to change (see Brehm & Fuegen, this volume). If we integrate positive or negative emotions elicited by a narrative into our associative networks, it seems plausible that implicit attitude change might occur. We have already suggested that identification with story characters leads to positive associations with particular beliefs. It seems plausible that on a purely implicit level, these positive responses may become integrated in the network of associations one already has regarding these beliefs. The individual need not be conscious of such positive associations, and indeed, may explicitly discount them (e.g., "The portrayal of African Americans in that movie was unrealistic"), but their inclusion in the greater network of associations should influence implicit attitudes and, quite possibly, behavior itself.

As we have already mentioned, there are those (including the U.S. government) who lobby Hollywood day in and day out to include pro-social messages in television shows (Quenqua, 2002). A survey of regular viewers of the popular prime-time medical drama *ER* (Brodie et al., 2001) found that viewers surveyed after watching a specific episode reported greater awareness of the health issue discussed in the episode than did viewers surveyed prior to the airing of the episode. Also, half of regular viewers reported that they discussed health issues from the show with family and friends, one-third reported that they used information from *ER* in making health decisions, and one in seven reported contacting a health professional about a health problem as a result of information in the show. Messages on everything from teen pregnancy to sexual assault to cancer prevention could be included in popular media (see also Diekman, McDonald, & Gardner, 2000). Even if the effect of such initiatives is statistically small, when distributed across millions of viewers, the impact could be widespread and substantial. With what other interventions can we reach millions of people willing to attend to our message?

The potential of narratives as a vehicle for communicating information is even more apparent when we consider the possibility of multiple message exposures. Many people enjoy particular genres of fiction (romance, mystery/crime, science fiction, medical drama, etc). For example, though romance novels may not be considered great literature, millions of people around the globe read these stories. In 2001, Harlequin Enterprises, a major publisher of romance novels, sold 150 million books in 94 international markets (Torstar Corporation, 2001). Specific narratives within a genre tend to follow the same general storyline and contain similar messages or themes. Diekman et al. (2000) conducted a content analysis of contemporary romance novels and concluded that these stories illustrate a "swept away myth" (p. 184) that love equals being swept away by passion. Unfortunately, such spontaneity results in romance novel protagonists having unprotected sex; Diekman et al. found that the vast majority (89.7%) of novels sampled failed to make any mention of condom use. Furthermore, in the limited number of stories in which safer sex was mentioned, almost half had the female protagonist rejecting condom use. Diekman et al. found that higher levels of romance novel reading were associated with less positive attitudes toward condoms and less intention to use condoms in the future. They also found that participants presented with romance novel excerpts in which the protagonists use a condom reported more positive attitudes toward condoms than did participants who read the same excerpts without mention of condom use. Thus, it seems clear that preference for a certain genre may lead readers to endorse beliefs pervasive in that genre—beliefs that may or may not be accurate or healthy.

We believe that the power of narratives in our culture is considerable, and failure to acknowledge this power would be irresponsible. Narrative may be a useful tool in overcoming resistance to persuasion, primarily because narratives may not throw up the barriers of closed-mindedness. Audiences should be receptive to a message that is presented in the context of a plausible, entertaining story. This can be beneficial, but when narratives are used to convey harmful messages (such as negative portrayals of minorities or positive depictions of smoking or unsafe sex) it can also be dangerous. Therefore, we should also be concerned with increasing resistance to narrative persuasion. As a potentially powerful tool for overcoming resistance to advocacy and rhetorical persuasive attempts, we feel that the study of narrative persuasion is not only fascinating, but also vitally important.

AUTHOR NOTE

Support for this project was provided in part by an Ontario Graduate Scholarship and a Centre for Behavioural Research and Program Evaluation, Canadian Cancer Society/National Cancer Institute of Canada Student Research Award awarded to the first author; a Social Sciences and Humanities Research Council Grant awarded to the second author; and a National Cancer Institute Research Grant awarded to the third author. The research discussed in this chapter was presented at the third annual meeting of the Society for Personality and Social Psychology, Savannah, GA, February, 2002.

REFERENCES

Brodie, M., Foehr, U., Rideout, V., Baer, N., Miller, C., Flournoy, R., & Altman, D. (2001). Communicating health information through the entertainment media. *Health affairs, 20,* 192–199.

Cave, H. B. (1942, June). Two were left. *American Magazine,* 133.

Chaiken, S., & Eagly, A. H. (1983). Communication modality as a determinant of message persuasiveness and message comprehensibility. *Journal of Personality and Social Psychology, 34,* 605–614.

Dal Cin, S., Gibson, B., Zanna, M. P., & Fong, G. T. (2003, August). Narrative persuasion and attitudes toward smoking. In T. C. Brock (Chair), *Models and Mechanisms of Narrative Persua-*

190   DAL CIN, ZANNA, FONG

sion. Symposium conducted at the 111th Annual Convention of the American Psychological Association, Toronto, ON.

Dal Cin, S., Zanna, M. P., & Fong, G. T. (February, 2002). Perceiver-based and stimulus-based individual differences in transportation. Symposium paper presented at the third annual meeting of the Society of Personality and Social Psychology, Savannah, GA.

Diekman, A. B., McDonald, M., & Gardner, W. L. (2000). Love means never having to be careful: The relationship between reading romance novels and safe sex behavior. *Psychology of Women Quarterly, 24,* 179–188.

Forbes, D. (2000, Jan. 13). Prime time propaganda. *Salon.* Retrieved September 12, 2002, from http://dir.salon.com/news/feature/2000/01/13/drugs/index.html.

Gerrig, R. J. (1993). *Experiencing narrative worlds.* New Haven, CT: Yale University Press.

Gibson, B., & Maurer, J. (2000). Cigarette smoking in the movies: The influence of product placement on attitudes toward smoking and smokers. *Journal of Applied Social Psychology, 30,* 1457–1473.

Green, M. C., & Brock, T. C. (2000). The role of transportation in the pervasiveness of public narratives. *Journal of Personality and Social Psychology, 79,* 701–721.

Green, M. C., & Brock, T. C. (2002). In the mind's eye: Transportation-imagery model of narrative persuasion. In M. C. Green, J. J. Strange, & T. C. Brock (Eds.), *Narrative impact: Social and cognitive foundations* (pp. 315–341). Mahwah, NJ: Erlbaum.

Green, M. C., Strange, J. J., & Brock, T. C. (Eds.). (2002). *Narrative impact: Social and cognitive foundations.* Mahwah, NJ: Erlbaum.

Greenwald, A. G., & Banaji, M. R. (1995). Implicit social cognition: Attitudes, self-esteem, and stereotypes. *Psychological Review, 102,* 4–27.

Internet Public Library. (2002, Jan. 16). *All-time bestselling books and authors.* Retrieved September 12, 2002, from http://www.ipl.org/div/farq/bestsellerFARQ.html.

Jacobs, R. N. (2002). The narrative integration of personal and collective realities in social movements. In M. C. Green, J. J. Strange, & T. C. Brock (Eds.), *Narrative impact: Social and cognitive foundations* (pp. 205–228). Mahwah, NJ: Erlbaum.

National Campaign to Prevent Teen Pregnancy. (2001, February). *Proposal to the John D. and Catherine T. MacArthur Foundation for the period October 1, 2001, through September 30, 2004.* Washington, DC: Author.

Nuland, S. (1994). *How we die.* New York: Knopf.

Oatley, K. (2002). Emotions and the story worlds of fiction. In M. C. Green, J. J. Strange, & T. C. Brock (Eds.), *Narrative impact: Social and cognitive foundations* (pp. 39–69). Mahwah, NJ: Erlbaum.

Oatley, K., & Gholamain, M. (1997). Emotions and identification: Connections between readers and fiction. In M. Hjort & S. Laver (Eds.), *Emotion and the arts* (pp. 263–298). New York: Oxford University Press.

Office of National Drug Control Policy, National Youth Anti-Drug Media Campaign (2000, July). Entertainment Industry Outreach. *Media Campaign Update Fact Sheets.* Retrieved September 12, 2002, from http://www.mediacampaign.org/newsroom/080299/update7.html

Pechmann, C., & Shih, C. F. (1999). Smoking in movies and antismoking ads before movies: Effects on youth. *Journal of Marketing, 63,* 1–13.

Petty, R. E., & Cacioppo, J. T. (1986). *Communication and persuasion: Central and peripheral routes to attitude change.* New York: Springer-Verlag.

Petty, R. E., & Krosnick, J. A. (Eds.). (1995). *Attitude strength: Antecedents and consequences.* Hillsdale, NJ: Erlbaum.

Quenqua, D. (2002, May 20). When Bush lobbies Bartlett. *PR Week, 20,* 15.

Sargent, J. D., Tickle, J. J., Beach, M. L., Dalton, M. A., Ahrens, M. B., & Heatherton, T. F. (2001). Brand appearances in contemporary cinema films and contribution to global marketing of cigarettes. *The Lancet, 357,* 29–32.

Sherif, M., & Hovland, C. I. (1961). *Social judgment.* New Haven, CT: Yale University Press.

Slater, M. D. (2002). Entertainment education and the persuasive impact of narratives. In M. C.

Green, J. J. Strange, & T. C. Brock (Eds.), *Narrative impact: Social and cognitive foundations* (pp. 157–181). Mahwah, NJ: Erlbaum.

Son Hing, L. S., Li, W., & Zanna, M. P. (2002). Inducing hypocrisy to reduce prejudicial responses among aversive racists. *Journal of Experimental Social Psychology, 38,* 71–78.

Strange, J. J., & Leung, C. C. (1999). How anecdotal accounts in news and fiction can influence judgments of a social problem's urgency, causes, and cures. *Personality and Social Psychology Bulletin, 25,* 436–449.

Sweeney, P. D., & Gruber, K. L. (1984). Voter information preferences and the Watergate affair. *Journal of Personality and Social Psychology, 46,* 1208–1221.

Torstar Corporation. (2002). *2001 Annual Report.* Retrieved September 12, 2002, from http://www.torstar.com/images/torstar/pdf/2001_annual_pt4.pdf.

Zanna, M. P. (1993). Message receptivity: A new look at the old problem of open- vs. closed-mindedness. In A. Mitchell (Ed.), *Advertising exposure, memory and choice* (pp. 141–162). Hillsdale, NJ: Erlbaum.

10

Forewarnings of Influence Appeals: Inducing Resistance and Acceptance

Jeffrey M. Quinn
Wendy Wood
Texas A&M University

According to conventional wisdom, "forewarned is forearmed." That is, warning of an impending request allows people to prepare for it and ultimately to resist it. For instance, advance knowledge that a telemarketer is about to call and deliver an unwanted sales pitch or that a friend is about to ask a burdensome favor should allow the target of such appeals to mount a successful defense. The idea that warnings generate resistance also is evident in reviews of persuasion research, which typically discuss forewarning effects along with other resistance techniques (e.g., Eagly & Chaiken, 1993). The assumption that warnings yield resistance can also explain a common practice in psychology experiments on attitude change. Experimenters often avoid warning participants of an impending persuasive communication, presumably to maximize participants' susceptibility to persuasion (Papageorgis, 1967, 1968).

In the present chapter, we consider whether warnings do in fact yield resistance to impending appeals—whether people who are forewarned are better able to resist temptation and stand firm in their beliefs. We review the experimental research on forewarnings, consider the various motives that warnings can induce, and evaluate how warnings affect thought about the issue in the appeal. In the reviewed research, some warnings informed recipients of a communicator's intent to persuade by noting that "you will hear a tape recorded message . . . designed to change your mind" (Hass & Grady, 1975, p. 462). Others specified the topic and position of the coming appeal, such as, "you will hear a tape recorded message advocating an increase in the New York City subway fare to 50 cents" (Hass & Grady, 1975, p. 462). Warning effects were then examined on people's attitudes before they received the appeal as well as on people's reactions to the appeal when it was delivered. At the end of the chapter, we consider the implications of forewarning research for the general phenomenon of resistance.

WARNINGS THAT INDUCE RESISTANCE: EVERYDAY INFLUENCE SETTINGS

In applied influence settings, forewarnings are used along with other interventions to instill resistance to subsequent counter-attitudinal attacks. Public health campaigns, such as those designed to prevent adolescent smoking, provide some of the clearest evidence of the effectiveness of these interventions. In the case of antismoking campaigns, the interventions typically are delivered in school and community settings to alert adolescents to social influences to smoke and to prepare them to resist these pressures. These programs might, for example, warn students of pressures to smoke from peers and from cigarette advertisers (Botvin & Kantor, 2000). Antismoking programs are multifaceted and typically include a variety of components in addition to forewarning. The programs might also provide information about smoking health risks and increase students' self-efficacy. When structured appropriately, the programs seem to be effective in reducing adolescent smoking (e.g., Botvin & Kantor, 2000; Bruvold, 1993; Rooney & Murray, 1996). Furthermore, warnings appear to contribute to this impact. The most effective treatments do not simply provide factual information on cigarette use but instead use a variety of social influence methods, including in particular warning of impending influence and teaching of resistance skills (Bruvold, 1993; Rooney & Murray, 1996).

Political news coverage is another everyday context in which forewarnings have been used to induce resistance. Specifically, "adwatch" programs conducted by television news media provide critiques of political advertisements to help voters identify and resist misleading information (Jamieson, 1992; Jamieson & Cappella, 1997; McKinnon & Kaid, 1999). Adwatches, like antismoking interventions, consist of warnings in conjunction with other components, such as the presentation of evidence supporting or refuting the arguments made in the ad. Warnings in adwatch coverage may take the form of spoken disclaimers alerting viewers that the information presented represents partisan advertisements and not actual news stories. Visual cues such as text overlays that label the ad's content as "misleading" or "false" also warn recipients to be wary of the arguments presented in campaign ads. In some empirical tests, adwatches increased viewer skepticism and reduced ad effectiveness (Cappella & Jamieson, 1994; Leshner, 2001; Pfau & Louden, 1994). However, in other tests, adwatches yielded a "boomerang" effect in the form of increased recall of an ad's arguments and increased favorability toward the candidate supported in the ad (Ansolabehere & Iyengar, 1996; Jamieson, 1992; McKinnon & Kaid, 1999; Pfau & Louden, 1994). These varying effects of adwatches are likely due to the varying content of the adwatch programs themselves. For example, the boomerang effect described above might occur when adwatches suggest that most of the claims made in a political ad are truthful or when they repeat the ad's arguments with minimal refutation or other commentary (Jamieson & Cappella, 1997).

In summary, warnings have the potential in real-world settings to prepare people to resist temptations for unhealthy behavior and to recognize inaccuracies in political campaigns. Yet, because warnings have typically been treated as one component of applied intervention programs, it is unclear whether warnings alone have an impact or whether their intervention effects emerge in combination with other program features. Experimental research that has examined the independent effects of forewarnings is more directly informative.

YOU'VE BEEN WARNED . . .

Past narrative reviews of the experimental literature have concluded that forewarnings can have a variety of effects in addition to resistance. McGuire (1969) characterized the effects of forewarnings of messages that are intended to persuade as "frustratingly elusive." He concluded that "there does seem to be a relationship begging to be found, and yet it seems to be hiding out in only certain cells of our experimental design" (p. 35). Other reviews have differentiated between types of warnings and concluded that forewarnings that convey just the *persuasive intent* of an appeal typically generate resistance, whereas forewarnings that specify the *message topic and stance* can generate resistance or susceptibility (Cialdini & Petty, 1981; Petty & Cacioppo, 1986). Eagly and Chaiken (1993) simply noted that these two types of warnings have widely varying effects depending on specific features of the warnings. More relevant to the focus of the present chapter is Petty and Wegener's (1998) discussion of how warnings confer resistance by directing people's thinking. They suggest that warnings of intent as well as warnings of topic and stance can reduce influence by negatively biasing people's thoughts about the attitude issue and the subsequent appeal. In sum, although narrative reviews of the experimental literature have recognized that warnings sometimes confer resistance, they have also noted that this resistance is not an inevitable outcome of exposure to warning.

Given the range of warning effects noted in past reviews, it is no surprise that researchers have used a number of theoretical perspectives to explain how warnings function (see Cialdini & Petty, 1981). Most theoretical accounts consider how warnings instigate particular motivational states that direct recipients' responses to an influence attempt. In this chapter we focus on three overarching motives that warnings might establish: (a) a conservative orientation to defend existing attitudes and important self-identities, (b) a desire to maintain positive relations with others and to convey certain impressions, and (c) a wish to understand reality and to hold valid judgments (Chaiken, Giner-Sorolla, & Chen, 1996; Wood, 2000). In brief, we argue that whether a warning generates resistance depends on the specific motives that it elicits in a given influence context.

Defense Motives.   Warnings of a counter-attitudinal attack can generate a defensive response by threatening recipients' existing attitudes and their important identities, such as their personal integrity (Petty & Wegener, 1998; Zanna, 1993; McGuire & Millman, 1965). Warnings in public health campaigns are often designed for this purpose, with the intent of motivating people to self-protection through rejection of risky, health-threatening behaviors. In general, defensively motivated individuals evaluate the available information, including their existing attitudes, the warning, the source, the context, and the message if available, to express a judgment that best meets their defense goals of protecting their attitudes and identities (Chaiken et al., 1996).

Warnings that elicit defensiveness can have a variety of effects on thoughts about the attitude issue and the impending appeal. In response to warnings that threaten existing attitudes with an impending attack, people may selectively attend to attitude-consistent information, selectively encode or retrieve such information, counterargue the impending message, and bolster existing attitudes and beliefs (e.g., Cialdini & Petty, 1981; Eagly, Chen, Chaiken, & Shaw-Barnes, 1999; Petty & Cacioppo, 1977). Another form of defensiveness may emerge when warnings elicit reactance because they appear to limit people's freedom to hold their favored position (Brehm, 1966; Hass & Grady, 1975). Then people may retain their original attitudes and resist the appeal in order to reestablish the threatened freedom, and they may do so with little thought about the message topic itself.

Some of the best evidence that warnings yield the resistance suggested by these defense theories emerged in Benoit's (1998) meta-analytic synthesis of prior experiments on the effects of warnings on persuasion. This review of 12 studies revealed that participants who were warned prior to the receipt of a message were less persuaded than were participants who received a message without warning (mean $r = .18$). Benoit also reported that warning-induced resistance was uniform across several potential moderating variables. However, this uniformity could be due to the small number of studies in his sample, which would have provided limited opportunity to explore potential moderators.

Although resistance may seem the most likely outcome of warning-induced defensiveness, McGuire and Millman (1965) suggested that warnings that threaten personal identity and self-esteem can yield the—somewhat surprising— outcome of preemptive attitude change toward the message. These researchers reasoned that warnings can make people anxious about being gullible or easily influenced when people believe that they are ultimately likely to be persuaded by the message. Then, the best strategy to preserve self-esteem is to shift preemptively toward the message to minimize its apparent impact. McGuire and Millman (1965) recognized further that preemptive shifts can both defend the self-concept and, when made public, secure the favorable impressions of others by not appearing to be influenced. However, they emphasized self-related motives such as maximizing self-esteem and minimizing discrepancies between real and ideal selves. In this spirit, we interpret such attitude change as a defensive maneuver intended to protect the self against being gullible rather than a self-presentational maneuver.

Impression Motives.   Under certain conditions, warnings can make people concerned about the impressions they convey to others. Forewarnings elicit impression motives when they alert recipients to the interpersonal consequences of expressing an opinion (Cialdini, Levy, Herman, & Evenbeck, 1973; Cialdini, Levy, Herman, Kozlowski, & Petty, 1976; Lundgren & Prislin, 1998). For example, antismoking interventions that warn teenagers of impending peer pressure to smoke can allow teens to develop response strategies that minimize social rejection. In general, impression-motivated individuals evaluate the available information to express a judgment that best conveys the desired impression (Chaiken et al., 1996). Research investigating impression motives has typically warned people of an impending discussion with another who holds opposing views (e.g., Cialdini et al., 1973; Cialdini et al., 1976). People then may express moderate attitudes because a moderate stance makes them appear broad-minded and responsive and allows them to use arguments from both sides of an issue to support their position in the impending discussion.

Validity Motives.   Warnings can make people concerned about the validity of their judgments when the warning indicates that the impending message selectively favors a certain position or is biased in some way. For example, warnings in the "adwatch" programs were designed to heighten viewers' awareness of biased information in political campaign ads. People motivated by accuracy concerns evaluate the available information in search of a judgment that best represents objective reality (Chaiken et al., 1996). Although experimental research has not evaluated this potential effect of warnings in much detail, research on bias correction has addressed judgment validity (Wegener & Petty, 1997). That is, when informed that a certain stimulus may have a biasing effect that threatens judgment validity (e.g., an especially attractive source), people have been found to correct for this effect and shift their attitudes to counteract the presumed bias.

In sum, past experimental research has documented a variety of effects of warnings, with some studies indicating that warnings induce resistance to an impending appeal and others indicating that warnings increase acceptance of the appeal. To explain these varying effects, theories of warning impact have identified a variety of motives likely to be instigated by warnings. Specifically, warnings that threaten people's existing attitudes are likely to instigate a defensive orientation and resistance to protect those attitudes. Warnings that threaten people's self-concepts by suggesting that they are vulnerable to influence are likely to instigate a defensive orientation and preemptive attitude change in order to reduce the apparent impact of the appeal. Warnings that focus people on the impressions they convey through their response to the message are likely to yield moderation toward a neutral, easily defensible position. To evaluate the plausibility of each of these interpretations, we conducted a meta-analytic synthesis of forewarning impact (Wood & Quinn, 2003).

Wood and Quinn's (2003) Research Synthesis

We conducted a comprehensive assessment of the direction and magnitude of forewarning effects on attitudes and examined how warning impact varies with the experimental conditions represented in forewarning studies. To accomplish this, we needed a broader sample of studies than Benoit's (1998) earlier investigation, which was limited to studies that evaluated warning impact on reactions to a persuasive appeal. Thus, we included experiments that assessed recipients' attitudes following the warning but prior to receipt of the appeal. These studies reveal how simply expecting an appeal influences attitudes. Overall, then, our review provided an estimate of warning impact prior to a message as well as warning impact on message persuasiveness.

We located eligible studies through a variety of mechanisms, including computerized databases (e.g., PsycInfo, ERIC, Dissertation Abstracts) and reference lists from previous reviews (e.g., Benoit, 1998; Cialdini & Petty, 1981). A total of 37 research reports were located that examined the effects on attitudes of warnings of persuasive appeals. Of these, 19 assessed attitudes after the warning but before message delivery. Several of these contained multiple experiments, yielding 25 separate studies in the *pre-message sample*. Eighteen reports assessed attitudes following delivery of both the warning and the message. Several of these also contained multiple experiments, yielding 23 separate studies in the *post-message sample*.

We analyzed pre-message and post-message samples separately to capture the unique effects of warnings in each paradigm. Prior reviews have given little reason to suppose that warning impact varies with the delivery of the message. For example, Cialdini and Petty (1981) claimed that the direction of forewarning impact "cannot be explained through an examination of whether . . . effects have been assessed in terms of pre- or postcommunication attitude change" (p. 221). Thus, initially we had few expectations that timing of assessment would influence warning impact.

To calculate effect sizes, we compared the attitudes participants expressed after the warning with the attitudes of a nonwarned comparison group. In the pre-message sample, the attitudes of both the warned and the nonwarned groups were assessed prior to the message. In the post-message sample, the attitudes of

TABLE 10.1
Effect Sizes Reported by Wood and Quinn (2003)

Study groupings		k[a]	Mean weighted effect size (d)[b]	95% Confidence Interval
Attitudes after warning but before message				
Full sample		20	0.37	0.29/0.46
Message canceled following warning		7	0.08	−0.09/0.25
Topic-only warnings		3	0.11	−0.25/0.46
Thought listing followed warning		4	−0.02	−0.19/0.15
Distraction following warning		2	0.61	0.27/0.95
Studies that manipulated outcome-relevant	High	3	−0.32	−0.61/−0.03
involvement of message topic	Low	3	0.07	−0.13/0.27
Attitudes following warning and message				
Full sample (compared with nonwarned controls who received message)		17	−0.38	−0.48/−0.28
Warning impact compared with no-message control conditions		7	0.22	0.06/0.37
Distraction between warning and message		3	0.20	−0.10/0.50
Distraction plus time delay between warning and message		3	0.05	−0.13/0.23
Thought listing between warning and message		3	−0.64	−0.94/−0.34
Studies that manipulated outcome-relevant	High	6	−0.96	−1.25/−0.66
involvement of message topic	Low	6	0.01	−0.25/0.23

[a] k = the number of study findings, and thus the number of effect sizes, in each mean effect size calculation.
[b] The ds are standardized difference scores representing shifts in the attitudes of forewarned participants in comparison with attitudes of those who were not warned. All mean ds were computed with each effect size weighted by the reciprocal of its variance, a procedure that gives more weight to effect sizes that are more reliably estimated (Hedges & Olkin, 1985). Negative effect sizes indicate that warnings were associated with greater resistance to the position advocated in the message compared with controls. Positive effect sizes indicate that warnings were associated with increased acceptance of the position advocated in the message in comparison with controls.

both the warned and nonwarned groups were assessed after the message had been delivered. Effect sizes were calculated for each study in terms of d, the mean difference between the warned and nonwarned groups' attitudes, divided by (for between-groups comparisons) the pooled standard deviation or (for within-group comparisons) the standard deviation of the difference between paired observations (Hedges & Olkin, 1985). Because the position of the impending appeal was always on the opposite side of the neutral point from participants' initial positions, agreement shifts toward the appeal were in the same direction as moderation shifts toward the scale midpoint. Thus, effect sizes were given a positive sign to signify change toward the appeal and/or the scale midpoint and a negative sign to indicate change away from the appeal and/or polarization.

Forewarnings That Induce Resistance. In general, warnings elicited resistance most consistently when attitudes were assessed following the
appeal (see bottom panel of Table 10.1). That is, people who received a warning
before a message were less persuaded by the message than those who received
a message without warning. In addition, this warning-induced resistance did not
appear to emerge from a reactance-like desire to reestablish freedom to hold
existing attitudes (see Brehm, 1966). In both the pre-appeal and the post-appeal
syntheses, warnings that specified an intent to persuade recipients, and thus that
specifically attacked their freedom, did not elicit greater resistance than warnings
that did not mention such an intent. The synthesis thus provided little evidence
that warning impact emerged from reactance-like motives.

Evidence that forewarning-induced resistance was a thoughtful process
emerged from studies that instituted a challenging cognitive task between the
warning and the appeal (e.g., solving mathematical and verbal problems). Such
tasks are distracting and reduce people's ability to build cognitive defenses
against the impending appeal (Eagly & Chaiken, 1993). Despite the general
finding that warning-induced resistance emerged when recipients' attitudes were
assessed after the warning and receipt of the message, no effect of warning
emerged in post-appeal studies that distracted participants between the warning
and the appeal (see Table 10.1). Distracted individuals apparently were unable
to muster the cognitive support to counterargue the impending appeal and were
no more likely than their nonwarned counterparts to resist the message.

Additional evidence of the thoughtful nature of warning-induced resistance
emerged with the studies that presented warnings on topics that were highly
involving in the sense that they concerned immediately important outcomes. For
these kinds of issues, recipients generally are highly motivated to scrutinize
message-relevant information (Johnson & Eagly, 1989). Warnings apparently
biased this processing in a negative direction. Thus, warnings on involving topics yielded strong evidence of resistance in both the pre-appeal and the post-
appeal paradigms (see Table 10.1). Further suggesting the role of thought in
generating attitudinal resistance, studies that explicitly instructed recipients to
report their thoughts following the warning obtained minimal attitude change
toward the impending appeal (see Table 10.1). Thus, warnings were especially
likely to yield resistance when they were given in conjunction with involving
messages or direct instructions to list thoughts. Under these conditions, the threat
posed by the warnings apparently biased recipients' processing and resulted in
attitudinal resistance.

Studies that instituted a time delay after the warning and thereby gave participants the opportunity to deliberate offer additional insight into the thoughtful
nature of warning-induced resistance. Forewarning researchers often incorporated time delays into their experimental procedures because delays supposedly
allow participants the opportunity to construct counterarguments prior to message receipt (Cialdini & Petty, 1981; Jacks & Devine, 2000). However, the
results of studies that used a time delay did not differ from those that did not,
indicating that in general time delays were not associated with resistance (see

similar results in Benoit, 1998). To investigate further the effects of time delay, we separately evaluated a subset of three studies that are commonly cited in narrative reviews as evidence that delays increase resistance (e.g., Cialdini & Petty, 1981). These three studies directly manipulated delay and thus provide direct evidence of the effectiveness of this technique (Freedman & Sears, 1965; Hass & Grady, 1975; Petty & Cacioppo, 1977, Experiment 1). Interestingly, all three studies used messages on highly involving topics, and therefore recipients should already have been motivated to think carefully about the message topic. In this subset of studies, a delay following the warning yielded greater resistance than when warnings were presented with no delay, suggesting that the time delay provided the opportunity to engage in thought. Thus, it seems likely that the null effects for time delay across the whole sample of studies were due to the primarily uninvolving topics typical of this sample. In general, the pattern of findings suggests that although delay provides the opportunity to think, this opportunity has little impact unless participants are already motivated to undertake such cognitive activity—by, for example, an involving topic.

The thoughtful resistance induced by warnings is similar to that found with research on *inoculation*, in which people who receive weak versions of an attacking message have been found to be protected against future threatening messages. Inoculation yields resistance because it motivates and enables cognitive refutation of counter-attitudinal appeals (Pfau, 1996; McGuire, 1964). The thoughtful resistance generated by forewarnings also bears some similarity to the cognitive processing mechanisms identified in research on motivated reasoning (Kunda, 1990). People who are motivated to arrive at a judgment that affords them the most favorable outcomes appear to engage in a biased memory search and to construct congenial beliefs in order to support that judgment. This cognitive bolstering allows people to resist evidence that counters their preferred positions (Kunda, 1990).

In general, the cognitive elaboration underlying warning-induced resistance should render recipients' attitudes relatively persistent and predictive of future behavior (Petty, Haugtvedt, & Smith, 1995). Thus, post-message warnings likely generated strong attitudes that would remain relatively resistant to future attack.

Forewarnings That Shift Attitudes Toward the Message.   We suggested earlier in this chapter that defensive responses to warnings do not always yield resistance. As McGuire and Millman (1965) argued, warnings that threaten recipients' identities can induce movement toward impending appeals. These preemptive shifts can minimize the threat of being gullible and changing one's attitude. Supporting this idea, preemptive change was the mean finding across the whole sample of studies when attitudes were assessed prior to message delivery (see top panel in Table 10.1). It is interesting to note that the shift toward the appeal was comparable in size to the resistance effect that emerged across the post-appeal sample of studies, suggesting that the magnitude of warning impact was uniform across the two paradigms, although opposite in direction. Furthermore, as would be expected if participants were responding to the threat of eventual attitude change, the preemptive attitude change was especially marked when the communication was reputed to be highly persuasive or was delivered by an expert source—conditions that should increase the likelihood that people believe they will be persuaded.

The pattern of pre-appeal attitude change appears to have been a relatively superficial response accompanied by minimal issue-relevant thought. Specifically, in the two pre-appeal studies that distracted participants after the warning was presented but before their attitudes were assessed, participants' attitude change was similar to that obtained when there was no distraction (see Table 10.1). Even though distraction presumably inhibited thought, it did not reduce the amount of movement toward the message. Thus, change toward the appeal plausibly reflected heuristic processing and recipients' use of rules such as "persuasive messages, expert sources . . . must be correct." Participants likely selected the rule that best met their defensive goals of maintaining a favorable self-view. Presumably, participants were unaware that using this rule generated attitude change; any awareness of preemptive agreement should reduce its effectiveness in defending self-esteem.

Additional evidence that warning-induced shifts toward the appeal were based on minimal issue-relevant thought emerged in the few studies that alleviated the threat of the impending appeal by canceling the message (see Table 10.1). When the message was canceled, preemptive attitude change disappeared, and participants' attitudes returned to their original positions. Thus, preemptive change represented an "elastic shift" or temporary response that emerged only while participants were anticipating the appeal (Cialdini et al., 1973). The elastic nature of attitude change provides important support for our argument that shifts toward the message emerged in response to defensive motives. Attitudes based solely on informational cues (e.g., expert sources, purportedly persuasive appeals) should have withstood cancellation because these cues would have remained available after the message threat was removed—and these cues might even have been strengthened by mention of the message in the cancellation manipulation. Additional evidence that informational processes alone did not account for anticipatory shifts toward the appeal was provided by studies that included an additional control condition in which participants were informed of the impending appeal but did not expect to be exposed to it themselves. Simply being informed about the existence of a counter-attitudinal appeal was not sufficient to change attitudes. Thus, the overall pattern of findings is consistent with the idea that anticipatory attitude change was a strategic response to the warning-induced threat to the self-concept.

One of the most interesting findings of the review is that warnings yielded very different patterns of attitude change before and after message delivery. Prior to the appeal, the threat represented in the warning generated change toward the message position, but upon receipt of the appeal it generated resistance (as we noted in our discussion of the post-appeal findings; see top panel of Table 10.1). These divergent effects of warning can be attributed to differences in the apparent target of the warning-induced threat prior to and during the appeal. Prior to the appeal, people apparently were motivated to defend a view of themselves as not being easily influenced. During and after receipt of the appeal, they apparently were motivated to defend their attitudes against the attacking message. This apparent shift in focus from defending the self to defending one's attitudes that accompanied delivery of the appeal could reflect a variety of factors. One is that people may not have been able thoughtfully to resist an appeal before learning what it said. In general, the idea that people can reduce threat in influence settings through both agreement and rejection has parallels in research on fear appeals. Fear-arousing components of messages have been found to increase persuasion or increase rejection, depending on such factors as the intensity of the threat and the available coping strategies (Gleicher & Petty, 1992; Baron, Logan, Lilly, Inman, & Brennan, 1994).

Conscious Awareness of Warning Impact. The research we reviewed on forewarnings did not address whether warnings operate consciously or nonconsciously. It seems plausible that some amount of conscious thought was involved in warning-induced resistance, given that resistance emerged from bolstering existing attitudes and refuting the advocated position. However, this thoughtful analysis might be undertaken as a deliberate defensive response or it might be spurred directly by perceptions of a communicator's persuasive intent with little explicit recognition of the need for defense (Dijksterhuis, 2001; Dijksterhuis & Bargh, 2001). Thus, people are not necessarily aware that they are motivated to defend their attitudes and resist the appeal in response to the warning. In contrast, we can be reasonably sure that preemptive shifts toward the appeal were enacted without conscious awareness. Our explanation that anticipatory shifts were undertaken to preserve self-esteem implies that the strategy operates outside of consciousness—any awareness of one's vulnerability to a persuasive attack and preemptive change to bolster the self would likely undermine the effectiveness of this strategy. In general, then, warnings may sometimes yield resistance when people consciously decide to defend their views or they do so nonconsciously. However, preemptive change toward the message most likely occurs with limited conscious awareness.

Impression Motives Instigated by Forewarnings

The suggestive evidence from our review that warnings elicit a defensive response can be contrasted with the possibility that warnings sensitize people to the impressions they convey to others (Cialdini et al., 1973; Cialdini et al., 1976). As we mentioned earlier in this chapter, warnings can instigate impression motives when they orient people to appear open-minded to others and to hold attitudes that will be defensible in discussions. To convey these favorable impressions, warned recipients may shift to neutral, midscale positions that appear unbiased and that allow them to use a range of arguments to explain their position.

Because the motivational states instigated by forewarnings typically were not assessed directly in the research, it is difficult to ascertain the specific defense- or impression-motivated state that warnings might have established in a given experimental context. As reviewers, we are functionally in the same position as the study authors, forced to infer the participants' motivational states from the pattern of attitude change findings. This failure to directly measure motives extends beyond the warning literature. Previous meta-analytic syntheses of persuasion and social influence also noted that the reviewed studies did not obtain direct measures of the motivational states instigating attitude change (e.g., Johnson & Eagly, 1989; Wood, Lundgren, Ouellette, Busceme, & Blackstone, 1994). Thus, in reviewing the warning literature we were unable to evaluate directly the possibility that attitudes shifted in response to specific motivational concerns instigated by a warning. We instead evaluated whether the pattern of attitude change outcomes was consistent with the idea that warnings elicited specific motives.

To evaluate impression motives, we compared the attitudes participants expressed when they expected to report their post-appeal attitudes publicly to others versus privately on a questionnaire. If attitude change is a relatively superficial attempt to convey certain impressions to others, then it should emerge primarily in public settings in which people can garner the social benefits of conveying particular impressions (Cialdini et al., 1973; Cialdini & Petty, 1981). However, across all studies in the review, attitude change was not greater with expectation of public rather than private attitude judgments. Additional evidence against an impression-motivated interpretation of attitude change prior to the appeal was provided by studies with warnings that specified only the topic and not the position in the impending appeal (see Table 10.1). Because impression-motivated attitudinal moderation requires just knowledge of the topic of the appeal, moderation shifts would be expected to emerge with topic-only warnings. However, we observed significant attitude shifts only in studies in which warnings indicated that the appeal would be counter-attitudinal, either by stating the message position or an intent to persuade. Thus, it appears that recipients agreed with the specific position in the impending appeal and were not engaging in impression-motivated moderation of their attitudes in expectation of *any* position that they might encounter on a topic.

Finally, we note that parsimony is an additional reason to favor defense over impression accounts of warning impact. Warning-induced defensiveness can explain both the acquiescence effects apparent prior to the appeal and the resistance effects that emerged following the appeal and when the message topic was highly involving. Thus, forewarnings of an impending counter-attitudinal attack appear to have motivated recipients to *defend* their existing attitudes and identities, rather than to *appear* in a favorable manner to others.

Although there was little overall evidence that impression concerns were responsible for the attitude shifts prior to the appeal, it remains plausible that certain types of warnings given in certain types of contexts can heighten concerns about the impressions conveyed to others. Specifically, Cialdini et al.

(1973) proposed that warnings would be especially likely to heighten impression concerns when they inform recipients of (a) an impending discussion on (b) an uninvolving topic with (c) a person who holds an opposing opinion. Two studies in Wood and Quinn's synthesis established these conditions in certain cells of their experimental designs (i.e., Cialdini et al., 1973; Deaux, 1968). Consistent with an impression interpretation of attitude change, in these specified conditions participants warned of a discussion on the message topic with another person shifted their attitudes toward midscale and the impending partner's position. These shifts were greater than those observed when warned participants expected to indicate their attitudes privately on a questionnaire. Thus, warnings of an impending *discussion* or *interaction* may operate differently than the warnings of an *attack message* in that the former sensitizes people to the impressions they convey to others whereas the latter highlights defensive concerns.

Although these two discussion warning studies in our synthesis found that people moderated their attitudes to an impending discussion, it is also possible that impression motives can lead to resistance under certain circumstances (Fitzpatrick & Eagly, 1981). Resistance is likely when discussions are framed as debates or competitions and a favorable impression can be attained by prevailing over a discussion partner. People also may resist when their initial attitudes are known by the discussion partner and changing their views would give the impression of inconsistency or compliance. In general, then, as with warnings that instigate defensive concerns, warnings that elicit impression motives are plausibly associated with a variety of attitudinal outcomes.

RESISTANCE AS AN OUTCOME OF FOREWARNING

The research reviewed in this chapter illustrates several attitudinal effects that result from warning of an impending counter-attitudinal appeal. Consistent with the expectations of practitioners who use warnings to forearm recipients and help them withstand a persuasive attack, forewarnings often produced defensive resistance to the message position. However, under certain conditions the same forewarning treatment had the opposite effect, eroding rather than enhancing resistance to a counter-attitudinal appeal. In this section of the chapter, we draw on the forewarning literature to develop answers to the general questions of what resistance is and when it is likely to occur. Our position is foreshadowed by the title of this section.

Formal definitions of resistance are difficult to find in the attitudes literature (see Jacks & O'Brien, this volume). Whereas some authors assert that resistance *is not* merely the inverse of persuasion (McGuire, 1964; Knowles, Butler, & Linn, 2001), few have defined exactly what resistance *is* (with notable exceptions of this volume; Petty & Wegener, 1998; Brehm, 1966). Resistance potentially can be treated as the *motive* to reject influence attempts and retain one's own views, as the *process* through which people reject and retain, and as a potential *outcome* of influence. As we explain, the pattern of attitude change that emerged in studies of forewarning suggests that resistance does not correspond to a particular motive or a particular process of rejection; it is best understood as an outcome of an influence attempt. In addition, we note that because the forewarning literature does not address another possible conceptualization of resistance—as a quality of an attitude or a person—we will not discuss this conceptualization here (see Briñol, Rucker, Tormala, & Petty, this volume).

Is Resistance a Motive?   Reactance theory provides a classic perspective on resistance to influence as an underlying motive (Brehm, 1966). According to this analysis, people desire to maintain freedom and, in influence contexts, to assert their own positions and oppose the appeal. Similarly, Jacks and O'Brien (this volume) define resistance as a motive to withstand an influence attempt. Yet, the warning literature illustrates the difficulties that emerge when resistance is defined as a motive. First, it is evident that this motive does not correspond to reactance. In the research synthesis, resistance was not heightened in circumstances that should have increased participants' reactance and desire to assert freedom through message rejection (i.e., when the warning mentioned an intent to persuade). Although a reactance-like motive may lead to resistance in some circumstances, it did not appear to account for resistance generated by forewarnings.

Instead of a general motive to resist, the results from forewarning studies suggest that multiple specific motives directed resistance and agreement (see also Wegener, Petty, Smoak, & Fabrigar, this volume). Specifically, resistance was found when warnings appeared to instigate defense motives in recipients. That is, resistance was pronounced when warnings apparently threatened participants' attitudes, as occurred when the warning topic was highly involving. That this specific defense motive did not represent a general desire to resist was evident in the pre-appeal literature, in which warning-induced threats to identity generated defensiveness in the form of preemptive agreement. Other research has indicated that, in addition to defense motives, warning-induced resistance can stem from a motivational concern with conveying specific impressions to others (e.g., Fitzpatrick & Eagly, 1981). That is, people resist when they wish to convey the impression of prevailing over an opponent in a debate or when their initial attitudes are known and change would signal compliance. Also, accuracy goals potentially could lead to resistance under some circumstances. We speculate that people motivated to be accurate will not resist a highly valid, credible message but will strongly reject a biased or one-sided position.

In summary, resistance in the forewarning literature did not emerge as a global reactance motive. Instead, resistance seemed to reflect situation-specific defense and impression motives, and potentially could reflect accuracy motives.

Is Resistance a Process?   Resistance as a process represents a negatively biased conscious or nonconscious reaction against an influence attempt that leads to rejection of the appeal. The classic example of resistance as a process involves thought generation as people counterargue appeals and bolster their existing views. Given that these mechanisms were critical to warning-induced resistance, it is tempting to define resistance in terms of this process. As we noted, when participants in post-message studies were distracted and apparently could not generate thoughts, warnings had little impact. Conversely, when participants were instructed to list their thoughts following the warning, they were especially successful at resisting the appeal.

Despite the evidence from forewarning that resistance emerged from a thoughtful evaluation of the impending appeal, other research has demonstrated that resistance implicates a variety of processing mechanisms. For example, resistance can involve emotional responses, as when feelings of irritation and other negative affective cues signal disagreement with the message (e.g., Zuwerink & Devine, 1996). The process of resistance also can involve reliance on heuristic rules that suggest rejection of a message (Zuckerman & Chaiken, 1998). All of these processes involved in resistance can result in rejection of an appeal. We speculate that less thoughtful rejection of appeals will be found with warnings that generate a stronger defensive reaction than is typical of the warnings in the literature we reviewed. We base this idea on studies of strong fear-inducing appeals that appear to elicit minimally thoughtful resistance processes, including defensive avoidance and discounting of the source and message (Jepson & Chaiken, 1990; Gleicher & Petty, 1992).

In summary, resistance mechanisms include a variety of thoughtful and less thoughtful processes as well as emotional reactions. At a general level, these mechanisms are not just involved in resistance and rejection of appeals but also are components of persuasion processes, as people thoughtfully or less thoughtfully accept messages and respond to them in emotionally positive ways.

Resistance Is Best Understood as an Outcome.   Attitudinal outcomes yield a clear, unambiguous indicator of resistance. Attitude outcomes are the gold standard for resistance: In our view, resistance does not occur without attitudinal evidence. In the warning literature, resistance is evident when the attitudes reported by warned participants are less favorable than those held by nonwarned participants. Theories explaining warning-induced resistance identify how this outcome is motivated by defense, impression, or accuracy concerns and how it is generated through various modes of processing (e.g., thoughtful or less thoughtful).

Our review of forewarning research identified several patterns of resistance when warned participants were compared with other, nonwarned ones. Prior to message delivery, when warnings concerned highly involving issues, resistance emerged as a "boomerang effect," or attitude shift away from an impending appeal. Boomerang shifts also emerged following message receipt when warned individuals had listed their thoughts prior to the appeal (and were compared with nonwarned controls who did not receive the message). Apparently, these experimental contexts spurred such persuasive cognitive bolstering of existing views and counterarguing of the appeal that people moved away from the expected position.

Resistance as attenuated agreement emerged following message delivery when warned participants shifted toward the message, but shifted to a lesser extent than nonwarned participants. Because messages in general were persuasive, the resistance-inducing effects of warnings reduced but did not eradicate message impact. In these experimental contexts, warnings apparently negatively biased message evaluation and thus decreased the amount of attitude change. It is interesting to note that although we are defining these outcomes as "resistance," in actuality the mean attitudinal effect even after a warning was a shift toward the message position.

Resistance as maintenance of original views given pressure to change was apparent prior to the appeal. That is, participants who listed their thoughts following the warning apparently engaged in bolstering of their own views and counterarguing of the impending appeal. Thus, they retained their views and did not demonstrate the shifts toward the appeal evidenced by participants who did not list their thoughts. In general, then, resistance outcomes generated by warnings were reflected in a variety of patterns of change, including boomerang shifts away from an impending appeal, reduced amounts of change toward the appeal, and no attitude change.

Outcomes Not Representative of Resistance.   Failure to change one's attitudes does not always signal resistance. Resistance occurs when individuals face pressure to change their attitudes. The three examples of resistance from the warning literature—a boomerang shift, reduced message persuasiveness, and attitudinal stability—all emerged in response to influence pressures that were in fact successful at changing the attitudes of nonwarned participants and other comparison groups. In contrast, attitude stability due to lack of pressure can be found when people are not exposed to any persuasive information, when they are exposed to attitude-congenial appeals, and when they are exposed to counter-attitudinal appeals with very weak arguments. Messages with weak arguments often link the attitude object to unfavorable or to neutral outcomes, and consequently information of this kind does not present much pressure to adopt the advocated position (for an opposing view of resistance, see Johnson, Smith-McLallen, Killeya, & Levin, this volume).

APPLYING FOREWARNING RESEARCH

The research reviewed in this chapter will be helpful to practitioners using forewarnings to instill resistance to influence. Practitioners' efforts will most likely be successful when they understand the motives instigated by their warning interventions and ensure that the context in which the warning is delivered allows recipients to satisfy those motives through resistance rather than acquiescence. To generate warning-induced resistance of the form obtained in the reviewed studies, practitioners should use warnings that (a) threaten attitudes, and (b) foster issue-relevant thought by highlighting the involving aspects of the issue or by explicitly instructing people to consider the issue and the impact of the message's counter-attitudinal position. Warnings should also be delivered in a context that is relatively free of distractions and thereby allows for systematic processing of relevant information.

Our findings also suggest that forewarning can be a persuasion tactic. Practitioners may attempt to use warnings to threaten recipients' identities rather than their attitudes in order to generate preemptive agreement (see also Sherman, Crawford, & McConnell, this volume, for a discussion of how future regret may generate compliance). However, in the reviewed research this acquiescence was a temporary and context-dependent response that disappeared when the threat was removed and the message was canceled. Thus, the compliance effects of warnings may be only short lived and may not represent enduring attitude change.

Warnings that threaten people's identities may not always lead to acquiescence, and may instead yield resistance when the identity involves an important social group. That is, when people identify strongly with a group, they are likely to be motivated to hold attitudes consistent with those of typical group members and inconsistent with those held by the outgroup. Following this logic, warnings are likely to instigate resistance when they associate an attitude position with an outgroup or derogated minority (e.g., ". . . keep in mind, this is what the outgroup would have you believe"). Similarly, resistance is likely when warnings claim attitude positions are typical of a valued ingroup (e.g., ". . . we are the ingroup and we believe x, not y"). The effects of specifying social identities in warnings could emerge because the identities act as simple persuasion cues (Pratkanis & Turner, 1996) or because the identities instigate thought about the message position (Pool, Wood, & Leck, 1998; Wood, Pool, Leck, & Purvis, 1996). The social identity effects of warnings are at present speculative and remain to be explored in subsequent research.

It would be premature for influence practitioners to attempt to instill resistance through warnings that sensitize people to the impressions they convey to others. The findings of our review provide only preliminary hints of the ways that warnings can enhance or reduce resistance by raising impression concerns. Attitudinal moderation toward midscale emerged in analyses on the two studies presenting warnings of an impending discussion with another person who held a counter-attitudinal position on a low involving issue. Furthermore, the conditions that lead to impression-motivated resistance are not well understood; this effect only emerged in one study that could not be included in the synthesis because it did not provide sufficient data to calculate effect sizes (Fitzpatrick & Eagly, 1981). Thus, an impression analysis of warning impact awaits further research.

Even less evidence is available about resistance generated by concerns with position accuracy. Our speculation that warnings could heighten accuracy concerns was based on research investigating techniques other than forewarnings.

Specifically, research on bias correction has demonstrated that a perceived threat
to the objectivity of one's judgment can lead to attitude shifts in a direction that
resists the potential bias (Wegener & Petty, 1997). However, it is unclear
whether warnings of potential bias have a general resistance effect. Much of the
research on bias correction has been conducted with issues of low involvement
(e.g., rating the desirability of vacationing in various locales; rating the attractiveness of various celebrities; Wegener & Petty, 1997), and it may be that
warnings of potential bias are motivating primarily when people do not have a
strong initial attitude or an initial commitment to a particular position. Additional
research will be needed to address the overall impact of forewarnings of potentially biased appeals along with the boundary conditions of such effects.

CONCLUSION

We have argued in this chapter that forewarned may indeed be forearmed, but
that forearming does not always involve resistance. Warnings of impending influence can generate resistance when they orient recipients to consider the threat
to their existing attitudes and undertake a cognitive defense, and when the warnings are presented in a context that does not distract people from careful thought.
In contrast, forewarnings can increase susceptibility to persuasion when they
focus recipients on the self-related implications of being influenced. That is,
when recipients are concerned about being gullible and losing integrity, then
they may preemptively agree with appeals in order to minimize eventual change.
Effective use of forewarnings in applied influence settings requires that practitioners consider the motives instigated by their interventions, the cognitive consequences of such events, and the contextual features that influence recipients'
responses. Practitioners with an understanding of warning effects have at their
disposal a means of arming individuals to resist harmful messages and thereby
to foster desirable outcomes such as improved public health and more accurate
political knowledge.

AUTHOR NOTE

Preparation of this chapter was supported by a grant from the National Institute
of Health to the second author (1R01MH619000-01). Correspondence concerning the chapter should be directed to Jeffrey Quinn or Wendy Wood who are
now at Duke University, Department of Psychology: Social and Health Sciences,
Durham, NC 27708. Electronic mail j.quinn@duke.edu or wwood@duke.edu.

REFERENCES

Ansolabehere, S., & Iyengar, S. (1996). Can the press monitor campaign advertising? An experimental study. *Press/Politics, 1,* 72–86.

Baron, R., Logan, H., Lilly, J., Inman, M., & Brennan, M. (1994). Negative emotion and message processing. *Journal of Experimental Social Psychology, 30,* 181–201.

Benoit, W. L. (1998). Forewarning and persuasion. In M. Allen & R. Priess (Eds.), *Persuasion: Advances through meta-analysis* (pp. 159–184). Cresskill, NJ: Hampton Press.

Botvin, G. J., & Kantor, L. W. (2000). Preventing alcohol and tobacco use through life skills training: Theory methods, and empirical findings. *Alcohol Research and Health, 24,* 250–257.

Brehm, J. W. (1966). *A theory of psychological reactance.* New York: Academic Press.

Brock, T. C. (1967). Communication discrepancy and intent to persuade as determinants of counterargument production. *Journal of Experimental Social Psychology, 3,* 296–309.

Bruvold, W. H. (1993). A meta-analysis of adolescent smoking prevention programs. *American Journal of Public Health, 83,* 872–880.

Cappella, J. N., & Jamieson, K. H. (1994). Broadcast adwatch effects: A field experiment. *Communication Research, 21,* 342–365.

Chaiken, S., Giner-Sorolla, R., & Chen, S. (1996). Beyond accuracy: Defense and impression motives in heuristic and systematic processing. In P. M. Gollwitzer & J. A. Bargh (Eds.), *The psychology of action: Linking cognition and motivation to behavior* (pp. 553–578). New York: Guilford Press.

Cialdini, R. B., Levy, A., Herman, C. P., & Evenbeck, S. (1973). Attitudinal politics: The strategy of moderation. *Journal of Personality and Social Psychology, 25,* 100–108.

Cialdini, R. B., Levy, A., Herman, C. P., Kozlowski, L. T., & Petty, R. E. (1976). Elastic shifts of opinion: Determinants of direction and durability. *Journal of Personality and Social Psychology, 34,* 663–672.

Cialdini, R. B., & Petty, R. E. (1981). Anticipatory opinion effects. In R. E. Petty, T. M. Ostrom, & T. C. Brock (Eds.), *Cognitive responses in persuasion* (pp. 217–235). Hillsdale, NJ: Erlbaum.

Deaux, K. K. (1968). Variations in warning, information preference, and anticipatory attitude change. *Journal of Personality and Social Psychology, 9,* 157–161.

Dijksterhuis, A. (2001). Automatic social influence: The perception-behavior links as an explanatory mechanism for behavior matching. In J. P. Forgas & K. D. Williams (Eds.), *Social influence: Direct and indirect processes. The Sydney symposium of social psychology* (pp. 95–108). Philadelphia: Psychology Press.

Dijksterhuis, A., & Bargh, J. A. (2001). The perception-behavior expressway: Automatic effects of social perception on social behavior. In M. P. Zanna (Ed.), *Advances in experimental social psychology* (Vol. 33, pp. 1–40). San Diego, CA: Academic Press.

Eagly, A. H., & Chaiken, S. (1993). *The psychology of attitudes.* Fort Worth, TX: Harcourt Brace Jovanovich.

Eagly, A. H., Chen, S., Chaiken, S., & Shaw-Barnes, K. (1999). The impact of attitudes on memory: An affair to remember. *Psychological Bulletin, 125,* 64–89.

Fitzpatrick, A. R., & Eagly, A. H. (1981). Anticipatory belief polarization as a function of the expertise of a discussion partner. *Personality and Social Psychology Bulletin, 7,* 636–642.

Freedman, J. L., & Sears, D. O. (1965). Warning, distraction, and resistance to influence. *Journal of Personality and Social Psychology, 1,* 262–266.

Gleicher, F., & Petty, R. E. (1992). Expectations of reassurance influence the nature of fear-stimulated attitude change. *Journal of Experimental Social Psychology, 28,* 86–100.

Hass, R. G., & Grady, K. (1975). Temporal delay, type of forewarning, and resistance to influence. *Journal of Experimental Social Psychology, 11,* 459–469.

Hedges, L. V., & Olkin, I. (1985). *Statistical methods for meta-analysis.* New York: Academic Press.

Jacks, J. Z., & Devine, P. G. (2000). Attitude importance, forewarning of message content, and resistance to persuasion. *Basic and Applied Social Psychology, 22,* 19–29.

Jamieson, K. H. (1992). *Dirty politics: Deception, distraction, and democracy.* New York: Oxford Press.

Jamieson, K. H., & Cappella, J. N. (1997). Setting the record straight: Do ad watches help or hurt? *Press/Politics, 2,* 13–22.

Jepson, C., & Chaiken, S. (1990). Chronic issue-specific fear inhibits systematic processing of persuasive communications. In M. Booth-Butterfield (Ed.), *Communication, cognition, and anxiety. [special issue]. Journal of Social Behavior and Personality, 5,* 61–84.

Johnson, B. T., & Eagly, A. H. (1989). Effects of involvement on persuasion: A meta-analysis. *Psychological Bulletin, 106,* 290–314.

Knowles, E. S., Butler, S., & Linn, J. A. (2001). Increasing compliance by reducing resistance. In J. P. Forgas & K. D. Williams (Eds.), *Social influence: Direct and indirect approaches* (pp. 41–60). Philadelphia: Psychology Press.

Kunda, Z. (1990). The case for motivated reasoning. *Psychological Bulletin, 108,* 480–498.

Leshner, G. (2001). Critiquing the image: Testing image adwatches as journalistic reform. *Communication Research, 28,* 181–207.

Lundgren, S., & Prislin, R. P. (1998). Motivated cognitive processing and attitude change. *Personality and Social Psychology Bulletin, 24,* 715–726.

McGuire, W. J. (1964). Inducing resistance to persuasion: Some contemporary approaches. In L. Berkowitz (Ed.), *Advances in experimental social psychology* (Vol. 1, pp. 191–229). New York: Academic Press.

McGuire, W. J. (1969). Suspiciousness of experimenter's intent. In R. Rosenthal & R. Rosnow (Eds.), *Artifact in behavioral research* (pp. 13–57). New York: Academic Press.

McGuire, W. J., & Millman, S. (1965). Anticipatory belief lowering following forewarning of a persuasive attack. *Journal of Personality and Social Psychology, 2,* 471–479.

McKinnon, L. M., & Kaid, L. L. (1999). Exposing negative campaigning or enhancing advertising effects: An experimental study of adwatch effects on voters' evaluations of candidates and their ads. *Journal of Applied Communication Research, 27,* 217–236.

Papageorgis, D. (1967). Anticipation of exposure to persuasive messages and belief change. *Journal of Personality and Social Psychology, 5,* 490–496.

Papageorgis, D. (1968). Warning and persuasion. *Psychological Bulletin, 70,* 271–282.

Petty, R. E., & Cacioppo, J. T. (1977). Forewarning, cognitive responding, and resistance to persuasion. *Journal of Personality and Social Psychology, 35,* 645–655.

Petty, R. E., & Cacioppo, J. T. (1986). The Elaboration Likelihood Model of persuasion. In L. Berkowitz (Ed.), *Advances in experimental social psychology* (Vol. 19, pp. 123–205). New York: Academic Press.

Petty, R. E., Haugtvedt, C. P., & Smith, S. M. (1995). Elaboration as a determinant of attitude strength: Creating attitudes that are persistent, resistant, and predictive of behavior. In R. E. Petty & J. A. Krosnick (Eds.), *Attitude strength: Antecedents and consequences.* (pp. 93–130). Mahwah, NJ: Erlbaum

Petty, R. E., & Wegener, D. T. (1998). Attitude change: Multiple roles for persuasion variables. In D. T. Gilbert, S. T. Fiske, & G. Lindzey (Eds.), *The handbook of social psychology* (4th ed., Vol. 1, pp. 323–390). Boston: McGraw-Hill.

Pfau, M. (1996). Inoculation model of resistance to influence. In B. F. Boster & G. Barnett (Eds.), *Progress in communication sciences* (Vol. 12, pp. 133–171). Norwood, NJ: Ablex.

Pfau, M., & Louden, A. (1994). Effectiveness of adwatch formats in deflecting political attack ads. *Communication Research, 21,* 325–341.

Pool, G. J., Wood, W., & Leck, K. (1998). The self-esteem motive in social influence: Agreement with valued majorities and disagreement with derogated minorities. *Journal of Personality and Social Psychology, 75,* 967–975.

Pratkanis, A. R., & Turner, M. E. (1996). Persuasion and democracy: Strategies for increasing deliberative participation and enhancing social change. *Journal of Social Issues, 52,* 187–205.

Rooney, B. L., & Murray, D. M. (1996). A meta-analysis of smoking prevention programs after adjustment for errors in the unit of analysis. *Health Education Quarterly, 23,* 48–64.

Wegener, D. T., & Petty, R. E. (1997). The Flexible Correction Model: The role of naive theories of bias in bias correction. In L. Berkowitz (Ed.), *Advances in experimental social psychology* (Vol. 29, pp. 141–208). New York: Academic Press.

Wood, W. (2000). Attitude change: Persuasion and social influence. *Annual Review of Psychology, 51,* 539–570.

Wood, W., Lundgren, S., Ouellette, J. A., Busceme, S., & Blackstone, T. (1994). Minority influence: A meta-analytic review of social influence processes. *Psychological Bulletin, 115,* 323–345.

Wood, W., Pool, G. J., Leck, K., & Purvis, D. (1996). Self-definition, defensive processing, and influence: The normative impact of majority and minority groups. *Journal of Personality and Social Psychology, 71,* 1181–1193.

Wood, W., & Quinn, J. M. (2003). Forewarned and forearmed? Two meta-analytic syntheses of forewarning of influence appeals. *Psychological Bulletin, 129,* 119–138.

Zanna, M. P. (1993). Message receptivity: A new look at the old problem of open- versus closed-mindedness. In A. A. Mitchell (Ed.), *Advertising exposure, memory, and choice. Advertising and consumer psychology* (pp. 141–162). Hillsdale, NJ: Erlbaum.

Zuckerman, A., & Chaiken, S. (1998). A heuristic-systematic process analysis of the effectiveness of product warning labels. *Psychology and Marketing, 15,* 621–642.

Zuwerink, J. R., & Devine, P. G. (1996). Attitude importance and resistance to persuasion: It's not just the thought that counts. *Journal of Personality and Social Psychology, 70,* 931–944.

11

Truth or Consequences: Overcoming Resistance to Persuasion with Positive Thinking

Blair T. Johnson
University of Connecticut

Aaron Smith-McLallen
University of Connecticut

Ley A. Killeya
Rutgers—The State University of New Jersey

Kenneth D. Levin
Remarketing Services of America

Truth or Consequences was a popular U.S. television quiz show that melded trivia game with stunt acts. Its host asked contestants silly questions and they had to answer them correctly before "Beulah the Buzzer" sounded. Failing to provide the "Truth," contestants faced the "Consequences," which meant having to perform an amusing and often embarrassing stunt. Just as this program combined pursuit of the truth—simple, logical knowledge—with some related consequences—bad or good experiences—so too do everyday pressures push us to hold seemingly truthful views that maximize our gains and minimize our losses and that permit us to approach or avoid some entity. Yet, just as contestants on *Truth or Consequences* experienced the pains of too little truth, in everyday life we have suffered the consequences of basing our attitudes or our behavior on evidence that seemed good at the time but later turned bad. Gamblers play the slots, convinced the next spin will win. Golfers buy the latest, greatest products in the hopes of giving their game that elusive edge. Politicians support policies that in retrospect are based on implausible principles with little chance of succeeding. In short, we often seem to act under the premise that we can "have our cake and eat it, too." People often leap before they look, although the reverse certainly happens as well.

Everyone, lay people and social psychologists alike, knows that "strong" arguments are more persuasive than "weak" arguments. If we take the strong versus weak contrast at face value, strong arguments induce persuasion but weak arguments do not. Put another way, presumably, persuaders who present cogent, rational arguments achieve the desired effect, whereas specious arguments fail to persuade. By this interpretation, weak arguments induce resistance in message recipients, who maintain their initial views and are not swayed. Yet beneath the surface, a more sophisticated interpretation is that, yes, strong arguments produce acceptance, but that weak arguments are not merely unpersuasive but actually can be *anti*-persuasive. In other words, weak arguments may sometimes move the message recipients' attitudes further away from the message position. Indeed, some research indicates that people who receive weak messages and who have a high degree of outcome-relevant involvement, a motivational state in which a person's attitude about a particular object is linked to an outcome about which they are highly concerned, demonstrate negative attitude change (Johnson & Eagly, 1989). The fact that negative attitude change, or "boomerang" effects, can occur in a relatively impersonal context presents important clues about the nature of attitudes in general and how to overcome resistance to persuasion.

In this chapter, we first synthesize data from argument quality studies that shed light not only on boomerang effects but also on the roles of message position valence and outcome-relevant involvement in persuasion. We then present experimental data exploring these effects. The basic thrust of our view is that the persuasive impact of argument quality, as it has been operationalized, is much less about logic than it is about valence. That is, persuasion is more about suggesting good rather than bad *consequences* (valence) for the message recipient than it is about creating impeccably logical—a.k.a truthful or likely— arguments. Much of this work supports the conclusion that the valence of actively generated cognitive responses to a message underlies persuasion. When the valence of these thoughts is positive (i.e., good consequences for the message recipient) then persuasion is likely to occur, but if the thoughts are negative there is evidence of true resistance—sticking to one's guns.

BOOMERANG VERSUS SIMPLE RESISTANCE

Although the two responses to persuasive communications discussed in this chapter, resistance and boomerang, are similar in that neither yield a positive result for the communicator, they are different in that *resistance* connotes that no meaningful change from initial attitudes appears following the reception of a message, whereas a *boomerang effect* implies significant attitudinal movement away from the message position. Traditionally, discussions of boomerang effects emerge in reference to two different frameworks, Reactance Theory and Social Judgment-Involvement (SJI) Theory. Reactance theory holds that boomerang effects can occur if messages threaten a perceived freedom not to believe, creating movement away from the advocated position (see Fuegen & Brehm, this volume; Sherman, Crawford, & McConnell, this volume). For example, a study by Worchel and Brehm (1970) presented messages that either contained or did not contain statements such as "you cannot believe otherwise" with regard to acceptance of the communist party in the United States. Providing such threats created movement away from what actually was a pro-attitudinal position. Yet, this explanation of resistance provides a poor fit for most persuasion data, given that nearly all studies' persuasive messages have omitted such pressing interpersonal statements. In sum, the reactance explanation provides little insight into the nature of argument quality except that strong arguments should not threaten individuals' freedoms.

SJI theory holds that perceptual displacements mediate persuasion (see Eagly & Chaiken, 1993, for a review). From this perspective (e.g., M. Sherif & Hovland, 1961), a person's existing attitudes provide an interpretive context for an incoming message. When the message position falls in, or very near to, a person's latitude of acceptance, the result is an attitudinal shift toward the position; that is, the message position is *assimilated*. If the position falls in the person's latitude of rejection, the message is regarded as more distant from one's own attitude than it truly is and no attitude change occurs; that is, the message position is *contrasted*, or in terms of this volume, *resisted*. SJI theory also predicts that, for those for whom involvement is very high, very discrepant messages might result in negative attitude change, or *boomerang*. SJI theorists regard highly involving attitudes as components of the ego or self-concept, that is, as aspects of the "self-picture—intimately felt and cherished" (C. W. Sherif et al., 1965, p. vi). Johnson and Eagly (1989) labeled this construct *value-relevant involvement* to differentiate it from outcome-relevant involvement. Yet, because this chapter is primarily concerned with the effects of persuasive communication involving outcome-relevant issues, unless we indicate otherwise, we will use the term "involvement" to refer to outcome-relevant involvement.

In general, being highly involved appears to motivate people to form accurate, albeit temporary, judgments about the issue in question. For example, investigators typically inform their high-involvement participants that the message is highly relevant to their short-term goals, whereas low-involvement participants learn that the message is relevant to another group and/or another time. In a seminal study, Petty and Cacioppo (1979, Experiment 2) examined college undergraduates' reactions to what has since become the most popular issue in persuasion research, the policy whereby passing a comprehensive examination in the student's major area should be a mandatory requirement for graduation. They informed their University of Missouri participants that they would be evaluating radio editorials sent in by colleges and universities across the country. In the low-involvement condition, the speaker advocated that the exams should be instituted at North Carolina State, thereby making the editorial of little interest to participants' own educational concerns; in the high-involvement condition, the speaker advocated that the exams be instituted at their own institution in the near future, thereby making the editorial of high interest. Recipients subsequently received either a strong or weak message in support of the message position.

Results showing that the argument quality manipulation had a much larger impact on attitudes for high- than for low-involvement provided support for one of the key predictions of the Elaboration Likelihood Model, which appeared soon thereafter. Specifically, under high message elaboration circumstances, attitudes should conform to message content (Petty & Cacioppo, 1986). Johnson and Eagly's (1989) review of 20 such studies generally confirmed this accuracy motivation: High (vs. low) outcome-relevant involvement promoted greater persuasion with strong arguments and generally promoted less persuasion with weak arguments. Although Petty et al. (1981) discussed the possibility that some of their weak-argument data may have reflected boomerang effects, this phenomenon has since then received little attention (for an interesting exception, see Zanna, 1994).

In sum, the foregoing literature further informs the nature of *resistance*, which we define as no attitude change in response to a message. People may resist persuasive attempts for a variety of reasons. Under conditions of low involvement, resistance may result from decreased motivation to cognitively engage with the issue and the arguments presented. When involvement is high, in contrast, resistance may be due to active counterarguing against the message content, in which case resistance implies the presence of a very persistent attitude that has stood a significant test (see Jacks & O'Brien, this volume). Additionally, people may resist persuasive messages because acceptance of a new position may require more cognitive restructuring than the person is willing to undergo (see Festinger, 1957). Our definition of resistance assumes that the target of the persuasive message actively receives the message, thereby ensuring that some amount of force was applied that could either be resisted or could produce attitudinal change. As the data presented in this chapter resulted from participants who actively received a message, observations of resistance cannot be explained by simple cognitive inertia.

META-ANALYSIS OF ACTUAL ATTITUDE CHANGE IN RESPONSE TO STRONG OR WEAK ARGUMENTS

That strong arguments are persuasive and that this pattern peaks under high involvement seem straightforward enough; what happens in relation to weak arguments is more complex. Message recipients under weak argument conditions face a potentially interesting dilemma: The message position suggests a conclusion at odds with its supposed supportive content. For example, suppose the weak version of an argument in favor of instituting comprehensive examinations is "the risk of failing the exam is a challenge most students would welcome" (e.g., Petty, Harkins, & Williams, 1980, Experiment 2). From the student participants' perspective, outcomes implied by this argument are plausibly negative (failing the exam, facing a new challenge), thus more logically supporting the reverse conclusion that comprehensives should *not* be instituted. The conflict between message position and message content faced by recipients of weak arguments might not be easily resolved without heightened motivation (and requisite ability) to think about the problem. Thus, increased involvement may be the key to pushing recipients to the message position logically implied by the message content that comprehensive exams are good, assuming recipients have the ability to do so. In contrast to these predictions having to do with counter-attitudinal message positions, under pro-attitudinal message position conditions, the negative valence implicit in weak arguments should prove less problematical to message recipients, who can, with sufficient motivation, generate their own attitude-supportive cognitive responses. Thus, consistent with our valence hypothesis, we anticipated showing fairly robust actual change in favor of a pro-attitudinal message position despite variations in the manipulated quality of supportive arguments, perhaps even heightened by increased involvement. Finally, under conditions of low involvement, we anticipated smaller argument quality-related changes.

If weak arguments actually have negative valence for the message recipient, then we should see that they tend to produce negative attitude change, despite a message position that requests change in the opposite direction. What is needed to assess such a question are measures of *actual* attitude change rather than post-test-only comparisons between strong and weak arguments. Unfortunately, studies in the argument quality literature almost never assess actual change by comparisons to baseline opinions or to a no-message control group. Yet, despite the size of this literature, we were able to address some important questions (for more details, see Johnson & Smith-McLallen, 2003).

We used a three-tiered strategy to locate our sample of studies. First, we conducted computer-based information searches in the PsycINFO (1967 to 2002) database using various combinations of the key words *argument quality, argument strength, no message, control group, pretest, pretest-posttest,* or *attitude change*. Next, an electronic request for articles that met our inclusion criteria was also posted on the Society for Personality and Social Psychology (SPSP) listserv. Finally, we reviewed the reference lists of numerous articles that were procured as a result of these searches. We included studies if: (a) they had both strong and weak arguments, as labeled by the researchers; (b) they included either a no-message control group, or in the case of within subjects designs, pretest and post-communication attitude measures toward the subject of the persuasive communication; and (c) they reported statistics from which effect sizes could be derived. Because such studies are difficult to locate based simply on their abstracts, which tend to omit such details, we obtained any study that had "argument quality" or "argument strength" in its abstract and then searched the document to determine whether the criteria were satisfied.

We excluded studies or portions of studies that created situations that do not well characterize this literature. For example, we excluded one case of experimentally induced high knowledge, but retained the low-knowledge control conditions (Johnson, 1994). Similarly, we excluded experimentally induced high fear, but retained the low-fear control condition (Smith, 1977). Only those studies meeting the inclusion criteria that were obtained by October, 2002, were included. Three of the studies (Friedrich, Fetherstonhaugh, Casey, & Gallagher, 1996; Johnson, 1994; Petty et al., 1981) used the modal persuasive issue in the literature, comprehensive examinations as a requirement for college graduation; other studies used the issues of "bending truth in interpersonal relationships" (Neimeyer et al., 1991), candidates for local political offices (Greer, 1996), government controls to minimize effects of acid rain (Lin, 1994), and unconditional amnesty for the Vietnam draft (Smith, 1977). All studies used college undergraduates as participants.

Among the dimensions that we coded from each study were low or high involvement when manipulated (in other cases, studies were labeled "other"); and whether the message position was pro- or counter-attitudinal. This latter coding was established by examining the mean attitude positions on the pretest or no-message control group: When the mean attitude toward the message position was on the negative side of the neutral point on the scale, it was regarded as counter-attitudinal; otherwise, it was pro-attitudinal.

In a separate analysis, we examined whether participants' ratings of these argument sets justified the labels of "strong" versus "weak." The mean argument ratings and standard deviations robustly justified scholars' labels of "strong" and "weak" for their sets of relatively strong or relatively weak arguments, and there were no deviations attributable to studies' use of a pro- versus counter-attitudinal message position or to use of high- or low-involvement conditions.

The effect sizes we used in this integration evaluated actual attitude change resulting from message exposure. The mean attitude for the strong or weak message condition was compared against the mean attitudes at pretest or in a no-message control group; this difference was divided by the pooled standard deviation or the standard deviation of the paired comparisons, respectively (see Johnson & Eagly, 2000). The g-values were translated into d-values by correcting them for bias that results from smaller samples. In studies that manipulated involvement (Johnson, 1994; Lin, 1994; Petty, Cacioppo, & Goldman, 1981) we calculated four separate effect sizes (i.e., high involvement/strong, high involvement/weak, low involvement/strong, low involvement/weak). The six experiments included in these three studies yielded 18 different comparisons, each of which was treated as a separate study in analyses. Analyses used conventional fixed-effects meta-analysis assumptions (see Johnson & Eagly, 2000).

First consider the results from pro-attitudinal message position studies, which Fig. 11.1's two left-most bars show. Despite the fact that these recipients perceived the strong arguments to be stronger than the weak arguments, the two versions produced a statistically identical amount of attitude change and in both cases the movement was statistically significant in the direction of greater ac-

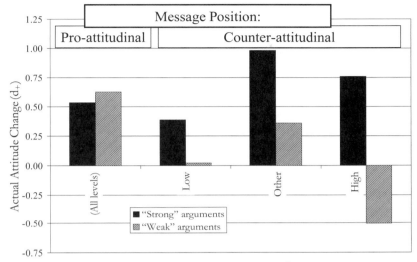

FIG. 11.1. Weighted mean effect sizes summarizing actual attitude change brought about in studies using "strong" (the darkened left bar within each cluster) and "weak" arguments (right bar in each cluster) with pro-attitudinal (left most pair) or counter-attitudinal (three right pairs) message positions. Counter-attitudinal studies are further divided by whether participants had low, other (i.e., no manipulation of involvement), or high outcome-relevant involvement (ORI) with message. (There was no impact of involvement within pro-attitudinal studies.)

ceptance of the message position. Moreover, the level of involvement induced within these studies had no relation to these results. Thus, it would appear that recipients of messages espousing pro-attitudinal positions find their own ways to support movement in the direction of the message, even if the accompanying arguments seem of poor quality.

The remaining bars in Fig. 11.1 show the varied role that argument quality played for the studies that used messages with counter-attitudinal positions, divided for whether involvement was manipulated to be low or high, or not varied ("other"). As a generalization across all of these comparisons, strong messages were significantly more persuasive than their weak counterparts and weak tended to be associated with resistance rather than boomerang. Yet this tendency for strong arguments to effect greater change than weak arguments depended on level of involvement, as the figure shows. Argument quality had no reliable impact when involvement was low (second pair of bars), but it had a significant impact when involvement was left unaltered or was high (see last two pairs of bars). Indeed, the last pair of bars in Fig. 11.1 illustrate the expected pattern of results for high involvement: Strong arguments elicited more and positive persuasion compared to weak arguments effect, which was directionally opposed. Both means differed significantly from zero, implying persuasion in the first case and the expected boomerang effect in the second. Finally, note that the amount of actual change elicited for highly involved recipients of counter-attitudinal message positions supported by strong arguments was statistically equivalent to that elicited for high outcome-relevant, pro-attitudinal positions. This combination of results suggests that strong counter-attitudinal messages have the same persuasive impact as pro-attitudinal communications because strong counter-attitudinal arguments are linked with positive outcomes for the recipient.

By examining *actual* rather than *relative* attitude change, this study afforded tighter generalizations about resistance or acceptance of a message in the face of identifiable message conditions. Our results suggest that people do not resist pro-attitudinal messages, just as they do not resist spontaneous self-generated positive thoughts. Indeed, these data confirm with different methods, a result shown experimentally by Killeya and Johnson (1998), that the negative impact of weak arguments can be overcome with convincing instructions to think only positive thoughts. Our data also confirmed, with different techniques and nearly independent data, the conclusion that Johnson and Eagly (1989) reached: High (compared to low) outcome-relevant involvement creates movement toward strong arguments and away from weak arguments. The present results go further in showing that, for such message recipients, persuasion in the direction of the message occurs with strong arguments, and boomerang away from the message position occurs with weak arguments. When involvement was low, there was no hint of boomerang in the face of weak arguments; the best that can be said is that these message recipients perhaps lacked the motivation to change their attitudes and resisted persuasion.

The actual attitude change observed for highly involved participants who received strong counter-attitudinal arguments was equivalent to the change that resulted for pro-attitudinal arguments (whether strong or weak). This result is consistent with our basic thesis that valence matters more than logic and suggests that strong arguments, when broken down, may actually be disguised versions of pro-attitudinal messages. These findings suggest that argument quality—as it has been represented in the literature to date—may be a mere proxy for valence. On the face of it, the conclusion that creating positive valence is crucial to overcoming resistance may not seem earth-shattering, but our finding that the resistance to weak arguments is overcome by positive valence has an intriguing implication. To wit, perceptions of veracity—a.k.a. sheer logic about the "truth value" of the presented arguments—matter relatively little compared to perceptions of valence (Levin et al., 2000). This conclusion flies in the face of many venerable theories, not the least of which is Fishbein's classic (1963) formulation of attitude as $\Sigma b \cdot e$, the sum of salient beliefs (b) about whether the entity possesses a characteristic multiplied by the evaluations (*e*) of those beliefs (see also Albarracín & Wyer, 2001; McGuire & McGuire, 1991). Yet, given that our meta-analysis's conclusions were based almost solely on persuasion outcomes, these data are ill-suited to assessing whether logicality, as assessed for example by the *b* component of the Σ*b* • *e* equation, underlies argument quality effects. To gather this evidence, we conducted a series of experiments.

EXPERIMENTAL EVIDENCE THAT VALENCE (USUALLY) MATTERS MORE THAN LIKELIHOOD

We conducted four studies that explicitly examined the logic that valence usually matters more than likelihood in persuasion (for more details, see Johnson, Smith-McLallen, Killeya, & Levin, 2003). Two of the studies explicitly examined whether valence or likelihood judgments are more closely related to perceptions of argument quality and the other two studies experimentally varied valence and likelihood of argumentation, examined perceptions of argument quality, and added persuasion measures; the last study also manipulated involvement.

Experiment 1—Judgments of Argument Strength, Valence, and Likelihood. In a fairly well-cited conference publication, Areni and Lutz (1988) were the first to question whether valence rather than likelihood may underlie argument quality's effects. These researchers examined the perceived strength—defined as likelihood—and the valence of arguments used in prior persuasion research. To make sure that recipients focused closely on the messages, instructions asked them to spend nontrivial amounts of time carefully studying the communications. Results showed that whereas valence of arguments differentiated strong from weak, there was no difference in judgments of the likelihood value of the information in the messages. Areni and Lutz therefore concluded that strong arguments elicited valence ratings that are more predominantly good than the weak arguments, and that likelihood matters little.

Our first experiment more specifically examined this valence hypothesis. Thirty-eight college students rated 24 quite commonly used arguments supporting the adoption of senior comprehensive exams. These arguments were developed by Petty et al. (1980, p. 87), who selected arguments based on cognitive response profiles. Eight arguments that had elicited predominantly favorable thoughts were their "strong" set; eight that elicited predominately unfavorable thoughts were "weak," and another eight that elicited even more unfavorable thoughts were "very weak." Using 15-point scales, participants were randomly assigned to judge the arguments along one of three dimensions, *valence* (end points: very bad to very good; *n* = 13), *likelihood* (very unlikely to very likely; *n* = 12), or *strength* (very weak to very strong; *n* = 13). We asked each group to do only one rating in order to avoid carryover effects in judgment and to simplify the task.

Collapsing over the arguments within each condition and using Petty et al.'s (1980) three a priori argument-quality conditions as a within-subjects factor and judgment condition as the between-subjects factor, a significant two-way interaction between the a priori strength group and the judgment condition emerged. "Strong" arguments were indeed seen as the strongest and the "very weak" arguments as the weakest, confirming Petty et al.'s initial argument-quality groupings in this sample. Also in line with our hypotheses, Petty et al.'s strong arguments received the highest valence ratings but the weak and very weak arguments had more negative valence. Analyses of likelihood judgments confirmed our hypothesis: The three levels of argument quality did not discriminate ratings of likelihood. More sensitive analyses using argument as the unit of analysis confirmed these findings; strength and valence correlated very highly, $r = .81$, whereas there was no link between strength and likelihood, $r = -.08$, and no link between valence and likelihood, $r = .02$. In sum, these data strongly support the conclusion that the perceived strength of arguments is strongly associated with perceived valence but not with perceived likelihood of arguments.

One might question whether the $\Sigma b \cdot e$ logic would better predict argument quality if the b (beliefs about the argument, is it strong or weak) and e (evaluations of the argument, is it good or bad) components were combined. That is, consistent with the $\Sigma b \cdot e$ logic, strong arguments might be those that are *both* good and likely, whereas weak arguments are those that are unlikely. In fact, this logic can be directly examined by regressing the mean strength judgments first on the mean valence and likelihood judgments and then on their interaction. The first step of this analysis offers the additional advantage of permitting a simultaneous assessment of both valence and likelihood's relation to argument strength judgments. This analysis confirmed the pattern reported in the preceding paragraph, with valence maintaining its impact on argument strength, but with likelihood having no relation; the interaction, added in the next step, proved nonsignificant.

That valence and strength are so tightly correlated confirms our expectation that *perceived strength* boils down to perceived *valence* of the arguments' content, consonant with Areni and Lutz's (1988) work. For practitioners in persuasion research, one implication of the close match between valence and perceived strength is that when subjects are presented with arguments differing in valence, they conceive of these differences as strength. This point has some import given that, in persuasion research, participants are often asked to rate arguments along a "strong–weak" dimension. What they may in fact implicitly be doing is rating them on a "good–bad" dimension. Since conducting this initial argument judgment study, we have obtained the same basic pattern in five more replications involving a total of four issues, two of which are "real-world" issues (e.g., U.S.–Arab relations) for which we obtained arguments from Web sites on the Internet. Across these studies, main effects of likelihood were quite rare, as were interactions of valence with likelihood. These results further suggest that when constructing persuasive messages, practitioners should not be overly concerned with creating arguments that suggest likely consequences for the message recipient. What these data failed to contain, however, was any active persuasion effort or measurement of persuasion. Our next two studies provided such data and further tested the hypothesis that information valence is more consequential to persuasion than information likelihood.

Experiment 2—Examining Valence and Likelihood as Factors in Persuasion. Evidence shows that when evaluating argument strength, valence matters more than likelihood; but because these studies have focused solely on argument judgments, there is to date no evidence about attitudes per se. Thus, we proceeded to conduct more traditional message-based persuasion experiments in which participants received a message position supported by argumentation and then completed the usual battery of measures. We stuck with the comprehensives issue for comparability with past research and continuity with Experiment 1. Thus, we selected arguments based on the ratings from the first experiment, completing the cells of a 2 (Valence: Good vs. Bad) $\times$ 2 (Likelihood: High vs. Low) factorial. The $\Sigma b \cdot e$ logic clearly predicts more positive attitudes in the face of good information that is likely to be true, and resistance or even boomerang in the face of bad information that is likely to be true. The unlikely combinations should be somewhere around neutral—unlikely information is a poor basis for one's attitudes.

In contrast, we expected that once again we would primarily see the valence effect in the persuasion data. Yet we also thought it likely that a "swallow-your-medicine" effect might occur with a bad but likely message. Under such circumstances, message recipients might interpret the arguments as bad-tasting medicine that must be taken in order to feel better later. With regard to the comprehensives issue, this logic implied, for example, that the tests may be stressful, but the benefit later in life may be better preparation for other competitions. Finally, we were intrigued by the combination that good but unlikely dimensions present. It is here that a "wishful thinking" effect may occur, such that although the arguments are unlikely to be true, the effects would be beneficial (cf. McGuire & McGuire, 1991; Albarracín & Wyer, 2001).

Participants were told that they would "be asked to read a short editorial on an important educational topic and to complete a series of scales and questions about the message." To maximize message scrutiny, the experimental booklet (falsely) stated that participants would later have to recall the arguments they read. The messages implied that the message was germane in an outcome-relevant fashion: The message position, which appeared at the beginning and the end of the message, was that "seniors at *this* university should be required to take a comprehensive examination in their major area as a requirement for graduation" (italics added). By heightening involvement for all participants, the research offered the possibility of addressing Areni and Lutz's (1988) speculation that likelihood plays a bigger role as elaboration likelihood increases.

Following were arguments that varied in *likelihood*, the chances that the stated consequences or antecedents are actually related to the argument, and *valence*, whether the consequences are genuinely desirable. Examples of the arguments follow:

Good/likely: Prestigious universities have comprehensive exams to maintain academic excellence.

Good/unlikely: Schools with comprehensive exams attract larger and more well-known corporations to recruit students for jobs.

Bad/likely: The difficulty of the exams will prepare one for later competitions in life.

Bad/unlikely: The risk of failing the exam is a challenge that most students would welcome.

These arguments were selected based on the ratings obtained in Study 1 and appeared in somewhat elaborated form along with another argument. After reading the message, participants rated their attitudes, engaged in a thought-listing task, and completed a series of ratings, including rating the arguments they had seen on their strength, likelihood and valence, with each of the two arguments they had seen rated separately.

As Fig. 11.2 illustrates, we found that good arguments were persuasive whether they were likely or unlikely, but bad arguments were persuasive only when they were judged as likely. Interestingly, only when arguments were both unlikely and bad was the mean attitude on the negative side of the midpoint, which is somewhat supportive of Areni and Lutz's (1988) speculation that under greater elaboration likelihood, argument likelihood can matter. Although we suspect that this pattern represents a boomerang effect, we cannot say with certainty in the absence of a measure of actual change. The fact that bad arguments can persuade when they are also likely does suggest a "bad-tasting medicine" effect: To wit, individuals may swallow the medicine given the knowledge that although the short-term effects may be bitter—that is, bad—the long-term effects will be far better. The rest of the persuasion pattern fails to support Areni and Lutz's speculation. Unlikely-but-good arguments were equally as persuasive as likely-and-good arguments. In short, a wishful-thinking effect emerged, despite relatively high elaboration likelihood.

We were especially intrigued by Experiment 2's demonstration that valence matters even for arguments that are unlikely to be true (as judged by the participants' peers) and we wished to explore possible boundary conditions of this valence effect. In particular, given that the valence effect occurred in the face of relatively high involvement with the issue, it was possible that it might not occur for participants with very low involvement, consistent with past demon-

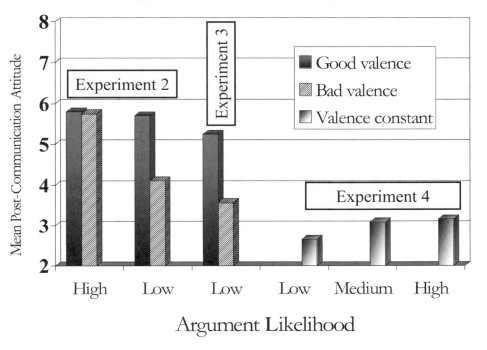

FIG. 11.2.   Mean post-communication attitudes as a function of argument likelihood (likely vs. unlikely to be true) and/or valence (good vs. bad). Experiment 2 had both factors; Experiment 3's data reflect only valence, as only the unlikely, good vs. bad pairing was used; Experiment 4's data reflect only likelihood, with valence constant.

strations of extent of processing × AQ interactions (e.g., Johnson, 1994; Killeya & Johnson, 1998; Petty & Cacioppo, 1979). In contrast, participants with very low involvement might actually process the arguments by using a valence heuristic, resulting in persuasion similar to that for high involvement.

Experiment 3—Bad Versus Good Yet Unlikely Arguments.
   Thus, Experiment 3 manipulated involvement, argument valence, and communicator credibility ($N = 167$). The persuasive messages were the unlikely, good versus bad, versions that appeared in Experiment 2; other methodological details also paralleled that study. Despite our evidence that our manipulations of involvement and credibility worked, the attitude data revealed no significant main effects or interactions involving these variables. The only significant effect was, again, the main effect of argument valence on attitudes such that good arguments elicited more positive attitudes than bad arguments. We conducted a path analysis to examine whether valence matters more than likelihood—in persuasion; in so doing we also examined processes plausibly associated with persuasion due to our strong arguments or resistance to persuasion due to weak

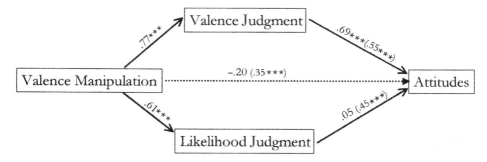

FIG. 11.3. This path analysis shows that the effect of argument valence on attitudes is completely mediated by judgments of valence (but not likelihood) of the arguments received (Experiment 3). (Values in parentheses are zero-order correlations.) ***$p < 001$.

arguments. As Fig 11.3 indicates, the valence manipulation affected both the ratings of argument valence and of argument likelihood, and it had a direct influence on attitudes. Although the arguments were preselected not to vary on likelihood, "good" arguments were still judged to be more *likely* than were "bad" arguments, which is correlational evidence of the same wishful-thinking effect that first emerged in Experiment 2. Controlling for the effects of argument ratings, the valence manipulations had no significant direct impact on attitudes. Instead, the persuasive impact of the valence manipulations was entirely carried by judgments of argument valence. Moreover, when added to the equation, the term for the valence of participants' thoughts proved nonsignificant in Experiment 3. As in Experiment 1, we also tested the combinatorial hypothesis that the interaction of the ratings of valence and likelihood mediates the effects of the valence manipulation on attitudes, but this term proved nonsignificant. Thus, the argument valence hypothesis again received the lion's share of support, although these data suggest that likelihood *can* play a role in persuasion.

Experiment 4—Varying Argument Likelihood Using a New Issue. Having shown robust valence effects across the first three experiments and only small likelihood effects, we decided a conceptual replication was in order in a potentially stronger attempt to show that argument likelihood can matter for persuasion. We selected another commonly used issue, tuition increases, and pretested arguments to vary from low to high likelihood of being true while remaining relatively constant on valence. Briefly, arguments were that an increase in tuition could be used "to provide course-related supplies. . . . and private bathrooms in every dorm room" (low likelihood), "to build underground tunnels for use during bad weather. . . . and to provide a subsidized taxi service to students" (moderate), and "to hire more faculty. . . . and to improve the quality and variety of food offered the dining halls" (high). We also varied communicator credibility orthogonally in the factorial design for our college undergraduate participants ($N = 107$). The only significant effect was a main effect for communicator credibility. Similar to results in the first two experiments, no significant likelihood effect emerged in analyses ($F < 1$; see last cluster in Fig. 11.2).

CONCLUSION

The studies in this chapter provide some insight into the potential roles of truth and consequences in persuasion. Our first study, the meta-analysis, examined the role of the valence of the message content and the message position as vital components in the recipe that creates strong or weak arguments. This recipe suggests that people will agree with message positions and message content that align with their prior attitudes. Consequently, counter-attitudinal message positions supported by "strong" arguments—viz, arguments that are positively valenced and therefore support initial attitudes—do indeed create persuasion. These patterns are, in the main, heightened by increasing outcome-relevant involvement, which presumably increases the motive to hold an accurate opinion about the issue. Messages fail to persuade when they present counter-attitudinal message positions supported by arguments that are weak—viz, arguments that are negatively valenced and therefore do not support initial attitudes. Such messages appear to create resistance for recipients with little motivation to process the message accurately and boomerang for those who do. Yet in consonance with social judgment-involvement theorists, we would offer the caveat that message position should matter more for individuals whose value-relevant involvement is high (cf. Johnson & Eagly, 1989; Johnson et al., 1995). The reviewed studies tended to examine relatively trivial issues as opposed to issues that may be more likely to tap into aspects of the self-picture, intimately felt and cherished. We suspect that actual attitude change for individuals with such involvements would show much greater resistance than that shown in the reviewed studies.

The four experiments we presented attempted to add to this picture by examining valence and likelihood of the arguments in two ways. One way simply compared judgments of arguments along valence and likelihood dimensions to determine which dimension best correlates with rated argument strength. In the main these data support a unitary view whereby valence is more closely related to argument strength than likelihood. The other way we examined valence and likelihood is by composing messages that varied on these dimensions, by examining persuasion patterns in response to these messages, and by determining whether these patterns were more plausibly explained by ratings of argument valence or likelihood. Across these experiments, the lion's share of data supported the conclusion of the judgment studies: Valence matters more than likelihood. Across the experiments, the interaction between valence and likelihood ratings played no role. Quite simply, good arguments imply approach and bad arguments imply avoidance. In Knowles and Linn's (this volume) terms, good arguments are the Alpha and bad arguments are the Omega.

If argument "strength" mainly boils down to argument "valence," does it challenge contemporary theories of persuasion? In fact, as Eagly and Chaiken (1993) discussed, renaming "argument quality" or "argument strength" effects "argument valence" effects may actually better match Petty and Cacioppo's assertion (e.g., 1986) that the *valence* of cognitive responses underlies persuasion. Note that researchers in this tradition rarely if ever pretest the arguments to show differing profiles of likelihood; the focus is almost always to develop "strong" arguments that elicit relatively favorable thoughts and "weak" arguments that elicit relatively unfavorable thoughts. Numerous studies have shown correlationally that the valence of cognitive responses listed after or during the message relates to post-communication attitudes (e.g., Johnson, 1994; Petty & Cacioppo, 1979), and Killeya and Johnson (1998) provided causal evidence of this effect. These researchers found that participants who were led spontaneously by their experimental instructions to think positively about a message were persuaded, even in the face of weak arguments. Thus, the resistance due to weak argumentation was overcome, with participants apparently self-persuading themselves to believe a specious message. Other participants who were not induced to think positively found the same message anti-persuasive.

More theoretical support for a valence interpretation of argument strength is suggested by research in other domains. Early evolution may well have favored a neural valence mechanism whereby organisms could swiftly determine whether to approach or avoid stimuli encountered in the environment, which needed only to be correct (likely) most of the time in order to become part of the genome. In contrast, a likelihood mechanism, if it were indeed a slower entity than the valence mechanism, would have been a more recent and more cerebral evolutionary development. If so, we should see that valence of the arguments is more correlated with argument strength for attitude entities that are known to be heritable, compared with those that are less heritable (see Tesser, 1993). Partially consistent with this perspective, Bargh, Chaiken, Govender, and Pratto (1992) found pervasive evidence across a large number of attitudes that even weakly held attitudes are automatically activated on the appearance of a prime. If attitudes have automatic evaluations, then it is plausible that the e components of attitudes are more salient than the b components. Yet to our knowledge, no one has directly tested this implication (see Pratto, 1994, for a review). Similarly, research on implicit attitudes suggests that automatically activated attitudes can be predictive of behavior (e.g., Marsh, Johnson, & Scott-Sheldon, 2001). Perhaps the most relevant evidence derives from person perception research. Following a dual-process model perspective, Gilbert and Malone (1995) reviewed research on the correspondence bias in person perception and supported a model whereby people first make internal attributions about a behavior, later correcting that attribution if they have sufficient ability and motivation to do so. Gilbert's (e.g., 1991) more general perspective on the process of belief suggests that at the time of comprehension, propositions are believed as true; only after this initial and swift acceptance are prepositions "unaccepted" or "certified." Yet it is unclear how this swift process would be evidenced in the persuasion context, where persons encounter many different propositions in the context of a single message.

Despite the bulk of evidence here favoring valence over likelihood as determining argument quality and persuasion, there are reasons to suspect that likelihood *can* play a role in defining argument strength and affecting attitudes, in consonance with the $\Sigma b \cdot e$ interpretation of attitude. For example, scientists are admonished and trained to pursue the truth (regardless of its consequences for their selves). Parents chronically judge whether their children are likely to be harmed by a potential situation and take action to prevent it. In the current studies, Experiment 2's bad but unlikely arguments were the least persuasive for our participants, who had a relatively high level of involvement with the issue. Possibly greater support for likelihood effects would be found if the arguments defined a greater range of likelihood values. Indeed, because of the subjective nature of the matter, arguments rarely have absolutely no truth value. It has been shown that message recipients may support their post-exposure attitudes with likelihood judgments that are not explicitly addressed by the message (e.g., Albarracín & Wyer, 2001). Similarly, Wegener, Petty, and Klein (1994) conducted two mood and persuasion studies in which participants' judgments of argument likelihood but not desirability were linked to attitudes. Because their studies' participants were in either happy or sad mood states and read only strong arguments, it is difficult to compare these results to the current research, which left mood unaltered and examined manipulations of argument quality.

The current research also did not explore some other conditions that may enhance the chances of finding likelihood effects, and here we point to mood and expertise. Individuals in positive moods should be more likely to follow affective valence in their judgments (the current valence manipulation) whereas those in negative moods should disregard valence in favor of sheer likelihood. For example, Gaspar and Clore (2002) found that people in happier moods tended to focus on the forest whereas those in sadder moods tended to focus on the trees. Indeed, Wegener et al.'s (1994) research found that positive moods infuse strong arguments with higher likelihood and negative moods with lower likelihood. Similarly, participants' expertise on the issue may well heighten the role of argument likelihood. Knowledge gains can decrease the impact of argument quality as it has typically been manipulated (Johnson, 1994); the implication is that valence should matter less and likelihood more for recipients with greater expertise. These expertise and mood explanations are deserving of further study because they could help to define the boundary conditions of valence and likelihood effects.

In closing, persuaders naturally need strong arguments in order to overcome resistance, but the question is how to achieve strong arguments and avoid weak arguments. The current research suggests that, generally speaking, formulating messages so as to suggest positive consequences to the recipients, or creating a motivational set that creates positive thinking about the message position, is far more important than making veridical statements. In short, persuasion results from the good and resistance from the bad. In subjective domains of communication and persuasion, the truth matters little when the consequences are clearly good or bad. Sound good?

AUTHOR NOTE

We thank David A. Kenny and Felicia Pratto for helpful comments and discussions regarding analyses in this chapter, and Dolores Albarracín and Lori A. J. Scott-Sheldon for comments on a draft of the chapter. This research was facilitated by National Institutes of Health grant R01-MH58563. Correspondence may be addressed to Blair T. Johnson, Department of Psychology, 406 Babbidge Road, Unit 1020, University of Connecticut, Storrs, CT 06269-1020. E-mail: blair.t.johnson@uconn.edu

REFERENCES

Albarracín, D., & Wyer, R. S. (2001). Elaborative and nonelaborative processing of a behavior-related communication. *Personality and Social Psychology Bulletin, 27,* 691–705.

Areni, C. S., & Lutz, R. J. (1988). The role of argument quality in the Elaboration Likelihood Model. *Advances in Consumer Research, 15,* 197–203.

Bargh, J. A., Chaiken, S., Govender, R., & Pratto, F. (1992). The generality of the automatic attitude activation effect. *Journal of Personality and Social Psychology, 62,* 893–912.

Eagly, A. H., & Chaiken, S. (1993). *The psychology of attitudes.* New York: Harcourt, Brace.

Festinger, L. (1957). *A theory of cognitive dissonance.* Evanston, IL: Row, Peterson.

Fishbein, M. (1963). An investigation of the relationship between beliefs about an object and the attitude toward that object. *Human Relations, 16,* 233–239.

Friedrich, J., Fetherstonhaugh, D., Casey, S., & Gallagher, D. (1996). Argument integration and attitude change: Suppression effects in the integration of one-sided arguments that vary in persuasiveness. *Personality and Social Psychology Bulletin, 22,* 179–191.

Gasper, K., & Clore, G. L. (2002). Attending to the big picture: Mood and global versus local processing of visual information. *Psychological Science, 13,* 34–40.

Gilbert, D. T. (1991). How mental systems believe. *American Psychologist, 46,* 107–119.

Gilbert, D. T., & Malone, P. S. (1995). The correspondence bias. *Psychological Bulletin, 117,* 21–38.

Greer, J. D. (1996). Unleashing the watchdogs on political advertising: The influence of need for cognition, argument quality, and source credibility on newspaper ad watch effectiveness. (Doctoral Dissertation, University of Florida, 1996). *Dissertation Abstracts International, 57,* 4178.

Johnson, B. T. (1994). Effects of outcome-relevant involvement and prior information on persuasion. *Journal of Experimental Social Psychology, 30,* 556–579.

Johnson, B. T., & Eagly, A. H. (1989). Effects of involvement on persuasion: A meta-analysis. *Psychological Bulletin, 106,* 290–314.

Johnson, B. T., & Eagly, A. H. (2000). Quantitative synthesis of social psychological research. In H. T. Reis & C. M. Judd (Eds.), *Handbook of research methods in social and personality psychology* (pp. 496–528). London: Cambridge University Press.

Johnson, B. T., Lin, H., Symons, C. S., Campbell, L. A., & Ekstein, G. (1995). Initial beliefs and attitudinal beliefs as factors in persuasion. *Personality and Social Psychology Bulletin, 21,* 502–511.

Johnson, B. T., & Smith-McLallen, A. (2003). *Effects of argument quality on actual attitude change: A research synthesis.* Unpublished manuscript.

Johnson, B. T., Smith-McLallen, A., Killeya, L. A., & Levin, K. (2003). *The good, the bad, and the likely: Components of argument strength and effects on message-based persuasion.* Unpublished manuscript.

Killeya, L. A., & Johnson, B. T. (1998). Experimental induction of biased systematic processing: The directed thought technique. *Personality and Social Psychology Bulletin, 24,* 17–33.

Levin, K. D., Nichols, D. R., & Johnson, B. T. (2000). Involvement and persuasion: Attitude functions for the motivated processor. In G. R. Maio & J. M. Olson (Eds.), *Why we evaluate: Functions of attitudes* (pp. 163–194). Mahwah, NJ: Erlbaum.

Lin, H. (1994). Communication goals as moderators of attitude accessability effects (Doctoral Dissertation, Syracuse University, 1994). *Dissertation Abstracts International, 56,* 567.

Marsh, K. L., Johnson, B. T., & Scott-Sheldon, L. A. J. (2001). Heart versus reason in condom use. *Zeitschrift für Experimentelle Psychologie, 48,* 161–175.

McGuire, W. J., & McGuire, C. V. (1991). The content, structure, and operation of thought systems. In R. S. Wyer, Jr., & T. K. Srull (Eds.), *Advances in social cognition* (Vol. 4, pp. 1–78). Hillsdale, NJ: Erlbaum.

Neimeyer, G. J., Macnair, R., Metzler, A. E., & Courchaine, K. (1991). Changing personal beliefs: Effects of forewarning, argument quality, prior bias, and personal exploration. *Journal of Social and Clinical Psychology, 10,* 1–20.

Petty, R. E., & Cacioppo, J. T. (1979). Issue involvement can increase or decrease persuasion by enhancing message-relevant cognitive responses. *Journal of Personality and Social Psychology, 37,* 1915–1926.

Petty, R. E., & Cacioppo, J. T. (1986). *Communication and persuasion: Central and peripherial routes to attitude change.* New York: Springer-Verlag.

Petty, R. E., Cacioppo, J. T., & Goldman, R. (1981). Personal involvement as a determinant of argument-based persuasion. *Journal of Personality and Social Psychology, 41,* 847–855.

Petty, R. E., Harkins, S. G., & Williams, K. D. (1980). The effects of group diffusion of cognitive effort on attitudes: An information-processing view. *Journal of Personality and Social Psychology, 38,* 81–92.

Pratto, F. (1994). Consciousness and automatic evaluation. In P. M. Niedenthal & S. Kitayama (Eds.), *The heart's eye: Emotional influences in perception and attention* (pp. 115–143). San Diego, CA: Academic Press.

Sherif, C. W., Sherif, M., & Nebergall, R. E. (1965). *Attitude and attitude change: The social judgment involvement approach.* Philadelphia: Saunders.

Sherif, M., & Hovland, C. I. (1961). *Social judgment: Assimilation and contrast effects in communication and attitude change.* New Haven, CT: Yale University Press.

Smith, M. J. (1977). The effects of threats to attitudinal freedom as a function of message quality and initial receiver attitude. *Communication Monographs, 44,* 196–206.

Tesser, A. (1993). The importance of heritability in psychological research: The case of attitudes. *Psychological Review, 100,* 129–142.

Wegener, D. T., Petty, R. E., & Klein, D. J. (1994). Effects of mood on high elaboration attitude change: The mediating role of likelihood judgments. *European Journal of Social Psychology, 24,* 25–43.

Worchel, S., & Brehm, J. W. (1970). Effect of threats to attitudinal freedom as a function of agreement with the communicator. *Journal of Personality and Social Psychology, 14,* 18–22.

Zanna, M. P. (1994). Message receptivity: A new look at the old problem of open- versus closed-mindedness. In A. A. Mitchell (Ed.), *Advertising exposure, memory, and choice* (pp. 141–162). Mahwah, NJ: Erlbaum.

12

Decreasing Resistance by Affirming the Self

Julia Zuwerink Jacks
Greensboro—North Carolina

Maureen E. O'Brien
Louisiana State University at Alexandria

"You're the coolest person I've ever met," she said to Heather. They were drinking sweet tea on the patio and staring into the fishpond, both tired from a long day of classes. Heather wasn't sure where her friend was going with this, but of course she didn't mind the flattery. "I mean, of all the friends I've met in college you've got to be the nicest," continued Jen. "You're warm, caring, honest. Like, who else would have run after that man to give him the $20 he dropped? I would have kept it. I mean, like he wasn't even good looking! What else have you done like that? It's so . . . it's so honest!"

Heather thought for a moment and remembered a few similar instances. She smiled as she recounted them to her friend. Come to think of it, she really was a good, honest person.

"What I don't get," said Jen after Heather was finished, "is how you could possibly be waffling on the question of whether or not to give African American students a better shot at getting into UNCG. I mean, why not? They deserve a break after the history of discrimination and wrong they've suffered in this country . . ." Jen continued with her arguments, and Heather listened with an open mind. The two talked till sunset, and in the end, Heather came around to Jen's point of view: African Americans should be given more scholarship opportunities.

This story illustrates the potential power of self-affirmations to increase vulnerability to persuasion. Heather was affirmed in a domain (i.e., honesty) that had nothing to do with the target issue (i.e., affirmative action) before Jen confronted her with persuasive arguments on that issue. Feeling good about herself in the unrelated domain, Heather was more open to Jen's arguments than she might otherwise have been. The self-affirmation reduced her resistance to persuasion.

In this chapter we will explore the self-affirmation procedure for reducing resistance to persuasion, and we will discuss some conditions under which the tactic does and does not work. Before explicating the theoretical framework behind this work, however, we offer a working definition of resistance.

WHAT IS RESISTANCE TO PERSUASION?

In our view, resistance to persuasion is not simply the inverse of persuasion. That is, resistance is not necessarily the same thing as not being persuaded (Cohen, 1964; McGuire, 1964). As Cohen put it, "In analyzing actual resistance to change, it is essential to examine evidence specifically gathered to bear upon resistance; resistance may not be a mirror image of acceptance, and the explicit study of [it] may highlight novel phenomena in the whole field of attitude change" (p. 121). Indeed, Cohen's observation presaged the collection of chapters in this volume, which represents a number of exciting research programs that are exploring "novel phenomena" related to resistance and persuasion (e.g., Tormala & Petty, this volume).

Despite this current interest, conceptual definitions of resistance are few and far between (for a rare exception, see Knowles, Butler, & Linn, 2001). This neglect in the literature is reflected in undergraduate textbooks as well. For example, we examined several introductory social psychology texts ($n = 8$), and not one of them offered a definition of resistance to persuasion. In this chapter, we define resistance to persuasion as *a motivated state in which the goal is to withstand the effects of a persuasive communication.* We assume that this motivation may be apparent in one's affective, cognitive, and/or behavioral responses to the persuasion attempt. That is, the motivation to resist may be expressed cognitively (e.g., by counterarguing), affectively (e.g., by getting angry or irritated), and/or behaviorally (e.g., by avoiding counter-attitudinal information). Predicting just how the resistance motive is expressed remains a matter for future investigation, however.

By defining resistance as a motivated state, we expressly mean to exclude cases in which individuals are merely not persuaded. For example, one could be unconvinced by a weak argument to adopt a novel attitude or to change one's brand of toothpaste. But in the absence of the motivation to avoid getting a new attitude or changing one's toothpaste, we would not say that resistance was operating. Thus, we concern ourselves primarily with cases in which the individual has a preexisting attitude that he or she is strongly motivated to maintain, and we use the term resistance motivation to refer to such cases. Unfortunately, the term resistance has been used, however, to refer to a failed persuasion attempt in which individuals likely did not have a preexisting attitude *or* an explicit motivation to resist attitude change. That is, "resistance" has been used to refer merely to the outcome on the attitude measure (i.e., lack of change). Although this use of the term resistance is understandable, we believe it might add confusion to the literature if resistance as an outcome versus a motivation is not properly distinguished. Thus, in both evaluating existing research and in planning new research, we suggest that greater clarity can be gained by specifying whether resistance is meant as an outcome, a motivation, or both.

When resistance as a motivation is operating, individuals will do whatever it takes to prevent change (Ahluwalia, 2000; Jacks & Cameron, 2003; Zuwerink & Devine, 1996). As indicated, this resistance may be manifested in individuals' cognitive, affective, and/or behavioral responses. Zuwerink and Devine (1996) have shown, for example, that both cognitive and affective responses contribute to the resistance process (see also Jacks & Devine, 2000). More recently, Jacks and Cameron (2003) have shown that individuals have a number of distinct strategies that they believe to be useful in resisting persuasion. Among these strategies, counterarguing, attitude bolstering, source derogation, and negative affect were the most preferred, and in one study, counterarguing was most effective in conferring resistance. Consistent with our view of resistance motivation, Ahluwalia (2000) has shown that among individuals who are committed to their attitude, if counterarguing or other biased processing strategies fail to reduce the impact of counter-attitudinal information, other resistance processes will "kick in." These include isolating or minimizing the implications of the damaging counter-attitudinal information on other aspects of the attitudinal representation (e.g., Clinton may have had sex with that woman, but he is still an effective leader). These more desperate resistance strategies were not observed among those less committed to their attitude. The point: Individuals have a number of resistance strategies at their disposal, and when motivation to resist is high, they will engage in a variety of these strategies in their efforts to resist change.

THE SELF-CONCEPT APPROACH

The general theoretical orientation that serves as our framework for understanding when an individual will be more or less motivated to resist persuasion is what we call the self-concept approach (Jacks & Cameron, 2002). Briefly stated, the self-concept approach assumes that a key motivator of resistance to persuasion is the need to protect the self-concept from threat and change. Stable self-conceptions, values, and attitudes provide individuals with a sense of control and predictability (Pittman & Heller, 1987). When this stability is challenged, individuals feel threatened and should resist change. A variety of theories (including dissonance, social judgment, and self-verification) and empirical findings are consistent with this reasoning (Abelson, 1986; Aronson, 1969; Cohen, Aronson, & Steele, 2000; Darley, 1938; Epstein, 1980; Festinger, 1957; Jacks & O'Brien, 2001; Johnson & Eagly, 1989; Katz, 1960; Lecky, 1945; Leippe, 1991; Lund, 1925; Rokeach, 1968, 1973; Rosenberg, 1979; Sherif & Cantril, 1947; Smith, Bruner, & White, 1956; Steele, 1988; Swann, 1990, 1997; Watson & Hartmann, 1939; Zuwerink & Devine, 1996). The self-concept approach predicts, generally, that individuals will be highly motivated to resist persuasion when their self-concepts are threatened in some way (either by the information itself or by other factors). In turn, manipulations that bolster one's self-concept or esteem should reduce the motivation to resist persuasion.

Self-Affirmation Theory and Resistance to Persuasion

Our more specific focus in this chapter is on the effects of self-affirmations (Steele, 1988) on persuasion dynamics in a classic communication-based persuasion paradigm. Self-affirmation theory is a useful means of examining persuasion dynamics within the more general self-concept approach because it provides an empirically validated way of manipulating the need to protect the self-concept (cf. Aronson, Cohen, & Nail, 1999). Self-affirmation manipulations are usually accomplished by having individuals complete a survey relevant to a personally important value (e.g., Steele & Liu, 1983) or describe why a particular value or characteristic is important to them (e.g., Cohen et al., 2000; Fein & Spencer, 1997). Research has shown that self-affirmations serve to "buffer" the self-concept and mitigate the need to engage in attributional analysis (Liu & Steele, 1986), the need to derogate others (Fein & Spencer, 1997), the need to ruminate about a frustrated goal (Koole, Smeets, van Knippenberg, & Dijksterhuis, 1999), and the propensity to justify one's dissonance-producing actions through attitude change (Steele, 1988; Steele & Liu, 1983; Steele, Spencer, & Lynch, 1993).

In addition, self-affirmed individuals have been shown to be more open to self-threatening health information (e.g., concerning the risk of AIDS among the sexually active) and less biased in their processing of such information compared to non-affirmed individuals (Reed & Aspinwall, 1998; Sherman, Nelson, & Steele, 2000). Finally, Cohen et al. (2000) have demonstrated that compared to non-affirmed individuals, self-affirmed individuals were more open to counter-attitudinal information. Specifically, they produced more favorable evaluations of attitude-disconfirming evidence, were less biased in their source evaluations, and were more vulnerable to persuasion following exposure to counter-attitudinal information. This latter attitude effect, however, was only significant in their second study. (It was insignificant in Study 1 and not examined in Study 3.) Nevertheless, their data are generally consistent with the view that self-affirmations undermine self-protective resistance processes and leave individuals more vulnerable to persuasion.

Dissonance Versus Persuasion Research

It is particularly interesting to note that the effects of self-affirmation manipulations on attitude change are different for dissonance versus persuasion research. Of course, self-affirmation theory (Steele, 1988) was first proposed as an alternative explanation to classic dissonance findings in a forced-compliance paradigm. In this paradigm, individuals are induced to choose freely to write a counter-attitudinal message, and doing so creates dissonance. When later asked to report their attitudes, free-choice participants change their attitudes to be consistent with their essay more than no-choice (i.e., no dissonance) participants. In a number of studies, Steele and his colleagues have demonstrated that self-affirmed individuals (compared to no-affirmation controls) do *not* change their attitudes in this forced-compliance dissonance paradigm (Steele, 1988; Steele & Liu, 1983; Steele et al., 1993). Theoretically, Steele and his colleagues argued that the self-affirmation opportunity repairs the self-concept, obviating the need for dissonance reduction through attitude change.

Research has also shown that self-affirmations are most effective in obviating the need for attitude change when they are *not* related to the dissonance-arousing act. For example, Aronson, Blanton, and Cooper (1995) have shown that following a dissonance induction, individuals chose *not* to affirm the self in the domain that had been threatened; instead, they preferred to affirm the self-concept in an unrelated domain. Further, Blanton, Cooper, Skurnik, and Aronson (1997) argued that self-affirmations make the standards that individuals have in that domain very salient. Therefore, affirmations that are relevant to dissonant behavior should *not* help reduce dissonance, but may, in fact, make people feel worse. In their research, when participants who had written a counter-attitudinal essay that contradicted the value of compassion were later affirmed on that value, the affirmation exacerbated dissonance and led to more attitude change compared to a no-affirmation control. Individuals who were self-affirmed in a domain unrelated to compassion, however, did *not* change their attitudes compared to no-affirmation controls. These findings suggest that only unrelated affirmations will mitigate the need for self-justifying attitude change in the dissonance paradigm.

Although disagreement still persists over the best explanation for dissonance effects (e.g., cognitive consistency, self-consistency, or self-esteem maintenance), this debate is not our focal concern. Rather, we are interested in the implications of self-affirmation theory and methodology for research in the persuasion domain. As already noted, Cohen et al. (2000) have shown that self-affirmations mitigate defensive processing, biased source evaluation, and resistance to attitude change. This last effect—greater attitude change in the self-affirmed versus no-affirmation condition—is the opposite of what has been found in the dissonance paradigm. Why? Self-affirmation theory argues that self-affirmations serve to "buffer" or bolster an individual's self-concept. Further, it is argued that self-affirmations can either *prevent* or *repair* potential damage to the self-concept (Aronson et al., 1999; Sherman et al., 2000). In the dissonance paradigm, self-affirmations serve as an "antidote" to self-esteem damage. In the persuasion paradigm, however, they presumably serve as an "inoculation" against such damage. To the extent that persuasive communications are threatening to the self and its cherished attitudes and beliefs, individuals should resist those communications. However, if self-affirmations inoculate the self against such threats, then counter-attitudinal communications should not evoke as great a sense of threat than might be the case for non-affirmed (non-inoculated) individuals. Consequently, self-affirmed individuals may process the persuasive message in a more open-minded, less defensive fashion, which should lead to greater vulnerability to persuasion (Cohen et al., 2000; Reed & Aspinwall, 1998; Sherman et al., 2000).

Self-Affirmations and Message-Compatibility

To date, studies showing that self-affirmations lead to less biased information processing and greater attitude change have, without exception, used self-affirmations that were not related to the persuasion domain investigated. Thus, this research demonstrates only that self-affirmations lead to less resistance when the self-affirmation has no bearing on the attitude issue. This situation is akin to the opening scene of this chapter. Heather was self-affirmed on the topic of honesty, which was unrelated to the affirmative action policy of offering African Americans more scholarship opportunities. Thus affirmed, she was vulnerable to Jen's persuasive arguments and changed her mind on the unrelated issue. We suggest, however, that self-affirmations will not always lead to greater persuasibility. Rather, we hypothesize that the relation between the self-affirmation and the counter-attitudinal message will determine whether persuasion or resistance prevails. Specifically, we hypothesize that self-affirmations will effectively undermine resistance to persuasion only when (a) the self-affirmation is *unrelated* to the persuasive message (as in Cohen et al., 2000), or (b) when the self-affirmation is *compatible* with the persuasive message. As an example of the latter condition, if one affirms the self as nonprejudiced, then one should be more open to attitude change in response to a nonprejudiced persuasive message (provided, of course, that the affirmation is important to the self; Steele, 1988).

Now imagine, instead, that after being self-affirmed as nonprejudiced, one encountered a prejudiced message (e.g., one arguing against gays in the military). In this case, the nonprejudiced self-affirmation is *incompatible* with the gist of the persuasive message. Under these conditions, we hypothesize that the self-affirmation will *not* undermine resistance. Rather, the self-affirmation in this case should, as in Blanton et al. (1997), make the standard (e.g., self as nonprejudiced) very salient and less likely to be violated. Thus, a message-incompatible self-affirmation should leave individuals resistant to persuasion compared to an unrelated self-affirmation. Importantly, we do not necessarily expect that a message-incompatible self-affirmation will lead to greater resistance than a no-affirmation control. Whether or not it will do so likely depends on the preexisting level of motivation to resist attitude change.

In the following sections we summarize the primary findings from our recent work on these issues. As will be seen, our data are generally consistent with the conceptualization we have laid out here. Following this presentation of the empirical evidence, we offer a more general discussion of the importance of this work for understanding the dynamics of persuasion and resistance to persuasion and suggest some practical implications of our findings.

EMPIRICAL EVIDENCE

Study 1: Unrelated and Message-Compatible Self-Affirmations

In our first study, participants were exposed to a counter-attitudinal message arguing in favor of giving African Americans more scholarship opportunities to attend college. The self-affirmation topic was either *unrelated* to this issue (i.e., honest) or it was *compatible* with the egalitarian gist of the message (i.e., non-prejudiced). We expected to find that self-affirmed individuals would be more persuaded by the counter-attitudinal message than their no-affirmation counterparts. We expected this effect whether the affirmation was compatible with or unrelated to the message.

In a prescreening session, introductory psychology students indicated their attitude toward recruiting more African American students to the university by offering them more scholarships on three 9-point semantic differentials (i.e., *good–bad, favorable–unfavorable, negative–positive*). Responses to these items were averaged such that higher scores indicated more favorable attitudes (Cronbach's alpha = .96). Approximately four weeks later, 110 individuals against scholarships for African Americans (scoring on average between 1 and 4) were recruited for participation by phone and/or electronic mail.

In the lab, we presented participants with two ostensibly unrelated studies. The first was presented as a brief pilot study that would be used for an experiment the following semester. Participants were then presented with the self-affirmation manipulation (see next section). After completing this "pilot study," participants were introduced to the "primary study," which concerned "how the length and technical aspects of journal articles may affect text evaluation," including "beliefs, thoughts, and feelings about the text." Participants then read a counter-attitudinal message in favor of providing scholarships for African American students as a means of recruitment. After reading the message, participants reported their attitudes toward this affirmative action issue along with their cognitive and affective responses to the message. The order in which attitudes versus thoughts and affect were assessed was counterbalanced. During debriefing, no participants indicated suspicion regarding the relationship between the first and second studies.

TABLE 12.1
Pretest and Posttest Attitude Scores as a Function of Affirmation Condition
(Study 1)

| | Pretest | | Posttest | | |
	M	SE	M	SE	Mean Change
Self-affirmation	2.70	0.17	3.58	0.26	0.88
No-affirmation	2.87	0.18	2.94	0.27	0.07

Self-Affirmation Manipulation. The affirmation topics were *nonprejudiced* and *honest*. Prescreening ensured that both of these topics were rated as high in personal importance (on a 15-point scale, $M = 12.45$, $SE = 0.29$ and $M = 14.01$, $SE = 2.21$, for nonprejudiced and honest, respectively). Thus, both topics were truly affirming for our participants (Steele, 1988). Instructions in the self-affirmation conditions asked participants to describe three examples of times they were personally successful at being either nonprejudiced or honest (cf. Cohen et al., 2000). Individuals in the no-affirmation condition were asked to describe three examples of how a *child* could display either trait. Thus, all participants thought about either nonprejudiced or honesty, but only those in the self-affirmation conditions considered the trait in self-relevant terms.

Results and Discussion. Data were analyzed in a 2 (Affirmation Condition: self-affirmation vs. no-affirmation) × 2 (Topic: compatible vs. unrelated) × 2 (Order: attitudes first vs. attitudes last) × 2 (Attitude Measure: pretest vs. posttest) mixed-model analysis of variance (ANOVA), with repeated measures on the last factor. This analysis revealed a significant Attitude Measure × Affirmation Condition interaction, $F(1, 101) = 5.65$, $p < .02$, (see Table 12.1). As expected, individuals in the self-affirmation conditions were more persuaded (mean change = 0.88) than their no-affirmation counterparts (mean change = 0.07). No interaction with affirmation topic was observed. Thus, as expected, whether individuals were self-affirmed in the unrelated or compatible domain, a self-affirmation led to more change than no affirmation.

Although we were encouraged by these results, a number of alternative explanations exist, all of which are particularly troublesome for the compatible (i.e., nonprejudiced) affirmation topic. For example, one concern is that the compatible self-affirmation served as a persuasive message itself. That is, it is possible that simply affirming the self as nonprejudiced would cause participants to change their attitudes to be more favorable toward giving African Americans more scholarship opportunities. Theoretically, then, self-affirmations may do little to influence self-protection motives and the openness with which persuasive messages are processed. Rather, self-affirmations may, in and of themselves, change attitudes. Alternatively, it is possible that the self-affirmations heightened consistency pressures such that participants were favorable toward the pro-African American message in order to respond consistently with the self-affirmation task. If this were true, then one would expect participants to change their attitudes in response to the self-affirmation manipulation (compared to no-affirmation) even in the absence of a persuasive message. Another possibility is that the self-affirmation manipulation served to heighten self-discrepancies in the prejudice domain. That is, being asked to think about one's successful non-prejudiced behaviors could also cause one to recall one's failures (Higgins, 1987), resulting in a salient self-discrepancy rather than self-affirmation. One way to reduce this discrepancy would be to assert one's nonprejudiced identity as soon as possible. Thus, individuals given an opportunity to report their attitudes toward the African American scholarships issue immediately following the self-affirmation manipulation (or the discrepancy-induction manipulation, if you will) should report *less* prejudiced attitudes toward this issue compared to no-affirmation controls.

All of these alternative explanations were addressed through the inclusion of no-message control conditions for the nonprejudiced affirmation topic. That is, we included two no-message control groups who either did or did not affirm the self on the trait *nonprejudiced*. Following this manipulation, both groups immediately reported their attitudes toward the affirmative action policy. An analysis comparing the no-message groups with the message groups in the non-prejudiced topic condition revealed a significant Attitude Measure $\times$ Affirmation Condition $\times$ Message Condition interaction, $F(1, 94) = 4.81$, $p < .04$. In the no-message control condition, the self-affirmation created a slight boomerang effect, such that individuals became *less* favorable toward giving African Americans more scholarships (pretest $M = 4.13$, posttest $M = 3.56$) than their no-affirmation counterparts (pretest $M = 3.13$, posttest $M = 3.45$). In contrast, self-affirmed individuals in the message condition became more favorable toward the policy (pretest $M = 2.36$, posttest $M = 3.09$) than their no-affirmation counterparts (pretest $M = 2.48$, posttest $M = 2.79$). Thus, the nonprejudiced self-affirmation alone did *not* produce attitude change in favor of the policy. Likewise, individuals did not feel compelled to respond to the attitude measures in a manner consistent with their nonprejudiced responses on the self-affirmation task. Nor does it appear that individuals were motivated by a desire to reduce self-discrepancies by reporting favorable attitudes toward African Americans. Only when self-affirmed individuals (in the nonprejudiced topic condition) were exposed to the actual persuasive message did they become more in favor of the affirmative action policy. These results strengthen the claim that the self-affirmations serve to buffer the self-concept against threat posed by the persuasive message, allowing greater openness to that message.

Ancillary Measures.   To understand how self-affirmations influence the persuasion process, we also measured participants' cognitive and affective responses to the persuasive message. Posttest scores were positively correlated with *positive mood* (an index of ratings of the extent to which the message made them feel *friendly, happy, positive, optimistic, content,* and *good*; alpha = .91), $r(106) = .41$, $p < .001$, and negatively correlated with *irritation* (a composite

index of the items *agitated, angry, annoyed, bothered, disgusted,* and *irritated*;
alpha $= .93$), $r(106) = -.61, p < .001$. However, there were no self-affirmation
effects on these indices, suggesting that self-affirmed individuals were no more
likely than their no-affirmation counterparts to be in a positive mood or to be
irritated by the message.

Two cognitive response indices were also analyzed. First, we examined valenced thoughts by subtracting the number of negative thoughts from the number
of positive thoughts and dividing by the total number of relevant thoughts. This
valenced thoughts index was positively related to posttest attitude scores, $r(109)$
$= .60, p < .001$, indicating that the more positive thoughts generated, the more
favorable were attitudes toward giving African Americans more scholarships.
However, there were no self-affirmation effects on this index either, indicating
that self-affirmed individuals were no more likely than non-affirmed individuals
to generate message-favorable thoughts. Furthermore, there were no effects on
a second index of the total number of relevant thoughts generated. Thus, the
self-affirmation manipulation did not influence cognitive responses to the message.

Summary.   We obtained the expected affirmation condition effect indicating that self-affirmed individuals were more persuaded than their no-
affirmation counterparts, and the topic of the affirmation did not modify this
effect. Thus, both unrelated and compatible affirmations had a similar positive
effect on attitude change. No-message control data helped to eliminate alternative explanations for this effect. The analyses of thoughts and affect indicated
that although thoughts, positive mood, and irritation were significantly related
to final attitudes, none of these constructs mediated the self-affirmation effect
on attitudes. These results cast doubt on a suggestion made by Cohen et al.
(2000) that positive affect may mediate self-affirmation effects. Further, they
suggest the possibility that self-affirmations influence attitudinal responses independently of cognitive and affective responses to the message.

Study 2: Unrelated and Message-
Incompatible Self-Affirmations

In this next study we wanted to examine the effects of a message-incompatible
self-affirmation on persuasion. To do so, we changed the counter-attitudinal
message to one that was *incompatible* with a nonprejudiced self-affirmation.
Specifically, we exposed participants to a counter-attitudinal message arguing
against allowing gays in the military. Because this message is prejudiced in
content, we expected individuals who were self-affirmed as nonprejudiced to be
more *resistant* to persuasion than individuals who were self-affirmed on the
message-unrelated characteristic of honesty. We did not make the strong prediction that the nonprejudiced self-affirmed group would be more resistant than
their no-affirmation counterparts because we suspected that resistance to this

counter-attitudinal message would already be generally high among most participants (Zuwerink & Devine, 1996). Thus, the key predictions were greater persuasion in the unrelated self-affirmation condition (i.e., honesty) compared to their no-affirmation control and greater resistance in the message-incompatible self-affirmation condition (i.e., nonprejudiced) relative to the unrelated self-affirmation condition (i.e., honesty).

Method. The method was essentially the same as in the first study. All individuals (30 males and 88 females) were recruited on the basis of their favorable attitudes toward allowing gays in the military (i.e., scoring 6–9 on a 9-point scale). Upon arriving at the laboratory, individuals affirmed the self (or not) on the trait honesty or nonprejudiced. Next, participants read a counter-attitudinal message arguing against allowing gays in the military and reported their attitudes, thoughts, and affect. The order in which attitudes versus thoughts and affect was assessed was again counterbalanced. During debriefing, no participants indicated suspicion regarding the relationship between the first and second studies, and an examination of the thought-listing protocols revealed no suspicious thoughts.

Results and Discussion. Data were analyzed in an Affirmation Condition × Topic × Order × Attitude Measure mixed-model ANOVA. The only significant effect in this analysis was a 4-way interaction, $F(1, 110) = 5.59$, $p < .02$. Unexpectedly, the order in which the dependent variables were measured significantly moderated the effects. Simple effects analysis indicated *no* significant effects when final attitudes were measured first, $ps > .16$. However, when final attitudes were measured last, the expected interaction between Attitude Measure, Topic, and Affirmation Condition was significant, $F(1, 56) = 4.24$, $p < .05$ (see Fig. 12.1). In this order condition, individuals self-affirmed in the unrelated domain were more persuaded by the anti-gay message (mean change = 1.88) than their no-affirmation counterparts (mean change = 0.62), $F(1, 26) = 3.28$, $p = .08$. In contrast, those who were affirmed in the incompatible domain were not more persuaded by the anti-gay message (mean change = 0.29) than their no-affirmation counterparts (mean change = 0.86), $p > .32$. Thus, as we expected, the self-affirmation did *not* enhance persuasion when the topic of the affirmation was incompatible with the persuasive message. Finally, as expected, those who were affirmed in the incompatible domain were more resistant to the anti-gay message compared to those who were affirmed in the unrelated domain, $F(1, 28) = 7.01$, $p < .02$. Thus, self-affirmations do not always lead to greater persuasibility. Rather, the topic of the self-affirmation is a critical moderator of the effect of self-affirmations on persuasion.

Thoughts and Affect. As in Study 1, we examined participants' cognitive and affective responses to the counter-attitudinal message. Posttest attitudes were correlated with *irritation*, $r(116) = .48$, $p < .001$, such that greater irritation was associated with greater resistance to the anti-gay message. (Recall

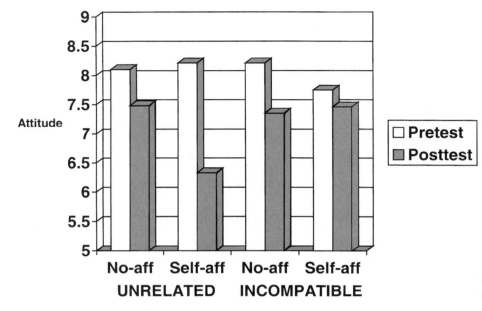

FIG. 12.1.   Pretest and posttest attitude scores as a function of Affirmation
Condition (self-affirmation vs. no affirmation) and Affirmation Topic (unrelated vs. incompatible) in Study 2. Means are for conditions in which attitudes were reported *after* thoughts and affect had been reported.

that in this study, higher attitude scores reflect greater resistance to the anti-gay
message.) However, *positive mood* was only marginally correlated with posttest
attitudes, $r(116) = -.16$, $p < .09$. As in the first study, there were no self-
affirmation effects on these indices. Posttest attitudes were also significantly
correlated with valenced thoughts, such that the fewer positive thoughts participants generated, the more they resisted the message, $r(118) = -.64$, $p < .001$.
However, as in the first study, there were no significant effects involving affirmation condition and topic on the valenced thoughts index, nor on an index of
the total number of relevant thoughts generated. Thus, as in Study 1, the effect
of self-affirmations on attitudes was not mediated by cognitive or affective responses to the message.

Study 3: Unrelated and Message-Incompatible Self-Affirmation (Conceptual Replication)

We were disappointed with the emergence of the order effect in Study 2 and
sought to test our hypotheses again using a different counter-attitudinal message
(anti-equality) and a different message-incompatible affirmation topic (freedom
instead of nonprejudiced). A conceptual replication was considered desirable

given that the key effects in Study 2 were observed only when attitudes were assessed after participants reported their thoughts and affective reactions to the message. Because neither thoughts nor affect significantly predicted final attitudes in Study 2, the reason for the obtained order effect is unclear, and we suspect that it is spurious. If the order effect does not replicate in Study 3, then we can more confidently conclude that it is not necessary to measure thoughts and affect first to obtain the predicted self-affirmation effects on attitudes.

In this replication we employed a message that argued against the value of equality (equal opportunity for all). To increase the generalizability of our results, we chose not to use nonprejudiced as our incompatible affirmation. Rather, individuals affirmed themselves (or not) on the value of *freedom.* (Honesty was again employed as the unrelated affirmation topic.) We reasoned that freedom and equality would be integrally related in the ideologies of our participants (Rokeach, 1973), so that affirming the value of freedom would lead to resistance to a message that explicitly argued against equal opportunity for all. Consistent with this reasoning, Prislin, Wood, and Pool (1998) reported that freedom was seen as "highly relevant" to equal rights. In addition, our own pilot participants reported that supporting the value of equality also implied supporting the value of freedom. Specifically, 18 individuals were asked to indicate whether supporting equality (equal opportunity for all) implies supporting ($+4$) or being against (-4) a variety of values (e.g., freedom, self-respect, social justice, honest). A zero point was labeled "supporting equality is unrelated to the value." Participants indicated that supporting equality implied significantly more support for freedom ($M = 3.50$, $SD = 1.15$) than honesty ($M = 1.44$, $SD = 1.65$), paired-samples $t(17) = 3.65$, $p < .01$. Thus, we hypothesized that a freedom self-affirmation would lead to greater resistance to a message that was opposed to equality compared to an honest self-affirmation.

Method.   After a prescreening session, individuals (17 males and 74 females) were recruited on the basis of their favorable attitudes toward equality (equal opportunity for all). The procedures followed were the same as those in the previous studies. Again, no suspicion was detected during debriefing or in participants' thought-listing protocols.

Results and Discussion.   Initial analyses revealed two outliers whose posttest scores were more than three standard deviations below the mean. Therefore, they were dropped from all analyses. Attitude data were analyzed in an Affirmation Condition × Topic × Order × Attitude Measure mixed-model ANOVA. This analysis revealed no order effects. The expected interaction between Attitude Measure, Affirmation Condition, and Topic was significant, $F(1, 81) = 4.93$, $p < .03$ (see Figure 12.2). No other ANOVA effects were significant. Compared to their respective no-affirmation controls, individuals who were self-affirmed in the unrelated domain were more persuaded by the anti-equality message and those who were self-affirmed in the incompatible domain were more resistant to the message. However, only the latter simple effect was

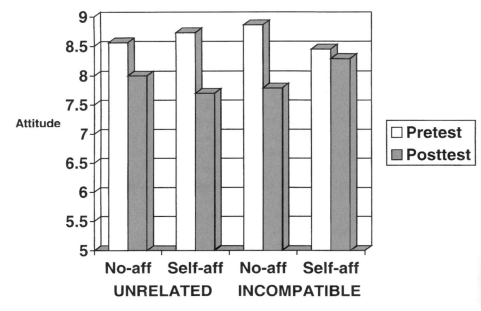

FIG. 12.2.   Pretest and posttest attitude scores as a function of Affirmation Condition (self-affirmation vs. no affirmation) and Affirmation Topic (unrelated vs. incompatible) in Study 3.

significant, $p < .02$. Importantly, individuals in the unrelated self-affirmation condition were more persuaded (mean change = 1.03) than those in the incompatible self-affirmation condition (mean change = 0.16), $p < .04$.

These findings replicate and extend those of Study 2 in showing that the topic of the self-affirmation is an important moderator of self-affirmation effects. When the topic of the affirmation is incompatible with the implications of the message, the affirmation does not increase persuasibility. Instead, such affirmations increase resistance to persuasion compared to self-affirmations that are unrelated to the message.

Thoughts and Affect.   As in the previous studies, we examined both cognitive and affective responses to the message. Neither irritation nor positive mood was significantly correlated with posttest beliefs, $ps > .22$, and there were no significant ANOVA effects for these affect indices. A valenced thoughts index significantly correlated with posttest beliefs, $r(89) = -0.52$, $p < .001$, such that more unfavorable thoughts were associated with greater resistance. (As in Study 2, higher final attitude scores reflect greater resistance to the message.) One significant ANOVA effect for this valenced thoughts index did emerge, however—an Affirmation Condition by Topic interaction, $F(1, 81) = 6.23$, $p < .02$. This interaction was such that individuals who were self-affirmed in the unrelated topic condition generated significantly fewer negative thoughts

($M = -0.38$, $SE = 0.10$) than their no-affirmation counterparts ($M = -0.71$, $SE = 0.14$), $p < .05$. However, they did *not* change their attitudes significantly more than their no-affirmation counterparts. Individuals who were self-affirmed in the message-incompatible condition, on the other hand, were significantly more resistant but they did not generate significantly more negative thoughts ($M = -0.51$, $SE = 0.11$) than their no-affirmation counterparts ($M = -0.28$, $SE = 0.10$), $p > .14$. This interaction is the first indication in three studies that self-affirmations may influence cognitive responses to the persuasive message. However, the pattern of significant effects in the thoughts data does not match that of the attitude data. Therefore, we cannot conclude that thoughts mediate the affirmation condition by topic interaction on attitudes. These manipulations did apparently influence thoughts, but not in a way that can explain their influence on attitudes.

Finally, an analysis of the total number of relevant thoughts generated revealed a main effect for topic, $F(1, 81) = 4.56$, $p < .05$. Individuals generated more relevant thoughts in the incompatible conditions ($M = 6.29$, $SE = 0.33$) than in the unrelated conditions ($M = 5.17$, $SE = 0.40$), $p < .05$. However, this effect cannot explain the self-affirmation effects on attitudes.

Meta-Analysis

Our two primary empirical hypotheses were that (a) an unrelated and/or message-compatible self-affirmation will lead to greater persuasion compared to no affirmation and (b) a message-incompatible self-affirmation will lead to greater resistance compared to an unrelated self-affirmation. Although the data from our three studies were generally supportive of these hypotheses, the effects were not always strong and, in one study, were modified by an unexpected order effect. Therefore, we conducted a mini meta-analysis to assess the average effect size (d) for each hypothesis (see Johnson, 1993; Johnson & Eagly, 2000). The effect sizes reported (Hedge's) are corrected for sample-size bias and yield somewhat smaller effect sizes than Cohen's ds.

For hypothesis (a) we also included the two relevant studies reported by Cohen et al. (2000; Studies 1 and 2). The weighted mean d across these five studies was 0.26, with a 95% confidence interval that does not include zero, 0.05/0.47 (Johnson & Eagly, 2000). By Cohen's standards this is a small effect size. Nevertheless, it is reliable (z value of $d = 2.46$, $p < .05$), and the homogeneity value, $Q(4) = 2.82$, *ns*, was small and nonsignificant, suggesting that the effect sizes are relatively consistent across studies. Thus, despite the weak showing in Study 3 and the order effect in Study 2, it appears that unrelated and/or message-compatible self-affirmations do reliably reduce resistance to persuasion.

The average effect size for hypothesis (b), calculated across our Studies 2 and 3, was -0.42, with a 95% confidence interval that does not include zero, $-0.82/-0.03$ (z value of $d = -2.13$, $p < .05$). Thus, the second hypothesis was supported across these two studies. In addition, a small and nonsignificant homogeneity value suggests that the studies appear to gauge only one population effect size. However, because only two studies were included, there was little power to detect deviations from the observed mean effect size.

GENERAL DISCUSSION

The research we have presented here suggests that Jen's strategy of affirming Heather's honesty before trying to change her affirmative action attitudes was a well-chosen one. Self-affirmations apparently have the power to attenuate the personal threat one feels at being confronted with a counter-attitudinal message. With the reduction of that threat, one is more vulnerable to the persuasive impact of the message. However, greater vulnerability is not the inevitable result of self-affirmations. As we have shown, whether or not self-affirmations create greater vulnerability to persuasion depends on the relationship between the topic of the self-affirmation and the gist of the persuasive message. If the topic of the self-affirmation is *incompatible* with the persuasive message, then self-affirmations do not lead to greater persuasion. Rather, they result in resistance compared to those who are self-affirmed on a message-unrelated topic. Thus, if Jen had made the mistake of affirming Heather for her individualism and/or work ethic, it is likely that such an affirmation would *not* have led to attitude change on the affirmative action policy. Rather, it likely would have promoted resistance to attitude change because these values are typically perceived as inconsistent with egalitarianism (cf. Katz & Hass, 1988).

Theoretical Issues

The Role of the Self-Concept. We favor a general self-concept approach to explaining why individuals are motivated to resist persuasion. This general theoretical account gleans from a number of "mini-theories" that converge on the point that individuals are motivated to protect their self-conceptions because they provide individuals with a sense of control and predictability. Our approach is also compatible with (but not identical to) reactance theory (Brehm, 1966), which argues that people are motivated to restore lost or threatened freedoms—even attitudinal freedom. In our view, it is a threat to the *self*, per se, that is the key to motivating resistance. Feedback, information, persuasive appeals, arguments with colleagues, parental advice, or remarks from one's therapist that threaten *self-conceptions* are expected to be met with resistance—a desire not to be influenced by the information, appeal, advice, or remark. Thus, an implication of our framework is that one way to increase the motivation to resist persuasion is to increase the perceived threat to the self.

A second implication of this framework, and one that is more central to the concerns of this volume on resistance and persuasion, is that one way to *decrease* the motivation to resist persuasion (and thereby enhance vulnerability) is to decrease perceived threat to the self. The self-affirmation research we have presented is supportive of this general strategy for decreasing resistance motivation. Theoretically, self-affirmations reduce the perceived threat of a counter-attitudinal message by increasing the resiliency of the self-concept. With the self-concept bolstered, the message seems less troublesome than it would otherwise seem, and it is more likely to be considered.

The Role of Affect and Cognition. Although our results are generally understandable within a broad self-concept approach to resistance, some unresolved theoretical issues remain. The existing persuasion literature clearly indicates that attitude change will be a function of one's favorable cognitive and affective reactions to a persuasive message (e.g., Petty & Cacioppo, 1986; Rosselli, Skelly, & Mackie, 1995; Zuwerink & Devine, 1996). We examined the impact of our self-affirmation manipulation on these processes in the hope of illuminating the effect of self-affirmations on the process of persuasion. However, in none of our studies did we find a significant relationship between self-affirmation condition (i.e., whether individuals were self-affirmed or not) and affect. That is, self-affirmed participants did not differ from their no-affirmation counterparts in the extent to which they experienced *irritation* or *positive mood* in response to the persuasive message. Although not reported here, we also examined three other distinct affective states (*dissonance*, *positive self-directed affect*, and *negative self-directed affect*) and found no evidence that these affective states mediated the effect of self-affirmations on final attitudes. Thus, self-affirmation effects appear not to be mediated by affective responses to the persuasion attempt. As mentioned previously, these results cast doubt on a suggestion made by Cohen et al. (2000) that positive mood (or positive self-regard) may be a mediator of self-affirmation effects.

Likewise, the self-affirmation effects we observed were not mediated by cognitive responses to the persuasive message. In the first two studies, we found no self-affirmation effects on cognitive responses. That is, self-affirmed individuals generated no greater or fewer favorable responses (or total responses) to the message than their no-affirmation counterparts in Studies 1 and 2. In Study 3, we did observe an affirmation condition by topic interaction on thoughts. However, the pattern of means did not completely match the pattern found in the attitude data. Thus, cognitive responses appear not to be essential in explaining how self-affirmations influence attitudinal responses to persuasive messages.

Alternative Explanations. What, then, is the process by which self-affirmations influence persuasion dynamics? One unlikely possibility is that the effects are due to the fact that self-affirmations heighten self-focus and increase the salience of one's attitudes. Previous research (Hutton & Baumeister, 1992) suggests that self-focus manipulations enhance resistance to persuasion by increasing the salience of one's attitudes. Although this explanation could account for the resistance found in our message-incompatible self-affirmation groups, it does not explain the enhanced persuasion found in our unrelated self-affirmation groups. Thus, self-focus alone is an insufficient explanation of our findings.

Another possible explanation is that merely thinking about the topic of the self-affirmation will have an impact on attitudes. This explanation was ruled out by our experimental design in two ways. First, we made sure that our no-affirmation control groups thought about the affirmation topic. That is, all individuals thought about honesty, nonprejudice, or freedom. The only difference between the self-affirmation and no-affirmation participants was that the former thought about these topics in a self-relevant way. Second, we included a no-message control group in the first study and showed that thinking about the topic of nonprejudice was not sufficient to produce attitude change (even when considered in a self-relevant way). Thus, topic salience alone is insufficient to account for the data.

Cohen et al. (2000) offered one additional explanation of self-affirmation effects on persuasion that deserves comment. Specifically, they suggested the possibility that "self-affirmations reduced resistance to persuasion by trivializing the importance of the attitude as a source of identity or self-worth" (p. 1161). Our data render this explanation implausible because, as we have shown, self-affirmations only reduce resistance to persuasion under certain conditions. If self-affirmations trivialize the importance of the attitude, then vulnerability to persuasion would be the result no matter what the topic of the self-affirmation (cf. Zuwerink & Devine, 1996, who showed that personally unimportant attitudes are more easily changed than important attitudes). A related but more plausible explanation is that the perceived personal importance of the *affirmation topic* is enhanced by the self-affirmation procedure.

Self- Versus Other-Generated Self-Affirmations.

Finally, one additional theoretical question concerns whether or not self-affirmations must be self-generated in order to be effective. In the scenario that opened this chapter, Jen induced Heather to affirm herself in the domain of honesty. That is, Heather was encouraged to generate and articulate instances in which she had behaved in an honest fashion. Likewise, in our experiments, we employed a self-affirmation manipulation that required individuals to generate their own examples of times they had lived up to the given characteristic (i.e., honesty, nonprejudice, or freedom). To what extent is this aspect of our procedure essential for obtaining self-affirmation effects in a persuasion paradigm?

From one perspective, it could be argued that self-generated affirmations will be most effective in producing effects in a persuasion paradigm. Consistent with this perspective, Aronson (1999) has argued, "where important attitudes, behavior, or lifestyle changes are concerned, self-persuasion strategies produce more powerful and more long-lasting effects than do direct techniques of persuasion" (p. 875). That is, when individuals generate their own reasons for attitude change, that change is more powerful and long-lasting. The same might be true in the present paradigm. That is, to create a self-affirmation powerful enough to overcome the motivation to resist persuasion, it may be necessary for individuals to generate their own self-affirmation. Being affirmed by someone else (e.g., an experimenter giving positive feedback on a valued trait) may be less effective in reducing the threat of a counter-attitudinal message. On the other hand, self-generated self-affirmations may not be any more or less effective than other-generated self-affirmations. In fact, previous research is consistent with this possibility. Cohen et al. (2000; Study 2) manipulated self-affirmation by giving some participants positive feedback regarding a bogus personality trait that they had been led to think was personally important. No-affirmation controls were not given any feedback concerning their "social perceptiveness." After exposure to counter-attitudinal information concerning capital punishment, self-affirmed individuals changed their attitudes more than their no-affirmation counterparts. Thus, it probably is not *necessary* for affirmations to be self-generated in order to observe their effects on attitude change. However, the possibility remains that the source of the affirmation (self versus other) may moderate the strength of self-affirmation effects.

Practical Implications

Attitude Change.   Although speculative at this point, we believe that our framework offers some practical suggestions for those concerned with either instilling resistance or overcoming it. In certain circumstances, the goal is to enhance resistance to persuasion (e.g., a mother who wants her child to resist the influence of tobacco ads or peer pressure to start smoking). In other circumstances, the goal is to enhance attitude change (e.g., a mother who wants her child to agree with an antismoking message; a tobacco company executive who wants to increase sales via persuasive advertising). When attitude change is the goal, our approach suggests that one should identify an affirmation topic that is important to the persuasion target but unrelated to the issue (or at least compatible with it) and then affirm the target on that dimension. For example, imagine that a local high school has arranged for a guest speaker to come in and speak to students about the dangers of smoking and/or giving in to peer pressure. To increase receptivity to the speaker's message, teachers could implement a self-affirmation exercise on the topic of honesty (presuming, of course, that honesty is important to most students). Such self-affirmations are unrelated to the message of resisting peer pressure and should lead to greater message receptivity compared to individuals who did not receive a self-affirmation. Our findings also suggest the possibility that more subtle self-affirmations (e.g., "that was a wonderful talk") may be effective in reducing resistance to subsequent persuasion (e.g., "let's eat Thai food for dinner").

This approach to attitude change is somewhat different from the typical approach offered by the dominant dual-process theories of persuasion (Chaiken, 1987; Petty & Cacioppo, 1986; Wegener, Petty, Smoak, & Fabrigar, this volume). These theories suggest that there are two routes to persuasion. The central or systematic route is based on careful cognitive processing of the persuasive message. To accomplish persuasion via this route, one must have strong cogent arguments that will inevitably lead to favorable cognitive responses among those who are motivated to think about the arguments. The peripheral or heuristic route is based on the influence of cues other than those relevant to the strength of the persuasive arguments. To accomplish persuasion via this route requires peripheral cues (e.g., an attractive source) or heuristics that will lead to agreement with the message without much thought (e.g., this is a credible speaker, she must be right). At this point, we do not know if and how self-affirmations interact with factors that influence the persuasion processes described by these models (e.g., source credibility, involvement, argument strength). Based on the fact that self-affirmations did not consistently influence cognitive responses, however, it seems most likely that self-affirmation effects represent a peripheral process. If so, factors that influence message processing (e.g., need for cognition, NFC) may moderate the effects of self-affirmations on persuasion. For example, individuals high in NFC may be less influenced by self-affirmations than their low-NFC counterparts (see also Briñol, Tormala, Rucker, & Petty, this volume).

Resistance. If enhancing resistance is the goal, our findings suggest that one should identify a self-affirmation topic that is *incompatible* with the objectionable message. For example, freedom and independence may be values that are incompatible with smoking. One who is addicted or who must smoke to be accepted is not, in a sense, independent or free. Thus, a parent might be well-advised to affirm, at an early age, a child's identity as free and independent. In the teenage years, the parent could encourage the teenager to self-affirm that identity, expecting that such affirmations will lead to greater resistance to pro-smoking influences.

This self-affirmation approach to increasing resistance to persuasion differs from existing approaches to inducing resistance, the most influential of which is McGuire's (1964) inoculation theory. The gist of this approach is that to increase resistance one must expose individuals to a weak version of the objectionable message. Once exposed, individuals will be motivated to generate counterarguments to such messages, thereby building up immunity to subsequent stronger attacks on their beliefs. In the present approach, prior exposure to persuasive arguments is not theoretically necessary to induce resistance. It is only necessary to self-affirm on a message-incompatible value or trait. Doing so should engage self-protection motives by making salient a valued source of identity that is incompatible with the objectionable message. Of course, it is likely that using multiple strategies for enhancing resistance (e.g., self-affirmations, inoculations) will be more effective than just taking a single approach.

CONCLUSION

In conclusion, we have considered persuasion dynamics using a self-concept approach, which argues that individuals resist attitude change when to change would threaten their self-conceptions. Consistent with this approach, we have shown that reducing perceived threat by affirming the self leads to greater vulnerability to persuasion. However, self-affirmations are not a panacea that will inevitably reduce resistance to persuasion. Rather, the effects of self-affirmations on persuasion depend on the relationship between the topic of the self-affirmation and the persuasive message.

AUTHOR NOTE

Funding for this research was provided by a National Science Foundation POWRE grant (Award Number 0074342) to the first author. We thank Joy Beck, Jenny Brown, Keena Dunham, and Misty McArthur for their help in collecting data. Special thanks to go to Trish Whitaker for her dedicated research assistance at every stage of the process.
Correspondence concerning this chapter should be addressed to Julia Zuwerink Jacks, Department of Psychology, UNCG, P.O. Box 26170, Greensboro, North Carolina 27402-6170. Electronic mail may be sent to jrjacks@uncg.edu.

REFERENCES

Abelson, R. P. (1986). Beliefs are like possessions. *Journal for the Theory of Social Behavior, 16,* 222–250.
Ahluwalia, R. (2000). Examination of psychological processes underlying resistance to persuasion. *Journal of Consumer Research, 27,* 217–232.
Aronson, E. (1969). The theory of cognitive dissonance: A current perspective. In L. Berkowitz (Ed.), *Advances in experimental social psychology* (Vol. 4, pp. 1–34). New York: Academic Press.
Aronson, E. (1999). The power of self-persuasion. *American Psychologist, 54,* 875–884.
Aronson, J., Blanton, H., & Cooper, J. (1995). From dissonance to disidentification: Selectivity in the self-affirmation process. *Journal of Personality and Social Psychology, 68,* 986–996.
Aronson, J., Cohen, G., & Nail, P. R. (1999). Self-affirmation theory: An update and appraisal. In E. Harmon-Jones & J. Mills (Eds.), *Cognitive dissonance: Progress on a pivotal theory in social psychology* (pp. 127–147). Washington, DC: American Psychological Association.
Blanton, H., Cooper, J., Skurnik, I., & Aronson, J. (1997). When bad things happen to good feedback: Exacerbating the need for self-justification with self-affirmations. *Personality and Social Psychology Bulletin, 23,* 684–692.
Brehm, J. W. (1966). *A theory of psychological reactance.* New York: Academic Press.
Chaiken, S. (1987). The heuristic model of persuasion. In M. P. Zanna, J. M. Olson, & C. P. Herman (Eds.), *Social influence: The Ontario symposium* (Vol. 5, pp. 3–39). Hillsdale, NJ: Erlbaum.
Cohen, A. R. (1964). *Attitude change and social influence.* New York: Basic Books.
Cohen, G. L., Aronson, J., & Steele, C. M. (2000). When beliefs yield to evidence: Reducing biased evaluation by affirming the self. *Personality and Social Psychology Bulletin, 26,* 1151–1164.
Darley, J. G. (1938). Changes in measured attitudes and adjustments. *The Journal of Social Psychology, 9,* 189–199.
Epstein, S. (1980). The self-concept: A review and the proposal of an integrated theory of personality. In E. Staub (Ed.), *Personality: Basic issues and current research* (pp. 82–132). Englewood Cliffs, NJ: Prentice-Hall.

Fein, S., & Spencer, S. J. (1997). Prejudice as self-image maintenance: Affirming the self through derogating others. *Journal of Personality and Social Psychology, 73,* 31–44.

Festinger, L. (1957). *A theory of cognitive dissonance.* Evanston, IL: Row, Peterson.

Higgins, E. T. (1987). Self-discrepancy: A theory relating self and affect. *Psychological Review, 94,* 319–340.

Hutton, D. G., & Baumeister, R. F. (1992). Self-awareness and attitude change: Seeing oneself on the central route to persuasion. *Personality and Social Psychology Bulletin, 18,* 68–75.

Jacks, J. Z., & Cameron, K. A. (2002). *Resistance to persuasion: What? When? Who? How? and Why?* Unpublished manuscript.

Jacks, J. Z., & Cameron, K. A. (2003). Strategies for resisting persuasion. *Basic and Applied Social Psychology, 25,* 145–161.

Jacks, J. Z., & Devine, P. G. (2000). Attitude importance, forewarning of message content, and resistance to persuasion. *Basic and Applied Social Psychology, 22,* 19–29.

Jacks, J. Z., & O'Brien, M. E. (2001). *Self, values, and resistance to persuasion.* Unpublished manuscript.

Johnson, B. T. (1993). *DSTAT 1.10: Software for the meta-analytic review of research literatures.* Hillsdale, NJ: Erlbaum.

Johnson, B. T., & Eagly, A. H. (1989). Effects of involvement on persuasion: A meta-analysis. *Psychological Bulletin, 106,* 290–314.

Johnson, B. T., & Eagly, A. H. (2000). Quantitative synthesis of social psychological research. In H. T. Reis & C. M. Judd (Eds.), *Handbook of research methods in social and personality psychology* (pp. 496–528). London: Cambridge University Press.

Katz, D. (1960). The functional approach to the study of attitudes. *Public Opinion Quarterly, 24,* 163–204.

Katz, I., & Hass, R. G. (1988). Racial ambivalence and American value conflict: Correlational and priming studies of dual cognitive structures. *Journal of Personality and Social Psychology, 55,* 893–905.

Knowles, E. S., Butler, S., & Linn, J. A. (2001). Increasing compliance by reducing resistance. In J. P. Forgas & K. D. Williams (Eds.), *Social influence: Direct and indirect processes* (pp. 41–60). Philadelphia: Psychology Press.

Koole, S. L., Smeets, K., van Knippenberg, A., & Dijksterhuis, A. (1999). The cessation of rumination through self-affirmation. *Journal of Personality and Social Psychology, 77,* 111–125.

Lecky, P. (1945). *Self-consistency: A theory of personality.* New York: Island Press.

Leippe, M. R. (1991). A self-image analysis of persuasion and attitude involvement. In R. C. Curtis (Ed.), *The relational self: Theoretical convergences in psychoanalysis and social psychology* (pp. 37–63). New York: Guilford Press.

Lui, T. J., & Steele, C. M. (1986). Attributional analysis and self-affirmation. *Journal of Personality and Social Psychology, 51,* 531–540.

Lund, F. H. (1925). The psychology of belief: A study of its emotional and volitional determinants. *Journal of Abnormal and Social Psychology, 20,* 63–81; 174–196.

McGuire, W. J. (1964). Inducing resistance to persuasion: Some contemporary approaches. In L. Berkowitz (Ed.), *Advances in experimental social psychology* (Vol. 1, pp. 191–229). New York: Academic Press.

Petty, R. E., & Cacioppo, J. T. (1986). The Elaboration Likelihood Model of persuasion. *Advances in Experimental Social Psychology* (Vol. 19, pp. 123–205). New York: Academic Press.

Pittman, T. S., & Heller, J. F. (1987). Social motivation. *Annual Review of Psychology, 38,* 461–489.

Prislin, R., Wood, W., & Pool, G. J. (1998). Structural consistency and the deduction of novel from existing attitudes. *Journal of Experimental Social Psychology, 34,* 66–89.

Reed, M. B., & Aspinwall, L. G. (1998). Self-affirmation reduces biased processing of health-risk information. *Motivation and Emotion, 22,* 99–132.

Rokeach, M. (1968). *Beliefs, attitudes, and values.* San Francisco, CA: Jossey-Bass.

Rokeach, M. (1973). *The nature of human values.* New York: Free Press.

Rosenberg, M. (1979). *Conceiving the self.* New York: Basic Books.

Rosselli, F., Skelly, J. J., & Mackie, D. M. (1995). Processing rational and emotional messages: The cognitive and affective mediation of persuasion. *Journal of Experimental and Social Psychology, 31,* 163–190.

Sherif, M., & Cantril, H. (1947). *The psychology of ego-involvements: Social attitudes and identifications.* New York: Wiley.

Sherman, D. A. K., Nelson, L. D., & Steele, C. M. (2000). Do messages about health risks threaten the self? Increasing the acceptance of threatening health messages via self-affirmation. *Personality and Social Psychology Bulletin, 26,* 1046–1058.

Smith, M. B., Bruner, J. S., & White, R. W. (1956). *Opinions and personality.* New York: Wiley.

Steele, C. M. (1988). The psychology of self-affirmation: Sustaining the integrity of the self. In L. Berkowitz (Ed.), *Advances in experimental social psychology* (Vol. 21, pp. 261–302). New York: Academic Press.

Steele, C. M., & Liu, T. J. (1983). Dissonance processes as self-affirmation. *Journal of Personality and Social Psychology, 45,* 5–19.

Steele, C. M., Spencer, S. J., & Lynch, M. (1993). Self-image resilience and dissonance: The role of affirmational resources. *Journal of Personality and Social Psychology, 64,* 885–896.

Swann, W. B., Jr. (1990). To be adored or to be known? The interplay of self-enhancement and self-verification. In R. M. Sorrentino & E. T. Higgins (Eds.), *Motivation and enhancement and self-verification* (Vol. 2, pp. 408–448). New York: Guilford Press.

Swann, W. B., Jr. (1997). The trouble with change: Self-verification and allegiance to the self. *Psychological Science, 8,* 177–180.

Watson, W. S., & Hartmann, G. W. (1939). The rigidity of a basic attitudinal frame. *Journal of Abnormal and Social Psychology, 34,* 314–335.

Zuwerink, J. R., & Devine, P. G. (1996). Attitude importance and resistance to persuasion: It's not just the thought that counts. *Journal of Personality and Social Psychology, 70,* 931–944.

13

Creating Critical Consumers: Motivating Receptivity by Teaching Resistance

Brad J. Sagarin
Northern Illinois University

Robert B. Cialdini
Arizona State University

Consumers have a paradoxical relationship with advertising. To our great personal detriment, we routinely resist health-related warnings from legitimate authorities such as the Surgeon General. At the same time, we readily accept advice from illegitimate authorities, even those who begin their appeal by admitting that "I'm not a doctor, but I play one on TV." This chapter describes three studies designed to tackle the latter problem—maladaptive gullibility. However, it turns out that that the former problem—misplaced skepticism—proved far easier to solve.

DEFINING RESISTANCE

There are many ways in which targets can resist a persuasive message. They can avoid the message through phenomena such as selective avoidance (e.g., not listening to a radio station because of the objectionable opinions expressed on that station) and coincidental avoidance (e.g., being out of the room when a commercial is aired). They can have an affective response such as anger, which leads to the outright rejection of the message. Or they can engage active cognitive processes that are triggered by the receipt of a persuasive message and function to lessen the probability of compliance or the magnitude of persuasion.

For the scope of the present investigation, we focus on this last type of resistance. Because this type of resistance always uses cognitive resources, it follows that (a) consumers, as cognitive misers, will not resist messages unless motivated to do so, and (b) resistance is a limited, depleteable resource, a perspective in keeping with the findings of Knowles and Linn (this volume). As a result, consumers' choice to resist or accept a persuasive message represents a tradeoff. On one hand, resisting carries the costs of the cognitive resources expended, plus the risks associated with missed opportunities. On the other hand, accepting a message carries the risk of being persuaded inappropriately—to the detriment of one's wallet and, possibly, one's self-image.

THE CHALLENGE FACING CONSUMERS

A mid-80s estimate suggested that, at the time, consumers were targeted by over 300 persuasive messages every day (Aaker & Myers, 1987). With the recent development of new marketing media such as Internet banner ads and pop-up windows, spam (unsolicited commercial e-mail), and m-marketing (mobile marketing to cell phones and pagers), as well as the increasing prevalence of traditional media, 300 is likely a substantial underestimate today.

In response to this daily onslaught, consumers must rely heavily on heuristics such as consensus information or the opinion of an expert. Cialdini (2001) describes the dilemma in this way:

> You and I exist in an extraordinarily complicated environment, easily the most rapidly moving and complex that has ever existed on this planet. To deal with it, we *need* shortcuts. We can't be expected to recognize and analyze all the aspects in each person, event, and situation we encounter in even one day. We haven't the time, energy, or capacity for it. Instead, we must very often use our stereotypes, our rules of thumb, to classify things according to a few key features and then to respond without thinking when one or another of these trigger features is present (p. 7).

Unfortunately, unscrupulous marketers can capitalize on consumers' reliance on these heuristics by manufacturing merely the veneer of consensus or the trappings of authority. Many consumers are fooled by such illegitimate heuristic information. Others may develop a chronic wariness or skepticism, protecting them from illegitimate heuristics, but also preventing them from accepting other messages that employ heuristics legitimately. Either approach carries costs— gullibility produces poor decisions; stubbornness, missed opportunities. As McGuire (1964) put it, "The best of both worlds would be to discover pretreatments that would make the person receptive to the true and resistant to the false" (p. 192).

HOW TO TELL THE TRUE
FROM THE FALSE

It is easier to agree with McGuire's perceptive assertion than to implement it. A pretreatment that enhances the likelihood of appropriate responding to "true versus false" persuasive messages would have to identify an effective rule for distinguishing the two types of messages. Unfortunately, determining what constitutes honest versus deceptive persuasive attempts is no easy task for a target. There is the obvious—a perceived discrepancy between what the material asserts and what the recipient knows to be true (MacKenzie & Lutz, 1989). But, in cleverly constructed communications, this discrepancy is not readily evident. Audiences of advertisements, for instance, frequently lack the experience or expertise to know whether a particular product or service is likely to meet the advertiser's claims. Instead, audience members must often rely on the depicted experience or expertise of individuals or other sources portrayed in the ad. Fortunately, a simple but effective rule may help audience members distinguish true authorities that should be adhered to from false authorities that should be resisted.

Persuasion practitioners have long recognized the power of authorities on the influence process (Cialdini, 2001), as have researchers (e.g., Aronson, Turner, & Carlsmith, 1963; Blass, 1991, 1999; Milgram, 1974). Accordingly, the source of information in many persuasive appeals is portrayed as an authority. Such portrayals, we contend, are more honest when the depicted authority is a genuine expert with special knowledge on the topic than when this is not the case.

By this account, a large number of authority-based advertisements would be considered objectionable. Actors regularly appear as physicians, attorneys, stockbrokers, or scientists and mouth their approval of commercial products and services. Indeed, sometimes spokespersons are chosen simply because they are associated with the fictional role of an expert. Performers from medical shows promote health products while those from police dramas describe the benefits of anticrime devices and so on. Even more worrisome, perhaps, is that the use of pseudo-authorities sometimes extends to legitimate news presentations. For instance, in a January 24, 2001 CNBC interview with the actor Martin Sheen, host Brian Williams seriously pursued a line of questions regarding Mr. Sheen's views of the appropriateness of presidential decisions to accept gifts and to pardon convicted criminals just before leaving office. Mr. Sheen dutifully offered his considered opinions in these matters even though his political credentials to that point were limited to playing the role of the U.S. president on the TV series "West Wing." Because, as these examples suggest, the public is regularly exposed to information presented by ersatz experts, we felt that a corrective was in order. Accordingly, we set about the task of constructing a treatment that would enable individuals to recognize and resist the influence of misplaced authority while continuing to accept the advice of those with true expertise.

We recognize that relevant expertise is not the only factor that can influence the legitimacy of an authority appeal. For example, a true expert who makes a specific statement on a relevant issue only because he or she has been paid to do so would also be an instance of the dishonest use of authority influence (Folkes, 1988). However, for the purposes of an initial investigation, we chose to focus on one basic distinction (the presence or absence of relevant expertise) and to leave other relevant distinctions for future research.

THE MOTIVATION AND ABILITY
TO RESIST

In his description of inoculation theory—one of social psychology's foremost theories of resistance to persuasion—McGuire (1964) described two critical components of a resistance-enhancing treatment: motivation and ability. Following McGuire's lead, we sought a treatment that would motivate influence targets to resist and that would enable them to do so effectively.

To implement McGuire's (1964) first component, motivation, we sought to identify a psychological dimension that would spur participants to resist illegitimate authority-based appeals. The task of identifying a crucial motivational dimension was complicated by the fact that the traditional reasons individuals reject incoming information—the information is discrepant from what recipients clearly know and/or prefer—often don't apply in advertising contexts. That is, much research has established that people resist the influence of information that conflicts with strongly held beliefs or attitudes (Petty & Krosnick, 1996; Visser & Krosnick, 1998), but many messages (e.g., the majority of those containing claims for this or that commercial product) do not challenge strong views or preferences.

A more suitable motivational construct—undue manipulative intent—emerges from an examination of a diverse set of literatures suggesting that individuals tend to reject information they perceive as designed to manipulate them unfairly (e.g., through deception). For example, studies of the behavior of human research participants indicate that participants are more likely to respond contrarily to the experimenter's wishes when they believe that the experimenter is trying to trick them (Christensen, 1977; Goldberg, 1965; Masling, 1966). Similar results have been observed in research on ingratiation. Although people tend to believe flattery and like those who provide it (Byrne, Rasche, & Kelly, 1974; Drachman, deCarufel, & Insko, 1978), ingratiation can backfire when it is clear that the flattery is a manipulative attempt to achieve ulterior goals (Jones & Wortman, 1973). In a trial setting, Fein, McCloskey, and Tomlinson (1997) demonstrated that pointing out a persuader's undue manipulative intent rendered the persuader's (otherwise convincing) message ineffective. Finally, in marketing contexts, researchers have found that persuasive impact is undermined if the influence agent is perceived as using manipulative tactics (Campbell, 1995; Ellen, Mohr, & Webb, 2000; Lutz, 1985; MacKenzie & Lutz, 1989).

For our purposes, the perception of undue manipulative intent seemed an ideal motivator of resistance to persuasion. First, it does not require that the message recipient be knowledgeable about the (often unknown) legitimacy of the specific claims made in the message. Instead, it only requires an assessment of whether the persuasive approach is legitimate. Second, to be effective, this perception is not restricted to the domain of strongly held attitudes. The idea of being duped or cheated is inherently resistance-inducing—by itself—because of evolved tendencies to avoid trickery (Cosmides & Tooby, 1992). Third, there is good evidence that this perception acts to blunt persuasion in the advertising and marketing arenas we wished to examine.

In addition to providing motivation, an effective treatment against illegitimate persuasive appeals must provide participants with the ability to distinguish between acceptable versus objectionable persuasive messages. It would be of limited value to foster the blanket rejection of all influence attempts, as unrelenting cynicism or stubbornness can be as costly as gullibility (Cialdini, 2001). In our case, then, an optimal treatment would afford participants a rule for discriminating between properly and improperly constituted authority-based communications. In addition, this rule should be relatively simple to learn and apply. Although multifaceted and complicated rule systems may cover a greater range of circumstances, they are frequently unsuitable for use because most people find such rule systems too difficult or cumbersome to employ, even in important, personally relevant domains (Kahn & Baron, 1995). Therefore, especially in the case of advertising and other mass media messages, which often occur in rapid-fire succession, a streamlined decision rule would be most useful. Finally, the treatment should take a form that could be easily incorporated into a variety of educational contexts. To deal with a society-wide offense, the corrective must be appropriate for wide-ranging implementation.

To these ends, we developed a brief (8–10 min.) treatment that offered participants a simple decision rule for classifying and responding to authority-based persuasive communications: Such appeals are objectionable and should be rejected if the depicted authority does not at least possess special expertise on the topic.

Although we consider this rule useful for influence targets to employ when faced with authority-based advertisements, it is important to acknowledge at this point that it is not our goal to assert the superiority of this particular rule according to any system of morals or ethics. Issues of what constitutes ethically proper versus improper conduct are difficult, highly subjective, and beyond the scope of our inquiry (See Boatright, 1992, for an appropriately textured treatment of many of these issues). Furthermore, it seems likely that the present results would generalize to an array of other rules—as long as the rules appear plausible and useful to influence targets. For example, while targets readily accepted the legitimate/illegitimate distinction presented in our treatment, they would likely reject a rule suggesting that messages printed on red paper should be accepted whereas messages printed on blue paper should be rejected.

Experiment 1

Experiment 1 sought to instill resistance to improperly constituted authority-based appeals by teaching participants a rule for discriminating between legitimate and illegitimate appeals and by suggesting to participants that ads containing illegitimate authorities are attempts to deceive consumers. Participants learned the rule through exposure to a brief treatment that provided examples of real magazine ads that would be considered acceptable or objectionable according to the rule.

Overall, we structured our treatment to leave participants (a) aware of the potential influence of authoritative sources, (b) able to discriminate between legitimate versus illegitimate authority appeals, and (c) motivated to discriminate against only the latter. However, another outcome seemed possible. It was conceivable that our treatment would only cause participants to perceive that advertisers invoking authority were attempting to control their choices. Should that be the predominant perception, participants might well demonstrate reactance (Brehm, 1966) against all subsequent authority-based ads. Reactance research has shown, for example, that messages containing highly controlling statements (e.g., "You as college students, must inevitably draw the same conclusion," p. 110) are less persuasive than equivalent messages without such statements. Such reactance would produce a less desirable societal outcome: reduced persuasion for all authority-based advertising, both legitimate and illegitimate.

In a test of these competing possibilities, participants either did or did not receive a treatment that taught them a rule for distinguishing between acceptable and objectionable forms of authority-based appeals and that characterized the objectionable forms as unduly manipulative in intent. All participants then rated a novel set of authority-based ads in terms of their undue manipulative intent and their persuasiveness. We predicted an interaction effect such that, compared to control condition participants, the treatment condition participants would find only the objectionable appeals within the new set of ads more manipulative and less persuasive.

Two hundred forty-one Arizona State University (ASU) undergraduates were randomly assigned to either the treatment or control conditions. The treatment consisted of a six-page discussion of the distinction between legitimate and illegitimate uses of authorities in advertising. The six-page control condition consisted of a discussion of the use of color and tone in advertisements, which was created to ensure that control and treatment participants would spend an equivalent amount of time examining the example ads. The crux of the treatment appeared in the first two paragraphs:

> Now we're going to look at some more magazine advertisements, but this time we're going to look at them from a different point of view. We're going to think about the ethics of the ads. Specifically we're going to examine whether the ads use authority in an ethical or an unethical way.

Many ads use authority figures to help sell the product. But how can we tell when an authority figure is being used ethically or unethically? For an authority to be used ethically it must pass two tests. First, the authority must be a real authority, and not just someone dressed up to look like an authority. Second, the authority must be an expert on the product he or she is trying to sell.

The five and a half pages that followed offered examples of ads that use authorities legitimately or illegitimately according to our criteria (see Sagarin, Cialdini, Rice, & Serna, 2002, for an extended discussion of the materials and results of these studies).

The text referred to six example ads selected from current periodicals. After reading the text, participants rated six additional ads (three containing legitimate authorities, three illegitimate) on two scales adapted from Campbell (1995). The first scale assessed the persuasiveness of the ad using items such as, "If you were to use this type of product in the future, how likely are you to choose this brand?" The second scale assessed the perception of undue manipulative intent, asking participants to indicate how closely they agreed with statements such as, "The advertiser seemed to be trying to inappropriately manage or control the consumer audience."

As predicted, presence of the treatment interacted significantly with legitimacy of the authority for both perception of undue manipulative intent, $F(1, 238) = 29.39, p < .001$, and ad persuasiveness, $F(1, 232) = 26.57, p < .001$. See Table 13.1.

An examination of the simple effects within the treatment by legitimacy of the authority interaction revealed that participants in the treatment condition perceived the ads containing illegitimate authorities as more unduly manipulative, $F(1, 238) = 7.61, p = .006$, and less persuasive, $F(1, 232) = 4.22, p =.041$, as compared to participants in the control condition. We also found that participants in the treatment condition perceived the ads containing legitimate authorities as less unduly manipulative, $F(1, 238) = 12.94, p < .001$, and more persuasive, $F(1, 232) = 16.21, p < .001$, as compared to participants in the control condition.

These results suggest that the treatment did not make participants more generally resistant to authority-based advertising. Instead, it made participants more discriminating about it on the critical legitimacy dimension. This finding stands in contrast to a reactance effect and to a reactance explanation of our findings. That is, according to reactance theory, resistance occurs when something is perceived as intending to direct or control one's perceived choices, thereby limiting one's freedoms to decide. Clearly, this is as much the intent of advertisements containing legitimate authorities as ads containing illegitimate authorities. Our results indicate that the treatment did not stimulate resistance to all attempts to direct and limit choices but only to attempts to do so by employing an improperly constituted authority.

This is not to say that the resistance effects observed in the present study bear no similarity to reactance. Both effects produce resistance, and both are likely to produce emotional responses such as anger. However, in contrast to the reactant influence target who resists in response to the perception, "You're trying to control me," the influence target who perceives undue manipulative intent resists in response to the perception, "You're trying to *fool* me." Both perceptions may elicit anger and resistance, but we believe the motivations, antecedents, and, possibly, origins of each differ sufficiently to warrant considering them related but distinct phenomena.

Besides conferring resistance to the illegitimate ads, the treatment had an additional effect: Ads with legitimate authorities came to be seen as more persuasive! Thus, participants learned not only to devalue inappropriate persuasive information, but also to enhance the value of appropriate messages. In fact, participants demonstrated substantially greater enhancement of legitimate authorities than derogation of illegitimate authorities. Control participants, in contrast, displayed unfocused, or, more properly, misfocused resistance, with their resistance resources misapplied toward legitimate messages. After receiving the treatment, however, participants were able to allocate their resistance resources more effectively. These participants resisted unduly manipulative ads (those containing illegitimate authorities), but they were released from the need to resist legitimate messages.

The release from resistance experienced by our treatment participants is reminiscent of the release from reactance displayed by the forward-looking participants in Sherman, Crawford, and McConnell (this volume). Similarly Fuegen and Brehm (this volume) found that weak reasons in favor of a counter-attitudinal proposal were more effective in reducing disapproval than strong reasons, because the weak reasons offered little challenge to the disapproval motive. In the present study, treatment and control participants received the same arguments from the legitimate authorities. But the perspective offered by the treatment reduced treatment participants' resistance motive.

While encouraged by the initial success of our brief treatment in instilling resistance to persuasion, we were concerned that the observed effects might have stemmed not from true resistance, but rather from the demand characteristics of our experimental setting. We had, after all, just told treatment participants how to identify "good" versus "bad" ads, and then asked them to rate a series of examples that fit our criteria for "good" and "bad" advertisements. Thus, it seemed possible that these participants responded as they did in an attempt to confirm what they presumed were the experimenter's expectations. We designed Experiment 2 to (a) address this concern and (b) test the enduring impact of our treatment outside of the laboratory context.

Experiment 2

Experiment 2 was intended to replicate and extend the results of Experiment 1. Participants in Experiment 2 rated legitimate and illegitimate authority-based ads both immediately after receiving the treatment and after a one- to four-day delay, in a separate setting unrelated to the laboratory context. The separation of the treatment and measurement contexts allowed us to assess the viability of demand characteristics as an alternative explanation.

The delay between the treatment and the test of its effectiveness offered a second benefit of more applied interest: an assessment of the perseverance of treatment impact. If we are to achieve the goal of instilling resistance to illegitimate authority-based appeals, the crucial treatment-taught distinctions must be retained and accessible to participants at later points in time when they are likely to encounter authority-based persuasive messages in other settings. Without evidence of durability and cross-situational robustness, the treatment would represent little more than an academic exercise of dubious practical value.

One hundred and thirty ASU undergraduates participated in Experiment 2. As with the previous experiment, participants were randomly assigned to either the treatment or control conditions and rated the same series of ads. Then, one to four days later, a research assistant, posing as a representative from the campus daily newspaper, administered a delayed questionnaire in the participants' psychology classes. This questionnaire asked respondents to evaluate the articles and advertisements in a new newspaper insert. Two of these advertisements were authority-based, one legitimate and one illegitimate. Respondents rated the ads on a four-question scale that included items such as "How did you like the ad?" with answers "I hated it; I disliked it; It was OK; I liked it; It was great!" and "Do you think that seeing this ad will make you more likely to use this product or service?" with answers "Definitely not; Possibly; Maybe; Probably; Definitely."

The impact of the treatment on immediate persuasion responses that we found in Experiment 1 was replicated in the present study. Presence of the treatment interacted with legitimacy of the authority with respect to the perception of manipulative intent, $F(1, 127) = 3.61$, $p = .060$, and with respect to the perceived persuasiveness of the ads, $F(1, 122) = 10.06$, $p = .002$. See Table 13.1.

The effects of the treatment also persevered one to four days after the experiment. As predicted, presence of the treatment interacted significantly with legitimacy of the authority in the delayed measure, $F(1, 51) = 4.04$, $p = .050$. See Table 13.1. Length of delay (one to four days) did not interact with the treatment effect, $F(3, 45) = 1.14$, $p = .344$, and an examination of the results for each day separately revealed that, if anything, the treatment produced more prediction-consistent results on days 2, 3, and 4 than on day 1.

Thus, the effects of treatment remained intact well after the end of the laboratory experiment and did not appear to decline, at least within the time period measured. The continued efficacy of the treatment outside of the laboratory context increases confidence that demand characteristics cannot account for the results and it suggests the practical value of treatments of this type. If the present treatment, using only a brief, written format, demonstrated significant effects days after its administration, an interactive, longer-term program (such as might be administered in schools) could have profound and long-lasting results.

Experiment 2 did produce one unexpected finding. While participants who received the treatment rated the ads containing legitimate authorities as signifi-

TABLE 13.1
Cell Means and (Standard Deviations) Within Each Condition

	Undue manipulative intent		Ad persuasiveness	
Condition	Legitimate authority	Illegitimate authority	Legitimate authority	Illegitimate authority
Exp. 1				
Control (*n* = 121)	2.38 (1.07)	2.23 (.99)	3.24 (.88)	3.56 (.74)
Treatment (*n* = 120)	1.90 (.97)	2.56 (.93)	3.69 (.89)	3.36 (.77)
Exp. 2				
Control (*n* = 65)	2.28 (1.05)	2.61 (1.02)	3.25 (.79)	3.36 (.80)
Treatment (*n* = 65)	1.98 (.96)	2.71 (.98)	3.67 (.79)	3.23 (.75)
Delayed control (*n* = 29)			2.68 (.61)	2.91 (.67)
Delayed treatment (*n* = 26)			2.99 (.77)	2.78 (.54)
Exp. 3 (n = 80/condition)				
Tone/color	2.42 (1.56)	2.61 (1.35)	3.31 (1.27)	3.31 (1.19)
No commentary	2.20 (1.19)	2.84 (1.42)	3.25 (.92)	3.18 (.91)
Asserted vulnerability	2.11 (1.43)	3.47 (1.33)	3.58 (1.06)	3.00 (1.02)
Demonstrated vulnerability	2.14 (1.24)	3.73 (1.42)	3.66 (1.12)	2.54 (1.36)

Note. Undue manipulative intent and ad persuasiveness were scored on 7-point scales from 0 to 6, with larger scores indicating more of the quality. The delayed measures of ad persuasiveness were scored on a 5-point scale from 1 to 5. One participant was removed from the analysis of the delayed measures of ad persuasiveness due to his or her statistical outlier status. The studentized deleted residual for this data point was -3.29, which falls far in the tail (99.8%) of the corresponding t-distribution, with 52 degrees of freedom (Neter, Wasserman, & Kutner, 1989).

cantly more persuasive as compared to controls, they did not resist the ads containing illegitimate authorities more effectively than did controls. Apparently, the treatment released participants from resisting legitimate authorities both in the lab and beyond, but it did not confer greater resistance to illegitimate authorities.

These results suggest that participants may have agreed with the characterization of illegitimacy presented in the treatment, but they may not have acted on it because they believed that they weren't susceptible to it ("I wouldn't have fallen for the unethical ads anyway."). Taylor and Brown (1988) argued that such overly positive illusions are common and can be adaptive. However, in the present context, this self-enhancement bias (Fiske & Taylor, 1991) may leave influence targets less likely to fend off inappropriate persuasive attacks. Indeed, as Fiske and Taylor put it, "Unrealistic optimism may lead people to ignore legitimate risks in their environment and fail to take measures to offset those risks." (p. 216). It seems possible, then, that our participants' sense of unique invulnerability to deceptive ads left them unmotivated to employ defenses against such ads.

Illusions of Invulnerability to Persuasion

To test our hypothesis that participants may have felt themselves uniquely resistant to the persuasive tactics that work on everyone else, we asked 888 undergraduates how much they believed television advertisements affect them, and we asked a separate 900 undergraduates how much they believed television advertisements affect the average ASU undergraduate. Participants responded on 0 to 6 scales for which 0 indicated "very strongly," 3 indicated "somewhat," and 6 indicated "hardly at all." As we suspected, participants rated themselves significantly less affected ($M = 3.56$) by television ads as compared to their peers ($M = 2.88$), $F(1, 1786) = 124.69$, $p < .0001$.

The results of this pilot study confirmed our concerns that participants maintained perceptions of personal invulnerability to advertising. Such "illusions of unique invulnerability" (Perloff, 1987) are widespread, leading, at times, to harmful or even fatal results. In the area of health psychology, the optimistic bias (Weinstein, 1980) appears as a discrepancy between perceptions of others' susceptibility to a disease and perceptions of one's own personal susceptibility to the illness. This bias can lead to negative health outcomes, as low levels of perceived personal susceptibility are associated with poor compliance with preventative health behaviors (Aiken, Gerend, & Jackson, 2001). In a study of HIV-infected women, Siegel, Raveis, and Gorey (1998) discovered that "perceived invulnerability to infection [was one of] the principle barriers to women recognizing their at-risk status" (p. 114).

Norris, Nurius, and Dimeff (1996) reported that college sorority women "held a high sense of invulnerability to victimization and an optimistic belief in their ability to resist sexual aggression" (p. 123). In a vivid demonstration of the tenacity of illusions of unique invulnerability, Snyder (1997) informed students that an upcoming classroom demonstration was designed specifically to expose their illusions regarding mortality risks. Despite the warning, the students discounted actuarial information and overestimated their age of death by nine years—an amount equivalent to the overestimates made by uninformed students.

Experiment 3

In Experiment 3, we sought to dispel these illusions of invulnerability by demonstrating in an undeniable fashion that participants can be fooled by ads containing counterfeit authorities. According to our pilot data, it appears that to motivate strong resistance, it is insufficient to argue that people in general can be unfairly manipulated. Therefore, we hypothesized that something else would be required to motivate the necessary resistance. One likely possibility emerged from an examination of the earlier-described research on health risks: Participants must learn that they are personally susceptible to the risk under consideration.

The results of our pilot study suggested that our participants were unmotivated to develop resistance to illegitimate ads because they regarded themselves as relatively invulnerable to the risk of being fooled. How might we convince them otherwise? Merely pointing out their vulnerability to a risk has not been a generally effective device for motivating individuals against it (Perloff, 1987; Snyder, 1997). For example, according to Aiken, Gerend, and Jackson (2001), "The public is inundated with information about cancer and with recommendations for cancer screening and prevention" (p. 727). Nevertheless, the National Health Interview Survey of 1994 reported that 44% of women over 50 had failed to have a mammogram within the previous two years (American Cancer Society, 1997; National Center for Health Statistics, 1996).

Aiken, Gerend, and Jackson (2001) specified three stages of perceived susceptibility to risk—a critical determinant of health behavior. "First, individuals are assumed to become aware of a health hazard (awareness), then to believe in the likelihood of the hazard for others (general susceptibility), and finally to acknowledge their own personal vulnerability (personal susceptibility)" (p. 730). Researchers attempting to increase compliance with health behaviors have sought to move people from stage 2 to stage 3. For example, Curry, Taplin, Anderman, Barlow, and McBride (1993) increased cancer screening in higher-risk women through the use of tailored personal, objective risk information.

Our pilot study demonstrated that many of our participants fell squarely into stage 2 of perceived susceptibility. They perceived that others were vulnerable to advertising but that they, themselves, were relatively immune. We anticipated that merely asserting participants' vulnerability to deceptive ads would leave many with their illusions intact. We predicted, however, that participants could be moved to stage 3 by arranging for them "to acknowledge their own personal vulnerability" (Aiken, Gerend, & Jackson, 2001, p. 730).

We were left, however, with the practical challenge of how to induce participants to acknowledge their own personal vulnerability. The labor-intensive task of providing participants with individualized, tailored personal risk information, as was done by Curry et al. (1993) to motivate cancer screenings, was impractical in the present setting. Instead, we sought a simple procedure that would unambiguously demonstrate vulnerability without increasing the time or effort necessary to administer the treatment.

Several studies within the literature on perceived risk indicate that one's level of prior personal experience with the risk factor can moderate optimistic bias (e.g., Helweg-Larsen, 1999; Norris, Smith, & Kaniasty, 1999; Van der Velde, Hooykaas, & Van der Pligt, 1992; Weinstein, 1980, 1987). These studies demonstrated that personal experience with a negative event—including earthquakes, hurricanes, illnesses, and sexually transmitted diseases—has the capacity to undercut one's illusion of unique invulnerability regarding future such events (See Weinstein, 1989, for a review). This finding is consistent with evidence indicating that learning based on first-hand experience is more powerful than that based on simple information (Epstein, 1998; Fazio & Zanna, 1981; Helweg-Larsen & Collins, 1997). Consequently, we included in Experiment 3 a procedure that gave some participants undeniable evidence that they had been susceptible to the persuasive impact of an illegitimate authority-based ad. We hypothesized that this procedure (the demonstrated vulnerability treatment condition) would give rise to a significantly stronger tendency to resist subsequent such ads than would a procedure similar to that of Experiments 1 and 2, in which participants' vulnerability was merely asserted.

Experiment 3 also provided an examination of the psychological mechanisms through which the instilled resistance operated. Consistent with prior research (Campbell, 1995; Lutz, 1985; MacKenzie & Lutz, 1989), we predicted that the resistance instilled by the treatment would be fully mediated by perceptions of undue manipulative intent. In other words, participants who are taught the distinction between legitimate and illegitimate authorities would come to see ads employing illegitimate authorities as unduly manipulative, and these perceptions would then lead to resistance.

We also sought to examine the mechanism whereby perceptions of undue manipulative intent lead to resistance. Drawing on the cognitive response model of persuasion (Greenwald, 1968) and, in particular, the finding that inferences of manipulative intent can lead to decreased persuasion via counterarguing (Petty, Ostrom, & Brock, 1981; Zuwerink & Devine, 1996), we anticipated that the effect of perceptions of undue manipulative intent on persuasion would be mediated, at least in part, by altered cognitive reactions.

To assess cognitive response, participants listed the thoughts they had in reaction to the ads. Subsequently, participants categorized these thoughts (as positive, negative, neutral, or irrelevant) in terms of their relation to the ad. Cognitive response-based resistance, which would manifest as increased counterargumentation, would appear as a greater quantity of negative thoughts and a lesser quantity of positive thoughts.

Although no a priori model was specified, Experiment 3 enabled an exploration of the possible mediators of the enhancement of the legitimate authority-based appeals.

In Experiment 3, participants rated two custom advertisements developed for the study. The ads each contained the testimony of an authority (one legitimate, one illegitimate) in the top half and a list of product features in the bottom half. For each ad, four versions of the list were developed that varied the strength (strong vs. weak) and number (two vs. six) of product features. The features were visually separated from the picture and testimony of the authority, had no relation to the testimony, and were manipulated independently of the legitimacy of the authority. These variables were included to examine whether participants in the different conditions processed ads using a different modality (central vs. peripheral, Petty & Cacioppo, 1986; Petty & Wegener, 1998, or heuristic vs. systematic, Chaiken, 1987; Chaiken, Giner-Sorolla, & Chen, 1996). More critically, these variables could determine whether participants exposed to the treatment (a) simply accepted or rejected an ad based on the legitimacy of the authority, or (b) factored the legitimacy of the authority into a more sophisticated appraisal of the ad that incorporated other ad features. This distinction is particularly important in light of the enhancement of advertisements containing legitimate authorities observed in Experiments 1 and 2. It would certainly be of no benefit to instill a mindless acceptance of the testimony of legitimate authorities (scenario (a) above). Far preferable would be a treatment that increased the salience of the legitimate authority's true expertise without discouraging scrutiny of the rest of the ad (scenario (b) above). Support for the former scenario would be found if feature strength had no effect on persuasion in the treatment conditions. A significant effect of feature strength in the treatment conditions, on the other hand, would offer support for the latter scenario.

Finally, we noted the possibility that our prior results could have stemmed not from the efficacy of the treatment, but rather from the inhibiting nature of our tone and color control condition. Specifically, though designed to be innocuous, the tone and color essay may have inadvertently focused participants away from the distinction between the legitimate and illegitimate authorities, on which they might have otherwise focused. To test this possibility, we added a second control condition that asked participants to look through the example ads but provided no commentary.

Three hundred twenty ASU undergraduates were randomly assigned to one of 32 conditions representing (a) the four treatments (the tone and color control condition, the no commentary control condition, the asserted vulnerability treatment condition, and the demonstrated vulnerability treatment condition), (b) the four versions of the rated ads that varied strength (strong versus weak) and number (two versus six) of product features, and (c) two levels of counterbalancing (representing the order in which the ads containing legitimate and illegitimate authorities were viewed and rated).

Tone and Color Control. As in Experiments 1 and 2, participants in the tone and color control condition received a packet discussing the cosmetic aspects of the accompanying ads.

No Commentary Control. Participants in the no commentary control condition received a brief packet that simply asked them to examine the accompanying ads.

Asserted Vulnerability Treatment. Participants in the asserted vulnerability treatment condition received a slightly modified version of the treatment packet of Experiments 1 and 2. Besides providing a set of sample ads and a working definition of ethical (vs. unethical) authority-based advertisements as had been done in the earlier experiments, it asked participants to consider whether they had been fooled by the unethical ads of manipulative advertisers:

> Take a look at ad #1. Did you find the ad to be even somewhat convincing? If so, then you got fooled. Unethical ads like this fool most people. But if we want to protect ourselves from being manipulated, we need to know what makes an ad ethical or unethical.
>
> Many ads, such as ad #1, use authority figures to help sell the product. But not all ads use authority figures ethically. For an authority to be used ethically it

must pass two tests. First, the authority must be a real authority, and not just someone dressed up to look like one. Second, the authority must be an expert on the product he or she is trying to sell. Let's use these tests to examine ad #1. What about that guy selling the Wall Street Journal Interactive Edition? He sure looks like a stockbroker. But where are his name and credentials? The ad doesn't give us any. For all we know this guy is just a model. This ad is unethical because it fails the first test. This guy is just dressed up to look like an authority.

When you looked at this ad, did you notice that this 'stockbroker' was a fake? Did you ask yourself whether you should listen to this so-called 'expert'? If you didn't, then you left yourself vulnerable to the advertisers that are trying to manipulate you.

Demonstrated Vulnerability Treatment. Participants in the demonstrated vulnerability treatment condition received a treatment packet that did more than simply assert their vulnerability to deceptive ads. It demonstrated that vulnerability by first instructing participants to examine a sample ad containing an illegitimate authority and to respond to a pair of questions concerning it. The initial question asked them to indicate how convincing they found it on a 7-point scale labeled: Not at all convincing (0), Somewhat convincing (1), Fairly convincing (2), Convincing (3), Quite convincing (4), Very convincing (5), and Extremely convincing (6). Results indicated that the great majority of participants rated the ad at least somewhat convincing. The second question asked participants which two aspects of the ad they found most important in making this decision and to write these reasons down in spaces provided. At this point the treatment packet was identical to that of the asserted vulnerability treatment condition except in two places. Rather than merely instructing participants to "Take a look at ad #1. Did you find the ad to be even somewhat convincing? If so, then you got fooled . . . ," the packet referred participants to their earlier-committed response to the ad: "Take a look at your answer to the first question. Did you find the ad to be even 'Somewhat convincing'? If so, then you got fooled . . ." Similarly, rather than merely asking "When you looked at this ad, did you notice that this 'stockbroker' was a fake?" participants were referred to their earlier responses to the question regarding the most important aspects of the ads that contributed to its convincingness: "Take a look at your answer to the second question. Did you notice that this 'stockbroker' was a fake?"

Participants in Experiment 3 rated the two new ads on the same scales used in Experiments 1 and 2. After rating each ad, participants were instructed to list the thoughts they had while examining the ad. Then, after rating and listing thoughts for both ads, participants were asked to categorize each thought as (a) "positive toward the ad," (b) "negative to the ad," (c) "neutral to the ad," or (d) "irrelevant to the ad." Participants listed a total of 2,367 thoughts, an average of 3.7 thoughts per ad. Cognitive response to each ad was calculated as the number of positive thoughts minus the number of negative thoughts.

The two control conditions did not differ significantly on any measured variable; consequently, we were assured that the control condition used in the previous studies had not served as an active treatment.

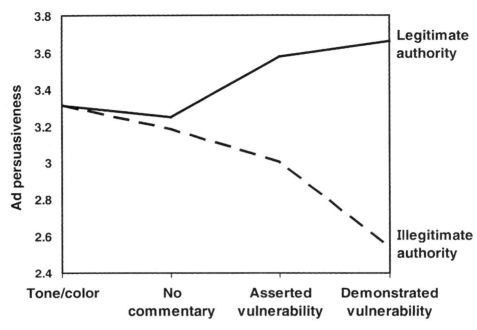

FIG. 13.1.   The effects of the resistance treatment and the perception of vulnerability on the perceived persuasiveness of advertisements containing legitimate and illegitimate authorities in Experiment 3.

The treatment once again interacted significantly with legitimacy of the authority with respect to perception of manipulative intent, $F(3, 311) = 11.01$, $p < .001$, and persuasiveness of the ads, $F(3, 297) = 9.75, p < .001$. See Table 13.1 and Fig. 13.1. Of particular note is the fact that the asserted vulnerability treatment and demonstrated vulnerability treatment differed significantly in their interaction with legitimacy of the authority with respect to ad persuasiveness, $F(1, 297) = 6.02, p = . 015$. An examination of the simple effects revealed that these two treatment conditions did not differ in their effects on the persuasiveness of the ad containing the legitimate authority, $F(1, 297) = .36, p = .548$; both were successful in enhancing the effectiveness of legitimate authority-based messages. However, these conditions did differ significantly in their effects on the persuasiveness of the ad containing the illegitimate authority, $F(1, 297) = 6.41, p = .012$.

Consistent with our previous findings, the asserted vulnerability treatment increased the persuasiveness of ads containing legitimate authorities, $F(1, 297) = 3.26, p = .072$, but did not confer significant resistance to ads containing illegitimate authorities, $F(1, 297) = 2.01, p = .157$, compared to control conditions. Once again, the treatment effectively enhanced the persuasive value of legitimate authorities but was less able to instill resistance to illegitimate authorities.

This particular weakness of the treatment was remedied, however, by the demonstration of personal vulnerability. An examination of simple contrasts revealed that the demonstrated vulnerability treatment produced significant resistance to ads containing illegitimate authorities, $F(1, 297) = 18.99$, $p < .001$, as well as significant enhancement of ads containing legitimate authorities, $F(1, 297) = 6.27$, $p = .013$, as compared to the control conditions. In fact, for the first time in our program of studies, the resistance effect was of greater magnitude than the enhancement effect. Thus, instilling resistance required more than merely asserting participants' vulnerability. Effective resistance required clearly demonstrating this vulnerability.

It is noteworthy that the asserted vulnerability treatment and demonstrated vulnerability treatment conditions did not differ significantly in their interaction with legitimacy of the authority with respect to perception of manipulative intent, $F(1, 311) = .66$, $p = .416$. This result fits well with our thinking, in that both conditions contained similar information about the manipulativeness of the authority appeals in the example ads. They differed only in information suggesting that participants would be susceptible to that manipulation.

To determine whether participants exposed to the treatment (a) mindlessly accepted or rejected the advertisements based on the legitimacy of the authority, or (b) incorporated the legitimacy of the authority into an overall appraisal of the ads, we ran a four-way (feature strength by feature number by treatment by legitimacy of the authority) ANOVA using ad persuasiveness as the dependent variable. Five significant effects emerged. The first two represented the effects of treatment discussed above.

The three additional significant effects included feature strength or number as factors. First, there was a significant main effect of feature strength indicating that ads containing strong features ($M = 3.43$) were more persuasive than ads containing weak features ($M = 3.03$), $F(1, 285) = 17.83$, $p < .001$. Second, feature strength interacted significantly with feature number such that six strong features ($M = 3.62$) were more persuasive than two strong features ($M = 3.25$) but six weak features ($M = 2.96$) were less persuasive than two weak features ($M = 3.10$), $F(1, 285) = 5.90$, $p = .016$. Third, feature number interacted significantly with legitimacy of the authority such that, for the ad containing the legitimate authority, six features ($M = 3.58$) were more persuasive than two features ($M = 3.32$), but for the ad containing the illegitimate authority, six features ($M = 2.99$) did not differ from two features ($M = 3.04$), $F(1, 285) = 4.33$, $p = .038$.

Overall, these results demonstrate that, even in the treatment conditions, participants considered the full advertisements in making their judgments. Thus, participants who learned to distinguish legitimate and illegitimate authorities did not mindlessly accept advertisements simply because they contained a legitimate authority. Nor did they automatically reject advertisements that employed ille-

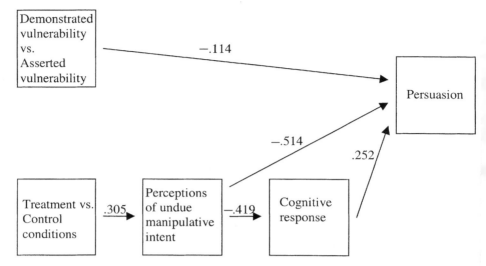

FIG. 13.2.   The mediation of resistance to the ad containing the illegitimate authority by perception of undue manipulative intent and cognitive response in Experiment 3. All paths have $ps < .01$.

gitimate authorities. Instead, participants rendered judgments that incorporated information on product features as well as an appraisal of the worth of the expert testimony.

Mediators of Resistance and Enhancement

Figure 13.2 represents the mediational model for the effect of treatment on resistance to the ad containing the illegitimate authority. After collapsing the two control conditions (discussed above), treatment is represented in the model by two orthogonal contrast vectors: (a) demonstrated vulnerability treatment (coded as 1) versus asserted vulnerability treatment (coded as −1) and (b) treatment conditions (coded as 1) versus control conditions (coded as −1). In the model, perceptions of undue manipulative intent and persuasion correspond to the undue manipulative intent and ad persuasiveness scales, respectively, and cognitive response represents the number of positive thoughts minus the number of negative thoughts.

We predicted that participants who learned the distinction between legitimate and illegitimate authorities would subsequently perceive advertisements containing illegitimate authorities as unduly manipulative. Furthermore, we predicted that these perceptions of undue manipulative intent would elicit a negative cognitive response toward the ads, and that this negative cognitive response would lead to resistance to the ads.

As can be seen in Fig. 13.2, the treatment caused a significant increase in perceptions of undue manipulative intent, and the increased perceptions of undue

FIG. 13.3. The mediation of the enhancement of the ad containing the legitimate authority by cognitive response in Experiment 3. All paths have $ps < .01$.

manipulative intent led to decreased persuasion, mediated in part by negative cognitive responses. The demonstration of vulnerability, on the other hand, had a direct effect on resistance. This model fit the data well according to a chi-square goodness-of-fit test (using EQS with maximum likelihood estimation on the covariance matrix), $\chi^2(5, N = 320) = 2.760, p = .737$, CFI $= 1.000$. The addition of missing paths does not significantly enhance model fit.

Although cognitive response partially mediated the effects of perceptions of undue manipulative intent on persuasion, a significant direct path remained. This suggests that the observed resistance was not a purely cognitive process. In a study of the effect of attitude importance on resistance to persuasion, Zuwerink and Devine (1996) reached a similar conclusion: "The results of this process analysis underscore that resistance to persuasion is both an affective and a cognitive affair, particularly for those who care deeply about their attitudes" (p. 936). It is unlikely that participants in the present experiment cared deeply about the advertised product—but they may well have cared deeply about the experience of being fooled (Cosmides & Tooby, 1992).

It is noteworthy that the unique resistance conferred by the demonstration of vulnerability was not mediated by perceptions of undue manipulative intent. As mentioned earlier, the demonstration of vulnerability was not designed to make illegitimate authority-based ads appear more manipulative. It was designed to make participants aware of their personal susceptibility to that manipulation. That demonstrated susceptibility had a direct effect on participants' willingness to reject the persuasiveness of illegitimate authorities.

For the enhancement effect, the most parsimonious exploratory model suggested that the enhancement of the ad containing the legitimate authority was mediated entirely by more positive cognitive responses to the ad (see Fig. 13.3). This model fit the data well, $\chi^2(1, N = 320) = 2.055, p = .152$, CFI $= .992$. The fact that different mediational models emerged for the resistance and enhancement effects may stem from the motivational nature of resistance. Because enhanced resistance consumes cognitive resources, participants required a high level of motivation (the demonstration of vulnerability) before allocating these resources. Enhanced receptivity, on the other hand, actually releases cognitive resources, and, as a result, participants may have been motivated to reduce their resistance to legitimate authorities once they learned that it was safe to do so.

A final difference between resistance and enhancement may stem from the different implications for the self of building or releasing resistance. Recognizing the need to build resistance required participants to accept the fact that they had been fooled in the past—a highly uncomfortable realization. Recognizing the advantages of releasing resistance simply required participants to accept a reason to let go of their skepticism—a substantially less taxing realization.

CREATING CRITICAL CONSUMERS

With the expanding prevalence and pervasiveness of advertising, our ability to critically distinguish messages that employ influence techniques appropriately from messages that counterfeit these techniques has become increasingly important. Until recently, social psychologists have had little to offer to those hoping to teach this critical distinction. The present research offers a first step. In three experiments, participants learned to distinguish between legitimate and illegitimate uses of authority in advertising. Compared to control groups, participants who learned this distinction demonstrated resistance against subsequent advertisements that employed authority illegitimately. Furthermore, compared to controls, these participants perceived legitimate uses of authority as less manipulative and more persuasive.

Originally, the treatment was expected to produce resistance to ads that employed authority illegitimately without affecting reactions to legitimate authorities. The results suggested, however, that the most robust effect of the treatment was the enhancement of the ads containing legitimate authorities. In contrast to instilling resistance, which required dispelling participants' illusions of invulnerability to counterfeit experts, the enhancement effects merely required describing the distinction between legitimate and illegitimate authorities.

Why might these seemingly parallel effects manifest so asymmetrically? Perhaps, in a sense, acceptance is the path of least resistance. When faced with an interpersonal request, saying no disappoints the requester, whereas saying yes pleases. Furthermore, Knowles and Linn (this volume) demonstrated that resistance is a resource that can be used up. As a result, influence targets may prefer to bank their resistance so it will be available when they truly need it. These factors (as well as the evidence of the present studies) suggest that convincing someone to resist is likely to be substantially harder than giving them an excuse to accept.

Motivating Receptivity by Teaching Resistance

The results of these three studies demonstrate the existence of an indirect but powerful influence technique. By pointing out plausible criteria that delineate the acceptable versus objectionable uses of a principle of influence (e.g., authority), acceptable uses of that principle (e.g., legitimate authorities) become more persuasive. In the present studies, these criteria were disseminated by a third party unrelated to the sponsors of the advertisements. A powerful extension of this technique could enable a clever advertiser to describe the relevant criteria and then employ an acceptable (and now enhanced) version of the corresponding principle.

The results of Experiments 1 and 2 suggested that, subsequent to learning the distinction between legitimate and illegitimate authorities, legitimate authorities were seen as less manipulative. Experiment 3 then offered evidence of the enhancement of legitimate authorities manifested via an increase in positive cognitive responses. This enhancement may, thus, represent both an increase in the perceived credibility of the legitimate authority and a decrease in the degree of negativity with which consumers typically perceive advertising (particularly television advertising, Mittal, 1994; Shavitt & Vargas, 2002).

The optimal treatment thus created critical consumers, ready to resist marketers who employ authority illegitimately but equally ready to reward those who provide genuine experts. This creates for marketers and consumers a win-win situation. Marketers are rewarded for providing useful heuristic information, while consumers are empowered to defend themselves against marketers who do otherwise.

AUTHOR NOTE

This research was supported in part by a National Science Foundation Graduate Fellowship to the first author. Some of the findings reported here were initially presented at the April 1997 meeting of the Western Psychological Association in Seattle, Washington, the January 1998 Kelley Graduate School of Business's Conference on Social Influence and Ethics in Organizations in Evanston, Illinois, the August 1998 meeting of the American Psychological Association in San Francisco, California, and the February 2000 meeting of the Society for Personality and Social Psychology in Nashville, Tennessee. A complete description of this program of research can be found in Sagarin, Cialdini, Rice, and Serna (2002). We thank Matthew Bogue, Scott James, Heather Magaw, Leah Peryer, Jeff Quinn, and Phylisa Smith for their help in conducting these experiments, Kelton Rhoads for his many insights during this research program, Rosanna Guadagno for her helpful review of earlier drafts of this manuscript, and the members of Arizona State University's Social Psychology Research Institute and Social Influence Interest Group and Northern Illinois University's Social-I/O Area for their commentary and guidance during the development and analysis of these experiments.

REFERENCES

Aaker, D. A., & Myers, J. G. (1987). *Advertising management.* Englewood Cliffs, NJ: Prentice-Hall.

Aiken, L. S., Gerend, M. A., & Jackson, K. M. (2001). Subjective risk and health protective behavior: Cancer screening and cancer prevention. In A. Baum, T. A. Revenson, & J. E. Singer (Eds.) *Handbook of health psychology* (pp. 727–746). Mahwah, NJ: Erlbaum.

American Cancer Society (1997). *Cancer risk report: Prevention and control, 1997.* Atlanta, GA: American Cancer Society. pp. 1–23.

Aronson, E., Turner, J. A., & Carlsmith, J. M. (1963). Communicator credibility and communicator discrepancy as determinants of attitude change. *Journal of Abnormal and Social Psychology, 67,* 31–36.

Blass, T. (1991). Understanding behavior in the Milgram obedience experiment. *Journal of Personality and Social Psychology, 60,* 398–413.

Blass, T. (1999). The Milgram paradigm after 35 years: Some things we now know about obedience to authority. *Journal of Applied Social Psychology, 29,* 955–978.

Boatright, J. (1992). *Ethics and the conduct of business.* New York: Prentice Hall General Reference and Travel.

Brehm, J. W. (1966). *A theory of psychological reactance.* New York: Academic Press.

Byrne, D., Rasche, L., & Kelley, K. (1974). When "I like you" indicates disagreement. *Journal of Research in Personality, 8,* 207–217.

Campbell, M. C. (1995). When attention-getting advertising tactics elicit consumer inferences of manipulative intent: The importance of balancing benefits and investments. *Journal of Consumer Psychology, 4,* 225–254.

Chaiken, S. (1987). The heuristic model of persuasion. In M. P. Zanna, J. M. Olson, & C. P. Herman (Eds.), *Social influence: The Ontario Symposium* (Vol. 5, pp. 3–39). Hillsdale, NJ: Erlbaum.

Chaiken, S., Giner-Sorolla, R., & Chen, S. (1996). Beyond accuracy: Defense and impression motives in heuristic and systematic processing. In P. M. Gollwitzer & J. A. Bargh (Eds.), *The psychology of action* (pp. 553–578). New York: Guilford.

Christensen, L. (1977). The negative subject: Myth, reality, or a prior experimental experience effect? *Journal of Personality and Social Psychology, 35,* 392–400.

Cialdini, R. B. (2001). *Influence: Science and practice* (4th ed.). Boston: Allyn & Bacon.

Cosmides, L., & Tooby, J. (1992). Cognitive adaptations for social exchange. In J. H. Barkow, L. Cosmides, & J. Tooby (Eds.) *The adapted mind: Evolutionary psychology and the generation of culture* (pp. 163–228). New York: Oxford University Press.

Curry, S. J., Taplin, S. H., Anderman, C., Barlow, W. E., & McBride, C. (1993). A randomized trial of the impact of risk assessment and feedback on participation in mammography screening. *Preventative Medicine, 22,* 350–360.

Drachmán, D., deCarufel, A., & Insko, C. A. (1978). The extra credit effect in interpersonal attraction. *Journal of Experimental Social Psychology, 14,* 458–467.

Ellen, P. S., Mohr, L. A., & Webb, D. J. (2000). Charitable programs and the retailer: Do they mix? *Journal of Retailing, 73,* 393–406.

Epstein, S. (1998). Cognitive-experiential self-theory. In D. F. Barone, M. Hersen, & V. B. Van Hasselt (Eds.). *Advanced personality.* New York: Plenum Press.

Fazio, R. H., & Zanna, M. P. (1981). Direct experience and attitude-behavior consistency. In L. Berkowitz (Ed.), *Advances in experimental social psychology* (Vol. 14, pp. 162–203). New York: Academic Press.

Fein, S., McCloskey, A. L., & Tomlinson, T. M (1997). Can the jury disregard that information? The use of suspicion to reduce the prejudicial effects of pretrial publicity and inadmissible testimony. *Personality and Social Psychology Bulletin, 23,* 1215–1226.

Fiske, S. T., & Taylor, S. E. (1991). *Social cognition.* New York: McGraw-Hill.

Folkes, V. S. (1988). Recent attribution research in consumer behavior: A review and new directions. *Journal of Consumer Research, 14,* 548–565.

Goldberg, P. A. (1965). Expectancy, choice, and the other person. *Journal of Personality and Social Psychology, 2,* 895–897.

Greenwald, A. G. (1968). Cognitive learning, cognitive response to persuasion, and attitude change. In A. G. Greenwald, T. C. Brock, & T. M. Ostrom (Eds.), *Psychological foundations of attitudes* (pp. 147–170). New York: Academic Press.

Helweg-Larsen, M. (1999). (The lack of) optimistic biases in response to the 1994 Northridge earthquake: The role of personal experience. *Basic and Applied Social Psychology, 21,* 119–121.

Helweg-Larsen, M., & Collins, B. E. (1997). A social psychological perspective on the role of knowledge about AIDS in AIDS prevention. *Current Directions in Psychological Science, 6,* 23–26.

Jones, E. E., & Wortman, C. (1973). *Ingratiation: An attributional approach.* Morristown, NJ: General Learning Corp.

Kahn, B. E., & Baron, J. (1995). An exploratory study of choice rules favored for high-stakes decisions. *Journal of Consumer Psychology, 4,* 305–328.

Lutz, R. J. (1985). Affective and cognitive antecedents of attitude toward the ad: A conceptual framework. In L. Alwitt & A. Mitchell (Eds.), *Psychological processes and advertising effects* (pp. 45–65). Hillsdale, NJ: Erlbaum.

MacKenzie, S. B., & Lutz, R. J. (1989). An empirical examination of the structural antecedents of attitude toward the ad in an advertising pretesting context. *Journal of Marketing, 53,* 48–65.

Masling, J. (1966). Role-related behavior of the subject and psychologist and its effect upon psychological data. *Nebraska Symposium on Motivation, 14,* 67–103.

McGuire, W. J. (1964). Inducing resistance to persuasion: Some contemporary approaches. In L. Berkowitz (Ed.), *Advances in experimental social psychology* (Vol. 1, pp. 191–229). New York: Academic Press.

Milgram, S. (1974). *Obedience to authority.* New York: Harper & Row.

Mittal, B. (1994). Public assessment of TV advertising: Faint praise and harsh criticism. *Journal of Advertising Research, 34,* 35–53.

National Center for Health Statistics (1996). *Healthy people 2000 review, 1995–1996.* Hyattsville, MD: Public Health Service.

Neter, J., Wasserman, W., & Kutner, M. H. (1989). *Applied linear regression analysis.* Homewood, IL: Irwin.

Norris, F. H., Smith, T., & Kaniasty, K. (1999). Revisiting the experience-behavior hypothesis: The effects of Hurricane Hugo on hazard preparedness and other self-protective acts. *Basic and Applied Social Psychology, 21,* 37–47.

Norris, J., Nurius, P. S., & Dimeff, L. A. (1996). Through her eyes: Factors affecting women's perception of and resistance to acquaintance sexual aggression threat. *Psychology of Women Quarterly, 20,* 123–145.

Perloff, L. S. (1987). Social comparison and illusions of invulnerability to negative life events. In C. R. Snyder & C. E. Ford (Eds.), *Coping with negative life events: Clinical and social psychological perspectives* (pp. 217–242). New York: Plenum.

Petty, R. E., & Cacioppo, J. T. (1986). *Communication and persuasion: Central and peripheral routes to attitude change.* New York: Springer-Verlag.

Petty, R. E., & Krosnick, J. A. (Eds.) (1996). *Attitude strength: Antecedents and consequences.* Hilsdale, NJ: Erlbaum.

Petty, R. E., Ostrom, T. M., & Brock, T. C. (1981). Historical foundations of the cognitive response approach to attitudes and persuasion. In R. E. Petty, T. M. Ostrom, & T. C. Brock (Eds.), *Cognitive responses in persuasion* (pp. 5–29). Hillsdale, NJ: Erlbaum.

Petty, R. E., & Wegener, D. T. (1998). Attitude change: Multiple roles for persuasion variables. In D. T. Gilbert, S. T. Fiske, & G. Lindzey (Eds.) *The handbook of social psychology* (4th ed., Vol. 1, pp. 323–390). New York: McGraw-Hill.

Sagarin, B. J., Cialdini, R. B., Rice, W. E., & Serna, S. B. (2002). Dispelling the illusion of invulnerability: The motivations and mechanisms of resistance to persuasion. *Journal of Personality and Social Psychology, 83,* 526–541.

Shavitt, S., & Vargas, P. (2002). The ad medium is the message: Public attitudes toward advertising depend on the ad medium. Manuscript submitted for publication.

Siegel, K., Raveis, V. H., & Gorey, E. (1998). Barriers and pathways to testing among HIV-infected women. *AIDS Education and Prevention, 10,* 114–127.

Snyder, C. R. (1997). Unique invulnerability: A classroom demonstration in estimating personal mortality. *Teaching of Psychology, 24,* 197–199.

Taylor, S. E., & Brown, J. D. (1988). Illusion and well-being: A social psychological perspective on mental health. *Psychological Bulletin, 103,* 193–210.

Van der Velde, F. W., Hooykaas, C., & Van der Pligt, J. (1992). Risk perception and behavior. *Psychology and Health, 6,* 23–38.

Visser, P. S., & Krosnick, J. A. (1998). Development of attitude strength over the life cycle: Surge and decline. *Journal of Personality and Social Psychology, 75,* 1389–1410.

Weinstein, N. D. (1980). Unrealistic optimism about future life events. *Journal of Personality and Social Psychology, 39,* 806–820.

Weinstein, N. D, (1987). Unrealistic optimism about susceptibility to health problems. *Journal of Behavioral Medicine, 10,* 481–500.

Weinstein, N. D. (1989). Effects of personal experience on self-protective behavior. *Psychological Bulletin, 105,* 31–50.

Zuwerink, J. R., & Devine, P. G. (1996). Attitude importance and resistance to persuasion: It's not just the thought that counts. *Journal of Personality and Social Psychology, 70,* 931–944.

14

Consumer Psychology and Attitude Change

Curtis P. Haugtvedt
The Ohio State University

Richard J. Shakarchi
The Ohio State University

Bendik M. Samuelsen
Norwegian School of Management

Kaiya Liu
The Ohio State University

The extent to which and the processes by which individuals are influenced by print, radio, television, interpersonal conversations, and Web sites (as well as future integrated technologies) is a fascinating area of study. As the various chapters in this book illustrate, as social psychologists make progress in understanding the nature of resistance to attitude change, new and very interesting questions about persuasion processes in general are raised. While many factors may be associated with strong attitudes, the extent to which individuals elaborate on the content of an initial persuasive appeal has been shown to be an important moderator of the extent to which and the processes by which they might resist subsequent opposing persuasive messages (see Petty, Haugtvedt, & Smith, 1995).

In this chapter we discuss some of our current work on factors related to message-relevant elaboration within a marketing context. Such elaboration has been shown to be a precursor to the development of attitudes that are more resistant to change. The first project we describe suggests that aspects of an advertisement that might normally be associated with reactance-like effects may prompt greater message-relevant elaboration (Shakarchi & Haugtvedt, 2003). Another line of research shows how the context in which a persuasive message appears might influence the extent of elaboration as well as the extent of resistance to subsequent opposing messages (Samuelsen, Haugtvedt, & Liu, 2002;

Samuelsen & Haugtvedt, 2003). In a final study, we present data using an individual difference measure of the extent to which participants tend to think about their own prior experiences when exposed to persuasive messages. The results of this study reveal that there may be optimal levels of self-referent thinking in some persuasion settings (Haugtvedt, Shakarchi, & Jarvis, 2002). After describing these new lines of research, we comment briefly on some possible boundary conditions as well as on future areas of research.

YOU HAVE NO CHOICE BUT TO ELABORATE

Marketers and other persuasive agents have many tools from which to choose when developing messages and campaigns designed to change attitudes or induce behavior. Knowles and Linn (this volume) point out that most marketing and advertising strategies attempt to induce people to purchase products by offering good prices, features, and other incentives. One such strategy is to offer a choice to the consumer, where none or few existed previously. Store brands often poise their brands as alternatives to products with limited competition; in fact, one major retail grocery chain (A&P) specifically refers to their brand as America's Choice.

But what are the implications of *limiting* consumer choice? Could this be used as an effective marketing or advertising strategy? We agree with Johnson, Smith-McLallen, Killeya, and Levin (this volume) that the use of reactance theory as an "explanation of resistance provides a poor fit for most persuasion data, given that nearly all persuasive messages omit such statements." However, advertising creates a context wherein statements that threaten freedom of choice can occur. In an attempt to gain consumers' attention and thus have a chance to create a strong memory of the target brand or product offering, advertisers often incorporate techniques that might not normally be implemented in laboratory research. Consumer research, therefore, might be fertile ground for investigating the effects of reactance.

A statement such as "You have no other choice" may, in fact, elicit more attention from consumers by its very nature of being reactive. One can readily imagine that a consumer might (internally) respond to such assertions by asking, "Why not?!" Although Sherman, Crawford, and McConnell (this volume) suggest that the resistant response of reactance may be an automatic process, another possibility may be that reactance creates an automatic motivation to scrutinize stimulus-relevant information for the validity of the assertion. If the assertion (restriction of freedom) is specious, such as when the assertion suggests that one of two equivalently favored choices is superior, then resistance will occur. However, if the assertion accurately represents the vast superiority of one choice over another, the assertion might help to focus recipients' attention on that superiority, thereby *increasing* persuasion—an Omega strategy to persuasion.

This hypothesis was tested by Shakarchi and Haugtvedt (2003). Seventy-four undergraduate students at the Ohio State University participated in this research in partial completion of course requirements. Participants were brought into a computer laboratory where the experiment was administered via MediaLab Research Software. Participants were informed that the researchers were interested in understanding how people interpret a variety of social information, such as they might encounter when reading a newspaper or magazine.

Participants were then exposed to a brief article describing personal digital assistant (PDA) features and functionality. (PDAs were chosen as the stimuli because prescreening indicated extremely limited experience with and knowledge of such products, therefore permitting more flexible manipulation of the stimuli.) After reading the article, participants saw one of four advertisements for a new Palm-OS™ PDA model. The advertisements varied orthogonally along two dimensions, Argument Strength (strong vs. weak) and Framing (choice vs. no choice). Strength was varied by manipulating the product attributes to be better than or worse than average PDA features, as described in the preceding article. Framing was manipulated by the catch-phrases that introduced the advertisement. Under the no-choice condition, participants were told: "YOU HAVE NO CHOICE" . . . "We made the decision for you.™"; under the choice condition, participants were told: "YOU HAVE A CHOICE" . . . "We've given you another choice.™" An image of the product was placed vertically between the two framing statements, and the product attributes were situated below these statements.

Following the advertisement, participants were asked to report their attitudes toward the advertised PDA, confidence in their attitudes, and their purchase intention and to give subjective reports of effort put into processing the advertisement and personal importance of PDAs. Need for cognition (18-item scale; Cacioppo, Petty, & Kao, 1984) was also assessed, as was the length of time participants spent reading the advertisement.

Our main interest was the effects of Framing and Strength on attitudes toward the PDA. An analysis of variance examined attitude as the dependent variable and Framing and Strength as the independent variables; the remaining measures were included as covariates. There was no significant effect for Framing, $F(1, 73) = 0.04$, $p = 0.840$, and none of the covariates were significant (all $ps > 0.05$). However, Argument Strength was significant, $F(1, 73) = 20.69$, $p < 0.001$. This main effect was qualified by the interaction of Framing $\times$ Argument Strength, $F(1, 73) = 10.12$, $p = 0.002$, as illustrated in Fig. 14.1

As evident from Fig. 14.1, the no-choice condition magnified the argument strength manipulation. This was true even when controlling for confidence in one's own attitudes, the relevance of the advertisement, self-reported effort spent processing the advertisement, actual time spent reading the advertisement, and need for cognition.

The implication of this research for understanding classical reactance is that, at least in the consumer domain, resistance is *not* the only potential outcome. Instead, consumers seem to challenge a statement that limits choice, and in fact

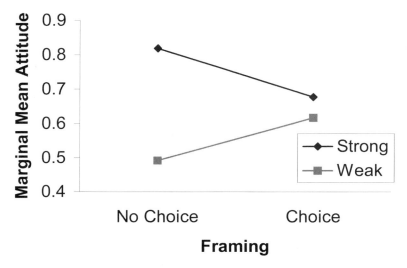

FIG. 14.1   Mean attitude as a function of Framing × Strength, with confidence, effort, importance, length of processing time, and need for cognition included as covariates.

read the information in more detail to gauge the credibility of that statement.

This research also suggests that there may be positive outcomes (persuasion) to assertions of limited choice. So long as the stimulus-relevant information supports the assertion, such an Omega strategy to persuasion may be very successful, magnifying the persuasive power of the relevant information. However, if the relevant information does not support the assertion (i.e., if the arguments are found to be weak), a greater degree of resistance is likely to occur than if no assertions had been made. The research is suggestive of a technique that might prompt consumers to think more carefully about message content. Attitudes formed or changed from such processes should be relatively more resistant to a counterpersuasive attempt by competitors. This idea, however, remains to be tested.

The factor that induced greater elaboration in aforementioned research was contained within the body of the advertisement. In the following section, we discuss how factors associated with the context in which an advertisement appears might influence the extent to which participants elaborate on the content of an advertisement.

THE POTENTIAL INFLUENCE OF
CONTEXT ON ELABORATION AND
RESISTANCE

The above study examined the influence of an explicit communication, where participants were likely quite aware of the statement. However, most advertisements occur in a more subtle context, simultaneously with other material such as programs on TV, editorial articles in magazines or newspapers, ads for other products, and so forth. Such materials within which ads are embedded are usually referred to as advertising context (cf. Soldow & Principe, 1981). The advertisement might appear in the middle of a feature story about war on terrorism or Thanksgiving traditions in rural North Dakota, or it might be interspersed in an article about a famous rock star in *Rolling Stone* magazine. Does advertising context influence the extent to which consumers will elaborate on message content? If so, are the attitudes formed by such processes relatively more resistant to opposing influences in future messages?

The question of how previous exposures (e.g., advertising context) affect perceptions of subsequent stimuli (e.g., an advertisement) has been addressed through the research using the concept of *priming*. Priming refers to "a procedure that increases the accessibility of some category or construct in memory" (Sherman, Mackie, & Driscoll 1990). Priming studies are concerned with the temporary activation of an individual's mental representations and how this internal readiness interacts with environmental information to produce perceptions, evaluations, and even motivations and social behavior (Bargh & Chartrand, 2000; Bargh, 1992, 2002). Segal and Cofer (1960) first used the term "priming" to refer to the effect of recent use of a concept in one task on the probability of using the same concept in a subsequent unrelated task (cf. Bargh & Chartrand, 2000). The basic assumption is that the accessible information will affect the subsequent processing of a message, or more precisely, that "primes" affect subsequent perceptions. Context is important for marketing issues. For example, Yi (1990a) found that prior exposure to contextual factors could prime certain product attributes and subsequently increase the likelihood that consumers will interpret product information in terms of these activated attributes, thereby affecting the evaluation of the advertised brand. Yi (1990b) also found that cognitive priming (i.e., priming a certain product attribute) determined the type of interpretation given to product information in a subsequent ad, and thereby guided consumers' evaluation of the advertised brand (see e.g., Yi, 1991; Soldow & Principe, 1981; Goldberg & Gorn, 1987; Coulter 1998, for additional studies of context effects). Because existing studies on priming have not included a manipulation of argument quality, it is unclear from the existing research if the observed effects of priming are due to a simple matching effect (e.g., a peripheral route process) or due to greater elaboration (a central route process). In an attempt to integrate the priming and attitude change literatures and methods, we (Samuelsen, Haugtvedt, & Liu, 2002) conducted an initial study. Our research was guided, in part, by the multiple-roles-for-variables postulate of the Elaboration Likelihood Model (ELM; Petty & Cacioppo, 1986). The multiple-roles-of-variables postulate in the ELM states that "variables can influence judgments (1) by serving as arguments relevant to determining the merits of an object or position, (2) by biasing the processing of attitude-relevant information (both of which are most likely when motivation and ability to scrutinize attitude-relevant information are high), (3) by serving as a peripheral cue (when motivation and ability is low), and (4) by itself affecting the level of scrutiny given to attitude-relevant information (when elaboration is not constrained by other factors to be particularly high or low)" (Petty & Wegener 1998; Petty, Cacioppo, Kasmer, & Haugtvedt, 1987). The role of priming in a given situation may depend on the baseline level of elaboration. Nonetheless, because of our inability to find studies with a combination of contextual priming and argument quality manipulations, we decided to conduct such a study. In our computer-based study (Samuelsen, Haugtvedt, & Liu, 2002), students were told that their task was to assess the readability and design of an Internet newspaper. Students were randomly assigned first to read an editorial from an Internet newspaper discussing a recent poll on young consumers' consumption patterns, emphasizing either functional needs or hedonic needs. Surrounding the story were words chosen to highlight main points of the story (functional words like quality, functionality, durability; or hedonic words like joy, pleasure, fun, exciting). All students were then exposed to an ad stressing functional benefits and attributes of a new brand of shampoo (a match to the functional prime, but a mismatch to the hedonic prime) in one of two versions: strong versus weak argument quality. The strong version of the shampoo advertisement contained arguments about vitamins, sun protection, dandruff prevention, and so on. The other version contained much of the same type of information, but in significantly weaker versions (e.g., will reduce dandruff if used less than three times a week; will keep your hair healthy as long as you stay out of wind and rain).

Thus, the study was a 2 (argument quality: strong vs. weak) $\times$ 2 (prime relevant, irrelevant) between-subjects factorial design. No differences in self-reported motivation were revealed on a typical involvement/personal relevance manipulation commonly used in persuasion research. Most interesting, however, is that a significant interaction between prime and argument quality ($F(1, 139) = 3.91$, $p < .05$) suggested that matching primes with message content led to greater levels of elaboration of message content. As seen in Fig. 14.2, when the prime was relevant to the subsequent target ad, the strong argument version led to more positive brand attitude than the weak argument version; when prime was irrelevant to the target ad, participants were less influenced by argument quality. This finding leads us to question the exact processes that produced the results of existing priming studies. The current study suggests that relevant primes can lead to more positive attitudes in the case of strong arguments because of greater elaboration of information. Relevant primes can also increase attitude change through a simpler matching process.

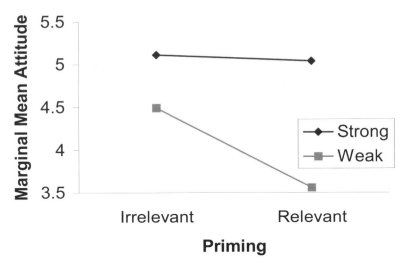

FIG 14.2   Mean attitude as a function of Priming × Strength.

One finding of Samuelsen et al.'s (2002) research is that in the strong argument conditions, brand attitude was identical across the relevant and irrelevant primes. Based on previous research (e.g., Haugtvedt, Schumann, Schneier, & Warren, 1994; Haugtvedt & Petty, 1992) and our hypotheses about the underlying processes, we were interested in assessing whether these equally extreme attitudes might have different attitude strength properties. Samuelsen and Haugtvedt (2003) thus conducted a study in which they examined how resistant these attitudes were to counterattack. To do this, they created two versions of a message pretested to contain strong or weak attacks on a brand of shampoo. Examples of strong attacks included: "More than half of those who tested it were unsatisfied" and "None of the testers wanted to change from their regular shampoo after the test-period." Examples of weak attacks included: "Some testers were unsatisfied with the shampoo" and "Some testers didn't like the shape of the bottle." Participants expressed their attitudes immediately after viewing the initial advertisement. They were then told that the company had solicited opinions about the products from employees and those results were on the following pages.

Brand attitudes were measured before and after the counter-message; the initial brand attitudes were identical in the two priming conditions, thus replicating the first experiment. However, a significant interaction ($F(1, 77) = 7.13$, $p < .01$) indicated that persons in the relevant priming condition were more resistant to the strong counterarguments than persons in the irrelevant prime condition.

Although the results are tentative and await more extensive analyses, the two experiments indicate that priming affects elaboration and that the attitudes based on elaboration were less influenced by counterpersuasive messages. A match between prime and target ad is beneficial if the advertising message is deemed cogent; otherwise, backfire (increased resistance) is likely to occur. When arguments are cogent, the context has the potential to induce an attitude more resistant to counterpersuasion.

INDIVIDUAL DIFFERENCES AND RESISTANCE TO PERSUASION

Haugtvedt, Petty, and Cacioppo (1992) suggested that the use of individual difference variables to operationalize theoretical constructs is an important but under-utilized approach for consumer psychology and marketing researchers. The use of individual difference measures in consumer research had fallen out of favor because reviews of studies in which researchers tried to predict behavior from knowledge of personality variables concluded that such studies were largely unsuccessful (for a review, see Kassarjian, 1971).

Perhaps, as Kassarjian (1971) speculated, part of the failure of past studies stemmed from adopting multidimensional personality measures with few attempts to validate the measures in the applied settings. Haugtvedt et al. (1992) suggested that one fruitful use of personality measures in basic consumer research would be to employ unidimensional personality measures that are related to processes theoretically relevant to attitude change and persuasion or in the attitude–behavior relationship. In this regard, need for cognition (Cacioppo & Petty, 1982) serves as an example of an individual difference variable that could be used to operationalize the motivation component in the Elaboration Likelihood Model (Petty & Cacioppo, 1981; 1986). In part, because of its relationship to a component of the ELM, need for cognition has also been shown to be relevant to the degree to which and the manner in which individuals resist persuasive attempts (Bagozzi, 1994; Haugtvedt & Petty, 1992; Haugtvedt & Wegener, 2002). In the following section, we describe a new individual difference measure, the propensity to self-reference (PSR: Haugtvedt, 1994), and discuss how it, too, may be relevant to understanding the processes underlying persuasion as well as resistance to persuasion.

Self-Referential Thought

How prior experiences and knowledge influence processes of attitude change and persuasion is a central theme throughout much theorizing in social psychology. Indeed, the cognitive response perspective posits that idiosyncratic thoughts are better predictors of attitude change and maintenance than is recall of message arguments. Consistent with this idea, Shavitt and Brock (1986) found that coding for self-originated thoughts improved predictions of attitude above traditional cognitive response polarity measures.

The Shavitt and Brock (1986) work focused on coding of cognitive responses naturally elicited by persuasive messages. In research on the topic of self-referencing, variables designed to increase or decrease the likelihood of self-related thoughts have been manipulated. For example, Burnkrant and Unnava (1989) presented college students with advertisements for a razor (see Petty, Cacioppo, & Schumann, 1983) that addressed the reader directly (e.g., "you") or indirectly (e.g., "people"). In addition, the quality of the product attributes was manipulated to be relatively strong and convincing or weak (see Petty, Cacioppo, & Schumann, 1983). As discussed in other chapters in this book, a manipulation of attribute or argument quality can provide insights as to the degree to which participants are elaborating on message content. Consistent with their predictions, Burnkrant and Unnava (1989) found that advertisements that addressed participants directly (e.g., "you"; high self-referencing) led to more extensive elaboration. Participants who received the strong argument version liked the product significantly more than participants who received the weak argument version. However, this was not the case for participants who were exposed to an advertisement that addressed the participants indirectly (e.g., "people"; low self-referencing). Burnkrant and Unnava (1989, 1995) suggested that the difference in the extent of elaboration may not have been due to differences in participant motivation. Rather, they argued that participants were more likely to use self-knowledge structures and prior personal experiences as a basis for elaborating on the advertising content to a greater degree when they were addressed directly.

While Burnkrant and Unnava's (1989) research suggests that higher levels of self-referencing should enhance message-relevant elaboration, research by Baumgartner, Sujan, and Bettman (1992) and Sujan, Bettman, and Baumgartner (1993) suggests that high levels of self-referencing might lead to lesser degrees of message-relevant elaboration. In a study employing an argument quality manipulation for wine, Sujan et al. (1993) found support for this idea. In their high self-referencing condition participants were asked to form an impression of the advertised brand in the context of an autobiographical memory; in the low self-referencing conditions no specific encouragement was provided. Consistent with their predictions, they found the greatest differentiation in argument quality for the low self-referencing condition.

These results appear to be inconsistent with the work of Burnkrant and Unnava (1989). One possible explanation of this inconsistency relates to the idea that some individuals might be so focused on their own prior experiences that processing of the stimulus material is reduced. Indeed, Sujan et al.'s (1993) preferred explanation for their findings is that participants in their high self-referencing condition were overwhelmed by the influence of emotions associated with past experiences, and were thus unable or unwilling to focus on the stimulus materials.

An individual Difference Approach to Self-Referencing

Haugtvedt (1994) was interested in developing a measure that would assess the degree to which individuals might differ in their natural propensity to think about their own prior experiences when exposed to persuasive materials. The starting point for this individual difference measure was the manipulation check items used in the Burnkrant and Unnava (1989) and Sujan et al. (1993) studies. Additional items were generated and a pool of 28 potential items were included in a questionnaire containing other individual difference measures and general questions focusing on attitudes toward a variety of products and issues. From the initial set of 28 items, 8 items loaded on a single factor thought to capture the extent to which persons draw on and integrate their own experiences when encountering persuasive messages. While we will not go into detail here, further scale development testing was conducted in which the contents of thoughts were examined for greater degrees of self-related experiences. The operation of propensity of self-reference is described in Shakarchi and Haugtvedt (this volume). Persons completing the PSR measure are asked to respond on a 1 (extremely uncharacteristic of me) to 5 (to extremely characteristic of me) scale to statements such as "I find that thinking back to my own experiences always helps me understand things better in new and unfamiliar situations." (See Table 14.1 for scale items)

Of most interest for our current discussion is a study (Haugtvedt, Shakarchi, & Jarvis, 2002) in which students were exposed to advertisements for a calculator. The stimulus materials used the indirect method of addressing participants (i.e., "people," as in Burnkrant & Unnava, 1989). Strong- and weak-argument versions of the calculator advertisement were also created and pre-tested. Strong arguments included such things as long battery life, comfortable keys, soft carrying case, and a clear display. The weak argument version noted short battery life, small keys, a plastic case, and a display that was somewhat difficult to read under low light conditions. Participants were led to believe that the purpose of the computer-based study was to obtain ratings of the advertisement copy for a new brand of calculator. The PSR measure was completed by students in a separate session. Consistent with our interest in gaining an understanding of the attitude change processes for low and high self-referencing, participants were categorized as low, moderate, or high in PSR based on a tercile split of their scores from the questionnaire. The 2 (Argument Strength: strong vs. weak) × 3 (PSR: low, medium, high) interaction effect was significant, $F(2, 73) = 7.34$, $p = .001$, as illustrated in Fig. 14.3.

To simplify exposition, two separate ANOVAs were conducted, one contrasting the low and moderate PSR groups and one contrasting the moderate and high PSR groups. Interestingly, the data comparing low to moderate PSR appear to mirror the data reported by Burnkrant and Unnava (1989), such that those moderate in PSR are more influenced by argument strength than are those low

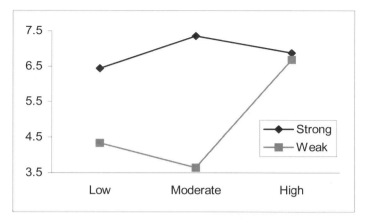

FIG 14.3   Effects of low, moderate, and high propensity to self-reference on attitudes as a function of argument strength.

in PSR. On the other hand, the comparison of the moderate to high PSR groups mirrors the data reported by Sujan, Bettman, and Baumgartner (1993), such that those moderate in PSR are more influenced by argument strength than are those high in PSR. Taken together, this study (Haugtvedt et al., 2002) found that individuals characterized as moderate in self-referencing engaged in the greatest degree of message-relevant elaboration (as indicated by the degree of difference in attitudes as a function of message strength). Such results are thus suggestive of an optimal level of self-referencing that will maximize the persuasive effect of a strategic communication. With low levels of self-referencing, individuals may not see the cogency or weaknesses in message arguments, but with high levels of self-referencing, individuals may be too focused on their own past experiences to appreciate fully the information contained in the persuasive materials. These results are preliminary and more detailed analyses of cognitive responses, etc., will be needed to verify this interpretation. It is interesting to note, however, that our study on the influence of self-referencing on persuasion seems related to the work of Dal Cin, Zanna, and Fong on transportability (this volume). However, the focus of their work is on the extent to which individuals are transported into a story, i.e., someone else's narrative. Our focus is on the extent to which individuals draw upon prior relevant experiences, i.e., their own narrative. Although both transportability and self-referencing reflect involvement in the persuasive communication, our own work suggests that some people create their own narrative based upon their own experiences, with little need for complex narrative development by the communication source. Future research in which three levels of self-referencing are created from factorial manipulations in the persuasive communication is planned.

CONCLUSION

The goal of many marketing communications is the creation and maintenance of positive attitudes toward a particular brand. Brand experiences and advertising that foster attitudes that are relatively more resistant to change may serve to maintain and enhance the worth of the brand (e.g., brand equity). Our goal in this chapter was to discuss new lines of research that we believe have implications for the creation of attitudes that will be more resistant to future changes. In this chapter, we provided a brief description of the way in which information in an advertisement might induce greater elaboration of message content. The Shakarchi and Haugtvedt (2003) study shows that telling participants that they have no choice regarding a product actually leads them to think more extensively about the product attributes. The Samuelsen et al. (2002) work focuses on the context in which a marketing communication appears. The results suggest that priming certain kinds of information might lead to greater elaboration of message content. While we have demonstrated that these results can be obtained, future research may reveal boundary conditions for such processes. Our interest was to see if the proposed processes would take place at moderate levels of participant motivation. We suspect that high levels of participant motivation would diminish the observed effects (everyone would be affected by argument quality) whereas low levels of participant motivation would lead to different results (the no-choice claim may be sufficient for a positive attitude or the simple matching of message content with a primed knowledge structure would lead to positive attitudes).

Similarly, the results observed in the propensity to self-reference study are contingent upon the existence of relevant prior experiences. Use of a less familiar object than a calculator would likely weaken the results. In addition, those individuals elaborating on message content by using their own experiences would likely be hampered by situations in which there is insufficient time to think. In our study, participants were able to examine the advertisements at their own pace. Future research should examine the influence of systematically manipulating the amount of time persons have to examine the materials.

The PSR individual difference measure may also have some important implications for other areas of persuasion and compliance. As noted earlier, the individual difference measure was developed to capture the processes activated by words used in advertising copy that might prompt thinking about personal experiences. It is also likely that various interpersonal compliance-gaining strategies prompt greater or lesser degrees of self-referencing.

Along the same lines, an intriguing study by Gregory, Cialdini, and Carpenter (1982) showed that requests asking persons to "imagine the benefits" of cable television were significantly more likely to subscribe one month later than persons simply told the "benefits of cable television." One possible explanation for these findings is that people were more likely to feel as if they had come up

TABLE 14.1
Propensity to Self-Reference Scale

1. I find that thinking back to my own experiences always helps me understand things better in new and unfamiliar situations.
2. I think it is easier to learn anything if only we can relate it to ourselves and our experiences.
3. When I read stories, I am often reminded of my own experiences in similar circumstances.
4. I often find myself using past experiences to help remember new information.
5. I think it is easier to evaluate anything if only we can relate it to ourselves and our experiences.
6. I always think about how things around me affect me.
7. In casual conversations, I find that I frequently think about my own experiences as other people describe theirs.
8. When explaining ideas or concepts to other people, I find that I always use my own experiences as examples.

with the idea and/or benefits of cable television if they were successful in imagining themselves enjoying the benefits. Part of the ability to imagine such benefits might be related to the extent to which persons are prompted to think about their own prior experiences at the time of the information presentation. Alternatively, some persons, (e.g., those high in PSR) may naturally reflect on their own prior experiences and thus be more susceptible to forgetting the source of the information. Even more interesting than the possibility that such individuals would be more likely to forget source information is the possibility that such individuals might be more likely to see themselves as the source of the information after some delay. If this kind of process is activated, it may have implications for understanding the sleeper effect as well.

In a related way, salespeople and other compliance practitioners often face an attribution problem because they are seen as benefiting when a consumer complies and purchases a product or service (Friestad & Wright, 1995). Because of this, consumers might discount the information presented by the salesperson as biased in some way. The use of factors that increase the likelihood of self-referencing might reduce the extent to which consumers discount salesperson information because the person will think that he or she generated the information by him/herself! Of course, there are likely situations in which seeing one's self as the source of information will lead to greater or lesser confidence of one's attitude. In any case, there appear to be many interesting avenues for future research as we continue in our quest to understand better the antecedents and consequences of attitude changes.

REFERENCES

Bagozzi, R. P. (1994) ACR Fellow Speech. *Advances in Consumer Research 21,* 8–11.
Bargh, J. A. (1992) Why subliminality does not matter to social psychology: Awareness of the stimulus versus awareness of its influence. In R. F. Bornstein & T. S. Pittman (Eds.), *Perception without awareness* (pp. 236–255). New York: Guilford.

Bargh, J. A. (2002). Losing consciousness: Automatic influences on consumer judgment, behavior, and motivation. *Journal of Consumer Research, 29,* (September), 280–285.

Bargh, J. A., & Chartrand, T. L. (2000). The mind in the middle. A practical guide to priming and automaticity research. In H. T. Reis & C. M. Judd (Eds.), *Handbook of research methods in social and personality psychology* (pp. 253–285). London: Cambridge University Press.

Baumgartner, M. H., Sujan, M., & Bettman, J. R. (1992). Autobiographical memories, affect, and consumer information processing. *Journal of Consumer Psychology, 1,* 53–82.

Burnkrant, R. E., & Unnava, H. R. (1989). Self-referencing: A strategy for increasing processing of message content. *Personality and Social Psychology Bulletin, 15*(4), 628–638.

Burnkrant, R. E., & Unnava, H. R. (1995). Effects of self-referencing on persuasion. *Journal of Consumer Research, 22*(1), 17–26.

Cacioppo, J. T., Petty, R. E., & Kao, C. F. (1984). The efficient assessment of need for cognition. *Journal of Personality Assessment, 48*(3), 306–307.

Coulter, K. S. (1998). The effects of affective responses to media context on advertising evaluations. *Journal of Advertising, 27*(4), 41–51.

Friestad, M., & Wright, P. (1995). Persuasion knowledge—Lay peoples and researchers beliefs about the psychology of advertising. *Journal of Consumer Research, 22*(1), 62–74.

Goldberg, M. E. & Gorn, G. J. (1987). Happy and sad TV programs: How they affect reactions to commercials. *Journal of Consumer Research, 14,* (December), 387–403.

Gregory, W. L., Cialdini, R. B., & Carpenter, K. M. (1982). Self-relevant scenarios as mediators of likelihood estimates and compliance: Does imagining make it so? *Journal of Personality and Social Psychology, 43*(1), 89–99.

Haugtvedt, C. P. (1994, February). *Individual differences in propensity to self-reference: Implications for attitude change processes.* Paper presented at the first Winter Meeting of the Society for Consumer Psychology, St. Petersburg, FL.

Haugtvedt, C. P., & Petty, R. E. (1992). Personality and persuasion: Need for cognition moderates the persistence and resistance of attitude changes. *Journal of Personality and Social Psychology, 63,* 308–319.

Haugtvedt, C. P., Petty, R. E., & Cacioppo, J. T. (1992). Need for cognition and advertising: Understanding the role of personality variables in consumer behavior. *Journal of Consumer Psychology, 1,* 239–260.

Haugtvedt, C. P., Schumann, D. W., Schneier, W., & Warren, W. (1994). Advertising repetition and variation strategies: Implications for understanding attitude strength. *Journal of Consumer Research, 21,* 176–189.

Haugtvedt, C. P., Shakarchi, R., & Jarvis, B. (2002). *Propensity to self-reference and attitude change processes.* Working paper. Fisher College of Business, The Ohio State University.

Haugtvedt, C. P., & Wegener, D. T. (2002). *Need for cognition and message order effects in persuasion.* Working Paper. Fisher College of Business, The Ohio State University.

Kassarjian, H. (1971). Personality and consumer behavior: A review. *Journal of Marketing Research, 8,* 409–418.

Knowles, E. S., & Linn, J. A. (2002). *Omega scale: A measure of resistance to persuasion.* Presented at the third annual meeting of the Society of Personality and Social Psychology, Savannah, GA.

Petty, R. E., & Cacioppo, J. T. (1981). *Attitudes and persuasion: Classic and contemporary approaches.* Dubuque, IA: Wm. C. Brown.

Petty, R. E., & Cacioppo, J. T. (1986). *Communication and persuasion: Central and peripheral routes to attitude change.* New York: Springer-Verlag

Petty, R. E., Cacioppo, J. T., Kasmer, J. A., & Haugtvedt, C. P. (1987). A reply to Stiff and Boster. *Communication Monographs, 54,* 257–263.

Petty, R. E., Cacioppo, J. T., & Schumann, D. W. (1983). Central and peripheral routes to advertising effectiveness: The moderating role of involvement. *Journal of Consumer Research, 10*(2), 135–146.

Petty, R. E., Haugtvedt, C. P., & Smith, S. M. (1995). Elaboration as a determinant of attitude strength: Creating attitudes that are persistent, resistant, and predictive of behavior. In R. E.

Petty & J. A. Krosnick (Eds.), *Attitude strength: Antecedents and consequences* (pp. 93–130). Hillsdale, NJ: Erlbaum.

Petty, R. E., & Wegener, D. T. (1998): Attitude change: Multiple roles for persuasion variables. In D. T. Gilbert, S. T. Fiske, & G. Lindzey (Eds.), *The handbook of social psychology.* New York: McGraw-Hill, 323–390.

Samuelsen, B. M., & Haugtvedt, C. P. (2003). Priming, elaboration, and resistance to counterpersuasion. Raw Data.

Samuelsen, B. M., Haugtvedt, C. P., & Liu, K. (2002). *Priming and persuasion: Elaboration of message content.* Working paper. Fisher College of Business, The Ohio State University.

Segal, S. J., & Cofer C. N. (1960). The effect of recency and recall on word association. *American Psychologist, 15,* 451.

Shakarchi, R., & Haugtvedt, C. P. (2003, June), Perceived restriction of choice and elaboration. Paper presented at the Midwest Marketing Camp, Columbus, OH.

Shavitt, S., & Brock, T. C. (1986). Self-relevant responses to commercial persuasion: Field and experimental tests. In K. Sentis & J. Olson (Eds.), *Advertising and consumer psychology, Vol 3.* (149–171). New York: Praeger.

Sherman, S. J., Mackie, D. M., & Driscoll, D. M. (1990). Priming and the differential use of dimensions in evaluation. *Personality and Social Psychology Bulletin, 16*(3) 405–418.

Soldow, G. F., & Principe, V. (1981). Responses to commercials as a function of program context. *Journal of Advertising Research, 21*(2), 59–65.

Sujan, M., Bettman, J. R., & Baumgartner, H. (1993). Influencing consumer judgments using autobiographical memories: A self-referencing perspective. *Journal of Marketing Research, 30,* 422–436.

Yi, Y. (1990a), The effects of contextual priming in print advertisements. *Journal of Consumer Research, 17,* (September) 215–222.

Yi, Y. (1990b), Cognitive and affective priming effects of the context for print advertisements. *Journal of Advertising, 19*(2), 40–48.

Yi, Y. (1991), The influence of contextual priming on advertising effects. *Advances in Consumer Research, 18,* 417–425.

Conclusion

15

The Promise and Future of Resistance and Persuasion

Eric S. Knowles
University of Arkansas

Jay A. Linn
Widener University

The 14 previous chapters have taught us a great deal about the phenomenon of resistance to persuasion and the processes by which it works. We have seen many faces of resistance and encountered many ways it can be identified and maneuvered.

As a set, these chapters have introduced new and exciting perspectives on the psychology of resistance and persuasion, particularly ways of increasing persuasion by reducing resistance. Most of the previous literature dealing with these two concepts, resistance and persuasion, has focused on how to increase the public's resistance to unwanted persuasion. Following the lead of McGuire (1964), most authors have sought ways to build, reinforce, activate, or motivate a person's ability to withstand persuasive assaults (Petty, Tormala, & Rucker, in press; Szabo & Pfau 2001). In a switch that parallels the shift 80 years ago from studying the evils of propaganda to studying the processes of attitude change, this volume introduces a less value-laden view of resistance, recognizing that (1) resistance is worthy of study in its own right, and (2) resistance is a critical element in creating as well as deterring persuasion, influence, and attitude change.

A LOOK FORWARD

As we move beyond this volume and look at its promise and prospect for the future, we can identify several areas where attention and research can be fruitfully applied.

Definition and Taxonomy. The authors of these chapters had an opportunity to hear each other present their ideas and to discuss the implications of them at a Symposium on Resistance and Persuasion held at the University of Arkansas. A plenary session at the end of this symposium concerned the look forward, what needed to be done next. One issue that all authors saw clearly was the need to deal with the diversity of definitions and meanings attributed to the term "resistance."

Different chapters in this volume rely on different meanings, or at least different operational definitions of resistance. Some chapters adopt behavioral definitions of stasis or boomerang movement in the face of persuasion (e.g., Quinn & Wood, this volume, Johnson et al., this volume) while others discuss an increasing unseen entity that doesn't become evident until a later countermessage is given (e.g., Tormala et al., this volume). Other authors adopt a primarily motivational definition (e.g., Knowles & Linn, this volume; Jacks & O'Brien, this volume), and other chapters include a strong cognitive, informational component (Sagarin & Cialdini, this volume; Wegener et al., this volume).

This diversity of definition is a strength of the field of resistance and persuasion, at least at this early stage of development. The diversity reflects the broad origin and applicability of the research, and to that extent reflects the underlying vitality of this approach to persuasion. However, the diversity can also be a limitation. One researcher's "resistance" may not be the same as another's. The findings from different approaches, relying on different meanings, might not integrate or index the same process.

The diversity in definition, then, presents a peril that deserves scrutiny, which can come in three ways. First, researchers and writers dealing with resistance and persuasion can give thoughtful attention to the definitions that are invoked and implied by their theories and operations. Being clear about what one means is the first line of defense. The clearer researchers can be, the clearer their similarities and differences can become. As a result of the discussions held at the end of the resistance and persuasion symposium, the authors of the chapters in this volume agreed to pay careful attention to the definitions and meanings of resistance used in their chapters. Each author in this volume was faithful to this promise, attending carefully to definitional issues in their work.

Second, thinking and research can focus directly on the taxonomic issues. We can develop a taxonomy of resistance to change. Several chapters in this volume begin this task. Knowles and Linn (introduction, this volume) suggest that reactance, scrutiny, distrust, and inertia are four types of resistance. A number of other chapters introduce distinctions that would be important to consider in a taxonomy of resistance. For instance, Briñol, Rucker, Tormala, and Petty (this volume) introduce a distinction between inertial resistance and bolstering–counterarguing resistance. Haugtvedt, Shakarchi, Samuelson, & Liu (this volume) suggest that the propensity to self-reference can be another source of resistance. Continued attention to the varieties and vicissitudes of resistance will serve the developing research well. The search for meaningful taxonomies is a process that we have seen over and over again bring clarity to a diverse field. We are reminded of all that Zajonc's (1965) elegant distinction between simple and complex situations did for the study of social facilitation.

Third, the diversity of definitions can become a topic for study itself. We see several examples of this remedy among the chapters in this volume. Two of the chapters employ meta-analytic strategies to assess statistically whether a set of findings are homogeneous or heterogeneous. A finding of homogeneity implies that the studies are investigating the same relationship and therefore share the same definition and processes. Any differences in terminology among studies in a homogeneous set are presumed to be semantic and trivial. Heterogeneity, on the other hand, implies that there are unacknowledged but meaningful differences among the studies in a set. Heterogeneity implies that there is a definitional distinction waiting to be uncovered. Another empirical strategy is to look at the convergent and discriminant validity among operationalizations of resistance. Shakarchi and Haugtvedt (this volume) present an empirical comparison of the various measures of resistance and resistance-related processes discussed in this book. Shakarchi and Haugtvedt find that the measures (need to evaluate, need for cognition, propensity to self-reference, Resistance to Persuasion Scale, consideration of future consequences, the Bolster–Counterargue Scale, and the Transportability Scale) all show good discriminant validity. Each measure references a separate resistance-related phenomenon.

Future studies of resistance and persuasion will do well to continue these three trends begun here: (a) being careful and clear about the meaning of resistance invoked and implied, (b) attending to taxonomies, distinctions, and comparability in resistance to persuasion, and (c) empirically investigating the convergence and discrimination among the concepts employed.

ORIGINS AND RELATIONS

Resistance is such a basic part of the persuasion process that social influence can't be the only occurrence of this phenomenon. The processes that produce resistance to persuasion have to be present in other ways, in other forms, in the human psychology. Another fruitful area for future inquiry is to identify and link the processes in this volume to other resistance-related processes in psychology.

Resistance to change is a topic that is more general than resistance to persuasion. Resistance to change is an active construct in both clinical psychology and in organizational psychology. Perhaps it is a testament to the broad applicability and importance of the concept of resistance that it is key both to the inner workings of the emotional mind (clinical resistance) and to the emergent dynamics of human collectives (organizational resistance).

Clinical Resistance. Freud (1969/1940) said, "The overcoming of resistances is the part of our work that requires the most time and the greatest trouble" (p. 36). In psychodynamic theory, resistance is an intrapsychic phenomenon, originating with repression and holding patients back from insight and integration. Wachtel (1982) established clinical resistance as a topic for serious consideration, applying it to both psychodynamic and behavioral approaches to psychotherapy. The phenomenon and treatment of resistance continue to be active topics in clinical psychology (Eagle, 1999; Leahy, 2000, 2001; Messer, 2002; Wachtel, 1999).

The clinical approach tends to define resistance either as the inability to achieve insight (e.g., "resisting interpretations"; Eagle, 1999) or as treatment noncompliance (Leahy, 2001). Arkowitz (2002) affiliated resistance with ambivalence. Resistance implies ambivalence, and treatment of ambivalence requires acknowledging and honoring both valences.

The study of resistance and persuasion can grow from an inspection and analysis of the clinical approaches to resistance. Knowles and Linn (this volume) relied on some of this literature, particularly work by Milton Erickson (1964; Erickson, Rossi, & Rossi, 1976), for examples and theoretical process involved in resistance to persuasion. Knowles and Linn's (this volume) approach–avoidance model is also closely related to Arkowitz's (2002) ambivalence approach to clinical resistance.

Organizational Resistance. The study of planned change, particularly planned change in organizations, also deals with resistance (Bennis, Benne, & Chin, 1985; Hannan & Freeman, 1984; Piderit, 2000). At its worst, organizational resistance has been used as "a not-so-disguised way of blaming the less powerful for unsatisfactory results of change efforts" (Krantz, 1999, p. 42). At its best, though, the analysis of resistance at the organizational level allows for more collaborative and effective planning and growth (George & Jones, 2001; Van de Ven & Poole, 1995).

Several recent discussions of organizational change have treated resistance in a differentiated and useful way. George and Jones (2001) proposed a seven-step process by which individuals in organizations change, and they suggested that movement between sequential stages can be impeded by different forms of resistance (e.g., rationalization, learned helplessness, denial, complacency, subtyping, minimizing). Piderit (2000) reviewed resistance in the organizational context and ended up linking the concept to ambivalence, reminiscent of Arkowitz's (2002) model of clinical resistance and Knowles and Linn's (this volume) model of persuasion. Piderit used the ambivalence model of resistance to draw several key implications for research and practice, including: (1) Looking at both positive and negative reactions is likely to lead to better prediction, (2) The variety of opinion that ambivalence implies will lead more to fully considered and eventually more optimal choices (Weick & Quinn, 1999), and (3) Positive and negative reactions to change are likely to evolve over time in a dynamical process (Vallacher & Nowak, 1994). The study of resistance and persuasion will benefit from linkage to the treatment of resistance at the organizational level.

Physiological Underpinnings. Resistance is such a basic component of many reactions to events and changes that it suggests a fundamental ambivalence toward change. Higgins's (1999, 2001) regulatory focus theory suggests a similar ambivalence. Higgins proposed that there are two fundamental orientations that people may take toward new ventures. The "Promotion Focus" attends to the opportunities in the venture. This focus is inherently optimistic and errs on the side of over-inclusiveness, emphasizing hits and avoiding errors of omission. The "Prevention Focus" attends to the dangers in the new venture. This focus is presumptively pessimistic and focuses on minimizing errors of commission. Higgins most often treats regulatory focus as a dichotomy, identifying which people employ or focus more on one than the other or which situations create one focus more than the other.

Ambivalence is the more basic point to regulatory focus theory. Any new venture calls upon both concerns—how to maximize the opportunities while minimizing the dangers. Both promotion and prevention are reasonable responses to change. Higgins's research suggests that these two foci attend to different features of the situation, operate by different processes, and lead to different behavioral and emotional outcomes. The differences, operating at the same time, become the ambivalence and must influence behavior through a dynamical interaction, even when one process is dominant.

The attention to opportunities and dangers in a new venture calls up a more fundamental distinction underlying action. Gray (1994), Fowles (1988), and others have identified neuro-chemical systems related to the activation of behavior that are separate from the systems involved in the inhibition of behavior. The "Behavioral Activation System," BAS as it is sometimes called, responds to the rewards and opportunities in the environment and initiates action toward them. Gray (1994, p. 41) located the BAS in basil ganglia and the dopamine system, specifically, "the basal ganglia (the dorsal and ventral striatum, and dorsal and ventral pallidum); the dopaminergic fibers that ascend from the mesencephalon (substantia nigra and nucleus A 10 in the ventral tegmental area) to innervate the basal ganglia; thalamic nuclei closely linked to the basal ganglia; and similarly, neocortical areas (motor, sensorimotor, and prefrontal cortex) closely linked to the basal ganglia."

In contrast, the Behavioral Inhibition System (BIS) imposes expectations on the environment and is responsive to discrepancies from the expected. The BIS responds to this information by inhibiting action. The BIS is associated with the amygdala and serotonin systems (Gray, 1994).

Evolution has given mammals two separate neurological information processing/action pathways, one that is responsive to the opportunities in the environment, the other that is responsive to the dangers in the environment. These systems are activated and operate in tandem. It should be no surprise, therefore, that ambivalence is a core feeling and reaction, that approach–avoidance conflicts are frequent and widespread (Carver & White, 1994).

ETHICS OF RESISTANCE AND PERSUASION

Books on persuasion and influence inherently and invariably raise ethical issues (Perloff, 2003). Is it ethical to devise and study ways to coerce people into doing what they would not do otherwise? As Singer and Lalich (1996) pointed out, persuasion comes in wide variation, from education to thought control, from collaborative discussion to coercive brainwashing. The key ethical elements of persuasion have to do with power, including its corollary, deception. Persuasion is ethically problematic when one party has social, political, or informational power over another. Compliance of the powerless runs the risk of being political submission rather than rational appraisal (Martin, 2002). Persuasion can use legitimate informational power (French & Raven, 1959; Friedrich & Douglass, 1998), as when one person tells unshared information to another. Deception is a less ethically appropriate form of informational power when the persuader keeps hidden the purpose or means of influence. Deception is a form of influence that maintains, yet hides, the differential in power (Bok, 1983). The influence agent knows what, when, and how the technique will apply, but the recipient does not.

Ethical issues in persuasion involve both the ends (the intention and purpose of the persuader) and the means (the appropriateness or deceptiveness of the tool or technique, the openness about purpose) of persuasion. Most advertising and public persuasion (editorials, talk radio, political speeches) are openly and blatantly persuasive (Barney & Black, 1994). The frankness of these appeals generally avoids the problem of hidden intent and moves the ethical discussion to considerations of manner. Are the advertisements being truthful and appropriate? Many claims are inappropriate, untruthful, misleading, or deceptive (Cialdini, Sagarin, & Rice, 2001), but as Sagarin and Cialdini (this volume) note, participants can be trained to identify misleading advertisements and to be less persuaded by them.

One definition of ethical persuasion is that it increases options rather than decreases them. Karl Wallace (1967) discussed the foundational values for ethical communication. The first value is the commitment to the worth and dignity of each individual. Ethical communications affirm this value. A second core value is a dedication to equality of opportunity. This value concerns freedom of choice and equal availability of information. In research ethics, informed consent embraces this second core value. Wallace's third value is the individual's freedom to determine, set, and achieve goals. Ethical communication honors and promotes this freedom. The fourth value assumes that people are free and autonomous agents within society. Individuals are to be treated as agents capable of gathering, evaluating, and acting on information in an autonomous and appropriate way. Erickson and Rossi (1975) commented that therapeutic persuasion usually went badly when it was composed for the advantage of the therapist, but often worked effectively when it was employed for the other person's benefit. Erickson and Rossi's statement is a shorthand summary of Wallace's four core principles of ethical persuasion.

The persuasion introduced and described in this book becomes available for persuaders to use, for good or for ill. Some techniques reported in this volume are inherently noncollaborative in their implementation (e.g., Knowles & Linn's, this volume, disrupt-then-reframe technique, or Haugtvedt, Shakarchi, Samuelsen, & Liu's, this volume, priming study). But even these techniques can be used to promote the target's goals and the target's access to opportunity. Other techniques discussed in these chapters appear to be more ethically neutral (e.g., acknowledging resistance, Knowles & Linn, this volume, or changing temporal perspective, Sherman, Crawford, & McConnell, this volume), but again, the issue is whether they are used to increase or decrease a target's options and opportunities.

Even techniques that are sponsored by concerns for ethical communication, such as Sagarin and Cialdini's (this volume) training of participants to identify unethical commercials, have unintended consequences that can make the technique manipulative. The conclusion seems clear: The ethics are in the user and the use, not in the technique. In this regard, we who read, study, and employ these techniques would do well to follow Wallace's (1967) four values underlying ethical communication.

APPLICATIONS

Looking at persuasion through resistance generates interesting theoretical insights and extensions. For instance, persuasion by reducing resistance seems to suggest a broader range of interventions than does persuasion by strengthening inducements. However, most of the interventions described in this book were aimed at either attitude change or relatively inconsequential behavioral compliance. One future direction for resistance and persuasion is to seek applications to more far-reaching and important domains of human behavior. Two domains seem fruitful for this extension.

Health Behavior.   Sanitation, anesthesia, and pharmaceutical revolutions in medicine have improved health and life expectancy. Behavioral health affords the next revolution in health. Diabetes, drug and alcohol abuse, cardiovascular diseases, and many other limitations to good health seem to rest primarily on unhealthful behaviors and behavioral decisions that people make. Major advancements in treating these diseases are likely to come from behavioral interventions (Chunn, 2002; Suls, Wallston, & Cotgreave, 2003).

These diseases are life-threatening problems precisely because citizens, even when they become patients, are resistant to making behavioral changes. For many of these problems, the treatment is clear and effective (Marlat & Witkiewitz, 2002). The problem is not the absence of a treatment, but the presence of resistance. Thus, one clear and helpful application for the principles, issues, theories, and techniques introduced in this volume is to reduce resistance to health-promoting behaviors.

Self-Regulation. Ambivalence is a condition that is felt, labeled, disliked, and counteracted. People often have an awareness of their ambivalence and yet a desire for one of the alternatives (Arkowitz, 2002). Phobias, avoidant behaviors, and other inhibitions would have this quality—"I know what I want, but I feel conflicted about doing it." In these cases, an understanding of resistance and persuasion might help people overcome their resistance and fulfill their desired purpose. Affirmation (Jacks & O'Brien, this volume), placing consequences in a more distant future (Sherman et al., this volume), devising double-binds (Knowles & Linn, this volume), or merely acknowledging the ambivalence (Knowles & Linn, this volume) might be strategies that can deactivate a person's resistance, making it easier for that person to follow through with his or her intention.

As this suggestion illustrates, knowledge of resistance and persuasion holds potential not only to change others, but also to change one's self. Many of these strategies explored in this volume can be added to one's self-persuasion.

We have only begun the study of resistance and persuasion. As this work unfolds, many additional insights and strategies for change will be developed. Our understanding of the change process and the repertoire of actions that affect this process has been broadened and invigorated by the chapters presented in this volume. But more, this volume reveals the great potential of this approach and it promises more benefits from the continued study of resistance and persuasion.

REFERENCES

Arkowitz, H. (2002). Toward an integrative perspective on resistance to change. *Journal of Clinical Psychology, 58,* 219–227.

Barney, R., & Black, J. (1994). Ethics and professional persuasive communications. *Public Relations Review, 20,* 233–248.

Bennis, W. G., Benne, K. D., & Chin, R. (Eds). (1985). *The planning of change* (4th ed.). New York: Holt, Rinehart and Winston.

Bok, S. (1983). *Secrets: On the ethics of concealment and revelation.* New York: Vintage.

Carver, C. S., & White, T. L. (1994). Behavioral inhibition, behavioral activation, and affective responses to impending reward and punishment: The BIS/BAS scales. *Journal of Personality and Social Psychology, 67,* 319–333.

Chunn, J. C., (Ed.). (2002). *The health behavioral change imperative: Theory, education, and practice in diverse populations.* New York: Plenum.

Cialdini, R. B., Sagarin, B. J., & Rice, W. E. (2001). Training in ethical influence. In J. M. Darley
    & D. M. Messick (Eds.), *Social influences on ethical behavior in organizations* (pp. 137–153).
    Mahwah, NJ: Erlbaum.
Eagle, M. (1999). Why don't people change? A psychoanalytic perspective. *Journal of Psycho-
    therapy Integration, 9,* 3–32.
Erickson, M. H. (1964). The confusion technique in hypnosis. *American Journal of Clinical Hyp-
    nosis, 6,* 183–207.
Erickson, M. H., & Rossi, E. L. (1975). Varieties of double bind. *American Journal of Clinical
    Hypnosis, 17,* 143–157.
Erickson, M. H., Rossi, E. L., & Rossi, S. (1976) *Hypnotic realities: The induction of clinical
    hypnosis and forms of indirect suggestion.* New York: Irvington.
Fowles, D. C. (1988). Psychophysiology and psychopathology: A motivational approach. *Psycho-
    physiology, 25,* 373–391.
French, J. R. P., & Raven, B. (1959). Bases of Social Power. In D. Cartwright (Ed.), *Studies in
    social power.* Ann Arbor: University of Michigan Press.
Freud, S. (1969/1940). *An outline of psycho-analysis* (trans. by James Strachey). New York: Norton.
Friedrich, J., & Douglass, D. (1998). Ethics and the persuasive enterprise of teaching psychology.
    American Psychologist, 53, 549–562.
George, J. M., & Jones, G. R. (2001). Towards a process model of individual change in organiza-
    tions. *Human Relations, 54,* 419–444.
Gray, J. A. (1994). Framework for a taxonomy of psychiatric disorder. In S. H. M. van Goozen,
    N. E. van de Poll, & J. Sergeant (Eds.), *Emotions: Essays on emotion theory* (pp. 29–59). Hills-
    dale, NJ: Erlbaum.
Hannan, M., & Freeman, J. (1984). Structural inertia and organizational change. *American Socio-
    logical Review, 49,* 149–164.
Higgins, E. T. (1999). Promotion and prevention as a motivational duality: Implications for eval-
    uative processes. In S. Chaiken & Y. Trope (Eds.), *Dual-process theories in social psychology*
    (pp. 503–525). New York: Guilford.
Higgins, E. T. (2001). Promotion and prevention experiences: Relating emotions to nonemotional
    motivational status. In J. P. Forgas (Ed.), *Handbook of affect and social cognition.* Mahwah,
    NJ: Erlbaum.
Krantz, J. (1999). Comment on "Challenging 'resistance to change'." *Journal of Applied Behavioral
    Science, 35,* 42–44.
Leahy, R. (2000). Sunk costs and resistance to change. *Journal of Cognitive Psychotherapy. 14,*
    355–371.
Leahy, R. (2001). *Overcoming resistance in cognitive therapy.* New York: Guilford.
McGuire, W. J. (1964). Inducing resistance to persuasion: Some contemporary approaches. In L.
    Berkowitz (Ed.), *Advances in experimental psychology* (Vol. 1, pp. 191–229). New York: Ac-
    ademic Press.
Marlatt, G. A., & Witkiewitz, K. (2002). Harm reduction approaches to alcohol use: Health pro-
    motion, prevention, and treatment. *Addictive Behaviors, 27,* 867–886.
Martin, R. (2002). *Propaganda and the ethics of persuasion.* Peterborough, ON: Broadview.
Messer, S. B. (2002). A psychodynamic perspective on resistance in psychotherapy: Vive la resis-
    tance. *Journal of Clinical Psychology, 58,* 157–163.
Perloff, R. M. (2003). *The dynamics of persuasion: Communication and attitudes in the 21st century*
    (2nd ed.). Mahwah, NJ: Erlbaum
Petty, R. E., Tormala, Z. L., & Rucker, D. D. (in press). Resisting persuasion by counterarguing:
    An attitude strength perspective. In M. R. Banaji, J. T. Jost, & D. Prentice (Eds.), *Perspectivism
    in social psychology: The yin and yang of scientific progress.* Washington, DC: American Psy-
    chological Association.
Piderit, S. K. (2000). Rethinking resistance and recognizing ambivalence: A multidimensional view
    of attitudes toward an organizational change. *Academy of Management Review, 25,* 783–794.
Singer, M. T., & Lalich, J. (1996). *Cults in our midst: The hidden menace in our everyday lives.*
    San Francisco: Jossey-Bass.

Suls, J. M., Wallston, K. A., & Cotgreave, P. A., (Eds.). (2003). *Social psychological foundations of health and illness*. Malden, MA: Blackwell.

Szabo, E. A., & Pfau, M. (2001). Nuances in inoculation: Theory and applications. In M. Pfau & J. P. Dillard (Eds.), *The persuasion handbook: Developments in theory and practice*. Thousand Oaks, CA: Sage.

Vallacher, R. R., & Nowak, A. (1994). *Dynamical systems in social psychology*. San Diego, CA: Academic Press.

Van de Ven, A. H., & Poole, M. S. (1995). Explaining development and change in organizations. *Academy of Management Review, 20,* 510–540.

Wachtel, P. L. (Ed.). (1982). *Resistance: Psychodynamic and behavioral approaches*. Cambridge, MA: Perseus.

Wachtel, P. L. (1999). Resistance as a problem of practice and theory. *Journal of Psychotherapy Integration, 9,* 103–117.

Wallace, K. (1967). An ethical basis of communication. In R. Johannesen (Ed.), *Ethics and persuasion* (pp. 41–56). New York: Random House.

Weick, K. E., & Quinn, R. E. (1999). Organizational change and development. *Annual Review of Psychology, 50,* 361–386.

Zajonc, R. B. (1965). Social facilitation. *Science, 149,* 269–274.

About the Contributors

Jack W. Brehm Professor Emeritus, University of Kansas. He previously taught at Yale University and Duke University. His research interests have centered on cognitive dissonance, responses to loss of freedom, and the intensity of emotion. Publications include: *Explorations in Cognitive Dissonance* (with A. R. Cohen; Wiley, 1962), *Perspectives on Cognitive Dissonance* (with R. A. Wicklund; Erlbaum Associates, 1976), *A Theory of Psychological Reactance* (Academic Press, 1966), and *Psychological Reactance: A Theory of Freedom and Control*, (with S. S. Brehm; Academic Press, 1982). E-mail address: jbrehm @ku.edu.

Pablo Briñol Ph.D., Professor of Psychology, Universidad Autónoma de Madrid (UAM), Carretera Colmenar Viejo, Km 15, 28049 Madrid, Spain. E-mail address: pablo.brinnol@uam.es. Dr. Briñol researches attitudes and persuasion at the Department of Social Psychology and Methodology (UAM) and also at The Ohio State University (http://www.psy.ohio-state.edu/gap/).

Robert B. Cialdini Received undergraduate, graduate, and postgraduate education in psychology at the University of Wisconsin, the University of North Carolina, and Columbia University, respectively. He has been elected president of the Society of Personality and Social Psychology and of the Personality and Social Psychology Division of APA. He is the recipient of the Distinguished Scientific Achievement Award of the Society for Consumer Psychology. E-mail address: robert.cialdini@asu.edu.

Matthew T. Crawford Ph.D., Social Psychology, Indiana University, 2002. Lecturer, Department of Experimental Psychology, University of Bristol, 8 Woodland Road, Bristol, BS8 1TN, United Kingdom. E-mail address: M.Crawford@bristol.ac.uk. Dr. Crawford's research focuses primarily on social perception, attitudes, counterfactuals, and anticipated regret.

Sonya Dal Cin   Ph.D. Candidate, Department of Psychology, University of Waterloo, Ontario, Canada N2L 3G1. E-mail address: sdalcin@watarts. uwaterloo.ca. Ms. Dal Cin is currently pursuing her Doctorate in Social Psychology. She studies the psychology of attitudes, particularly health behavior change, and the persuasive effects of narratives.

Leandre R. Fabrigar   Ph.D., Social Psychology, The Ohio State University, 1995. Associate Professor, Department of Psychology, Queen's University, Kingston, Ontario, K7L 3S2, Canada. E-mail address: fabrigar@psyc.queensu.ca. Dr. Fabrigar teaches and conducts research in the areas of attitudes, persuasion, social influence, and statistical methodology.

Geoffrey T. Fong   Ph.D., Social Psychology, University of Michigan, 1984. Associate Professor, Department of Psychology, University of Waterloo, Waterloo, Ontario, Canada N2L 3G1. E-mail address: gfong@uwaterloo.ca.

Kathleen Fuegen   Ph.D., Social Psychology, University of Kansas, 2002. Assistant Professor at The Ohio State University at Lima. Her research examines the intensity of attitudes, how stereotypes are activated and applied in various settings, and social comparison. Please address correspondence to 4240 Campus Drive, The Ohio State University at Lima, Lima Ohio 45804. E-mail address: fuegen.1@osu.edu.

Curtis P. Haugtvedt   Ph.D., Social Psychology, University of Missouri. Associate Professor of Marketing at Fisher College of Business, The Ohio State University, Columbus, OH 43210. His research has focused on attitude strength, particularly as it affects attitude persistence and resistance. He is former Associate Editor of the *Journal of Consumer Psychology* and served as President of the Society for Consumer Psychology, APA Division 23 (1999–2000). His E-mail address is: haugtved@cob.ohio-state.edu.

Julia Zuwerink Jacks   Ph.D., Social Psychology, University of Wisconsin—Madison, 1995. She currently teaches at Guilford College, 5800 W. Friendly Ave., Greensboro, NC 27410. Her main research interest is in resistance to persuasion. Dr. Jacks enjoys sharing stories about her four very cute children (some of whom are more resistant to persuasion than others). E-mail address: jjacks@guilford.edu.

Blair T. Johnson   Ph.D., Social and Personality Psychology, Purdue University, 1988. Professor, Department of Psychology, University of Connecticut, Storrs, CT 06268-1020. E-mail address: blair.t.johnson@uconn.edu. Read more about his work on social influence at http://johnson.socialpsychology.org.

Ley A. Killeya (Killeya-Jones)   Ph.D., Social and Developmental Psychology, Rutgers University, 1999. Research Project Manager, Division of Addiction Psychiatry, UMDNJ, Piscataway, NJ 08854. E-mail: killeylh@umdnj.edu. Dr. Killeya-Jones' interests include adolescent prevention issues and substance abuse prevention and policy.

Eric S. Knowles   Ph.D., Social and Personality Psychology, Boston University, 1971. Professor, Department of Psychology, University of Arkansas, Fayetteville, AR 72701. E-mail address: eknowles@uark.edu. Dr. Knowles teaches, researches, and consults about resistance-reducing change strategies. Read more about his work at www.uark.edu/~omega.

Kenneth D. Levin   Ph.D., Social Psychology, Syracuse University, 2002. Dr. Levin is currently Manager of Customer Analytics at Remarketing Services of America (RSA) in Buffalo, NY. Dr. Levin uses advanced analytic techniques to help RSA's clients improve their marketing productivity through customer insight.

Jay A. Linn   Ph.D., Experimental Psychology, University of Arkansas, 2003. Dr. Linn is an Assistant Professor at Widener University, Chester, PA, where he teaches industrial/organizational and social psychology. He conducts research and consults on the nature of resistance to change and Omega persuasion strategies. He also has a strong interest in cultural social psychology. E-mail address: linn_jay@yahoo.com

Kaiya Liu   Ph.D. student in Communication, The Ohio State University. He studies the interplay of affect and cognition in person perception and attitude change. E-mail address: liu.262@osu.edu.

Allen R. McConnell   Ph.D., Indiana University, 1995. Associate Professor, Department of Psychology, Miami University, Oxford, OH 45056. E-mail address: mcconar@muohio.edu. Interests: self-concept formation and representation, impression formation, social cognition, stigma, social influence, judgment and decision making. For more information go to www.users.muohio.edu/mcconnar/.

Maureen E. O'Brien   Ph.D., Social Pychology, The University of North Carolina at Greensboro, 2003. She is currently an Assistant Professor of Psychology at Louisiana State University in Alexandria. Her main research interests involve attitude functions and prejudice. Dr. O'Brien enjoys traveling and playing the guitar. E-mail address: mobrien@lsua.edu.

Richard E. Petty   Ph.D., Social Psychology, The Ohio State University, 1977. Distinguished University Professor, Department of Psychology, The Ohio State University, Columbus, OH 43210. E-mail address: petty.1@osu.edu. Dr. Petty's primary research focus concerns understanding the processes underlying change in people's conscious and unconscious beliefs, attitudes, and behaviors. For more information go to: www.psy.ohio-state.edu/petty

Jeffrey M. Quinn   Doctoral student, Duke University, Department of Psychology: Social and Health Sciences, Durham, NC 27708. E-mail address: j.quinn@duke.edu. Jeff's research interests include resistance to persuasion, habitual behavior, and behavioral control.

Derek D. Rucker   B.A. from the University of California-Santa Cruz, where he worked with Dr. Anthony Pratkanis. He is currently completing his Ph.D. in Social Psychology at The Ohio State University where he is working with Dr. Richard Petty. Derek studies attitudes, persuasion and social influence, and social cognition, as well as research and statistical methodology. E-mail address: rucker.46@osu.edu.

Brad Sagarin   Ph.D., Social Psychology, Arizona State University, 1999 and B.S., Computer Science, Massachusetts Institute of Technology, 1988. He is an assistant professor of psychology at Northern Illinois University. His research interests include attitude change, resistance to persuasion, deception, jealousy and infidelity, evolutionary psychology, human sexuality, and statistical approaches to missing data and noncompliance. E-mail address: bsagarin@niu.edu.

Bendik M. Samuelsen   Assistant Professor in Marketing at the Norwegian School of Management. His research interests focus on persuasion, especially as applied to advertising and brand management contexts. E-mail address: bendik.samuelsen@bi.no.

Richard J. Shakarchi   Ph.D., The Ohio State University, 2002. Dr. Shakarchi is currently a Senior Research Scientist at The Ohio State University, teaching and conducting research on consumer behavior, social cognition, persuasion, and pharmaceutical marketing and policy. E-mail address: shakarchi.1@osu.edu.

Steven J. Sherman   Ph.D., Social Psychology, University of Michigan, 1967. Professor, Department of Psychology, Indiana University, Bloomington, IN 47405. E-mail address: sherman@indiana.edu. Research interests: social cognition; judgment and decision making; counterfactual thinking; impression formation and change of individuals and groups.

Aaron Smith-McLallen   M.A., Social Psychology, University of Connecticut, 2002. Doctoral candidate, Department of Psychology, University of Connecticut, Storrs, CT 06268-1020. E-mail address: aaron.smith-mclallen @uconn.edu. Mr. Smith-McLallen studies attitude structure and attitude change as well as social cognitive aspects of social influence.

Natalie D. Smoak   M.S., Social Psychology, Purdue University, 2001. Currently a Ph.D candidate, Department of Psychology, Purdue University, degree expected May 2004. E-mail address: ndove@psych.purdue.edu. Research interests include stereotypes and prejudice (with a specific focus on racism and sexism), bias correction, and health psychology.

Zakary L. Tormala   Ph.D., The Ohio State University, 2003. Assistant Professor, Department of Psychology, Indiana University, Bloomington, IN 47405. E-mail address: ztormala@indiana.edu. Dr. Tormala's primary research interests focus on attitudes, persuasion, and resistance, with particular emphasis on the role of meta-cognition in these areas.

Duane T. Wegener   Ph.D., Social Psychology, The Ohio State University, 1994. Professor, Department of Psychological Sciences, Purdue University, West Lafayette, IN 47907-2081. E-mail address: wegener@psych.purdue.edu. Dr. Wegener teaches and conducts research on attitude change (including attitudinal approaches to numerical anchoring and to prejudice), mood management, bias, and bias correction.

Wendy Wood   Ph.D., Social Psychology, University of Massachusetts, 1980. Professor, Department of Psychology: Social and Health Sciences, Duke University, Durham, NC 27708. E-mail address: wwood@duke.edu. Dr. Wood's research interests include influence, habits and behavior generation, and sex differences. She uses meta-analytic synthesis techniques as well as primary research to investigate these topics.

Mark P. Zanna   Ph.D., Social Psychology, Yale University, 1970. Professor, Department of Psychology, University of Waterloo, Ontario, Canada N2L 3G1. E-mail address: mzanna@watarts.uwaterloo.ca. A Fellow of the Royal Society of Canada and Editor of *Advances in Experimental Social Psychology*, Professor Zanna studies the psychology of attitudes, currently focusing on overcoming resistance to persuasion. Read more about his work at www.psychology.uwaterloo.ca/people/mzanna/.

Author Index

Numbers in *italics* indicate pages with complete bibliographic information.

D

Dal Cin, S., 9, 105, 106, *113,* 124,
    183, 187, *189, 190,* 293
Dalton, M. A., 187, *190*
D'Anello, S. C., 42, 47, *63*
Darby, B. I., 122, 125, *145*
Darley, J. G., 237, *255*
Davidson, A. R., 15, *34*
Davis, B. P., 131, 132, *144*
de Vries, N., 151, *174*
Deaux, K. K., 203, *211*
deCarufel, A., 262, *280*
Deci, E. L., 158, *173*
Dermer, M., 19, 29, *34*
DeSteno, D., 19, 29, *34,* 85, 90, 100,
    102, 103
Devine, P. G., 15, *38,* 66, 80, *81, 82,*
    95, *102, 104,* 200, 207, *211,*
    237, 238, 245, 251, 252, *256,*
    257, 271, 277, *282*
Diekman, A. B., 188, 189, *190*
Dijksterhuis, A., 203, *211,* 238,
    256
Dillard, J. P., 122, 134, 141, *145*
Dimeff, L. A., 269, *281*
Ditto, P. H., 161, *171*
Dolinski, D., 122, 128, *145*
Dollard, J., 118, 119, 126, *145*
Douglass, D., 306, *309*
Drachman, D., 262, *280*
Driscoll, D. M., 287, *297*
Duncan, C. P., 120, *145*
Dunn, M., 20, 30, 32, *37*

E

Eagle, M., 304, *309*
Eagly, A. H., 15, 16, 27, 28, *34,* 40,
    62, *63,* 120, *145,* 159, *171,* 180,
    189, 193, 195, 196, 200, 204,
    205, 206, 209, *211,* 216, 217,
    218, 220, 229, 230, *232,* 238,
    249, *256*

Ekstein, G., 229, *232*
El-Alayi, A. G., 150, *172*
Elkes, R., 163, *171*
Elkin, R. A., 27, *35*
Ellen, P. S., 262, *280*
Epstein, S., 237, *255,* 270, *280*
Erickson, M. E., 124, 128, 131, 132,
    136, 139, 141, *145,* 304, 307,
    309
Evans, L., 23, *34*
Evenbeck, S., 197, 202, 203, 204,
    211

F

Fabrigar, L. R., 5, 6, 7, 9, 17, 19, 24,
    25, 27, 28, 31, 33, *34, 35, 36,*
    37, 52, 80, 83, 85, 149, 168,
    206, 253, 302
Faison, E. W. J., 127, *145*
Fazio, R. H., 15, *34,* 67, *81,* 270,
    280
Fein, S., 238, *256,* 262, *280*
Festinger, L., 27, *35,* 40, *63,* 66, 67,
    81, 88, *102,* 122, 128, *145,* 157,
    171, 218, *232,* 237, *256*
Fetherstonhaugh, D., 220, *232*
Fisch, R., 137, *148*
Fishbein, M., 14, *33,* 40, *62,* 71, *81,*
    223, *232*
Fisher, R., 163, *173*
Fiske, A. P., 158, *171*
Fiske, S. T., 268, *280*
Fitzpatrick, A. R., 205, 206, 209, *211*
Flay, B. R., 30, 31, *35,* 95, *102*
Fleming, M., 27, *35*
Flournoy, R., 188, *189*
Floyd, J. 132, *144*
Folkes, V. S., 262, *280*
Fong, G. T., 9, 105, 106, *113,* 124,
    183, 187, *189, 190,* 293
Forbes, D., 176, *190*
Forster, J., 68, *82,* 119, 141, *145*
Fowles, D. C., 305, *309*

Subject Index

Forewarning (*continued*)
  self-esteem, 196, 203
  self-identitiy, 195, 196, 209
  thoughtful process of, 200
  and time delay, 200–201
  topic involvement, 200
  valid judgments, 195
  validity motives, 197
Future focus, 150
Future regret, 150
Future thinking
  behavior and, 164
  bias, 165
  compliance, 163, 165
  conditional reference frame, 165

measures, 106–108
persuasion and, 87
resistance strategies, 96
resistance to persuasion, 83, 87–88, 105
transportability, 183
Inoculation Theory, 4, 14, 77–78, 262

L

Likelihood
  expertise, 231
  mood, 231
  truth, 231

H

Health behaviors, 307

I

Illusions of invulnerability
  acknowledging personal
      vulnerability study
    argument quality, 271
    cognitive response model, 271
    influence of arguments number, 271
    manipulative intent, 271
    method, 270–273
    prior experience, 270
    results, 274
    vulnerability, 270–273
  pilot study, 269
  self-enhancement bias, 268
Individual differences
  authoritarian personality, 87
  cognitive rigidity, 87
  consistency, 88
  consumer research and, 290
  defensive confidence, 88
  elaboration, 16

M

Manipulative intent
  defined, 262
  legitimate/illegitimate appeals, 265
  motivates resistance, 262–263
Minority Influence, 78
Meta-cognition
  argument quality, 91
  bias, 86, 94
  confidence, 85
  elaboration, 89–90, 92–93, 100
  false feedback, 92
  nature of belief, 84
  need for cognition, 91
  openness to change/conservation, 86
  personality, 85
  persuasibility, 86, 89–91, 94, 100
  resistance strategies, 97
  resistance to persuasion, 89, 93
  self-confidence, 95
  self-efficacy, 89
  self-transcendence/self-
      enhancement, 86
  situational factors, 94
  value judgment of belief, 84
Motivation
  defense motivation, 23